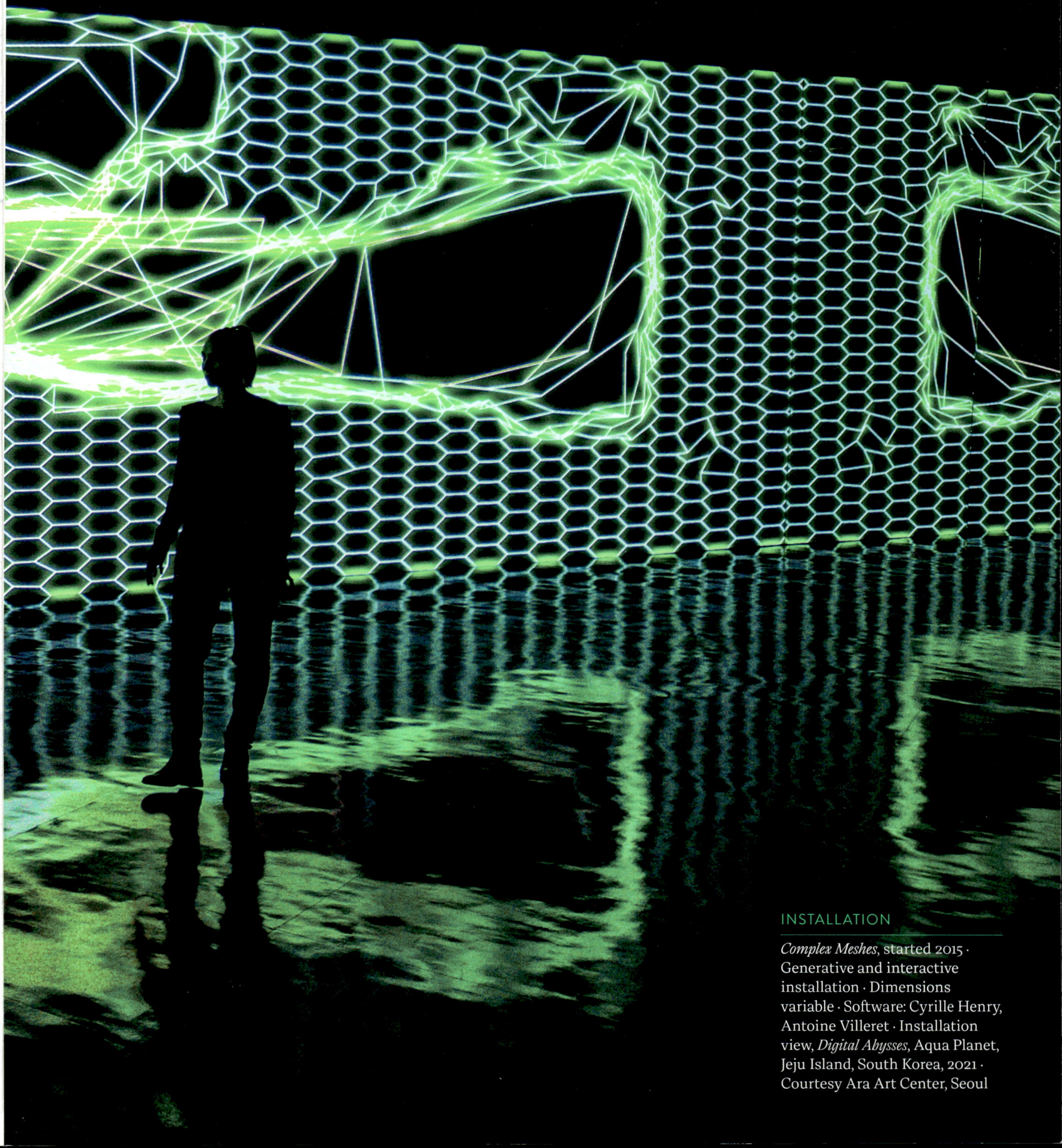

INSTALLATION

Complex Meshes, started 2015 ·
Generative and interactive
installation · Dimensions
variable · Software: Cyrille Henry,
Antoine Villeret · Installation
view, *Digital Abysses*, Aqua Planet,
Jeju Island, South Korea, 2021 ·
Courtesy Ara Art Center, Seoul

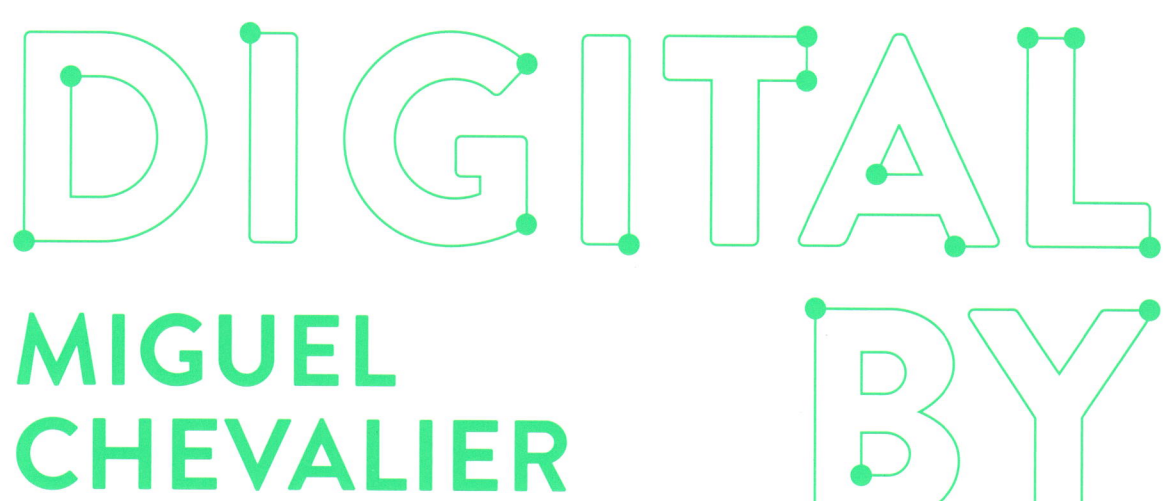

DIGITAL BY NATURE

MIGUEL CHEVALIER

EDITED BY
ROGER DIEDEREN AND
FRANZISKA STÖHR

HIRMER

KUNSTHALLE
MÜNCHEN

Foreword

● With *Digital by Nature: The Art of Miguel Chevalier*, the Kunsthalle München proudly presents the first major solo exhibition in Germany dedicated to the groundbreaking work of Miguel Chevalier (born 1959 in Mexico City, lives and works in Paris). In a career spanning four decades, Chevalier has been internationally recognized as one of the pioneering figures in the field of virtual and digital art, showing his creations all over the world. At a time when digital technologies have become deeply embedded in everyday life, this exhibition offers an opportunity to engage with the work of an artist who not only anticipated these transformations, but who has continuously used digital media as a source of aesthetic innovation and philosophical reflection. Miguel Chevalier has been exploring the artistic potential of the computer since the early 1980s. Long before terms like "virtual reality," "interactive installation," or "AI-generated art "entered the cultural mainstream, he was already employing algorithmic processes and digital codes to create dynamic, immersive environments. His practice is marked by a tireless curiosity for new technologies and a desire to reimagine the relationship between art, science, and nature. At the same time, Chevalier's work is deeply informed by art history. His digital universe is not detached from tradition, but rather in continuous dialogue with longstanding themes and motifs—from Islamic geometry to baroque ornamentation, from modernist abstraction to biomorphic surrealism.

Today, immersive exhibitions have gained enormous popularity worldwide. However, most of them are spectacles that merely put digitized pieces by long-deceased artists in motion. This exhibition is fundamentally different. *Digital by Nature* presents original works by a living artist who has dedicated his career to developing a visual language that is native to the digital realm. Rather than adapting preexisting imagery, Chevalier creates generative environments and installations that evolve in real time and often respond directly to the public's presence. In this way, his art offers not just a visual but a physical and emotional experience—an invitation to participate, to move, to observe, and to wonder.

The exhibition highlights the richness and diversity of Chevalier's artistic approach. Alongside large-scale projections and interactive environments, visitors encounter videos, digital prints, sculptures, tapestries, and drawings, and many of these artworks

ROGER DIEDEREN
Director
Kunsthalle München
September 2025

4 (FOREWORD)

are realized through advanced technologies such as 3D printing and robotics. Across all these media, Chevalier's works examine the connections—and tensions—between the natural and artificial, the organic and the digital. His virtual gardens bloom with glowing, algorithmically generated plants; his "digital organisms" pulse and transform like living beings. With these creations, he opens up a poetic space in which the boundaries between biology and technology, between machine logic and beauty, begin to dissolve.

At its core, *Digital by Nature* is about transformation. It asks how technology shapes our perception and how art can help to see our world anew. It reminds us that the digital does not have to be cold, sterile, or detached. In the hands of an artist like Miguel Chevalier, it becomes something tactile, dynamic, and deeply human. The Kunsthalle München is delighted to present this journey through an oeuvre that is at once intellectually engaging and visually enchanting.

I am deeply grateful to Miguel Chevalier not only for his visionary spirit but also for his extremely kind and generous approach to working together. My gratitude very much extends to his collaborators as well: Nicolas Gaudelet, Emilie Lesne, Thomas Granovsky, Pascal Maillard, Elise Michel, Cyrille Henry, Ollie Smith, Claude Micheli, Samuel Twidale, Antoine Villeret, Ludovic Mallégol, Jacopo Baboni Schilingi, and Gabriel Chouvet, who have been exceptionally helpful and committed to making this such a rich and varied project.

Once again, it was a great pleasure to plan and realize this exhibition with Franziska Stöhr, curator at the Kunsthalle München. Her ability to create a convincing trajectory for Chevalier's very distinctive works was impressive, and her structuring of this publication, as well as the texts she wrote for it, command the greatest respect. I would also like to thank our curatorial assistant Jasmin Gierling, not only for her texts but also for her dedicated support throughout the work on the exhibition and catalog. Thanks to the excellent collaboration with graphic designer Florian Frohnholzer, this book captures Chevalier's aesthetic in an outstanding way. Holger Steinemann's and James Copeland's critical editing contributed significantly to the precision of the texts. Lisa Contag once again provided the eloquent translation into English. Kerstin Ludolph, Jutta Allekotte, Cordula Gielen, and Hannes Halder have supervised this publication for Hirmer Publishers in a very constructive and pleasant manner. As with several previous exhibitions at the Kunsthalle München, Martin Kinzlmaier has brought his refined sense of design and color to bear. This has once again resulted in a truly spectacular presentation that perfectly showcases Chevalier's work. I would also like to express my heartfelt thanks to the institutional and private lenders who have so generously made their objects and artworks available and thus made it possible to contextualize certain ideas and systems that lie at the core of Chevalier's art.

Last but not least, I would like to emphasize how grateful I am to all the wonderful staff at the Kunsthalle and the Hypo-Kulturstiftung, who approach every exhibition with great enthusiasm and tireless energy. And finally, I wish to express my heartfelt thanks to the Board of the HypoVereinsbank, which has been strongly committed to the Hypo-Kulturstiftung and the Kunsthalle since 1985. As the Kunsthalle now celebrates its 40th anniversary in 2025 and, as with all 120 extraordinary exhibitions shown here before, *Digital by Nature* would simply not have been possible without this exceptional patronage. It is therefore with great pleasure that I invite you now to immerse yourself in Miguel Chevalier's universe, where code becomes color, data becomes form, and the digital becomes nature.

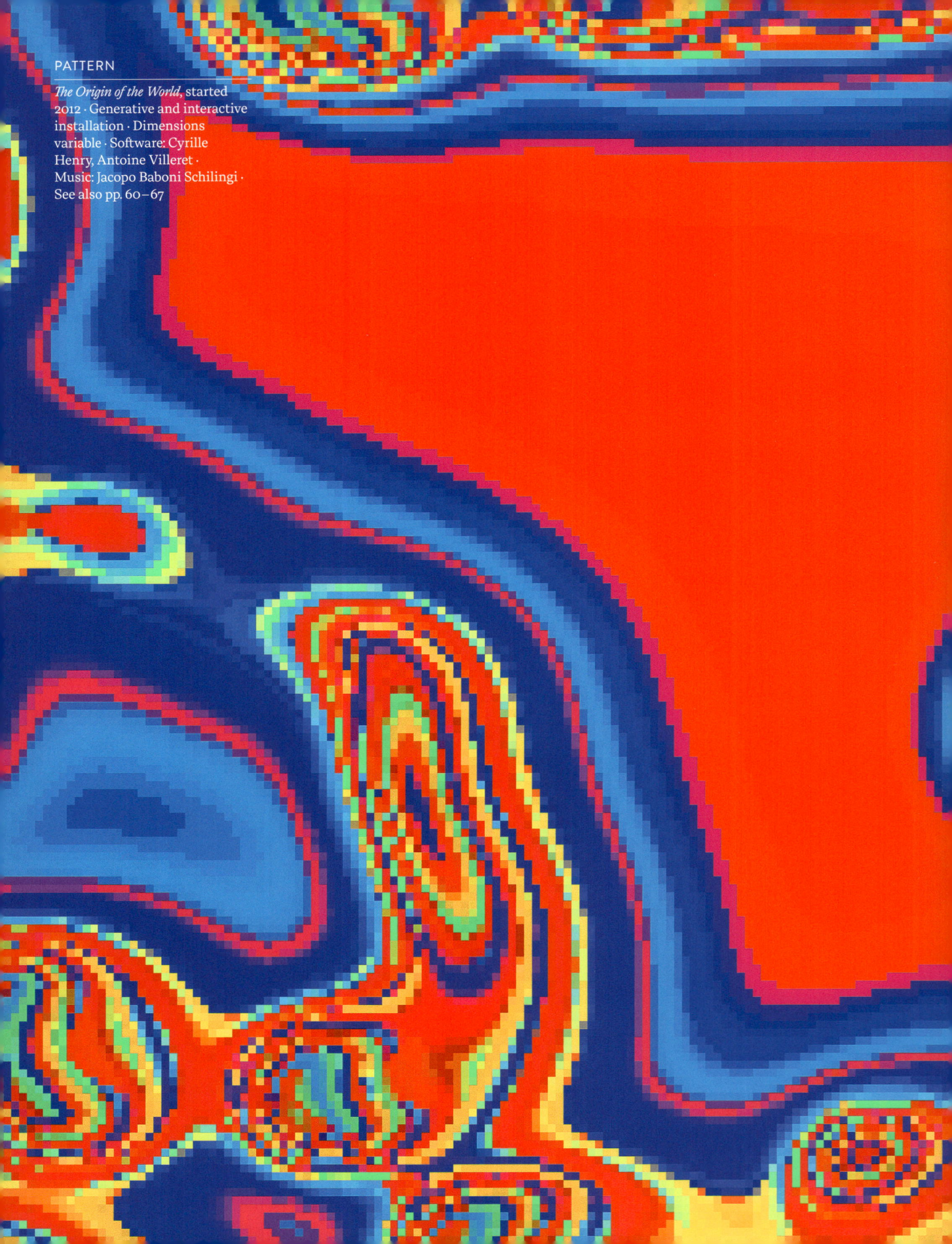

PATTERN

The Origin of the World, started 2012 · Generative and interactive installation · Dimensions variable · Software: Cyrille Henry, Antoine Villeret · Music: Jacopo Baboni Schilingi · See also pp. 60–67

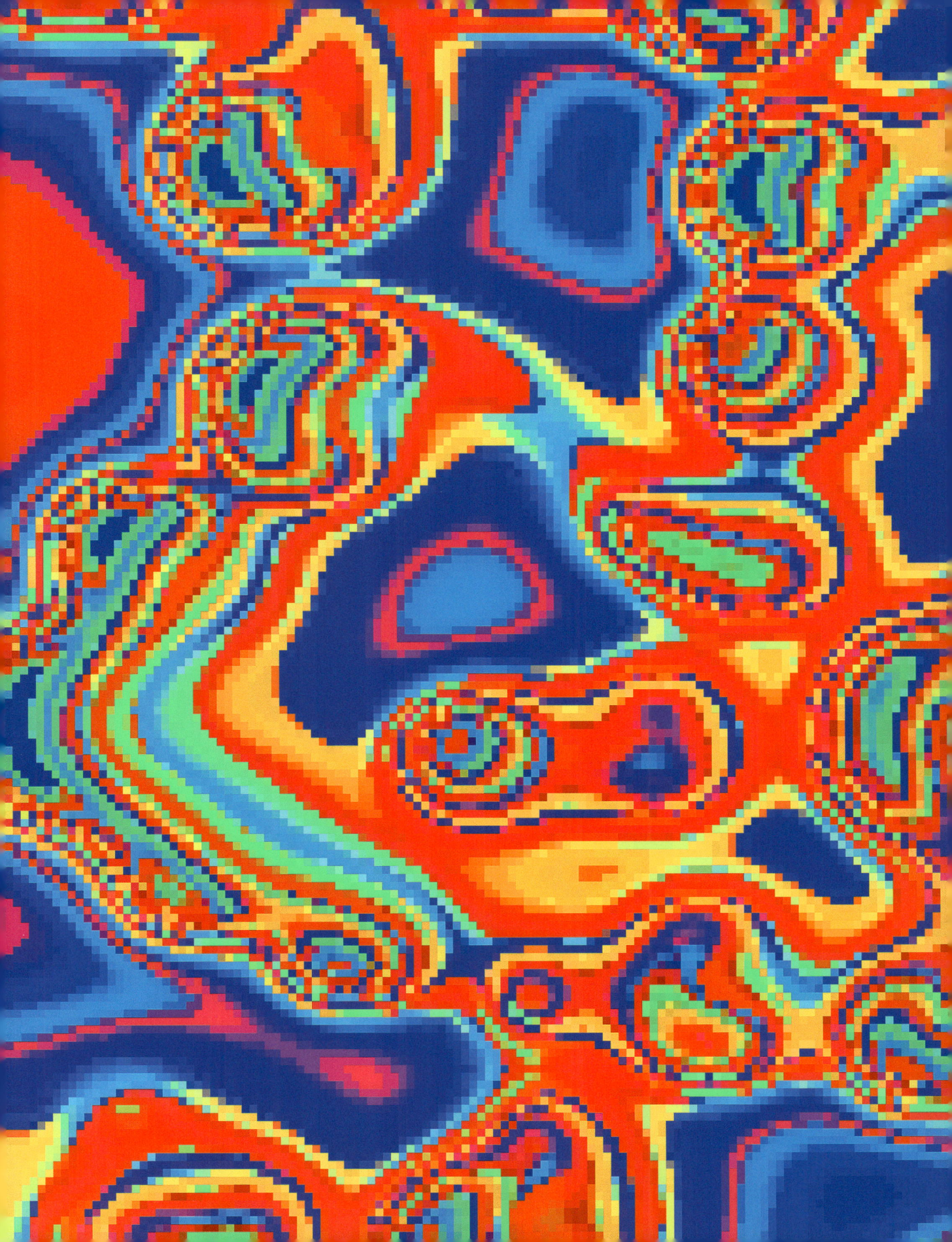

The Computer as Creative Tool

MIGUEL CHEVALIER
IN CONVERSATION WITH
FRANZISKA STÖHR

FRANZISKA STÖHR You studied in Paris and between 1981 and 1983 received degrees in visual art and archeology. But it seems that the most important experience took place not in Paris but in New York, in 1983 at the Pratt Institute and in 1984 at the School of Visual Arts. It was in New York that you first had the chance to draw with software programs and animate your images. The computer has become your core medium since then. How did you work at the beginning of your artistic career, and what convinced you that the computer was the right tool for expressing yourself artistically?

MIGUEL CHEVALIER Before my time in New York, I mainly worked with traditional media. However, my curiosity had already pushed me, starting in the late 1970s and early 1980s, to experiment with various techniques, blending drawing, photography, photocopying, painting, and even scratching on slides or 35 mm film. I sought to create a hybrid artistic language, inspired both by the animated creations of Norman McLaren (1914–1987) and the films of Man Ray (1890–1976), such as the one where he randomly threw pins onto the film emulsion, using manual gestures as creative tools.

At that time, my work was deeply experimental. Images projected on television screens were photographed, then the slides were reworked by hand by removing parts of the gelatine coat and repainting these exposed areas. These manual interventions echoed the practices of the second half of the nineteenth-century and early twentieth-century photographers who painted directly onto film to achieve vivid colors that couldn't be produced through purely photographic techniques. With the modified slides, I created sequences of images, which I projected onto walls and was thus able to present them as large-scale installations (see also p. 43). Afterwards, to preserve these creations, I explored screen-printing, which materialized my works on various surfaces such as plywood, chipboard, Plexiglas, and glass. This enabled me to create connections between painting, photography, and video grids, laying the groundwork for all the digital variations that subsequently became possible. I also captured electronic snow on television screens by recording it on a video tape—the moving image when no signal is received—using these random flows as artistic material. These experiments bridged the analog and digital worlds while questioning the boundaries of moving images. Later, at the Pratt Institute and the School of Visual Arts, my first encounters with drawing software were a revelation: I realized that computers would allow me to create ever-evolving works, to play with time, light, and motion, which was impossible in this way with classical media.

> I realized that computers would allow me to create ever-evolving works, to play with time, light, and motion, which was impossible in this way with classical media.

FS Before the mid-1980s, computers were very large and not easily available to artists. When you returned to Paris after living in the US, where did you find one to work on, since you didn't yet have a personal computer?

MC In the early 1980s, gaining access to computers was a real challenge. The machines, expensive and bulky, were primarily reserved for scientific laboratories and television networks. Thanks to the support of engineer Serge Equilbey (b. 1950), who had an appreciation for art, I was permitted to use the powerful computers at the CNRS (Centre National de la Recherche Scientifique) from midnight to six in the morning. This not only gave me the opportunity to use the technology in general but also enriched my thinking about the possibilities offered by computers. These interdisciplinary collaborations still play a key role in the development of my work today, allowing me to imagine a new dialogue between art and technology. Back then it enabled me to begin exploring the creative potential of these tools, which were still very rarely used in the arts. Computing was largely misunderstood and seldom accepted in the community, except for a few visionary figures like art critic Pierre Restany (1930–2003), founder of the Nouveau Réalisme movement, who was a fervent supporter of my research as early as 1988.

● FS In 1985, you bought your first personal computer, an Amiga 1000 made by the American company Commodore. Were there any programs you could use to start creating your art or was it necessary to program everything yourself?

● MC The acquisition of my first Amiga 1000, along with a scanner, a video camera, and a printer, marked a significant financial investment and a pivotal moment in my artistic journey. For the first time, I achieved autonomy, freeing myself from the constraints of institutional mainframes and their complex interfaces used for modifying and generating images, while also allowing me to save them on magnetic tape. The Amiga was for me far more than a tool: it was an extension of my thought process, a gateway into a new creative space—a hybrid medium, positioned between the tangible and the virtual.

The graphics editor Deluxe Paint, although rudimentary by today's standards, was revolutionary at the time. It enabled me to draw and paint with light without requiring programming skills. Despite its limitations in functionality and color palette, it offered an unprecedented visual language. Drawing with a mouse—as graphic tablets had yet to be invented—posed a technical challenge but also an opportunity to redefine the artistic gesture, giving rise to a personal aesthetic: my own poetics of ▸ pixels (p. 28) and the digital. This exploration bridged traditional painting with digital processes, photography, video, and emerging algorithmic possibilities.

This moment revealed an essential conceptual dimension for me: the interaction between the artist and the machine is not merely an act of production but a genuine dialogue. Each image became a space for experimentation, challenging the boundaries between manual and automatic, between materiality and immateriality. This synergy between human intention and algorithmic potential laid the groundwork for an innovative artistic language, where each work exists at the intersection of gesture, idea, and system.

> The Amiga was for me far more than a tool: it was an extension of my thought process, a gateway into a new creative space—a hybrid medium, positioned between the tangible and the virtual.

VIDEO STILL →

Binary State, 1990–91 · Video, color, sound, 5 min. · Music: Fred Wallich, production: Grand Canal, CICV Montbéliard Belfort

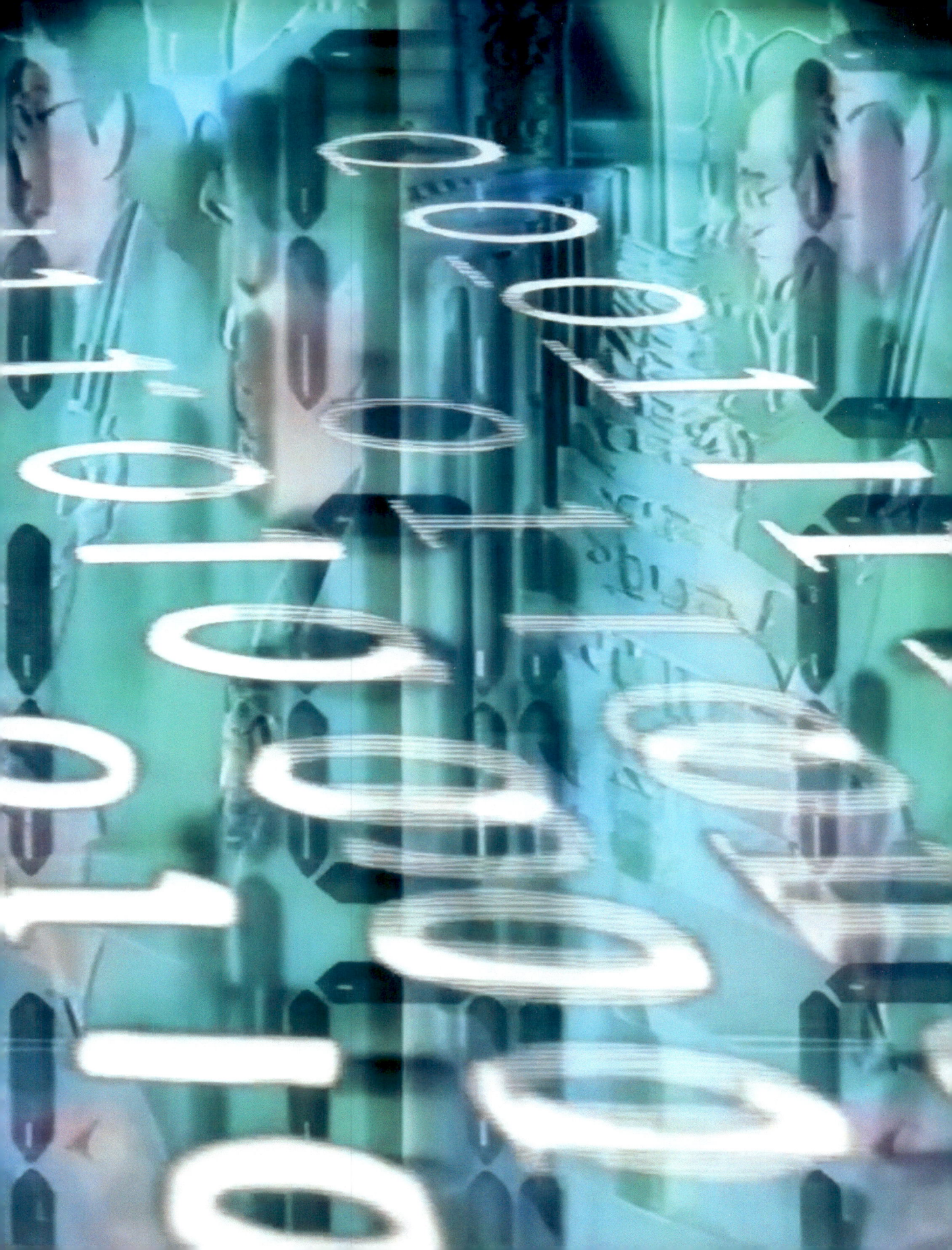

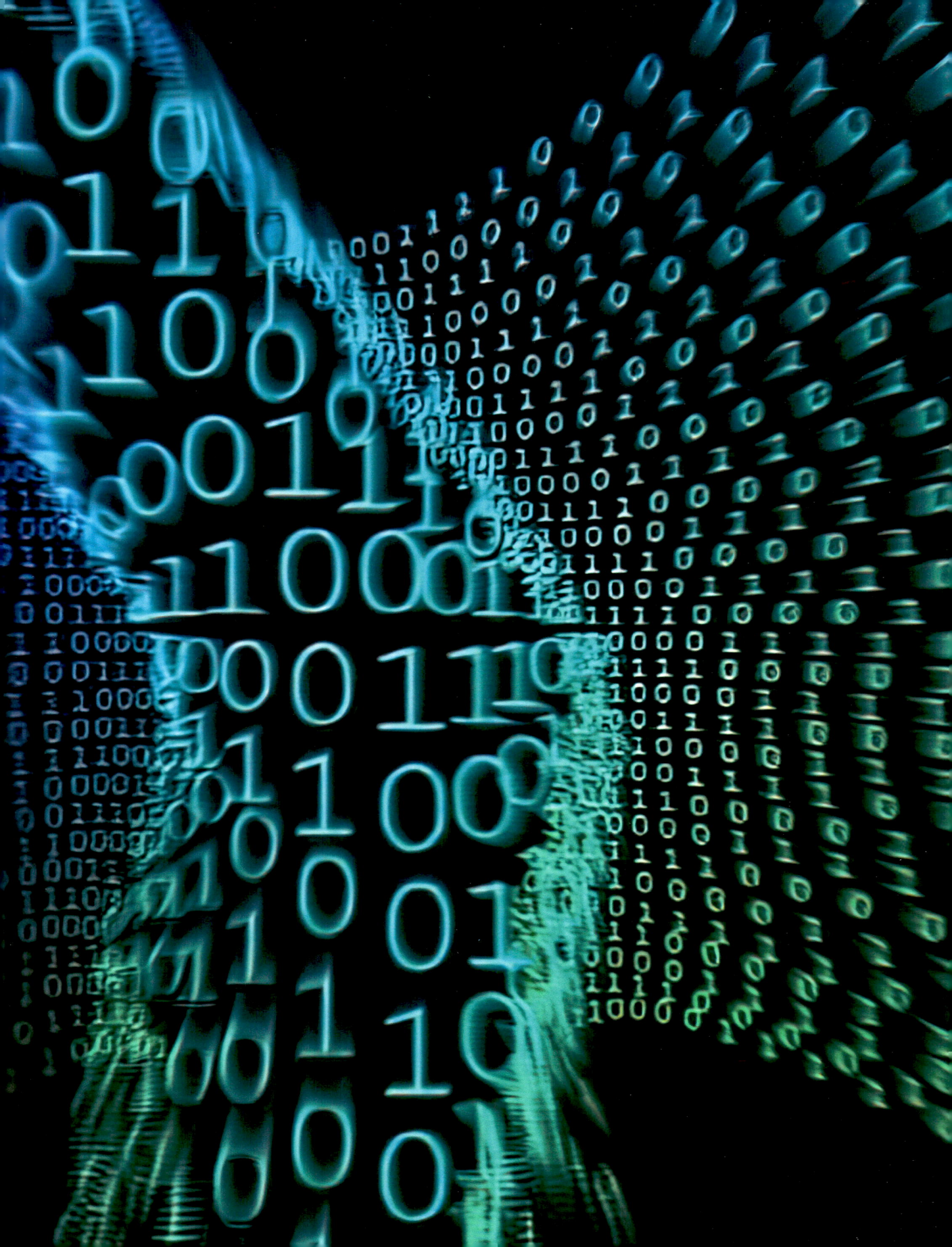

Binary Wave 4K, 2004–22 ·
Video 4K, color, no sound, 41 min.

● FS Looking back at the 1980s and early 1990s, was there much of an exchange among artists working in this field?

● MC Exchanges between artists exploring the digital realm only happened amongst a small group, but they occurred on a high conceptual level. In France, the tiny community holding these profound and stimulating dialogues included people like Piotr Kowalski (1927–2004), Edmond Couchot (1932–2020), Michel Bret (b. 1941), Maurice Benayoun (b. 1957), and Jeffrey Shaw (b. 1944). However, these connections remained predominantly on a national scale, as communication options were still very limited compared to today. Further interactions mainly took place during modest exhibitions, conferences, and symposiums abroad where I would present my research through slides. Such occasional international meetings were invaluable for presenting our visions, sharing methodologies, and debating emerging ideas.

● FS Two important early exhibitions focusing on computer art took place as early as 1968: *Cybernetic Serendipity: The Computer and the Arts* at the Institute of Contemporary Arts in London, followed by presentations in Washington, DC, and San Francisco, as well as *Tendencies 4: Computers and Visual Research* at the Museum of Contemporary Art in Zagreb. People like Frieder Nake (b. 1938), Georg Nees (1926–2016), and A. Michael Noll (b. 1939) are considered to be founding fathers of digital and algorithmic computer graphics. Already in 1963, Nake developed a program at the Technical University of Stuttgart that made it possible to link the institute's computer (ER 56 by SEL) with the Z 64 Graphomat, the newly acquired and already legendary drawing machine by inventor Konrad Zuse (1910–1995). How accessible was information about computer-based art for you in the 1980s?

> The interaction between the artist and the machine is not merely an act of production but a genuine dialogue.

● MC Such Information back then was scarce and fragmented, but a few key events had a decisive impact on my practice as a young artist. The exhibition *Electra*, organized by Frank Popper (1918–2020) and Marie-Odile Briot (1939–1998) at the Musée d'Art Moderne de la Ville de Paris in 1983–84, was one of the most remarkable for its ambition, diversity, and ability to make these new approaches accessible to a broad audience. It demonstrated how electronics and new technologies were transforming the field of contemporary art. Another key exhibition was *Les Immatériaux* (1985) at the Centre Pompidou, conceived by Jean-François Lyotard (1924–1998) and Thierry Chaput (1949–1990). This interdisciplinary event, with its profound intellectual depth, explored the transformations of the postmodern world under the influence of new technologies, rethinking matter, knowledge, and communication. It offered an innovative reflection on the future of creation. These exhibitions opened new avenues of thought for me by highlighting the dialogues between art, science, philosophy, and technology.

However, outside these exceptional moments, ▸digital art (p. 27) remained an unexplored territory, poorly documented and misunderstood within the art world, particularly at a time when there was a strong return to painting and a growing interest in street art. Scientific publications and the rare exchange networks between

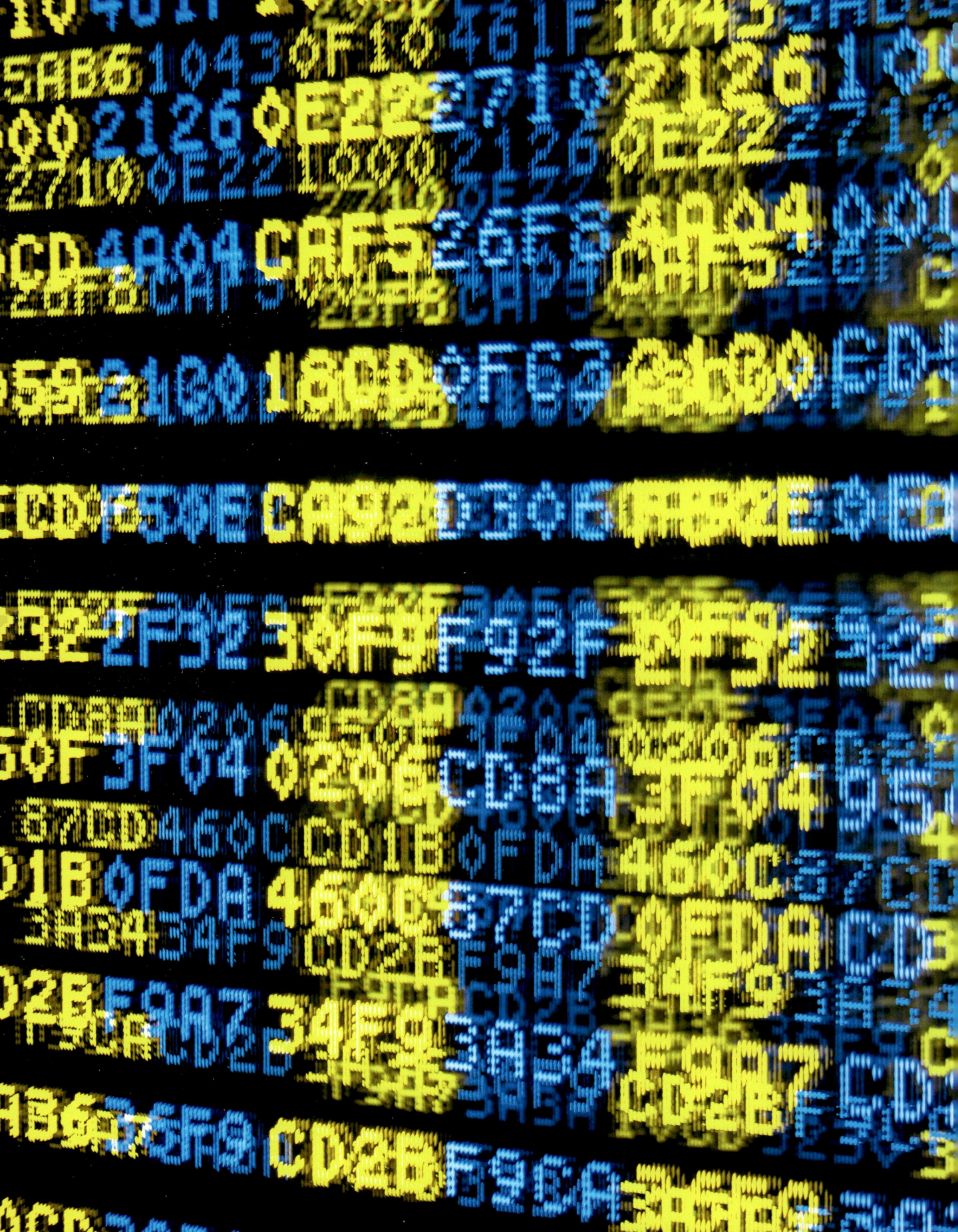

← OBJECT

Infinite Hexadecimal Memory Window, 1992 · Silkscreen on mirror, neon lighting, metal box · 100 × 100 × 15 cm (39 3/8 × 39 3/8 × 5 15/16 in.) · Detail from p. 74

artists, scientists, and engineers became essential anchors. The lack of a dense informational structure led me to embrace experimentation as a method, developing direct dialogues with pioneering figures such as Vera Molnár (1924–2023), Manfred Mohr (b. 1938), Catherine Ikam (b. 1942), Edmond Couchot, Fred Forest (b. 1933), and Jean-Pierre Vasarely, known as Yvaral (1934–2002). These exchanges expanded my understanding of the potential of the digital medium, not merely as a technical tool but as a conceptual space to explore.

This context of limited information also reinforced the idea that digital art could not simply rely on traditional artistic paradigms. It required a redefinition of creation and its foundations: a delicate balance between technological innovation and profound aesthetic reflection. Ultimately, it was a transitional period marked by an urgency to lay the first foundations of digital art.

● FS Your oeuvre ranges from aspects of digital art to themes of nature in relation to ecology and humans. In your earlier pieces, you explore the means of the digital world, for instance the ▸ binary system (p. 26), which consists only of sequences of 0 and 1, or the pixel or the ▸ voxel (p. 29). Can you share with me your thoughts on creating pieces like *Flip Flop* (1987; p. 70), *Infinite Hexadecimal Memory Window* (1992; p. 74), *Binary State* (1990–91; pp. 72–73), *1m3* (1992; p. 82), and *Infinite Pixels* (2010–12; pp. 75–77)?

● MC In my early works, using pixels or voxels, such as in the piece *1m3*, were primarily explorations aimed at decoding and delving into the fundamental principles of the digital realm. They allowed me to familiarize myself with the core elements of digital imagery—the pixel, binary code, and algorithmic structures—that now form the foundation of my artistic language. For example, *Infinite Hexadecimal Memory Window* embodied an attempt to translate the abstraction of digital systems into a visual form, thus materializing concepts like infinity and variation.

In my early works, using pixels or voxels, such as in the piece *1m3*, were primarily explorations aimed at decoding and delving into the fundamental principles of the digital realm.

These works, although modest in appearance today, were in fact experiments within a technological field that was still in its infancy. They embodied a desire to tame these new tools and transform them into a fully fledged artistic medium capable of expressing a unique and singular aesthetic. Through them, I explored abstract notions such as modularity, movement, and the tension between the visible and the invisible, while questioning our relationship with digital technologies.

These pieces continue to resonate and have influence in my current work. They represent the seeds of a broader reflection on recurring themes in my practice: the relationship between nature and artifice, between control and emergence, or between fixity and movement. They remain essential landmarks for me, a kind of conceptual matrix for my entire artistic universe. Much like Pop Art and the Nouveau Réalisme movements in the 1960s, which powerfully captured shifts brought about by the rise of consumer society, my works reflect the stakes of a pivotal moment marked by the emergence of digital technology. They bear witness to the profound transformations that this revolution brought to our relationship with images, materiality, memory, and, more broadly, with reality itself.

PATTERN →

The Origin of the World,
started 2012 · See also pp. 60–67

● FS In a certain way, these early works are connected to later pieces like *The Origin of the World* (started 2012; pp. 60–67) but also your deep-sea pieces, which focus on things that are usually invisible to us. For example, *The Origin of the World* explores microstructures like microscopic cells and pixels. Some of the *Digital Abysses* (started 2018; pp. 122, 124–31) are inspired by creatures that live so deep in the sea that humans are rarely confronted with them. Throughout the centuries, art has greatly helped scientists visualize the invisible time and again. What is it about this kind of revelation that interests you so much?

● MC I am deeply drawn to what is imperceptible to the naked eye because it invites us to explore hidden dimensions of our existence, whether they originate from the natural world or the digital realm. Revealing the invisible—whether it be the microscopic universe of plankton, marine microorganisms, cellular structures, or even pixels—brings us closer to the fundamental mysteries that govern life. These discrete elements, although inaccessible to our immediate perception, play a crucial role in the balance and complexity of our world.

In my work, I strive to transcend this invisibility by transforming it into a visual and sensory experience through digital tools. This approach goes beyond mere scientific or technical exploration; it also questions our relationship with the minute, the elusive, and all that lies beyond our direct understanding. By making the invisible visible, I aim not only to evoke wonder and introspection but also to highlight the fragility of our place within these interconnected and infinite ecosystems. My work is an invitation to contemplate what elements, despite being imperceptible, profoundly shape our reality and our connection to the living world.

● FS In 1975, the mathematician Benoît Mandelbrot (1924–2010) coined the term *fractal* (from the Latin *fractus*, "broken," or *frangere*, "to break into pieces"), which refers to certain natural or artificial structures or geometric patterns. This is something you have dealt with quite a lot, for example in *Fractal Flowers* (started 2008; pp. 108, 110–21), *Fractal Arborescence* (started 2023; pp. 144–51), the *Digital Crystals* (started 2018; pp. 134–39), or the *Digital Abysses*. ▶ Fractals (p. 27) show a high degree of scale invariance or self-similarity. This is the case, for example, when an object consists

> I am deeply drawn to what is imperceptible to the naked eye because it invites us to explore hidden dimensions of our existence, whether they originate from the natural world or the digital realm. Revealing the invisible—whether it be the microscopic universe of plankton, marine microorganisms, cellular structures, or even pixels—brings us closer to the fundamental mysteries that govern life.

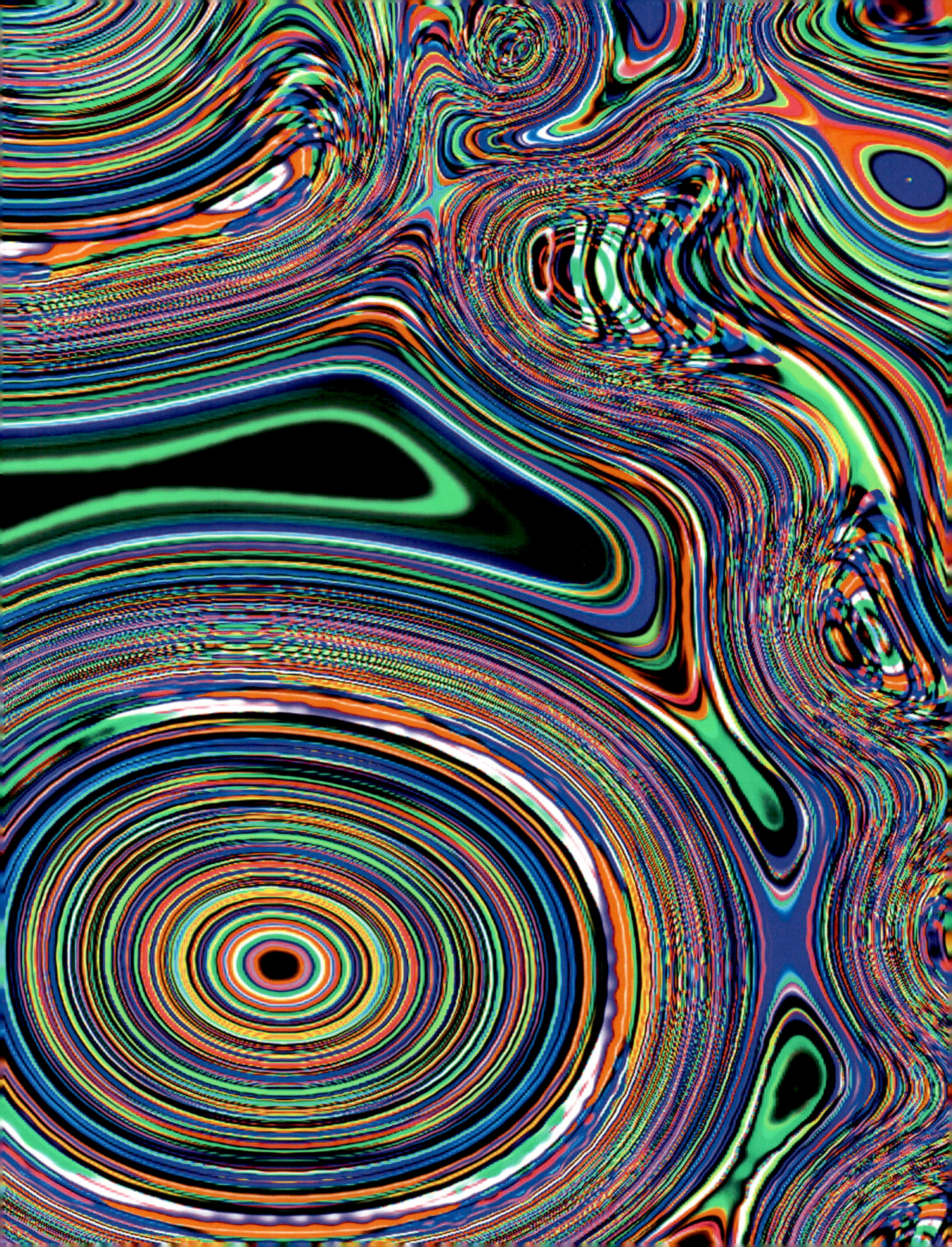

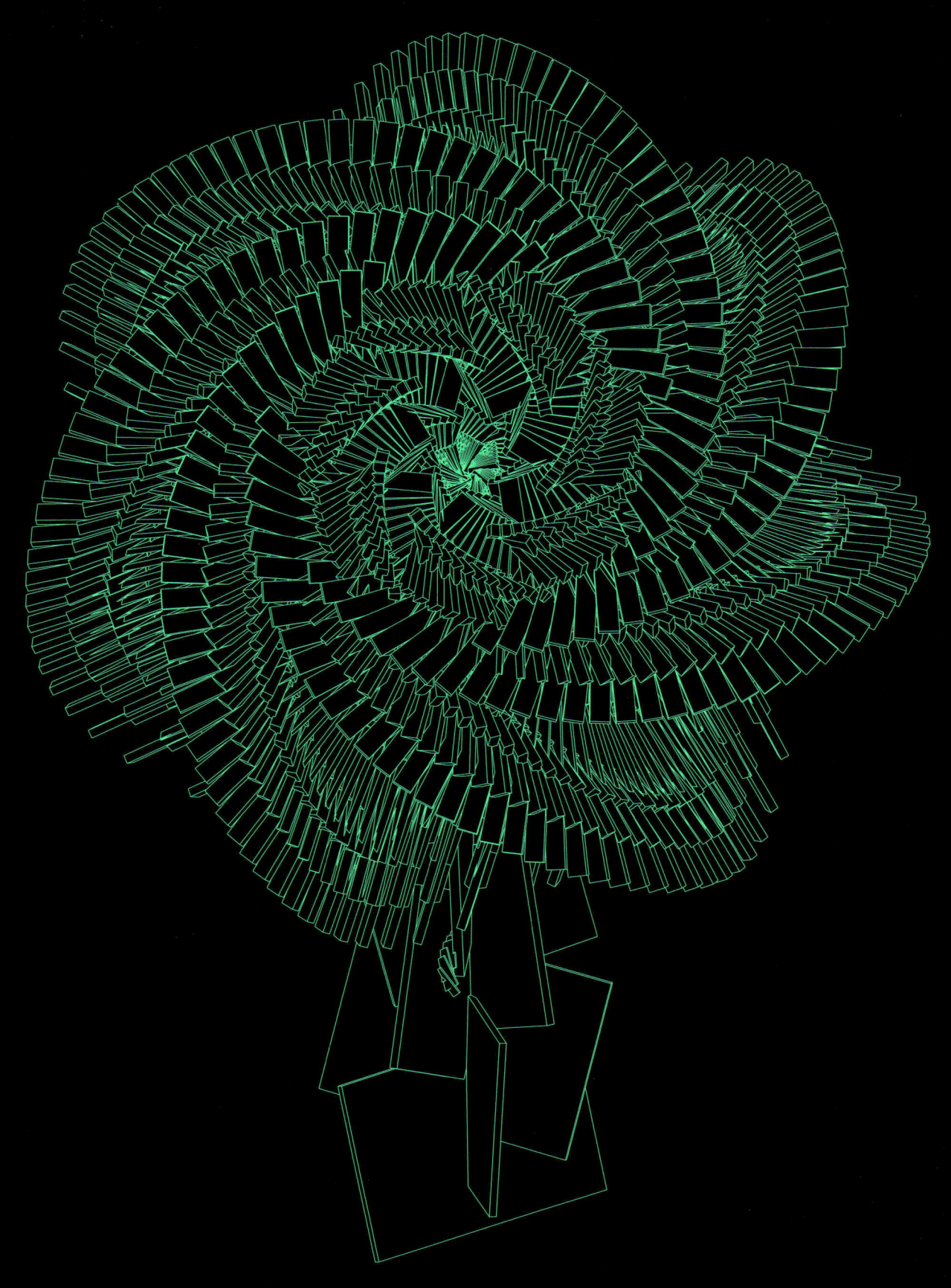

Lilus Arythmeticus named by Euclid, 2008 · From the series *Fractal Flowers*

of several scaled-down copies of itself. The fractal can be found in nature—for example the structure of a fern, romanesco broccoli, and corals, but also of certain snail shells—and is an important element for mathematical calculations. What interests you about this subject?

● MC What fascinates me about fractals is their ability to reflect the infinite and complex structures of nature while embodying a rigorous geometric beauty. They serve as a bridge between chaos and order, revealing how simple patterns can, through iteration, generate forms of striking complexity.

Fractals captivate me also because of their universality: they are found everywhere, from ferns and trees to nervous systems and rock formations. They represent a kind of hidden language of nature, a symbiosis between science and aesthetics. This dual aspect—scientific and artistic—gives them a compelling dimension, both rational and poetic.

In works of mine such as the *Fractal Flowers*, they become a way to explore the infinite facets between the vegetal and the mineral, to play with their scales, and to reinvent nature. They allow me to create visual universes where every detail contains a depth that unfolds gradually, as if the viewer were diving into an endless mirror. These forms, at once familiar and alien, stimulate the imagination and challenge our relationship with space, time, and the very act of creation.

> Fractals captivate me also because of their universality: they are found everywhere, from ferns and trees to nervous systems and rock formations. They represent a kind of hidden language of nature, a symbiosis between science and aesthetics.

● FS To me it seems as if the theme of nature is becoming ever more important in your work, especially its artificiality, which is created by human intervention, but also its fragility. Is it your intention to make people reflect on the systems and environment we live in?

● MC Absolutely, art is a powerful medium to raise awareness about the fragility and richness of our ecosystem. Through my works, I strive to foster an understanding of the complex interactions between humans and nature while highlighting the impacts of technology on our environment. By combining aesthetics and reflection, my work aims to strengthen the collective sense of responsibility to preserve and revalue our natural heritage, which is unique and essential to our global survival and balance.

> Art is a powerful medium to raise awareness about the fragility and richness of our ecosystem.

● FS Although your work is always digitally based, the sensory experience in the real world is very important for you, too. Can you please elaborate why this is the case?

MC While digital art may sometimes appear immaterial, it has the power to fully engage the senses and create a deep emotional connection. In my installations, several elements play a crucial role in achieving this: the monumental scale of the space and the projected moving image evoke a sense of total immersion in the work. Moreover, the possibility of interaction strengthens the bond between the artwork and the viewers. It transforms the viewers into active participants, allowing them to undergo a unique and personal experience, while blurring the boundaries between creator and receiver. My art aims at creating moments of introspection, not only inviting the viewers to contemplate but also to observe themselves observing. The interaction also aims to create an emotional and intellectual connection by addressing universal themes and human dimensions that resonate with everyone. The objective is to offer immersive experiences that touch, inspire, and broaden artistic perspectives while enriching our perception of the world.

FS You work a lot with generative processes. In general, these can be found not only in computer software but also in nature. Generative means "having the power or function of generating, originating, producing, or reproducing", in biology it means "of or relating to the production of offspring", and in computing it means "using ▸ artificial intelligence (p. 26) algorithms to create complete units of content (such as text compositions, images, audio, or video) based on a broad corpus of material." These processes include a certain degree of chance. Chance seems to be a driving force in your work: on the one side, ▸ algorithms (p. 26) generate the projected moving images based on images that you prepare, meaning the projected images are ever evolving and never look the same. But visitors also can interact with your installations, bringing in another form of chance and influencing the appearance of the artwork. Why is the accidental important for you?

> Chance introduces a dimension of unpredictability into my digital works.... [It] acts as a creative force, capable of generating infinite variations and unique forms that could never arise from strict control or rigid planning.

MC Chance introduces a dimension of unpredictability into my digital works. It reflects the very nature of life, which is a blend of determinism and contingency, of structure and surprise. Chance acts as a creative force, capable of generating infinite variations and unique forms that could never arise from strict control or rigid planning.
In my installations, chance allows for the creation of dynamic and ephemeral experiences. It also triggers reflection on our human condition: just as our birth and personal encounters are shaped by random elements, chance in my creations symbolizes the fragile and unpredictable beauty of existence. Finally, by integrating chance into programmed digital systems, I aim to blur the boundaries between the artificial and the living, creating generative works that are in constant evolution.

FS Do your algorithms sometimes surprise you?

● MC Yes, very often. Algorithms have this incredible ability to produce unexpected results, sometimes beyond what I had envisioned or imagined. For example, the behavior of cellular automata, the structures generated by Voronoi diagrams, or the intricate patterns of fractals regularly astonish me with their formal and conceptual richness.

These are not merely happy accidents; they genuinely enrich my artistic vision. They reveal internal dynamics within the algorithms that, although guided by defined parameters, occasionally elude complete anticipation. It is within this space that much of the value of working with these systems lies: they become creative partners, opening up new avenues that I might not have explored otherwise. This dimension of unpredictability is important to me, as it fuels a perpetual quest and keeps my creative process alive and constantly evolving.

● FS As mentioned above, working with a generative process includes the possibility of chance. Is this what interests you most in applying artificial intelligence? And how do you divide the work between you and the AI?

● MC I share the creative process with artificial intelligence by setting a precise framework that guides and channels its capabilities. This starts with writing carefully crafted ▸ prompts (p. 29), which steer the artistic direction, as well as feeding the AI with my own creations and visual or conceptual references. In return, the AI generates variations and sometimes proposes unexpected solutions, thus becoming a true collaborator in the process.

This dialogue between the artist and the machine is both stimulating and unpredictable: it can lead to disappointing or uninteresting results, but it can also bring about wonderful discoveries that open up new perspectives. When the AI's proposal has potential, I work to refine and enrich it, transforming it into something even more extraordinary.

This dialogue between the artist and the machine is both stimulating and unpredictable: it can lead to disappointing or uninteresting results, but it can also bring about wonderful discoveries that open up new perspectives. When the AI's proposal has potential, I work to refine and enrich it, transforming it into something even more extraordinary. This evolving interaction embodies a hybrid collaboration, where human and artificial intelligence mutually enrich each other to push the boundaries of artistic creation.

● FS In recent years, artists have experimented a lot with AI to understand what its possibilities might be. Aren't we now entering a phase where the field of experimentation needs to develop into a field of defined artistic decisions showing how artists use AI in order to help visitors better understand the role of technology in the work? Often, the viewer is not given any insight in the difference between where the artist was at work and where the AI.

What are the advantages, from your point of view, of integrating AI, and how can it become more than a trendy tool?

● MC It is essential that AI serves a precise artistic intention, rather than being a mere technical feat or an alluring novelty. AI relies on the prompts formulated by the user: every keyword and hierarchy of ideas influences the outcome. Without a strong vision or idea, AI is merely an inert instrument, comparable to a pencil lying next to a blank sheet of paper.

Far from stifling creativity, AI allows for the exploration of new forms; it represents a new language and a novel aesthetic. However, its use demands constant dialogue between the artist and the machine: precise writing of prompts, the ability to respond to generated proposals, and a critical eye to refine and guide the process.

Artificial intelligence does not replace the artist; it transforms the creative process. Art now resides in this interaction—in the way one organizes, interprets, and co-creates with the machine. Like the avant-gardes of the twentieth century, AI disrupts conventions and enriches the artistic vocabulary, inviting us to rethink our relationship with tools, processes, and creativity itself.

This conversation took place in Paris on January 28, 2025.

DIGITAL FILE →

Meta-Nature AI, started 2023 · Generative and interactive installation · Dimensions variable · Software: Claude Micheli · See also pp. 160, 162–71

DRAWING → →

Complex Meshes 8, 2022 · Felt-tip pen on paper, drawn by a robot · 50×65 cm (19 11/16×25 9/16 in.)

AI relies on the prompts formulated by the user: every keyword and hierarchy of ideas influences the outcome. Without a strong vision or idea, AI is merely an inert instrument, comparable to a pencil lying next to a blank sheet of paper.

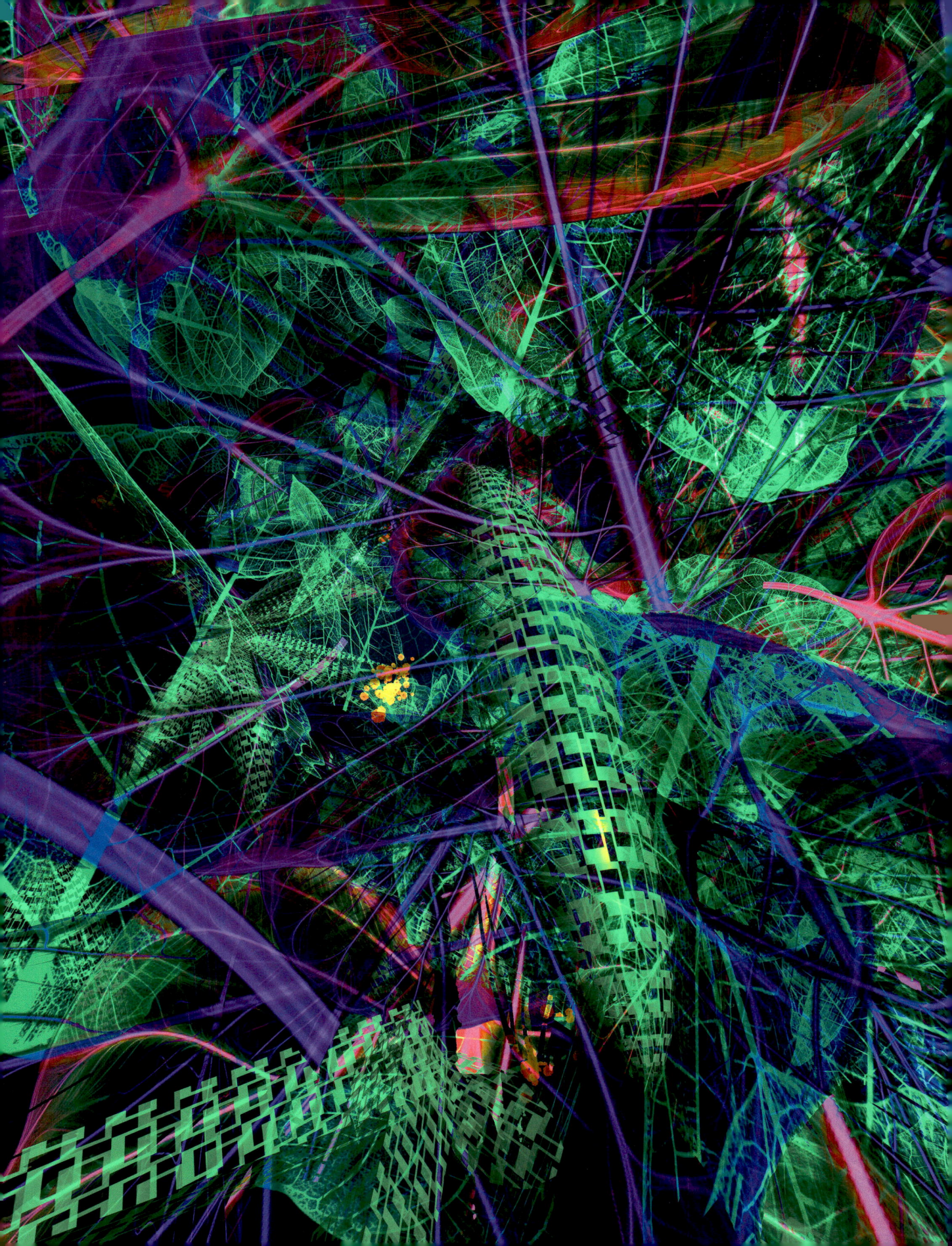

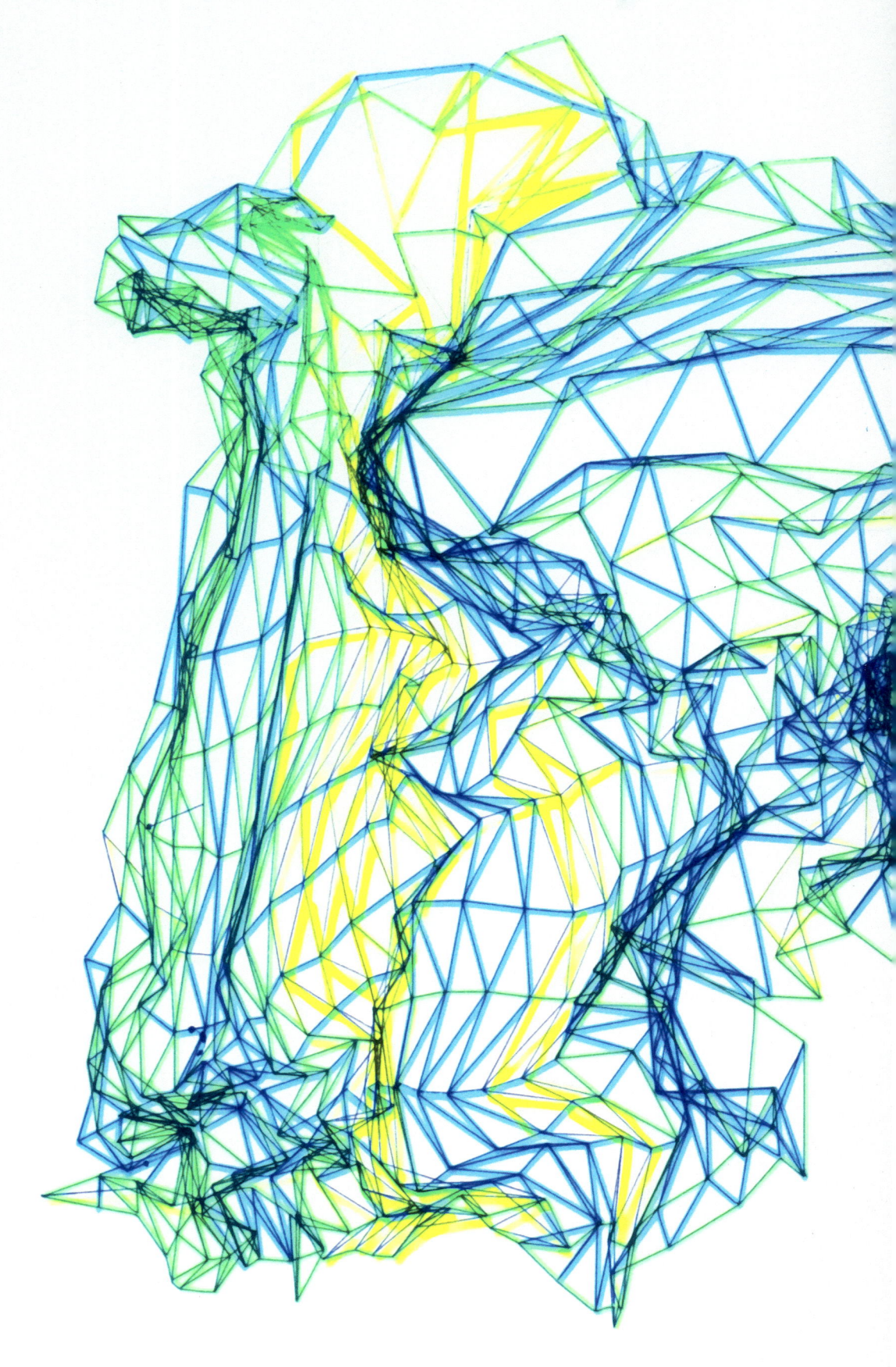

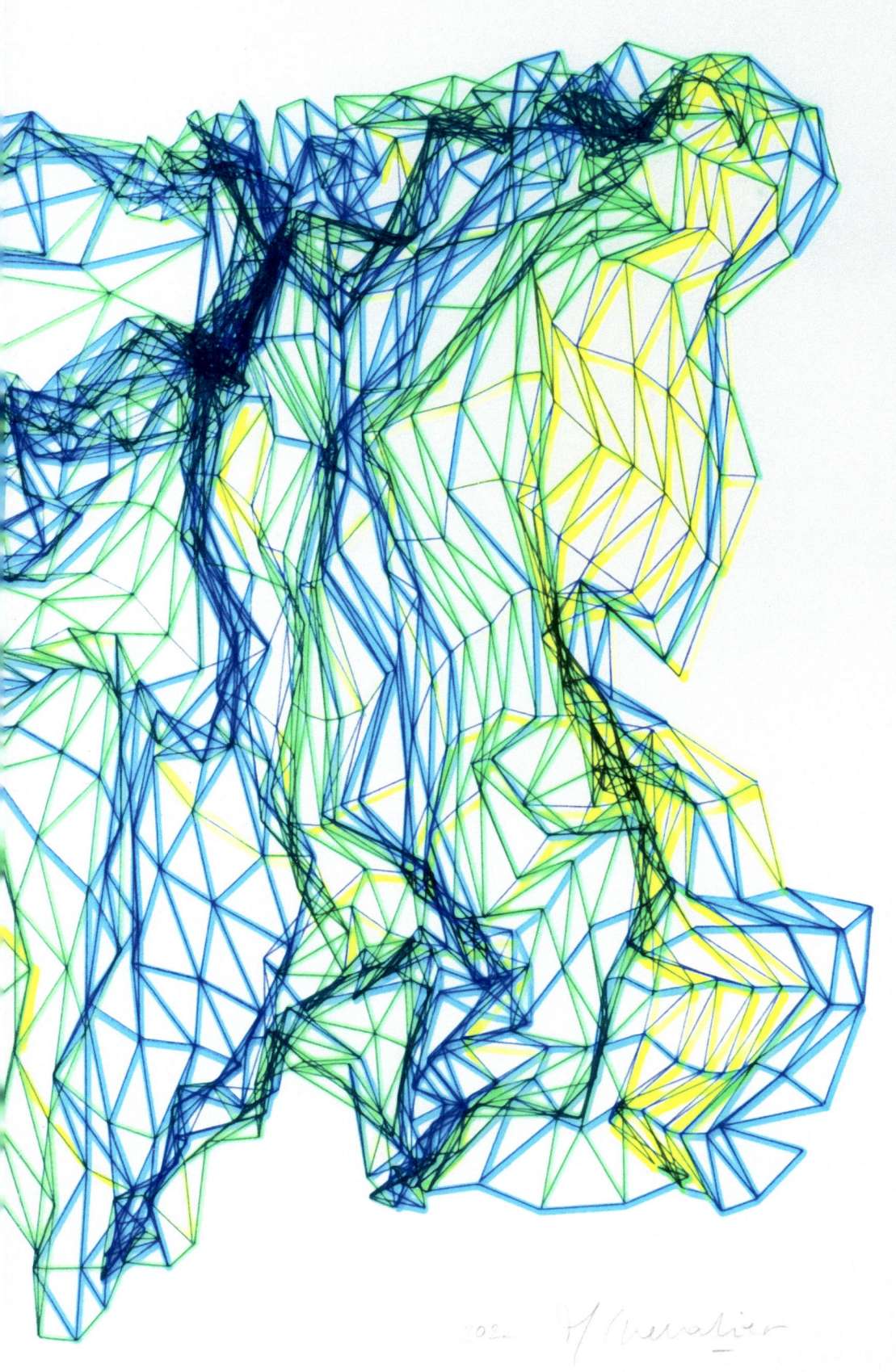

2022   M Chevalier

Glossary

Algorithm

Algorithms are fundamental to computer science and computer technology. An algorithm is a set of rules or instructions. It may consist of a sequence of simple "if–then" statements or more complex mathematical equations. Algorithms help collate data, retrieve information,

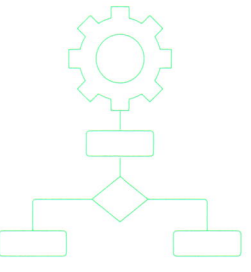

make decisions, and recognize patterns. They can also be used to create digital works of art. So-called nature-inspired optimization algorithms are based on natural processes. They help solve optimization, search, and learning problems in computer science. For example, "ant colony" optimization algorithms, which are based on the behavior of real ants in their search for food, are used for more efficient supply and logistics chains.

Artificial Intelligence

Artificial intelligence (AI) is a machine's ability to simulate human skills such as learning, planning, and logical thinking, as well as creative processes. Artificial intelligence uses data to learn how to read information and solve problems. In contrast

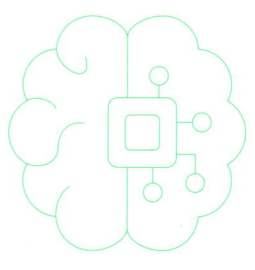

to ▸ machine learning, it can also deal with unstructured data and unforeseen events. While predictive artificial intelligence leverages existing data with the help of systematic ▸ algorithms and machine learning to recognize patterns and draw conclusions from them, generative artificial intelligence is able to generate new content such as text, images, videos, or music. If an AI model is trained with one-sided data, this has an impact on its performance or results. AI-based systems can either be installed in physical devices (for example in robots, drones, or autonomous cars) or operate in a purely software-based form in virtual space (for example in search engines, facial or speech recognition systems, and image analysis software).

Binary System

The word "binary" comes from the Latin *bini*, meaning "double" or "in pairs." The binary system uses only two digits, 0 and 1, to represent all numbers (see also p. 28 the overview of decimal, binary, and ▸ hexadecimal system). It is the basic language of computing systems and is used to convey data or instructions in an unambiguous and machine-readable form. This ensures high reliability and speed for computers and communication systems. Data is stored on a computer as binary code and can then be converted into forms of text or images suitable for display on a screen, for example. The earliest dual systems are known to date back to the third century BCE, but it was not until the twentieth century that the binary system with the two digits 0 and 1 became the basis for computer technology.

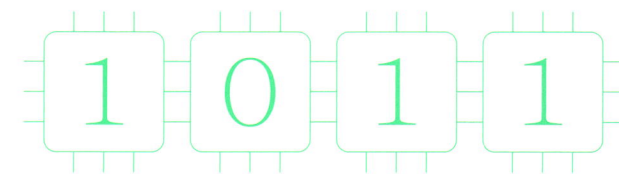

Bit

The word "bit" is formed from the words "binary" and "digit." A bit is the smallest binary unit of information and forms the basis for all larger data units in computer technology. In the ▸ binary system, a bit consists either of the value 0 or 1.

Crystal

A crystal is a solid that occurs in nature, but can also be grown artificially. Its atoms or molecules are not randomly distributed, but are arranged in repeating units—they form a crystal lattice. Crystals can

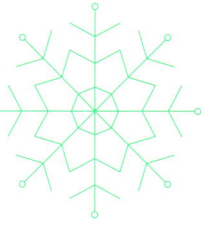

be created from liquids or gas. Snow, for example, consists of water crystals that develop from water vapor. However, crystals can also form under pressure, such as diamonds, which develop from carbon under pressure and heat. Not every crystal is a ▸ mineral, not every mineral is a crystal.

Digital Art

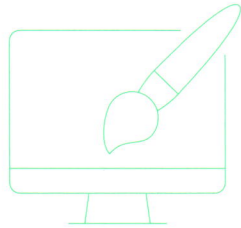

The word "digital" is derived from the Latin *digitus*, meaning "finger." The term thus refers to finger-counting. Digital devices use numerical values to display information by means of an electronic process that generates, stores, and processes data in two states: Off (0) or On (1). Digital art utilizes digital technologies as a central part of the artistic process. The media are extremely diverse and range from digital photography, computer graphics, and video art to generative works that develop infinitely with the help of ▸ algorithms, and to works that are created by the artist in collaboration with ▸ artificial intelligence. In all cases, the creation of an artwork requires hardware, such as a computer or a digital camera, and corresponding software.

Fractal

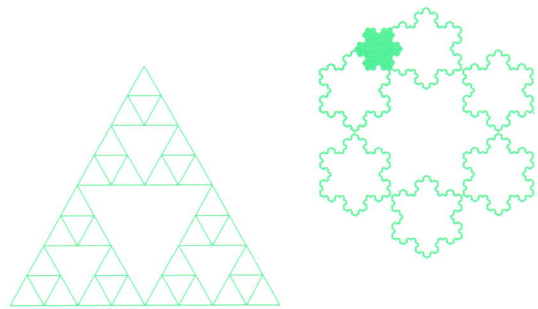

The word "fractal" is derived from the Latin *fractus*, meaning "broken," which in turn comes from the verb *frangere*, meaning "to break into pieces." The term was coined in 1975 by mathematician Benoît Mandelbrot (1924–2010). It is used to describe geometric shapes that appear infinitely the same at different scales. Scientists refer to this as self-similarity. Fractal patterns can often be found in nature, for example in snowflakes, ferns, and even the broccoli variety known as romanesco, whose individual florets always reflect the vegetable's overall shape. Abstract fractals can be generated by computers. They often bear the names of their creators: Mandelbrot set, Hilbert curve, Sierpinski triangle,

or Koch snowflake. However, fractals also have a practical application in technology, for example in cell phone antenna design.

Generative Art

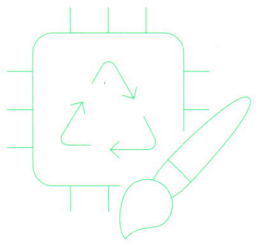

The word "generative" is derived from the Latin *generare*, meaning "to generate." Generative art refers to artistic processes where artists from the fields of music, literature, and visual arts provide a machine, such as a computer, with a set of rules, based on which the computer produces a work of art using ▸ algorithms or mathematical formulas. Artists can decide whether to leave all decisions in this process to the machine or to integrate some pre-defined decisions into the set of rules. In either case, they consciously relinquish some control in the creative process. The result is not fully predictable, as endless variations of the initial idea are possible. Artistic exploration of chance as an extension of the creative process started at the beginning of the twentieth century and was further developed after the middle of the century in the interplay between systematic rules and chance. Beginning in the 1960s, artists began to use the computer as an artistic tool (see also pp. 35–37), which enabled these methods to develop even greater potential.

Generative Artificial Intelligence

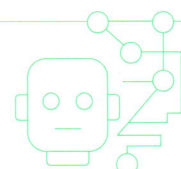

▸ Artificial Intelligence

Herbarium

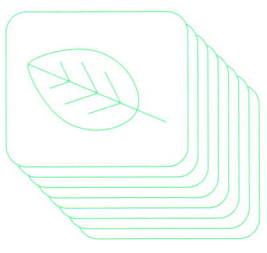

An herbarium (from the Latin *herba*, meaning "herb") is a systematically organized collection of pressed and dried plants and plant parts. The so-called herbarium specimens are usually mounted onto sheets of paper and stored in folders. Some scientific collections also hold wet preserved specimens; in such cases, plants are stored in alcohol. Other materials such as loose seeds, pollen, dried fruits, algae, and fungi are also preserved. On this basis, data sets, botanical illustrations, photographic images, and other forms of information are created for further research.

Hexadecimal System

The word "hexadecimal" is made up of the Greek *hexa* ("six") and the Latin *decem* ("ten"). The hexadecimal system is a numbering system. Unlike the decimal system, which we use for everyday calculations, the hexadecimal system uses the numbers 0 to 9, but replaces 10 to

0	1	2	3
4	5	6	7
8	9	A	B
C	D	E	F

15 with A to F. In contrast to the ▸ binary system, which only uses the digits 0 and 1 to symbolize numbers, there are sixteen symbols to represent numbers here. For example, if a piece of information has eight digits in the binary system, the same information can be represented with two digits in the hexadecimal system. Large numbers can therefore be represented with fewer digits when using this system, making them faster to write and easier to read in computer science.

	DECIMAL SYSTEM	BINARY SYSTEM	HEXA-DECIMAL SYSTEM
Zero	0	0 0 0 0	0
One	1	0 0 0 1	1
Two	2	0 0 1 0	2
Three	3	0 0 1 1	3
Four	4	0 1 0 0	4
Five	5	0 1 0 1	5
Six	6	0 1 1 0	6
Seven	7	0 1 1 1	7
Eight	8	1 0 0 0	8
Nine	9	1 0 0 1	9
Ten	10	1 0 1 0	A
Eleven	11	1 0 1 1	B
Twelve	12	1 1 0 0	C
Thirteen	13	1 1 0 1	D
Fourteen	14	1 1 1 0	E
Fifteen	15	1 1 1 1	F

Machine Learning

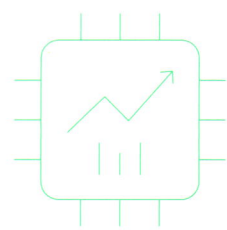

Machine learning is part of the broader concept of ▸ artificial intelligence. In machine learning, an ▸ algorithm is fed with data. The more data it has as a basis, the more precise its decisions can be. The computer trains and improves itself as the amount of data increases, instead of having to be explicitly programmed for a specific task. However, there is an essential difference between machine learning and artificial intelligence: while artificial intelligence can deal with unforeseen events (unstructured data), machine learning can only process predictable events (structured data) in a targeted manner. An example from everyday life is that an algorithm detects when money is withdrawn from an account at an unusual location, potentially enabling it to uncover fraud, which becomes possible through the training of machine learning.

Minerals

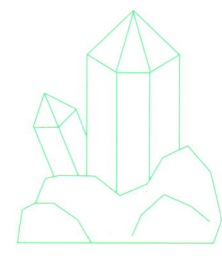

The term "mineral" refers to natural substances that are formed through geological processes. At 95 percent, silicates make up the largest part within the mineral families. They consist of oxygen and silicon and contain magnesium, aluminum, calcium, iron, and other metals. Minerals are usually solid at room temperature, with the exception of mercury, for example, which is liquid. Minerals are made up of either atoms or molecules. However, not every mineral is a ▸ crystal, just as not every crystal is a mineral. Sugar, for example, forms crystalline structures but was not formed in a geological process. The opal gemstone originates from a geological process but does not form a crystalline structure. The focus of research into minerals is on their chemical composition, while crystals are studied for the physical arrangement of atoms in the crystal lattice.

Pixel

The word "pixel" is formed from the combined abbreviations of "picture" ("pic") and "element" ("el"). A pixel is the smallest unit of a digital image. It contains the three primary colors red, green, and blue (RGB). These have different intensities,

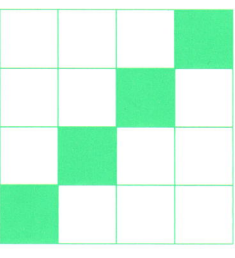

allowing different colors to be generated. If, for example, 3266 × 2449 is specified as the dimension of an image, this refers to the number of pixels regarding width and height. Different resolutions, resulting in the according image size, can also be defined. If, for example, a print quality of 300 dpi (dots per inch) is specified for the stated dimensions of 3266 × 2449, this results in a printed size of 27.7 × 20.7 centimeters. At only 72 dpi, this would result in a size of 115.2 × 86.4 centimeters.

Prompt

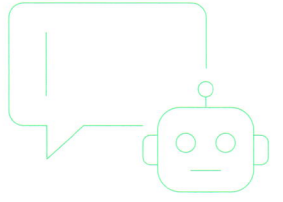

A prompt is an instruction a human gives to ▸ artificial intelligence. It is used to instruct an AI model to generate a specific text, create an image, or perform a specific task, for example. The prompt can be provided in the form of text, image, audio, or other data formats. The AI analyzes the input and generates a response based on what it has learned during previous training. Generally, result quality depends on how precisely the prompt is formulated.

Virtual Reality

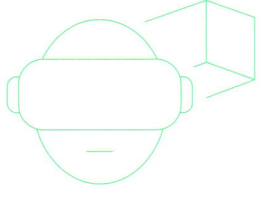

Virtual reality (VR) refers to a visual environment that is created using computer graphics. Users usually access VR via VR glasses, or move around in a 360-degree presentation. The user has the full visual experience of being transported to a different place. Virtual reality is usually interactive; users can move around the virtual environment with the help of a controller or gestures, and, if intended, also act in it. While the individual perspective can be changed when using glasses, it is fixed in the 360-degree presentation.

Virtuality

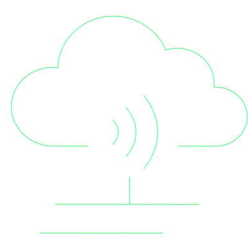

The word "virtuality" is derived from the Latin *virtus*, meaning masculinity, virtue, morality, but also power and ability in the sense of spiritual strength. Virtuality is a form of existence that is immaterial and exists only as digital or electronic information. Virtuality therefore refers to something that is potentially or seemingly real without actually existing materially—for example in digital simulations or computer-generated environments.

Voxel

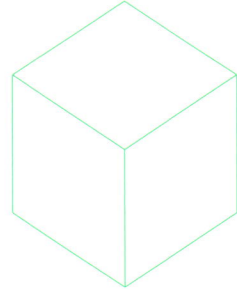

The word "voxel" is formed from the combined abbreviations of "volume" and "element." A voxel is the smallest addressable element in a three-dimensional digital representation and could be regarded a three-dimensional ▸ pixel: a "volume element" corresponding to the two-dimensional image element pixel.

PATTERN →

Pixel Wave, started 2011 · Generative and interactive installation · Dimensions variable · Software: Cyrille Henry, Antoine Villeret · See also pp. 78–81

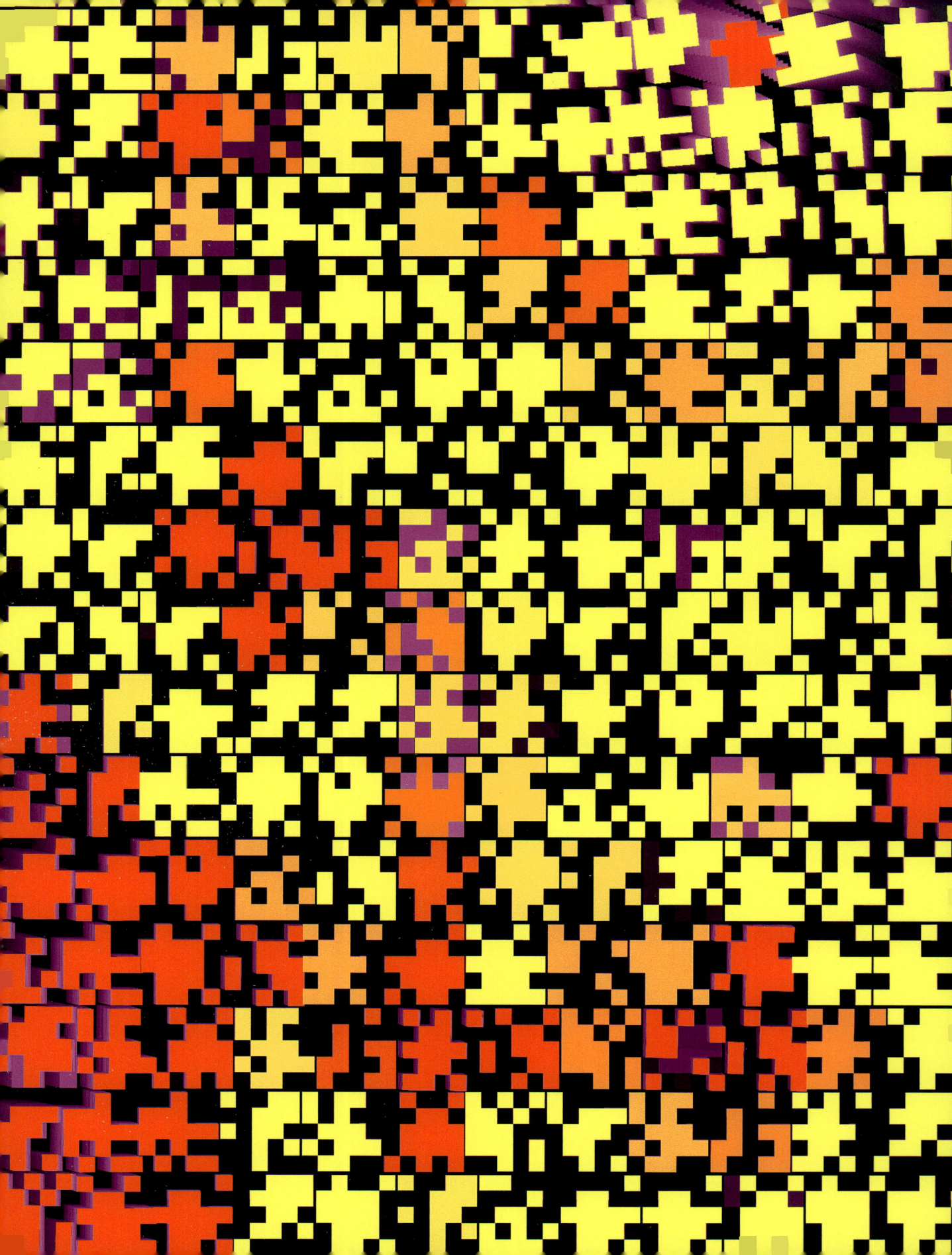

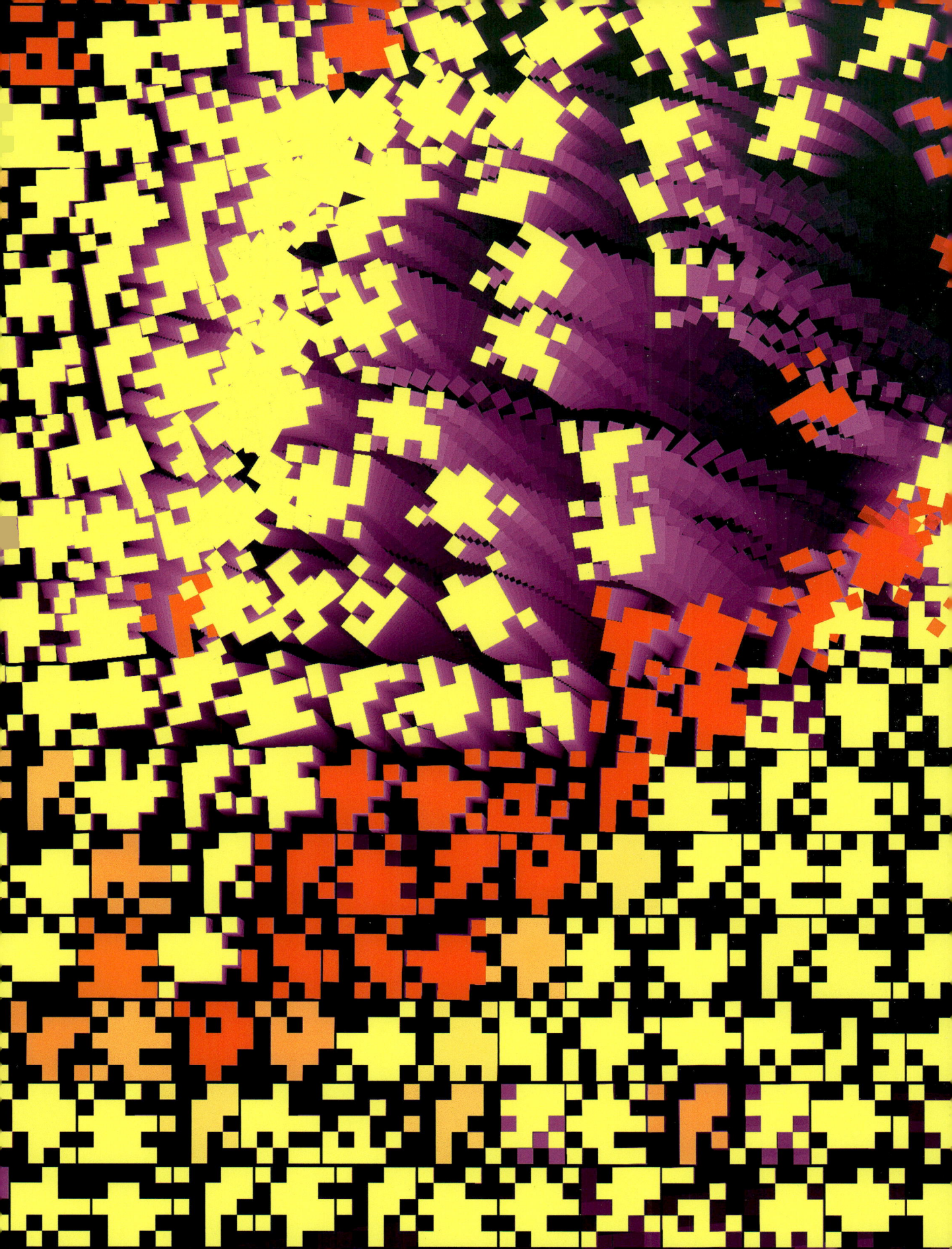

FRANZISKA STÖHR

On Authorship, Chance, and Interaction

MIGUEL CHEVALIER'S METHOD THROUGH THE LENS OF ART HISTORY

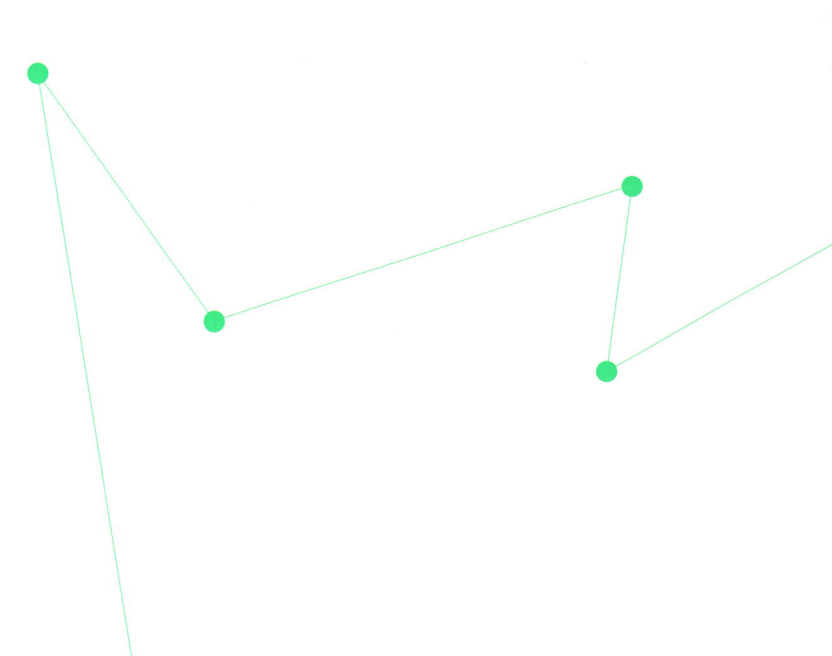

Miguel Chevalier has been working with the computer as a creative medium since the 1980s. Although his works originate in the digital realm, the sensory and physical experience of his art is an equally important aspect for him. His current work includes sculptures and drawings that he produces employing 3D printing and robotics, machine-produced embroideries and handmade tapestries, videos, and generative projections on a monumental scale. In the latter—using ▸ algorithms (p. 26) based on motifs created by the artist—a computer continuously generates moving images, almost all of which viewers help shape interactively through their body movements.

Chevalier's early works were primarily pictorial inventions, whether in the form of prints, sculptures, or videos where he explored the digital world's fundamental elements, such as ▸ pixels (p. 28), the ▸ binary system (p. 26), or algorithms. Since the 2000s, he has increasingly expanded his oeuvre to include themes associated with our globally connected world, the relationship between nature and technology, and the relationship between humans and the environment. Celebrating the diversity of nature, he also reminds us of its existentially important role and fragility. Chevalier's thinking and methodological work are characterized by his cross-genre engagement with a wide variety of art historical discourses, particularly in the twentieth and twenty-first centuries. His main focus is on the shared authorship of artist and machine, the interplay between automated processes and chance as an extension of one's own creativity, the further development of the concept of the picture plane, and interaction with the public.

This essay sheds light on Miguel Chevalier's methods and looks back at corresponding discourses and predecessors in art history.[1] Introductions to the individual chapters and the short texts beginning on page 54 focus on groups of works and selected pieces by the artist.

Shared Authorship with a Machine and Chance as a Creative Partner

Since first coming into contact with computers in the 1980s, Miguel Chevalier has been fascinated by the idea of producing works that continuously evolve and make use of time, light, and movement as central creative elements. Additionally, he has long been interested in working with algorithms that he has created, seeing how they at times produce unforeseen results.[2] From the onset, he regarded the computer as a creative counterpart capable of enriching his own thinking and artistic work. Other devices, such as drawing robots, 3D printers, and embroidery machines, expanded his range of tools over time. His oeuvre thus follows in the tradition of artists who explored working with machines while also investigating the nature of authorship and chance as a creative partner.

Historically, the interplay between art and machines by no means began with the computer. One need only think of Leonardo da Vinci's (1452–1519) or Albrecht Dürer's (1471–1528) perspective machines (figs. 1–2); Pierre and Henry-Louis Jaquet-Droz's (1721–1790; 1752–1791) humanoid automata, which could make music, write, and draw with the help of templates (fig. 3); or, to give a literary, and thus fictional, example, Alfred Jarry's (1873–1907) novel *Gestes et opinions du docteur Faustroll, pataphysicien*

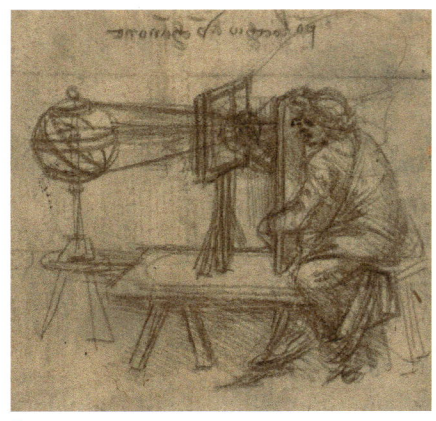

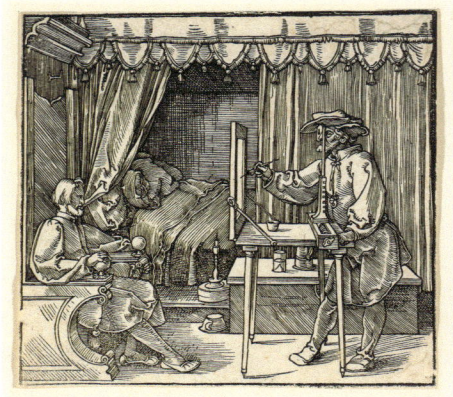

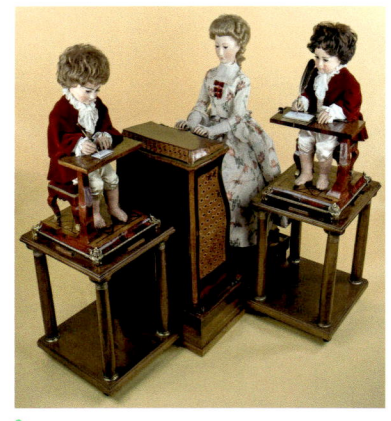

(*Exploits and Opinions of Dr. Faustroll, Pataphysician*), in which a machine splashes walls with paint.[3] A distinction, however, must always be made as to whether the machine is merely an instrument, such as the perspective machine, or whether it actually becomes part of a creative process, as is detailed below.

With the rise of industrialization, machines in general gained importance. In the context of the visual arts, they also provided the impetus to question traditional notions of the artistic genius and unique works of art and to distribute the creative process among several actors. Media theorist Lev Manovich (b. 1960) has pointed out that collective authorship is not exclusively associated with new media and works from traditional painters' workshops or the construction of medieval cathedrals were already based on this principle.[4] In the twentieth century, however, tendencies emerged that sought to radically rethink the creative artistic process from a critical perspective. The machine was an ideal counterpart for this. The Constructivists demanded that artists should become engineers; at the *First International Dada Fair* in Berlin in 1920, the Dada movement, using the slogan "Art is dead. Long live the new machine art of Tatlin," declared traditional painting and sculpture matters of the past while paying tribute to Constructivist Vladimir Tatlin (1885–1953).[5]

Artistic engagement with the deconstruction of the artistic genius and its idiosyncrasies was further enriched by other forms of shared authorship and machine production, for example the contributions of László Moholy-Nagy (1895–1946), who instructed a factory on how to execute his enamel piece *EM 2 (Telephone Picture)* (1923; fig. 4) by telephone.[6] In addition, there was a general interest in machine production which allowed for the omission of artistic idiosyncrasies altogether—whether in the case of Donald Judd (1928–1994), who had works such as *Untitled* (1967; fig. 5) entirely constructed in factories, or Andy Warhol (1928–1987), who had pieces reproduced en masse via screen-printing and said of himself, "The reason I paint this way is

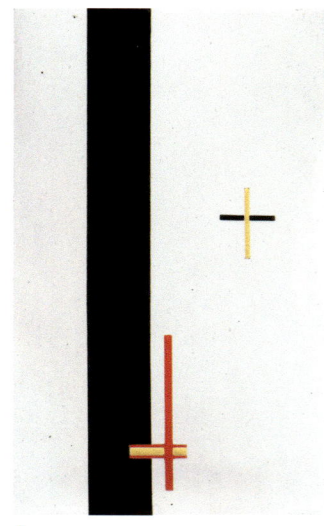

FIG. 1

Leonardo da Vinci · *Codex Atlanticus*, f. 5 recto, ca. 1480–82 · Silverpoint on paper · Veneranda Biblioteca Ambrosiana, Milan · Detail

FIG. 2

Albrecht Dürer · *Artist Drawing a Portrait of a Man*, undated · Woodcut · 13.3 × 14.9 cm (5 1/4 × 5 7/8 in.) · The Metropolitan Museum of Art, New York

FIG. 3

Pierre and Henry-Louis Jaquet-Droz et al. · *The Illustrator*, ca. 1770–73 · 76 × 39.9 × 42.6 cm (29 15/16 × 15 11/16 × 16 3/4 in.) · *The Musician*, 1772–74 · 137 × 66.8 × 88.5 cm (53 15/16 × 26 5/16 × 34 13/16 in.) · Pierre and Henry-Louis Jaquet-Droz · *The Writer*, 1768–73 · 76 × 40.5 × 43 cm (29 15/16 × 15 15/16 × 16 15/16 in.) Musée d'Art et d'Histoire de Neuchâtel

FIG. 4

László Moholy-Nagy · *EM 2 (Telephone Picture)*, 1923 · Porcelain enamel on steel · 47.5 × 30.1 cm (18 3/4 × 11 7/8 in.) · The Museum of Modern Art, New York

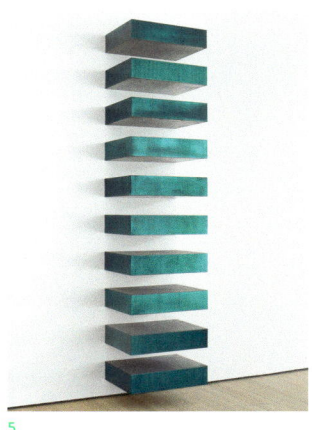

5

because I want to be a machine, and I feel that whatever I do and do machine-like is what I want to do."[7]

When it comes to the relationship of art and machines, it is particularly the artists who used machines to set art in motion, while still keeping the viewer in mind, that hold significance for Miguel Chevalier. Specifically, he has cited Marcel Duchamp (1887–1968) as an inspiration, in particular his kinetic objects such as the so-called *Rotoreliefs* (1935; fig. 6), motorized discs whose circular motifs only form complete spirals in the viewer's perception.[8] The art historian Söke Dinkla (b. 1962) perfectly sums up this connection: "Artist and artwork thus share their formerly authorial position not only with their viewers, but also with the machinery that is ultimately the prerequisite for the altered perception."[9] Jean Tinguely's (1925–1991) drawing machines, which he created beginning in 1959 under the title *Méta-Matics*, are also an important reference here. Driven by an electric motor, they produced random abstract drawings. Some of the machines could also be operated by the public (fig. 7).[10] Tinguely emphasized an aspect that is also essential for Chevalier: "For me the machine is first and foremost an instrument that allows me to be poetic. If you respect the machine and engage with it, it is perhaps possible to produce a 'happy' machine, and by happy I mean 'free.'"[11] Finally, Nicolas Schöffer (1912–1992), the French representative of reactive kinetic art, is a point of reference in this context. He constructed cybernetic sculptures that produced sounds or actions in relation to environmental influences. *CYSP 1* (1956), for example, reacted to changes in color of the ground (white/black) and sound environment. The sculpture moved freely in space, the colored panels rotated around their own axes.[12] At the Festival de l'Art d'Avant-Garde in Le Corbusier's Cité Radieuse in Marseille, the sculpture interacted with ballet dancers, evoking a human–machine collaboration with the two parties on equal footing (fig. 8).[13]

The computer opened up countless new possibilities in this respect. While today's computer-based art has grown substantially more complex due to advanced programs and high storage capacities, early computer art consisted of simple graphics and first had to find its place within the visual arts.[14] In the 1970s, for example, American artist Kenneth Knowlton (1931–2022) noted, "It is still too early to call what we

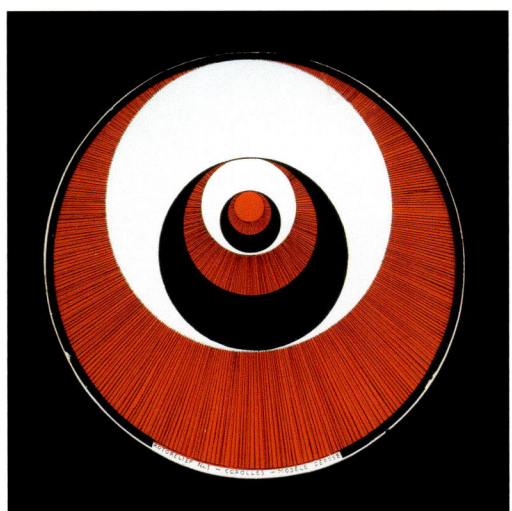

6

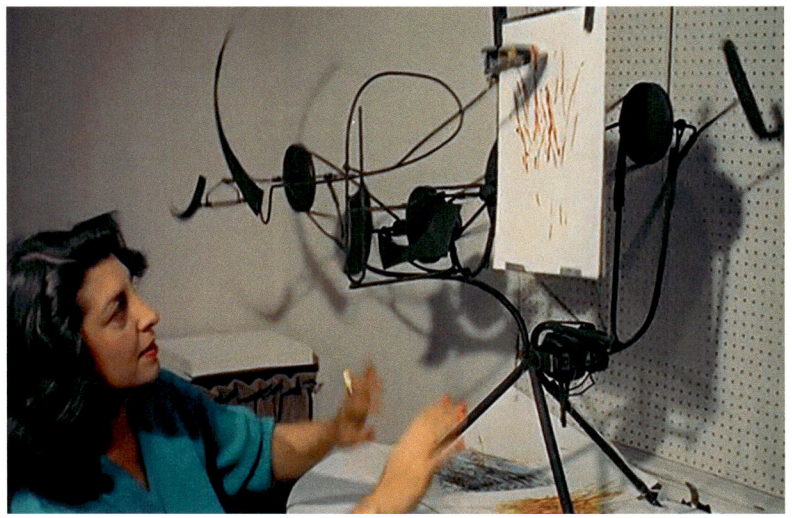

7

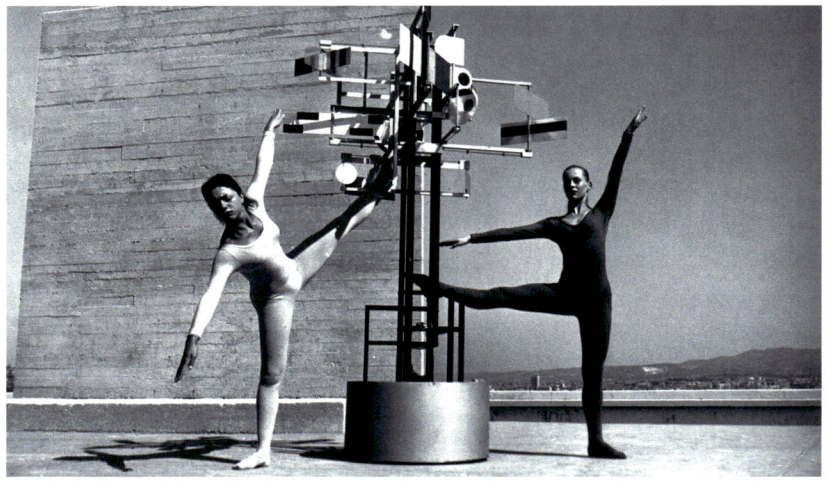

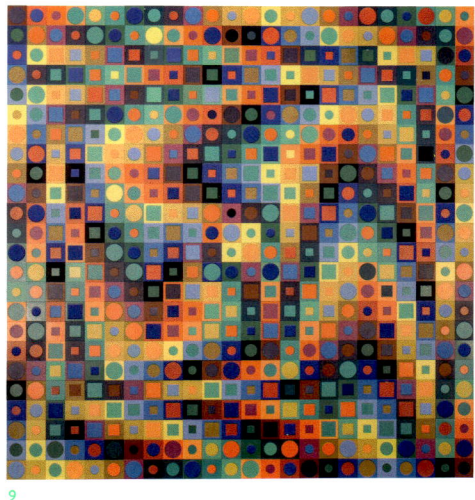

8

9

are producing with the computer 'art.' It will certainly remain so for a long time to come, because the complexity of the processes is highly tempting, but also quite a hindrance for the artist."[15] This discourse continued into the 1980s. Karin Guminski (b. 1959), author of the book *Kunst am Computer* (Art on the computer), also points out the problem of accessibility in this context: "You had to be particularly persistent and maintain the right contacts with research institutions if you wanted to work on one of the computers and get good results out of a machine. This was only possible for artists who were fascinated by computers per se."[16] Miguel Chevalier was lucky enough to have access to computers at the Pratt Institute and the School of Visual Arts during two stays in New York in 1983 and 1984, and in Paris at the Centre National de la Recherche Scientifique, when scientists were not using them at night. In 1985, he finally acquired his first personal computer (see also p. 10). For him, this meant complete freedom to explore the relationship between artist, machine, and the public. When Chevalier invites the viewers to influence his computer-guided drawings, but also the projections, through their own body movements, he is interested in joint creation in the vein of Tinguely or Schöffer, but also in the individual's, and thus the recipient's, ephemeral perception, much like Duchamp.

For most artists, the element of chance means an unforeseeable and therefore productive extension in the creation of works "that are not exclusively shaped by the ideas of their creators."[17] However, Eva-Marina Froitzheim has emphasized that it is always the artists who pave the way for chance, which "can find its way into a work of art from the outside, through various materials or external parameters, or occur intrinsically as a result of the creative process as a specific, unrepeatable aesthetic component. Unlike in the natural sciences, however, there is no objective chance within the realm of art. Wherever chance is consciously or unconsciously sought out or integrated, it is always a matter of chance being guided by the artist."[18] Chance is not necessarily linked to machines; it had already found its way into the visual arts via other techniques, for example decalcomania, which was invented in eighteenth-century England and later developed further by the Surrealists. In this semi-automatic, random process, wet paint is transferred from one surface to another. Another example also used by the Surrealists is the method of automatic writing, an

FIG. 8

Tania Bari and Marie-Claire Carrié from Maurice Béjart's ballet ensemble dance with Nicolas Schöffer's sculpture *CYSP 1* on the roof terrace of Le Corbusier's Cité Radieuse during the Festival de l'Art d'Avant-Garde in Marseille, August 8, 1956.

FIG. 9

Victor Vasarely · *MAJUS*, 1964 · 576 × 576 cm (226 3/4 × 226 3/4 in.) · Fondation Vasarely, Aix-en-Provence

intuitive form of emotionally grounded authorship without the intervention of a critical ego. One of the most prominent artists to further develop this technique in painting was Jackson Pollock (1912–1956), who created his so-called "drip paintings" from the 1940s onwards. Bending over a canvas spread out on the floor, he let the paint drip onto the fabric by gesturing with the brush.

In this context, Chevalier refers to artists who combined a clear vocabulary of forms with the principle of chance. These include Victor Vasarely (1906–1997), who, inspired by Auguste Herbin (1882–1960), also invented a so-called "alphabet plastique" for his painting. Herbin's system from 1942 assigned each letter to a specific shape, color, and musical note, providing him with a defined vocabulary for his painting. Vasarely's system, fully formulated around 1959, was based on a grid into which geometric shapes in different colors were inserted. He used "two reds, two yellows, two purples, three blues, three greens, white, black, grey; and the figures, very precisely, two squares, two circles, two diamonds, two half-discs, two double sticks, six ellipses as well as a triangle."[19] This created an infinite number of possible combinations for his at times seemingly illusionistic works (fig. 9). One last artist should also be named in this context: Sol LeWitt (1928–2007) created written instructions for his wall pieces to be realized by other people. These instructions always included some leeway in terms of implementation, so the works would never be identical when reproduced (fig. 10). Although these wall pieces are located in the field of painting, like Miguel Chevalier's generative computer-based works they are based on a system that can be used to create an infinite number of compositions.

Among the computer art pioneers, Chevalier particularly highlights Vera Molnár (1924–2023). She was given access to a computer at a Sorbonne research laboratory in 1968. In the years before, she had begun to develop handmade compositions following strict mathematical rules, from which a clear sequence of instructions for the drawing process was derived—in essence this already corresponded to the principle of algorithms. In the computer she finally found her ideal medium. Molnár deliberately allowed what she defined as "1% disorder" to affect this system in order to integrate chance into her work (fig. 11).[20] She also repeatedly intervened in the creation process to influence the result according to her artistic sensibility.[21] With his endlessly evolving works, Chevalier goes one step further by limiting his ability to influence the projections; he is only involved at the beginning, and the computer and visitor then complete the work's production together.

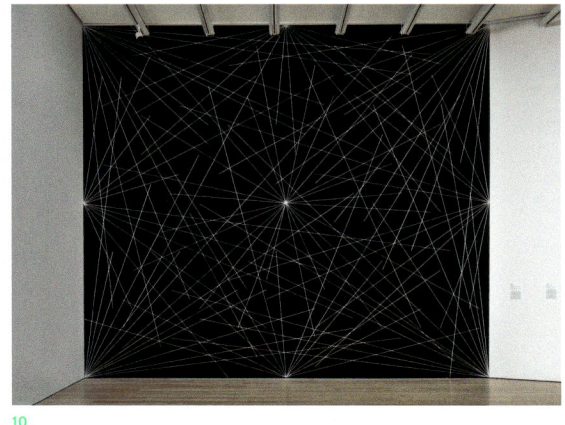

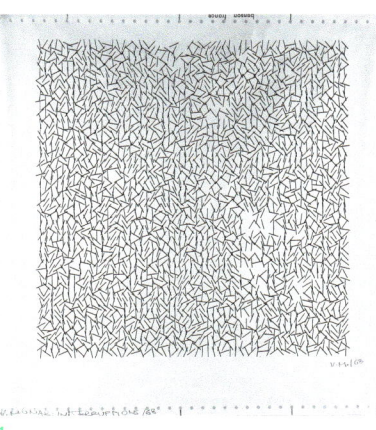

10

11

Borderless Images, Immersion, and Interaction

Early on, Miguel Chevalier took an interest in further developing the concept of the picture plane, which today mainly finds expression in his large-scale projections. Remarkably, it was primarily painters who inspired him in this respect. Having grown up in Mexico, he was familiar with the large-format murals of Diego Rivera (1886–1957) and David Alfaro Siqueiros (1896–1974) (fig. 12; see also p. 43). Moreover, in Europe there was a discourse about dissolving the boundaries of the classical two-dimensional canvas, as Lucio Fontana (1899–1968), for example, had promoted with his slashed works (fig. 13). Also of great importance to Chevalier is the work of Claude Monet (1840–1926), particularly the eight water lily paintings (1914–26; fig. 14) in the two elliptical halls of the Orangerie in Paris, which completely surround visitors. Monet wanted to create "the illusion of an endless whole, of a wave without horizon and without shore."[22] As Chevalier has explained, "Claude Monet captivated me with his exploration of time, light, and immersion. His *Water Lilies* transcend traditional painting by becoming a sensory experience, where the viewer is literally immersed in his pictorial environment. This deeply resonated with my desire to create immersive works that envelop visitors."[23]

At the beginning of his career, Chevalier still worked with slide projectors. Projections on a monumental scale, as presented by him today, were not yet possible at the time: projectors neither offered sufficient resolution nor were they affordable. It was not until the 1990s, as the quality of the devices improved and gradually became more affordable, that large-scale projections increasingly found their way into media art.[24] The idea of bringing the moving image into the exhibition space on an oversized scale had previously been realized by representatives of video art such as Nam June Paik (1932–2006) or Marie-Jo Lafontaine (b. 1950) through video sculptures that spread the moving images across several monitors (fig. 15). Paik's statement from 1965 of

FIG. 12

Diego Rivera · Murals on Secretaria de Educación Pública, Mexico City, ca. 1922–28

FIG. 13

Lucio Fontana · *Concetto spaziale – Attese*, 1962–63 · Oil on canvas · 92 × 73 cm (36 3/16 × 28 3/4 in.) · Städel Museum, Frankfurt am Main

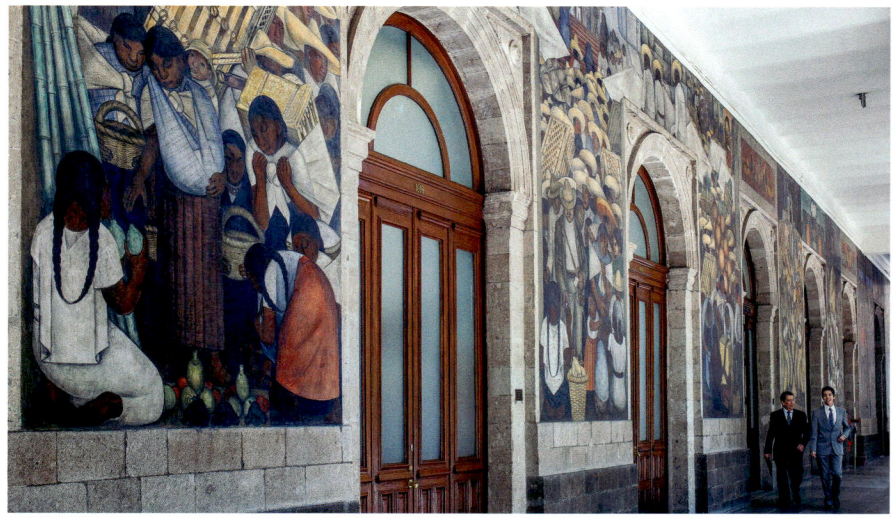

12

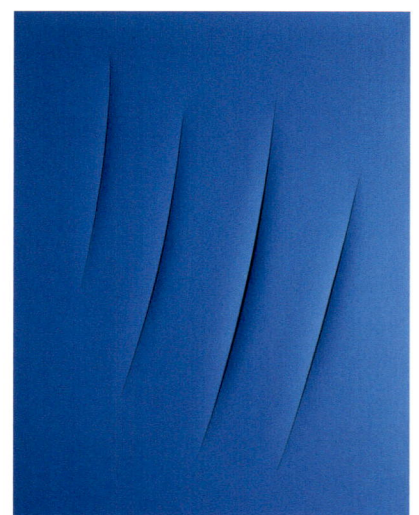

13

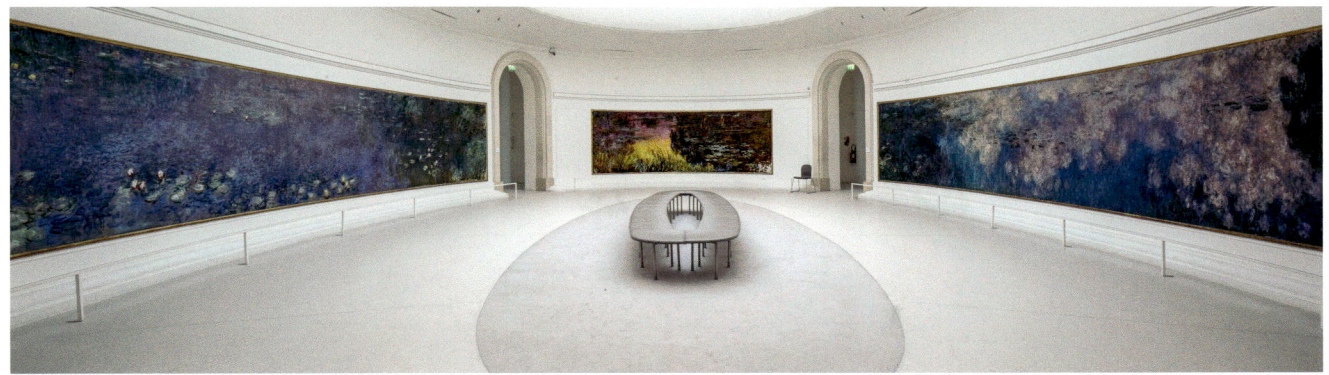

14

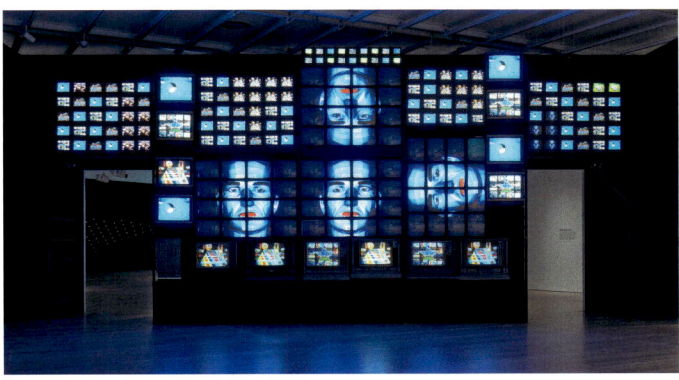

15

FIG. 14

Claude Monet · *Water Lilies*, 1914–26 · Installation view, Musée de l'Orangerie, Paris

FIG. 15

Nam June Paik · *Fin de Siècle II*, 1989 · Seven-channel video installation, 207 televisions, sound · 426.7 × 1219.2 × 152.4 cm (168 × 480 × 60 in.) · Whitney Museum of American Art, New York

the cathode-ray tube (meaning the television set) replacing the canvas is in fact also echoed in Miguel Chevalier's methodical, cross-genre thinking.[25]

In Chevalier's oeuvre, a distinction must be made between works that are finalized, such as his drawings or sculptures, and those that are ongoing. In the first case, the themes of shared authorship and chance usually only concern the relationship between artist and machine. Visitors contribute to the artwork in drawings such as those for *Complex Meshes* (started 2022; pp. 90–93), where the images are created based on people's movements in the interactive installation. The interactive projections, on the other hand, generally have neither a beginning nor an end. The images are always generated anew on the basis of a data set created by Chevalier, and are combined using an algorithm in such a way that no identical repetitions are produced. Chevalier does not formulate a narrative in his moving image works. Rather, his abstract works embody an idea, represent a theme such as the encounter of the digital and the analog realm in *The Origin of the World* (started 2012; pp. 60–67), or are a symbolic expression of our increasingly connected world, such as in *Complex Meshes* (started 2015; pp. 96, 98–105). The public therefore never misses a beginning in the exhibition space and is not given any instructions by the artist as to how long they should engage with these works. What is essential for Chevalier, however, is that the visitors change the artwork itself through their body movements and thus participate in the creative process (see also p. 20). In this, he was influenced by Yves Klein (1928–1962), who, with his *Anthropometries*, expanded the technique of painting to include the human body itself: following his instructions, women applied the shapes of their bodies, which were covered in blue paint, as imprints on the canvas (fig. 16). Also worth mentioning are the GRAV group of artists (Groupe de Recherche d'Art Visuel, 1960–68), whose environments and kinetic objects consciously involved visitors in the artistic experience; the interactive (but not digitally based) installations by Jesús Rafael Soto (1923–2005; fig. 17); and Niki de Saint Phalle (1930–2002) with her colorful walk-in sculptures in the Giardino dei Tarocchi (fig. 18).

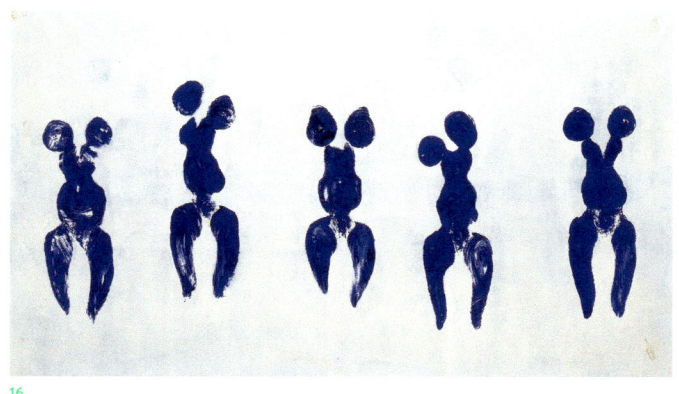

16

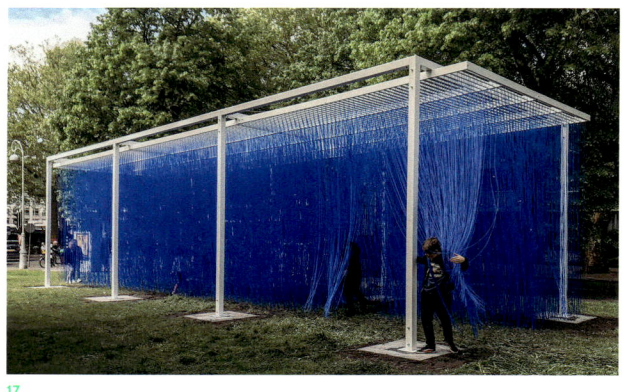

17

Lev Manovich has pointed out that interaction can also be a miscommunication between the author and the user—in this case artist and audience—since the author "has no idea about the assumptions and intentions of a particular user" and the user in turn "often also does not know anything about this work, what is supposed to do, what its interface is etc."[26] Chevalier avoids this potential problem by opening up the possibility of interaction, so the work is greatly enriched by more complex forms, however it also exists without the involvement of the public. If we look back at the beginnings of interactive art, we return once more to the early twentieth-century avant-garde. As Söke Dinkla explains, the avant-garde reacted to the "widening gap between the mass public and the art public."[27] Futurist and Dada artists were already attempting to liberate the public from its observational role, be it by inviting visitors to further work on drawings during the 1920 Dada exhibition in Cologne, or in Marcel Duchamp's legendary 1938 *Exposition Internationale du Surréalisme* in Paris, in which visitors had to illuminate the works themselves using flashlights.[28] These movements thus had a decisive influence on the visual arts' further development. In the second half of the twentieth century, closed-circuit video art installations—such as those by Bruce Nauman (b. 1941) or Dan Graham (1942–2022), in which visitors could see themselves broadcast live in the exhibition space for the first time (fig. 19)—or happenings in which people were invited to join in, gave significant impetus to the aspect of participation.[29]

When looking at Chevalier's methodological approaches to shared authorship with machines, chance as an extension of artistic creativity, the concept of immersion, and interactivity with the public, the richness and abundance of the traditions undergirding his works becomes clear. In his search for new technologies that he could harness for his art, these traditions are always present: "Each of these artists, in their own way, has enriched my thinking about form, content, and the role of art in our lives. They have encouraged me to continuously push the boundaries of my medium and to explore the intersections of art, science, technology, and humanity."[30]

Regardless of the types of works artists create with computers, what Karin Guminski stated over two decades ago still applies today: the computer is "by no means an automaton ... that can produce images without human intervention. Irrespective of what type of computer image genre, the image creator always brings his or her own person into the design in some way. Their actions are controlled by consciousness. The human consciousness is therefore always involved."[31] Looking back at the development of art

FIG. 16

Yves Klein · *Anthropometry of the Blue Period (ANT 82)*, 1960 · Dry pigment and synthetic resin on paper mounted on canvas · 156.5 × 282.5 cm (61 5/8 × 111 3/16 in.) · Centre National d'Art et de Culture Georges Pompidou, Paris

FIG. 17

Jesús Rafael Soto · *Pénétrable BBL bleu, ex. № 5/8*, 1999 · Plastic threads · Installation view, Artzuid, Amsterdam, 2019

FIG. 18

Niki de Saint Phalle et al. · Il Giardino dei Tarocchi, Garavicchio, Italy, 1979–96

FIG. 19

Dan Graham · *Present, Continuous, Past(s)*, 1974 · Mirrored wall, video camera, monitor with time delay · Ca. 244 × 366 × 244 cm (96 × 144 × 96 in.) · Courtesy the Estate of Dan Graham and Marian Goodman Gallery

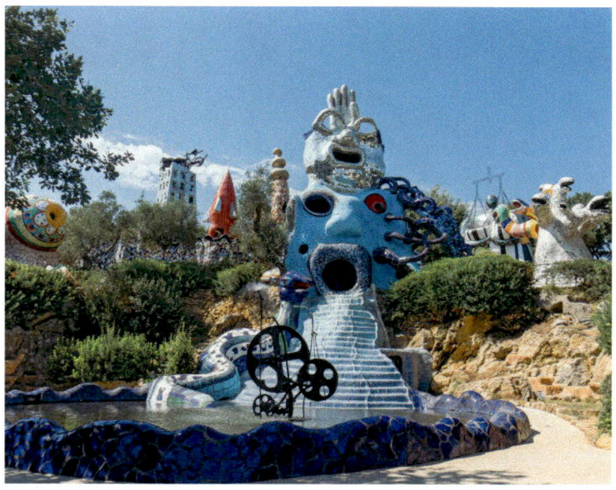

18

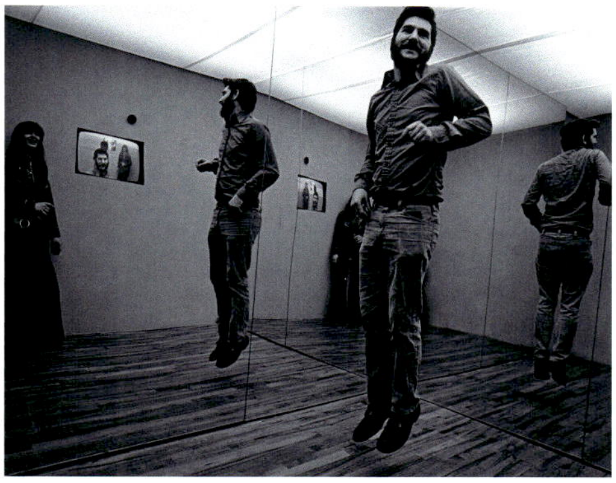

19

and technology over the past hundred years, ever-increasing computing capacities, better graphic display options, and machines that open up ever more creative solutions raise significant expectations as to what the visual arts will produce in the future. Miguel Chevalier shares none of the concerns some people have about ▸ artificial intelligence (p. 26): "Artificial intelligence does not replace the artist; it transforms the creative process. Art now resides in this interaction—in the way one organizes, interprets, and co-creates with the machine. Like the avant-gardes of the twentieth century, AI disrupts conventions and enriches the artistic vocabulary, inviting us to rethink our relationship with tools, processes, and creativity itself."[32]

1 Unless stated otherwise, all information regarding Miguel Chevalier's sources of inspiration is based on conversations he had with the author on June 27, 2024, and January 28, 2025.
2 Cf. Franziska Stöhr's interview with Miguel Chevalier in this volume, pp. 8–23, here pp. 20–21.
3 Cf. Katharina Dohm and Heinz Stahlhut, "Art Machines Machine Art. The Spirit in the Machine," in *Art Machines—Machines Art*, ed. idem, exh. cat. Schirn Kunsthalle Frankfurt, Frankfurt am Main; Museum Tinguely, Basel (Heidelberg: Kehrer 2007), pp. 17–25, here p. 18.; Peter Frieß, *Kunst und Maschine. 500 Jahre Maschinenlinien in Bild und Skulptur*, PhD diss., Munich, 1991/92 (Munich: Deutscher Kunstverlag 1993), pp. 52–62.
4 Cf. Lev Manovich, "Who Is the Author? Sampling / Remixing / Open Source," https://manovich.net/content/04-projects/035-models-of-authorship-in-new-media/32_article_2002.pdf (accessed June 11, 2025).
5 Cf. Dohm and Stahlhut, "Art Machines Machine Art" (see note 3), p. 19; Justin Hoffmann, "Artist Becomes Machine Becomes Artist," in Dohm and Stahlhut, *Art Machines—Machines Art* (see note 3), pp. 26–35, here p. 26.
6 Cf. Dohm and Stahlhut, "Art Machines Machine Art" (see note 3), p. 19; https://www.moma.org/collection/works/78747 (accessed June 5, 2025).
7 "What Is Pop Art? Answers from 8 Painters, Part I, Jim Dine, Robert Indiana, Roy Lichtenstein, Andy Warhol," interview by G. R. Swenson, *Art News* (November 1963), https://www.artnews.com/art-news/news/top-ten-artnews-stories-the-first-word-on-pop-183/ (accessed June 10, 2025).
8 Reference should also be made here to Marcel Duchamp's film *Anémic Cinéma* (1926), made in collaboration with Man Ray.
9 Söke Dinkla, *Pioniere interaktiver Kunst von 1970 bis heute. Myron Krueger, Jeffrey Shaw, David Rokeby, Lynn Hershman, Grahame Weinbren, Ken Feingold*, PhD diss., Hamburg, 1995 (Ostfildern: Cantz 1997), p. 26 (translated).
10 One of the machines in operation is shown in the 1959 documentary short film *Robot Art*, https://www.britishpathe.com/asset/35927/ (accessed May 6, 2025).
11 *The Assembled Human*, ed. Nadine Engel, Anna Fricke, and Antonia Krezdorn, exh. cat. Folkwang Museum, Essen (Bielefeld/Berlin: Kerber 2019), p. 244.
12 Miguel Chevalier in a conversation with the author on June 27, 2024; cf. also Agnes Ferenczi, "Nicolas Schöffer and the Birth of Cybernetic Art," https://www.katevassgalerie.com/blog/nicolas-schoeffer (accessed June 5, 2025).
13 Ibid.
14 Cf. Karin Guminski, *Kunst am Computer. Ästhetik, Bildtheorie und Praxis des Computerbildes*, PhD diss., Munich, 2001 (Berlin: Reimer 2002), pp. 62–64.
15 Kenneth Knowlton, quoted in Guminksi, *Kunst am Computer* (see note 14), p. 63 (translated).
16 Guminski, *Kunst am Computer* (see note 14), p. 64 (translated).
17 Dietmar Guderian, "Auf dem Weg zum Zufallsbild" (1969, published in 1986), in *Text zu Mappe von herman de vries "random"*, edition galerie hoffmann (Friedberg, 2016), unpaginated; quoted in idem, "Art in Search of Chance," in *[Un]erwartet. Die Kunst des Zufalls*, ed. Ulrike Groos and Eva-Marina Froitzheim, exh. cat. Kunstmuseum Stuttgart (Cologne: Wienand 2016), pp. 37–41, here p. 40.
18 Eva-Marina Froitzheim, "On Chance in Art and Methods of Making this Visible," in Groos and Froitzheim, *[Un]erwartet* (see note 17), pp. 25–31, here p. 26. "Objectively random" refers to events with an unidentifiable cause. This may be due to limited knowledge or because there is no objective reason. In other words, there is no reason why an event takes place at a certain place at a certain time in a certain way; cf. Gerhard Vollmer, "Zufall in der Biologie," https://www.spektrum.de/lexikon/biologie/zufall-in-der-biologie/72005 (accessed June 5, 2025).
19 Pauline Mari, "Victor Vasarely: Un humaniste moderne," https://www.fondationvasarely.org/victor-vasarely/ (accessed June 5, 2025; translated).
20 Cf. "Vera Molnár. Hungarian, 1924–2023," https://ropac.net/artists/231-vera-molnar/ (accessed June 5, 2025).
21 Cf. Guminski, *Kunst am Computer* (see note 14), p. 128.
22 "The Water Lilies by Claude Monet," Musée de l'Orangerie, https://www.musee-orangerie.fr/en/node/197502 (accessed June 5, 2025).
23 Miguel Chevalier in a conversation with the author on January 28, 2025.
24 Cf. Franziska Stöhr, *endlos. Zur Geschichte des Film- und Videoloops im Zusammenspiel von Technik, Kunst und Ausstellung* (Bielefeld: transcript, 2016), pp. 187–88, n. 385.
25 Nam June Paik, "Electronic Video Recorder," in *Nam June Paik. Videa 'n' Videology, 1959–1973*, ed. Judson Rosebush, exh. cat. Everson Museum of Art, Syracuse, and Galerie Bonino, New York (Syracuse: Everson Museum of Art, 1974), p. 11.
26 Manovich, "Who Is the Author?" (see note 4).
27 Dinkla, *Pioniere interaktiver Kunst* (see note 9), p. 25 (translated).
28 Ibid., pp. 25–26. The original plan was to activate the lighting with the help of light barriers. As this was not feasible, flashlights were chosen. Due to frequent theft of the flashlights, normal lighting was eventually used again.
29 Cf. ibid., pp. 37–40.
30 Miguel Chevalier in a conversation with the author on January 28, 2025.
31 Guminski, *Kunst am Computer* (see note 14), p. 61.
32 Miguel Chevalier in a conversation with the author on January 28, 2025.

JASMIN GIERLING

Transformation Through Projection

MIGUEL CHEVALIER'S INSTALLATIONS IN THE PUBLIC REALM

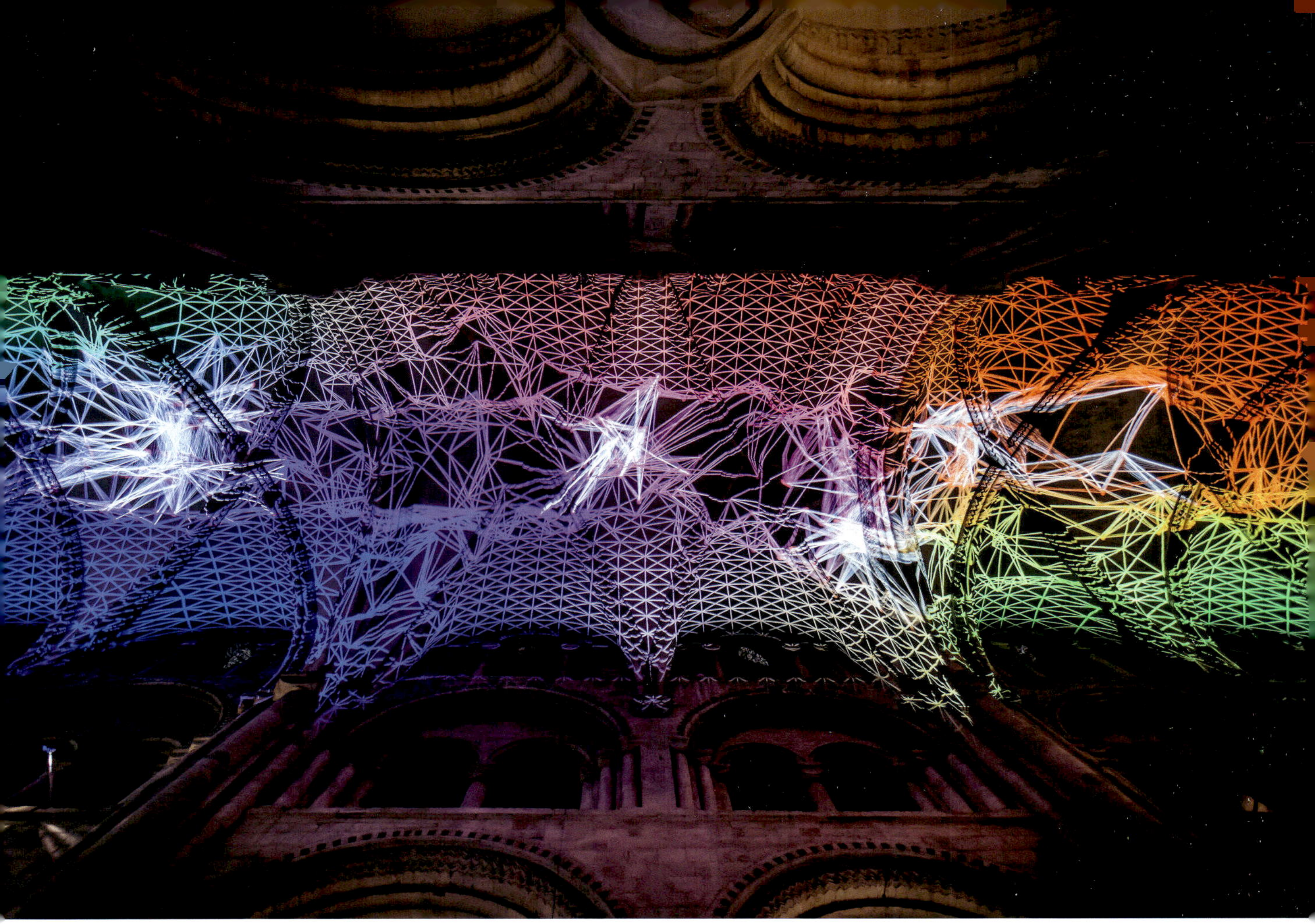

INSTALLATION

Complex Meshes, started 2015 ·
Generative and interactive
installation · Dimensions
variable · Software: Cyrille Henry,
Antoine Villeret · Music: Jacopo
Baboni Schilingi · Installation
view, Lumiere festival, Durham
Cathedral, United Kingdom, 2015

▶ VIDEO

● Since the early 1980s, Miguel Chevalier has been exploring the urban space as a site for his projections and installations. Working outside the museum is particularly important to him, as it allows his art to be accessible to a broad public. He was especially influenced by the monumental, socially critical murals of Diego Rivera (1886–1957; p. 38, fig. 12) and David Alfaro Siqueiros (1896–1974), which he discovered during his childhood in Mexico.[1] In his first large-scale installation, Chevalier's approach toward working digitally was already apparent: in 1984, the artist presented *From Stained Glass to the Digital* at the Cathédrale d'Images (a former stone quarry, now Les Carrières des Lumières) in Les Baux-de-Provence in the South of France. As video projectors were then rare, expensive, and of poorer image quality than monitors or slide projectors, he opted for the latter. Eight synchronized devices automatically projected looped series of thirty slides each onto the walls and floors. They featured superimposed images of fragmented and pixelated rose windows from Gothic cathedrals. As early as 1988, Chevalier created *Performance*, a monumental installation on the facade of the Panthéon in Paris, executed with large stage projectors.[2] He himself described this project as paving the way for his "future works, where ▶ digital art (p. 27) engages in a dialogue with architectural environments to create unique sensory experiences in public spaces."[3] In keeping with the rapid progress of technology since the 1980s,

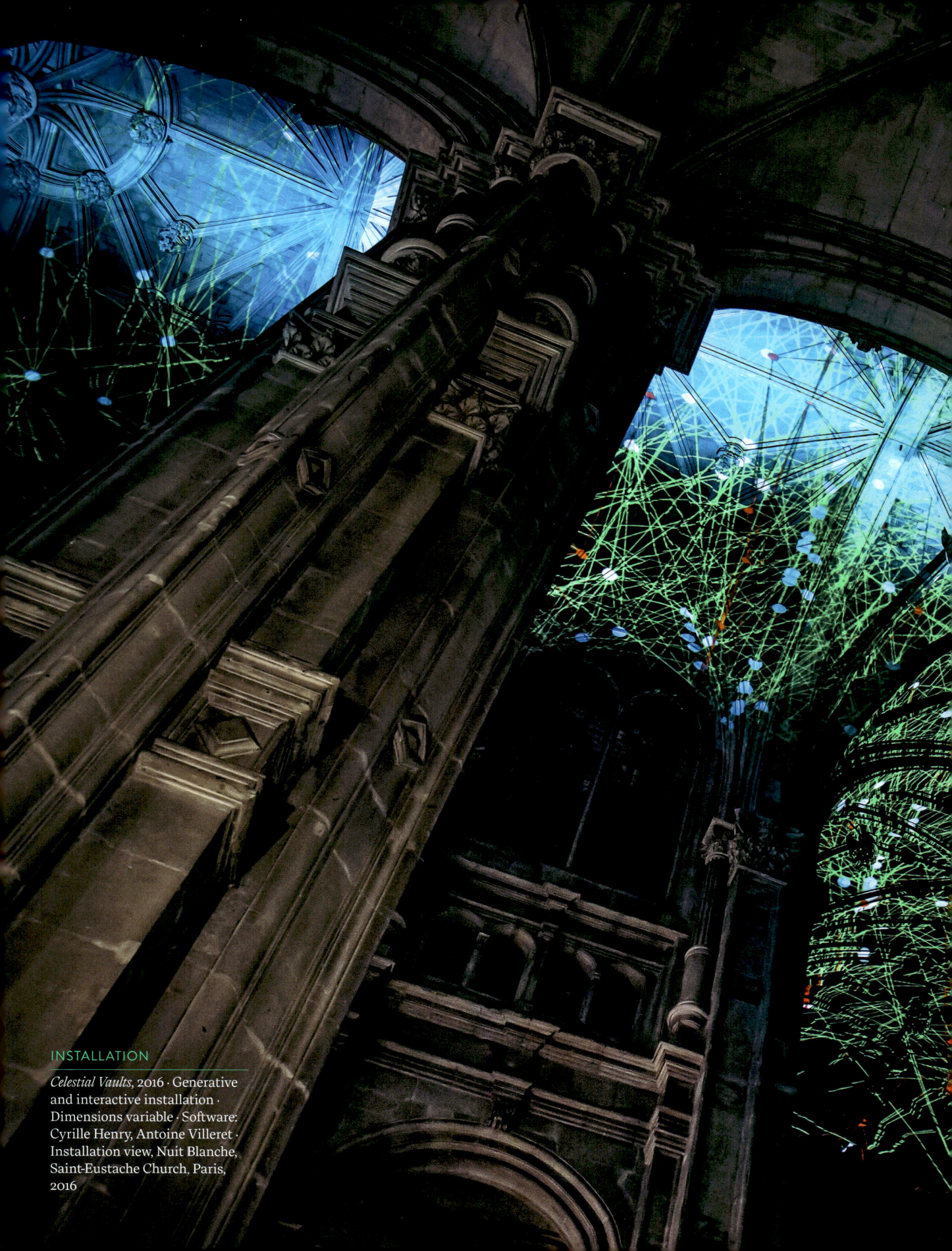

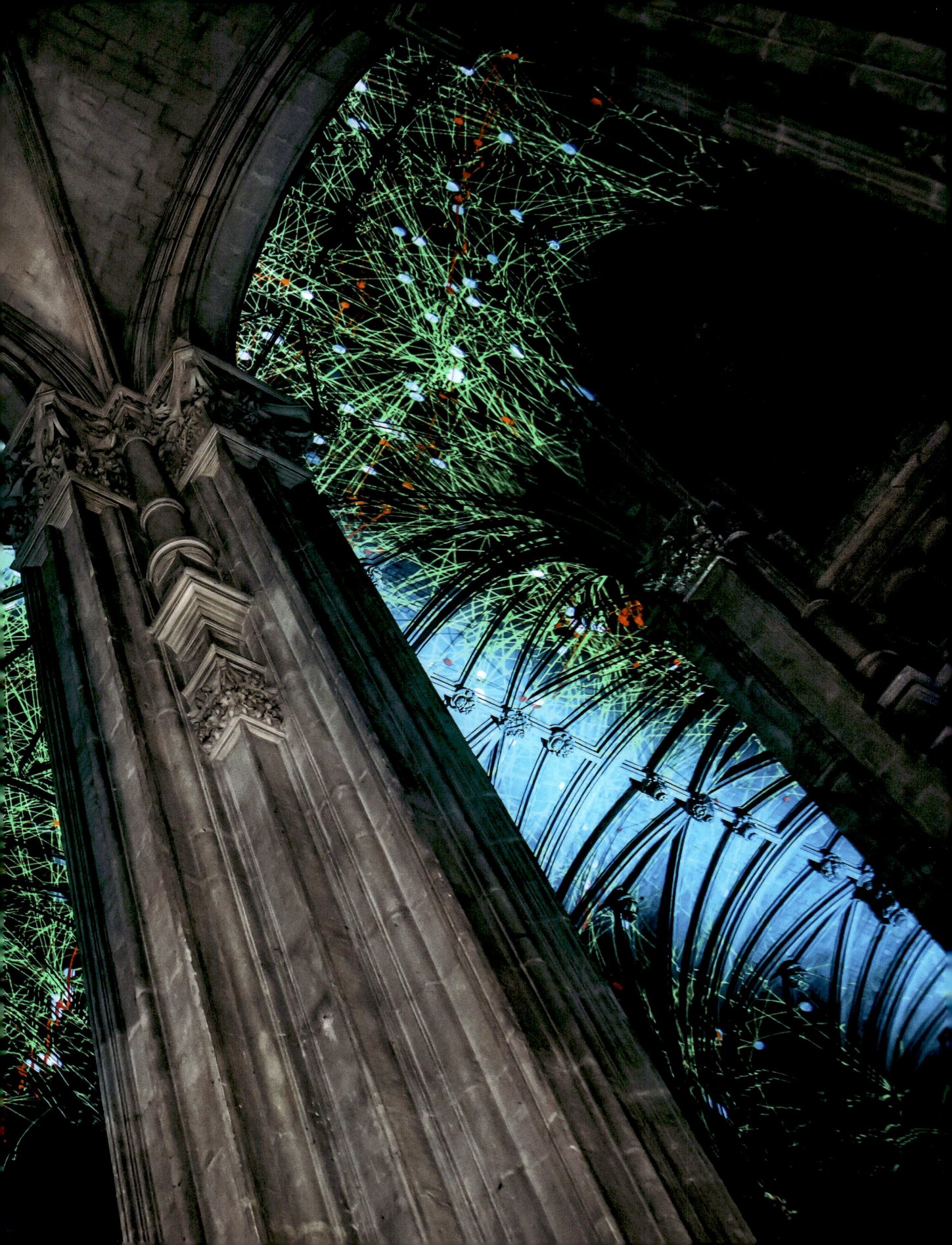

he has regularly added generative and interactive elements to his works, involving visitors through their body movements.

For Chevalier, an installation's architectural environment is an integral part of its genesis. Each piece is adapted to its respective place: "I create or adapt a custom-made artwork, following the inspiration of the location, its memory, its traffic stream, and in intimate connection with the architecture and public space. An installation is never isolated: It interacts with perspectives, pedestrian flows, and peripheral views. Buildings become surfaces, but not passive canvases."[4] In addition to its architectural quality, a facade also serves as a carrier medium.[5] It becomes a field of reference for accessing the artwork, while the installation can complement the narrative of the built environment in return by evoking associations with the spatial context. As philosopher Juliane Rebentisch (b. 1970) states, "site-specific installation art aims at the thematic interweaving of the literal and the social site. It reflects its institutional, social, economic, political, and/or historical framework conditions *by* formally intervening in architectural and landscape conditions."[6] A facade that is turned into a projection surface is thus not merely a decorative element but becomes part of the artwork itself.[7] The architectural surface transforms into a screen.[8] Chevalier uses this screen in different ways. The three works discussed below show his diverse approaches to the interaction of architecture or urban space and art installation: the interior of a medieval church, an object inserted into the urban space, and the exterior facade of a contemporary building serve as projection surfaces in these examples.

Digital Mesh and Gothic Ribbed Vault

As part of the Lumiere festival, Chevalier presented an interactive light installation at Durham Cathedral (1093–1133) for four days in November 2015. *Complex Meshes* (started 2015; p. 43) was projected onto the central nave's ribbed vault (height: 22 meters) and extended over six bays between the baptismal font at the entrance and the crossing. Sensors registered the movements of visitors and the projected patterns were modified in real time to create new structures. Physical participation thus influenced the visible outcome of the installation. This interactive spatial experience was complemented by an auditory component with music composed by Jacopo Baboni Schilingi (b. 1971).

Chevalier's decision to create this work for Durham Cathedral was based on the formal aesthetic similarities between Romanesque and Gothic architecture and *Complex Meshes*, because "both follow a mathematical and modular logic, with vertical momentum and rhythmic repetition."[9] Typically, Gothic buildings are characterized by pointed arches and a high cross-ribbed vault that could only be erected with the help of external buttresses onto which the vault's thrust was distributed. This innovation made it possible to design a new, seemingly floating interior. Chevalier's installation in the cathedral thus combined modern technology with medieval high-tech statics. *Complex Meshes* consists of polygonal mesh structures that differ in size, shape, and color. In fluid movements, these individual digital meshes interlock and overlap. Black voids are created in between, suggesting a vaulted opening to the sky and thus also alluding to the ceiling frescoes depicting night skies often found in Gothic cathedrals:[10] "I wanted to create a work that deals with the sacred and at the same time offers

INSTALLATION

Origin of the World Bubble, 2018 ·
Generative installation projected
on an inflatable sphere ·
Diam. 11 m (36 ft.) · Software:
Cyrille Henry · Installation view,
Lumiere festival, Oxford Circus,
London, 2018

▶ VIDEO

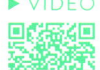

a contemporary vision of spiritual elevation."[11] In an almost completely darkened environment, the architectural structure disappeared under the "fresco of light."[12] Only rarely could the arches or keystones be made out below the installation. The vault now functioned as a screen; the constructed mass appeared to be veiled by a curtain of light art. The principle of dissolving walls was also pursued in Gothic architecture through the use of large, pointed arches and tracery windows. Chevalier's manner of staging the projection in the church interior was a contemporary implementation of this maxim.[13]

Organic Pixel Worlds in the Urban Space

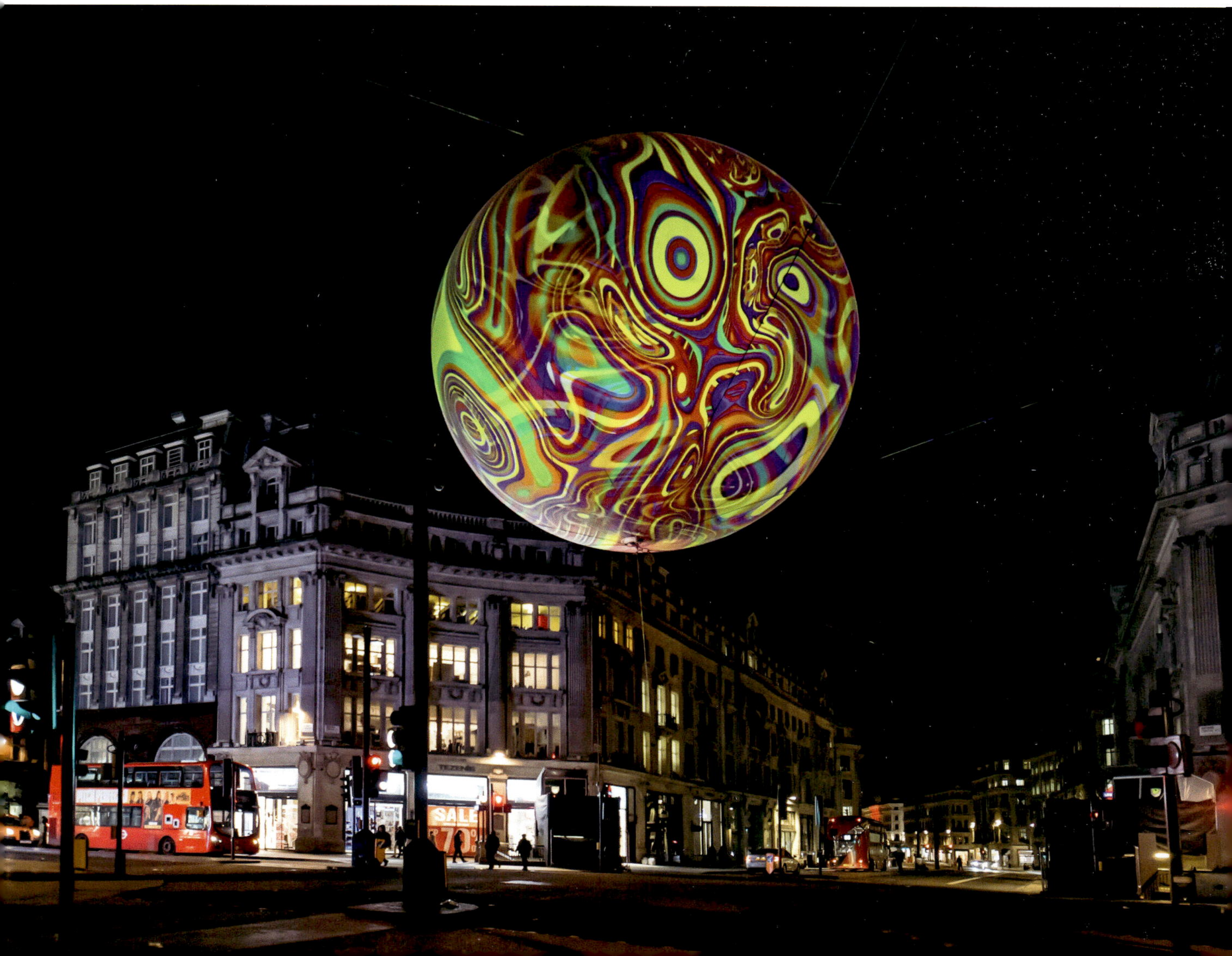

Oxford Circus in London is a busy traffic hub where pedestrians, cars, and double-decker buses pass each other continuously. The intersection of Regent Street and Oxford Street has the appearance of being a circular plaza due to the four corner buildings' inwardly curved facades. During the Lumiere festival in London in January 2018, an inflated sphere with a diameter of eleven meters was installed above the middle of this circle for three days, onto which Chevalier's *The Origin of the World* (started 2012) was projected. In this work, cell-like formations and organic structures merge into new shapes and mix with artificial graphic elements such as ▸ pixels (p. 28). The shapes join and separate in bright colors and at different speeds, reminiscent of the pop-cultural aesthetics of the 1960s and 1970s and creating a nearly psychedelic effect. The 360-degree installation was thus in a state of continual transformation.

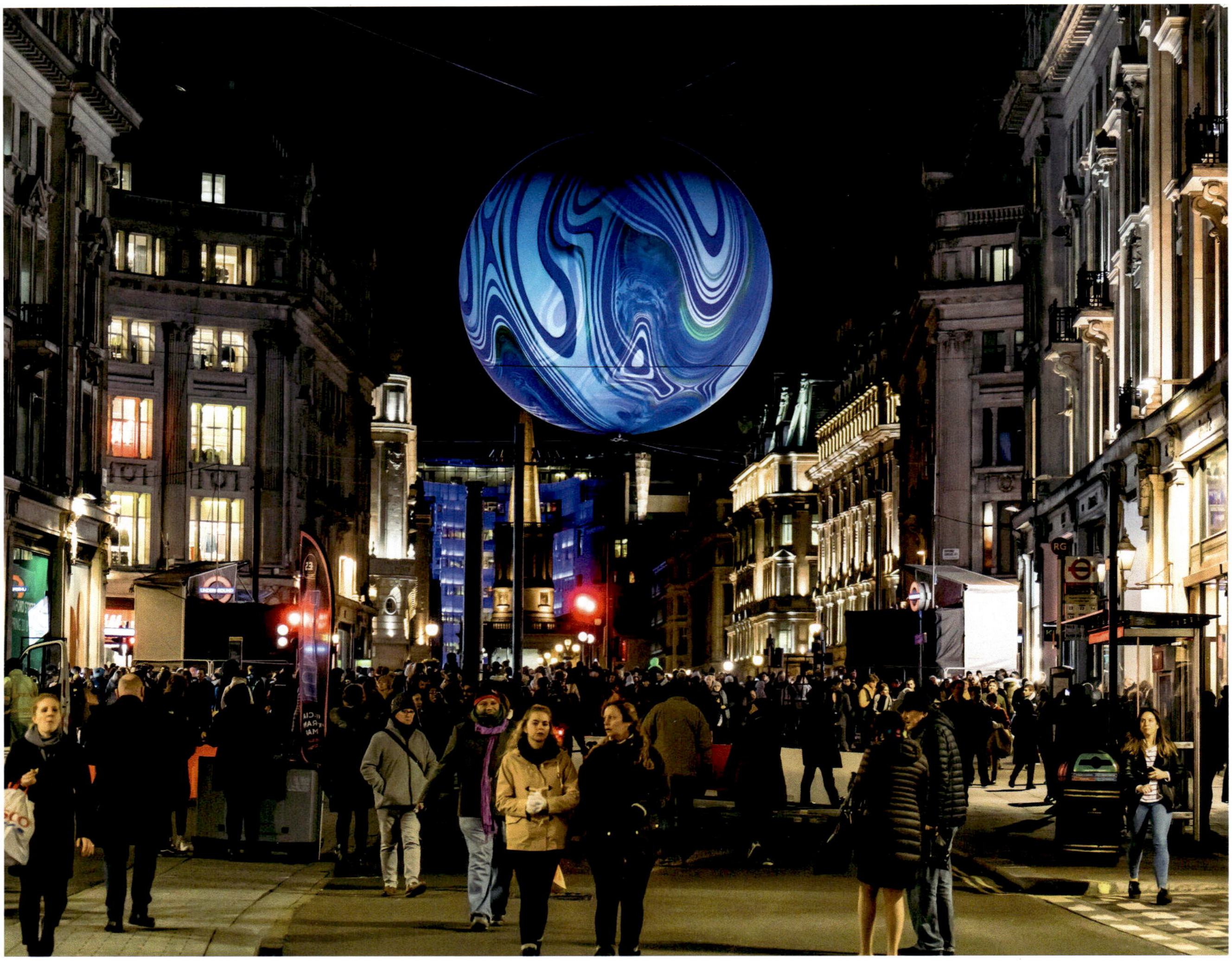

The sphere perfectly reflected the area's spatial structure. In the dark, it even appeared to float freely, as it was only attached to the surrounding buildings with wire cables. Nevertheless, the *Origin of the World Bubble* stood out clearly against the neoclassical facades due to its bright hues and modern patterns. Although no architectural surface was projected upon, the placement of the bubble meant that the artwork interacted with the urban environment. The sphere also alluded to the earth as a planet with living organisms, consisting of a "universe of cells."[14] Chevalier's recurring principle of mixing the analog reality with digital representation is evident in this work: "An organic world or a pixelated one—this artificial universe seems to meet the universe of living beings."[15]

INSTALLATION ↑

Origin of the World Bubble, 2018 · Generative installation projected on an inflatable sphere · Diam. 11 m (36 ft.) · Software: Cyrille Henry · Installation view, Lumiere festival, Oxford Circus, London, 2018

INSTALLATION →

The Origin of the World, started 2012 · Generative and interactive installation · Dimensions variable · Software: Cyrille Henry, Antoine Villeret · Installation view, Noor Riyadh festival, King Abdullah Financial District, Riyadh, Saudi Arabia, 2023

▶ VIDEO

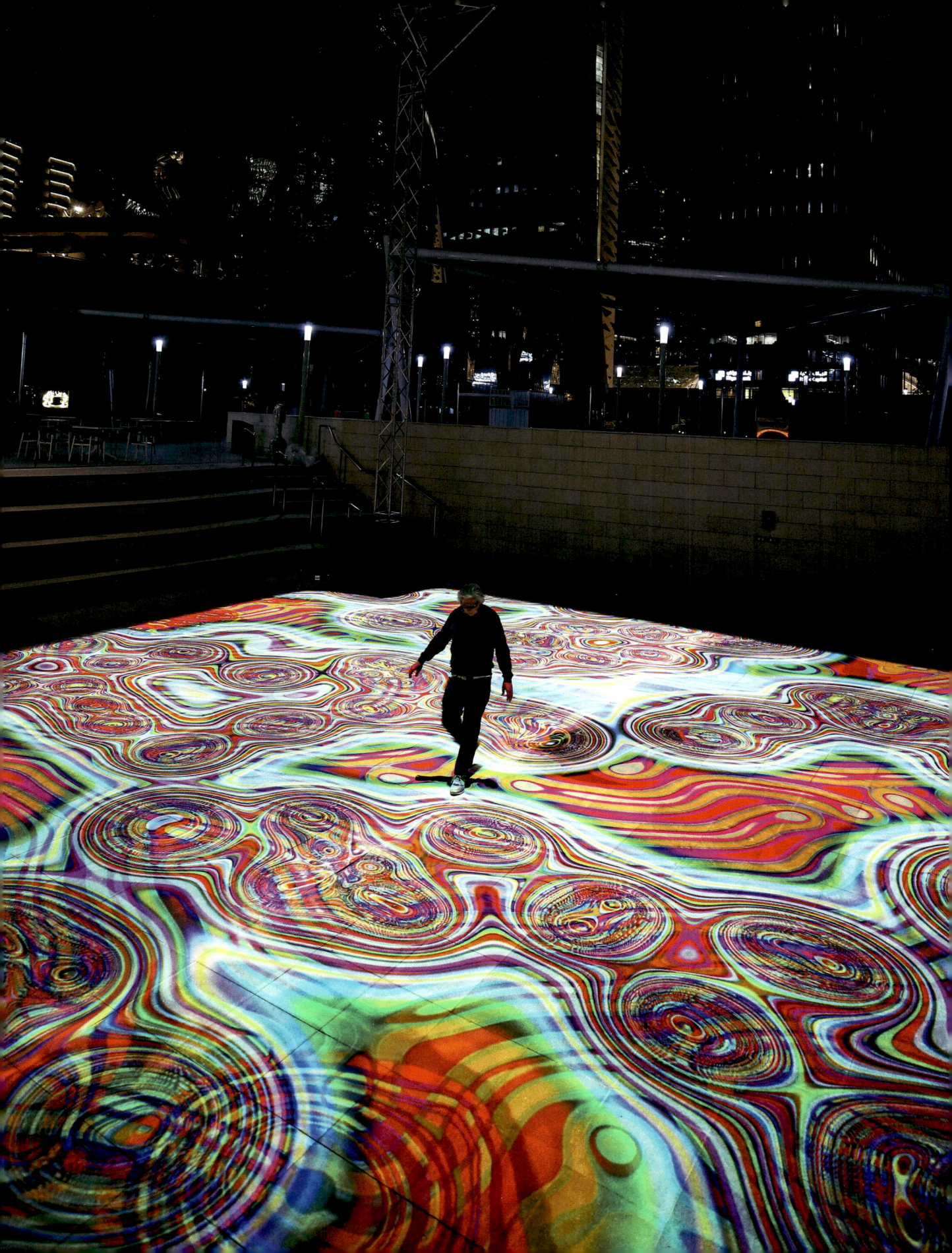

A Virtual Garden on a Facade

INSTALLATION →

Meta-Nature AI, started 2023 · Seamless loop, video, color, sound, 10 min. · Software, music: Claude Micheli · Installation view, Seoul Light DDP, Dongdaemun Design Plaza (architect: Zaha Hadid) · Courtesy Ara Art Center, Seoul, South Korea, 2023

▶ VIDEO

Dongdaemun Design Plaza (2007–14) in Seoul was planned by Zaha Hadid (1950–2016) as a large cultural hub. Hadid's fluid, organic design language gives the building a sculptural quality. In 2023, *Meta-Nature AI* (started 2023; pp. 51–53) was projected onto this curved structure for eleven days — in this case as a ten minute video loop, accompanied by the music of Claude Micheli (b. 1957). The work addresses the coexistence of the natural and the artificial: Chevalier created a "virtual ▶ herbarium (p. 27)."[16] He collected images of flowers and leaves, then complemented them with AI-generated imagery of plants (pp. 160, 162–71). The elements of this digital garden swiftly moved across the building's curved volume. They passed through the four seasons, visualizing the beauty and transience of vegetation.

Meta-Nature AI thus was in a dialogue with the organic shape of the building embedded in a designed landscape architecture. As visitors strolled through the area, they could constantly gain new perspectives on the installation; depending on the vantage point, the architectural surface almost seemed to dissolve due to the projection's depth effect. The trompe l'oeil quality created an immersive experience, suggesting an extension of the real space.

Miguel Chevalier's installations in public spaces not only enable a democratic approach to art but also always open up a concrete reference to the built environment. A dialogue unfolds between the work, the form, and the history of a place in the urban space. Supposed opposites, such as the abstract projection in a medieval church, organic shapes in a dense urban space, or a digital garden on a facade in the middle of a metropolis combine to generate new images. Chevalier has been creating a growing number of interactive installations in public spaces that react to the visitors' movements, for example *Magic Carpets* (started 2014), which are light projections on the ground where the movements of passersby influence the shapes' design, causing them to drift apart or merge together. Miguel Chevalier's thinking, which always combines past and present, analog and digital, as well as art and technology, manifests itself particularly clearly in these works.

1 Miguel Chevalier in a conversation with Franziska Stöhr, January 28, 2025; cf. also Elisabeth Couturier, "Miguel Chevalier: Roving Virtual-Image Artist " (2015), https://t1p.de/d2vpn (accessed June 11, 2025).
2 Miguel Chevalier worked with projectors from the company Pani.
3 Miguel Chevalier in a conversation with Franziska Stöhr, January 28, 2025.
4 Email from Miguel Chevalier to the author, April 24, 2025.
5 Cf. Bärbel Schlüter, *Im Raum der Fassade. Temporäre Installationen* (Munich: Edition Metzel, 2014), p. 58.

6 Juliane Rebentisch, *Ästhetik der Installation* (Frankfurt am Main: Suhrkamp, 2003), p. 233 (translated).
7 Cf. Giuliana Bruno, *Surface: Matters of Aesthetics, Materiality, and Media* (Chicago and London: University of Chicago Press, 2014), p. 93.
8 Cf. also Dave Colangelo: "The … monumental projection places the moving image in a direct relationship with its surroundings, thus invoking an extra-diegetic, spatial montage with the city, multiplying contingency and ambivalence, and thus extending the boundaries and characteristics of architecture and monumentality."

Dave Colangelo, *The Building as Screen: A History, Theory and Practice of Massive Media* (Amsterdam: Amsterdam University Press, 2020), p. 52.
9 Email from Miguel Chevalier to the author, April 24, 2025.
10 Such a design should not only symbolize heaven and the proximity to God associated with it, but also create a spiritually charged sphere.
11 Email from Miguel Chevalier to the author, April 24, 2025.
12 "Complex Meshes 2015,"https://www.miguel-chevalier.com/work/complex-meshes-2015 (accessed June 12, 2025).

13 *Complex Meshes* and other works with a similar aesthetic were installed in other medieval cathedrals or public buildings.
14 Email from Miguel Chevalier to the author, April 24, 2025.
15 "Origin of the World Bubble 2018," https://www.miguel-chevalier.com/work/origin-of-the-world-bubble-2018 (accessed June 12, 2025).
16 "Meta-Nature AI, 2023,"https://miguel-chevalier.com/work/meta-nature-ai (accessed June 12, 2025).

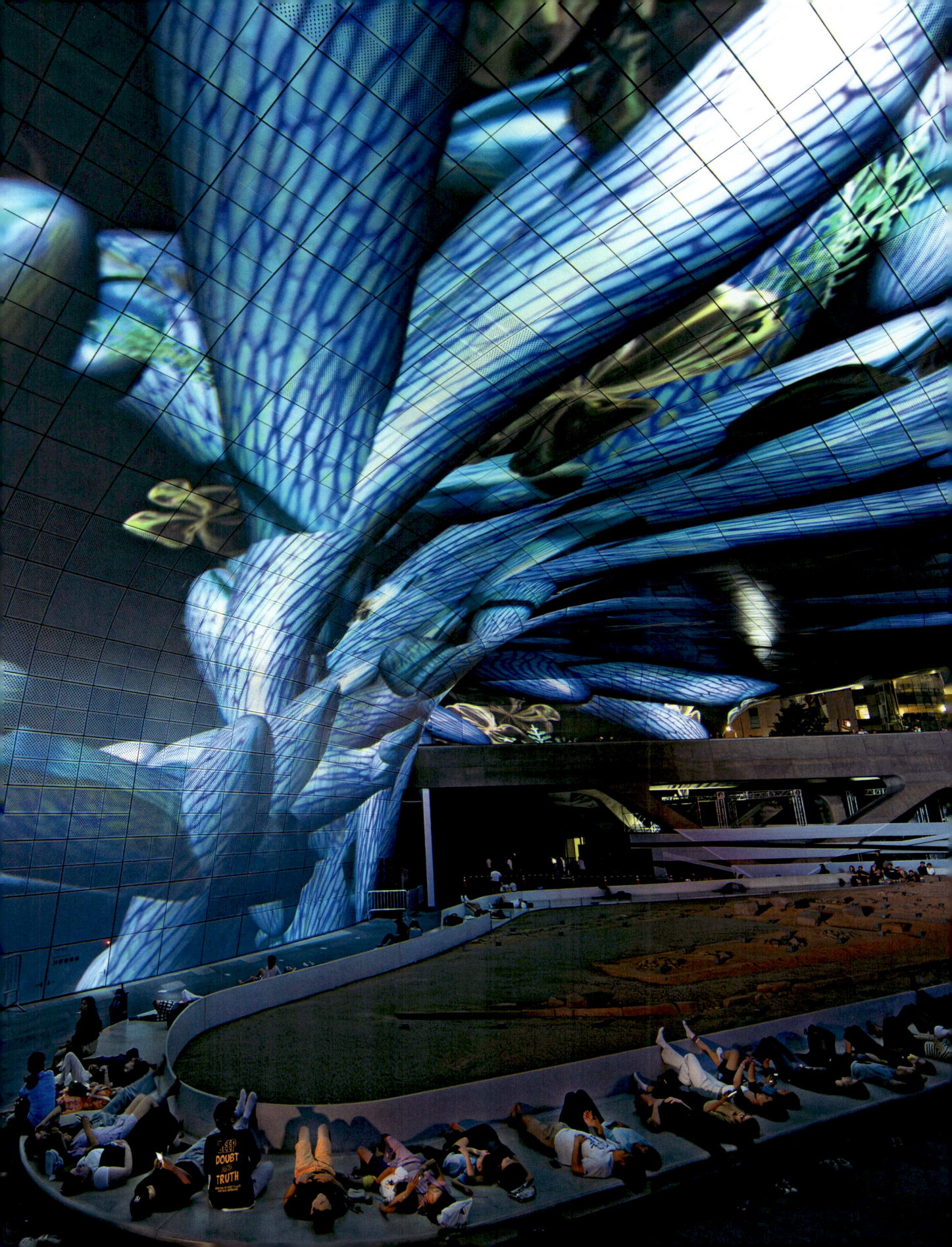

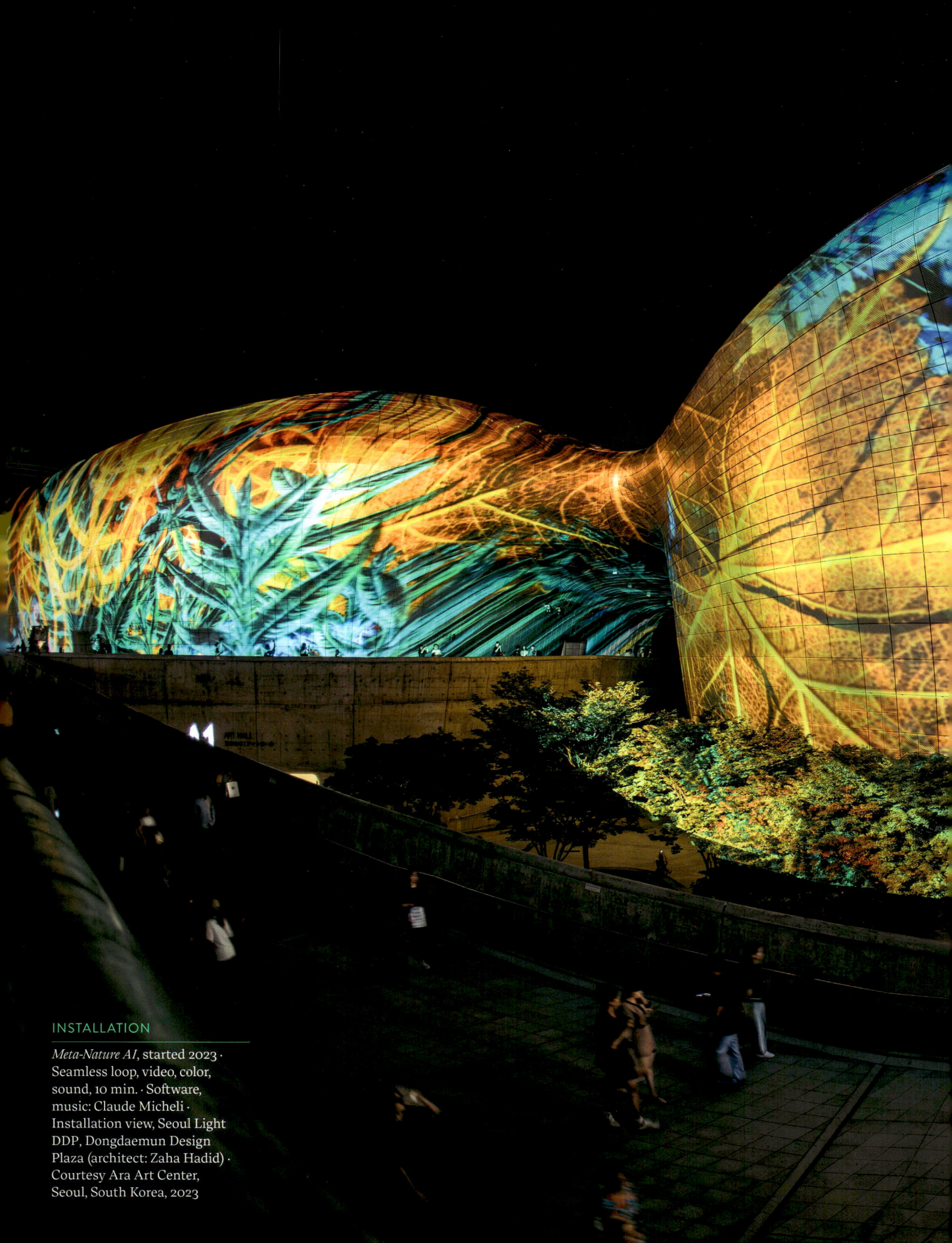

INSTALLATION

Meta-Nature AI, started 2023 ·
Seamless loop, video, color,
sound, 10 min. · Software,
music: Claude Micheli ·
Installation view, Seoul Light
DDP, Dongdaemun Design
Plaza (architect: Zaha Hadid) ·
Courtesy Ara Art Center,
Seoul, South Korea, 2023

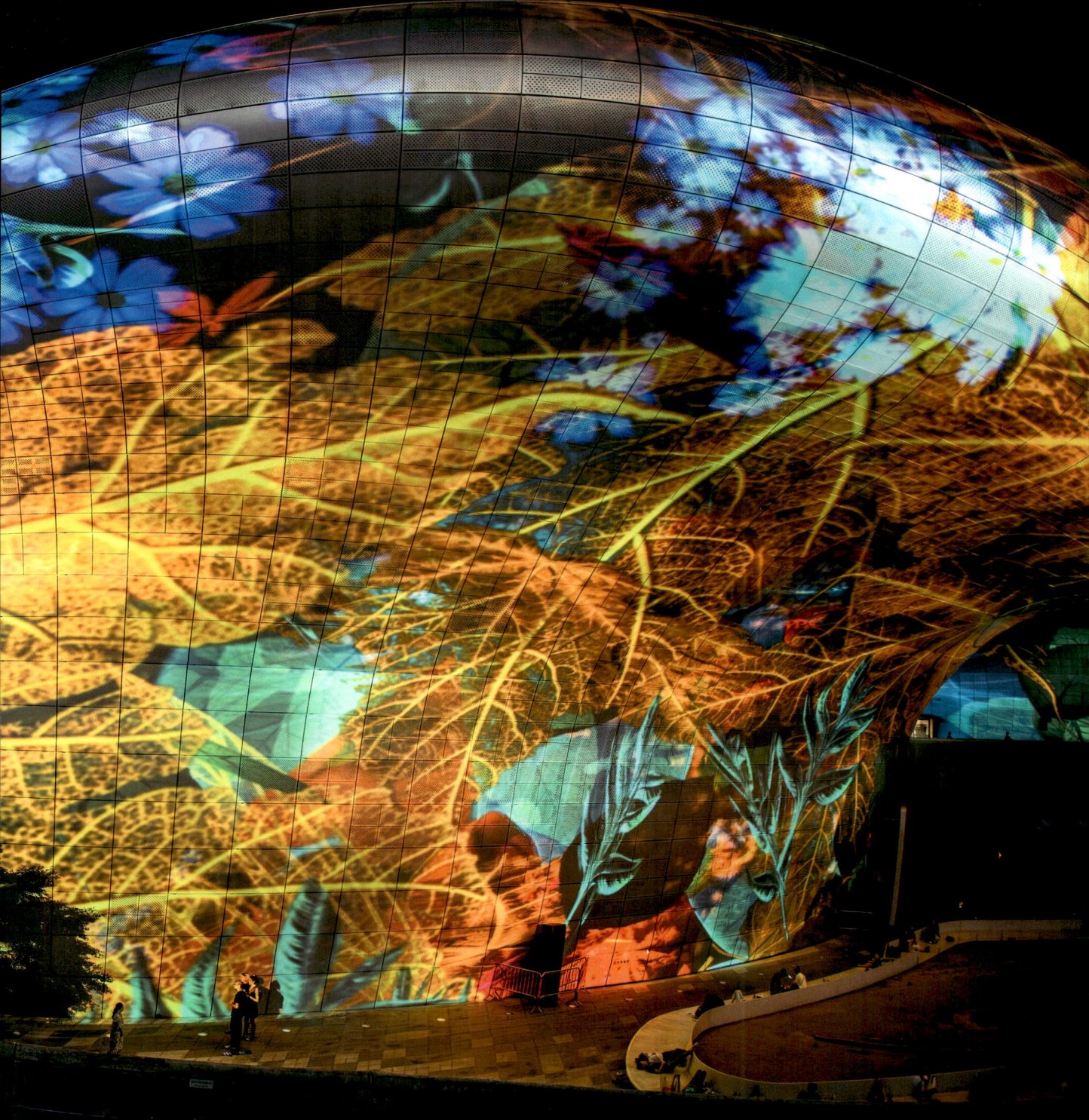

FUNDAMENTAL DIMENSIONS

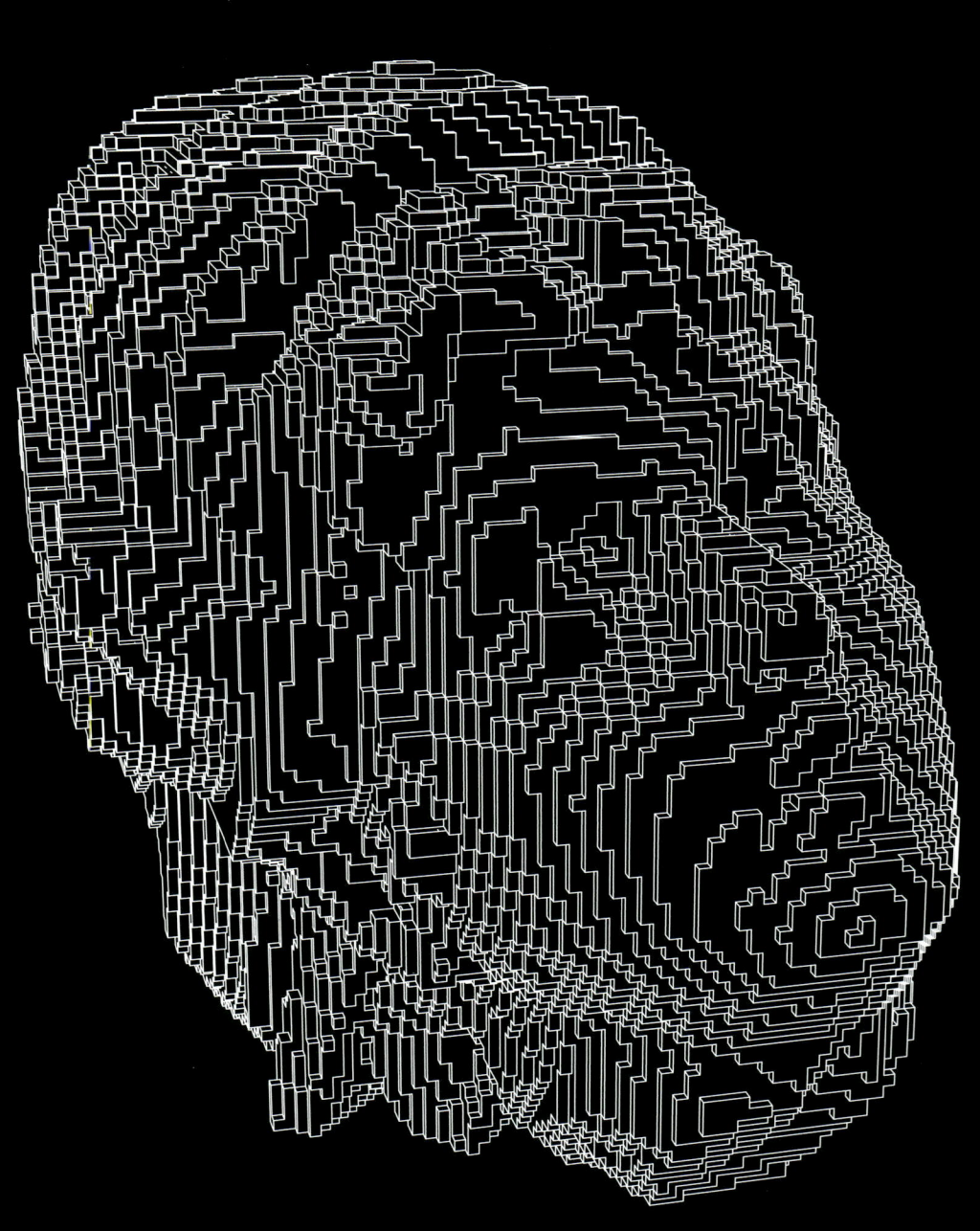

Janus, 2016 · Engraving
on Dibond · 62.8×50 cm
(24 3/4 × 19 11/16 in.)

Miguel Chevalier's work unfolds between the poles of past and future, analog and digital. These aspects become particularly apparent in *Janus* (2013; p. 57) and *The Origin of the World* (started 2012; pp. 60–67).

Hailing from Roman mythology, the figure of Janus is emblematic of these dualities. The two-faced god symbolizes both beginnings and endings, looking at once toward the past and the future. Picking up on this traditional representation, Chevalier created a 3D-printed sculpture from silica sand and synthetic resin, thus transforming the 2D ▸ pixel (p. 28) into a ▸ voxel (pixel in volume; p. 29). In this way he expresses his fundamental interest in the history of art and culture. Realizing them with new technologies, he makes visible the frequent integration of technological advancements into the visual arts. The gaze that is simultaneously directed forward and backward is programmatic for the artist's thinking.

The Origin of the World also combines two apparent opposites: micro-organisms, as they occur in our ecosystem, and pixels, the digital language's smallest elements that form grid-based images. Both are usually invisible to the naked eye, yet they are essential building blocks of their respective worlds. In Miguel Chevalier's work, cellular forms move, divide, fuse, and are continuously interlaced or overlaid by pixelated image creations.

Chevalier here refers to the scientist Alan Turing (1912–1954). In 1952, Turing presented a model that has remained fundamental for developmental biology to this day. In his essay "The Chemical Basis of Morphogenesis," he explains how patterns form in nature—such as zebra stripes or leopard spots. This model is based on two substances that, through alternating dominance, allow the emergence of patterns like black and white stripes, thus forming organized visual structures. *The Origin of the World* is based on more than seventy motifs created by the artist. In this generative work, an ▸ algorithm (p. 26) combines the various patterns and sets them in motion so that they continue to evolve endlessly and in ever-changing ways. The work also features generative and interactive music, created expressly for this purpose by composer Jacopo Baboni Schilingi (b. 1971). It reacts both to the images and to the visitors (see also p. 60).

In multiple ways Chevalier thus takes up Turing's model, in which two always differing counterparts produce a joint result, be it through the moving image, where elements of biology and the digital world meet, or through the interaction of image and music, or the interplay of the generative artwork and visitor activity. Ultimately, the artist formulates a sensory and complex equivalent for the foundations of our existence. (FS)

Left: *Janus (Yellow)* · Right: *Janus (White)* · Both 2019 · Felt-tip pen on paper, drawn by a robot · Each 40 × 29.7 cm (15 3/4 × 11 11/16 in.)

Top: *Janus (Green)*, 2024 · 3D-printed scultpure, synthetic resin · 30 × 40 × 25 cm (11 13/16 × 15 3/4 × 9 13/16 in.) · Bottom: *Janus*, 2013 · 3D-printed sculpture, synthetic resin, silica sand, fluorescent pigment · 100 × 90 × 85 cm (39 3/8 × 35 7/16 × 33 7/16 in.) · Installation views, *Pixels: Miguel Chevalier*, Grand Palais Immersif, Paris, 2024

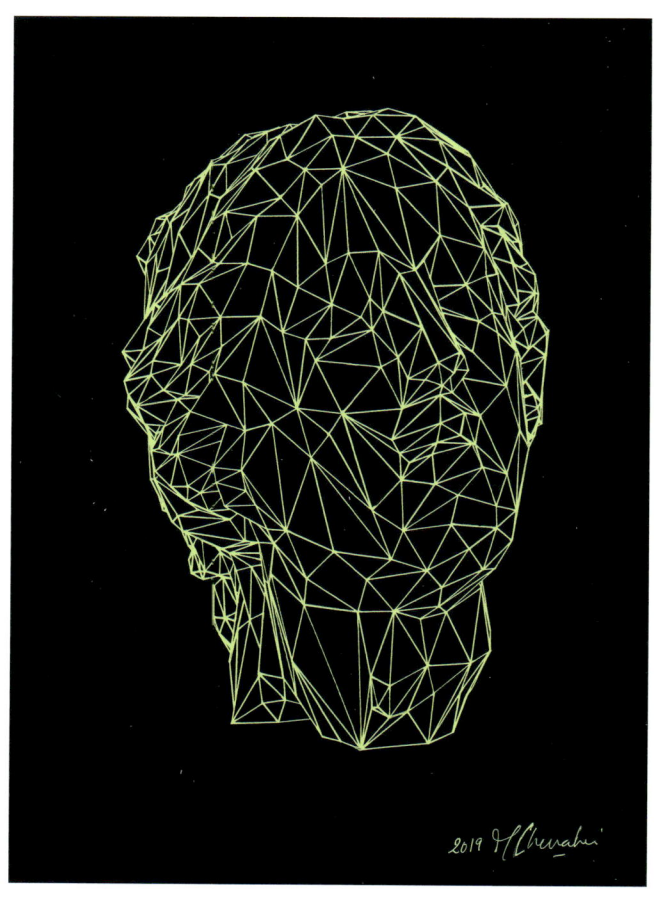

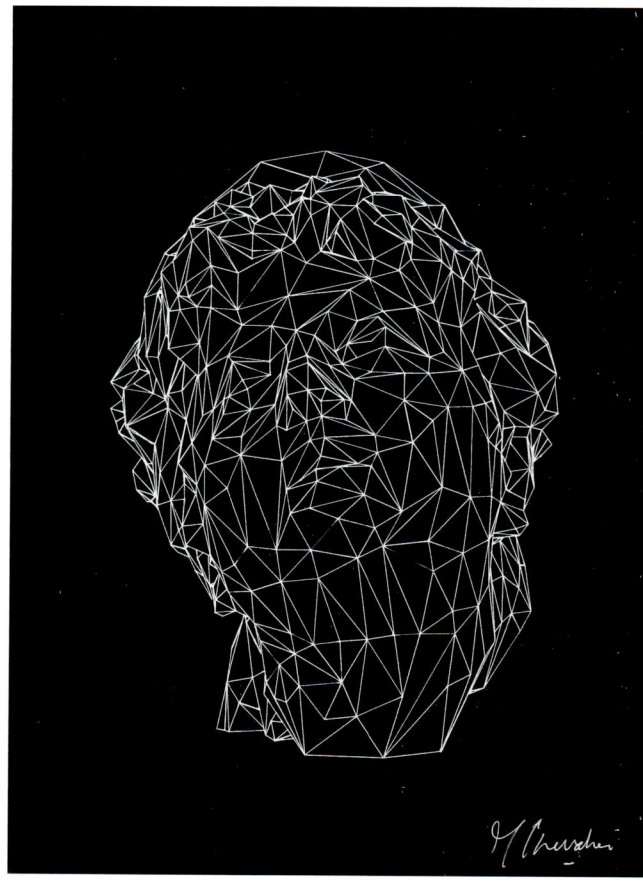

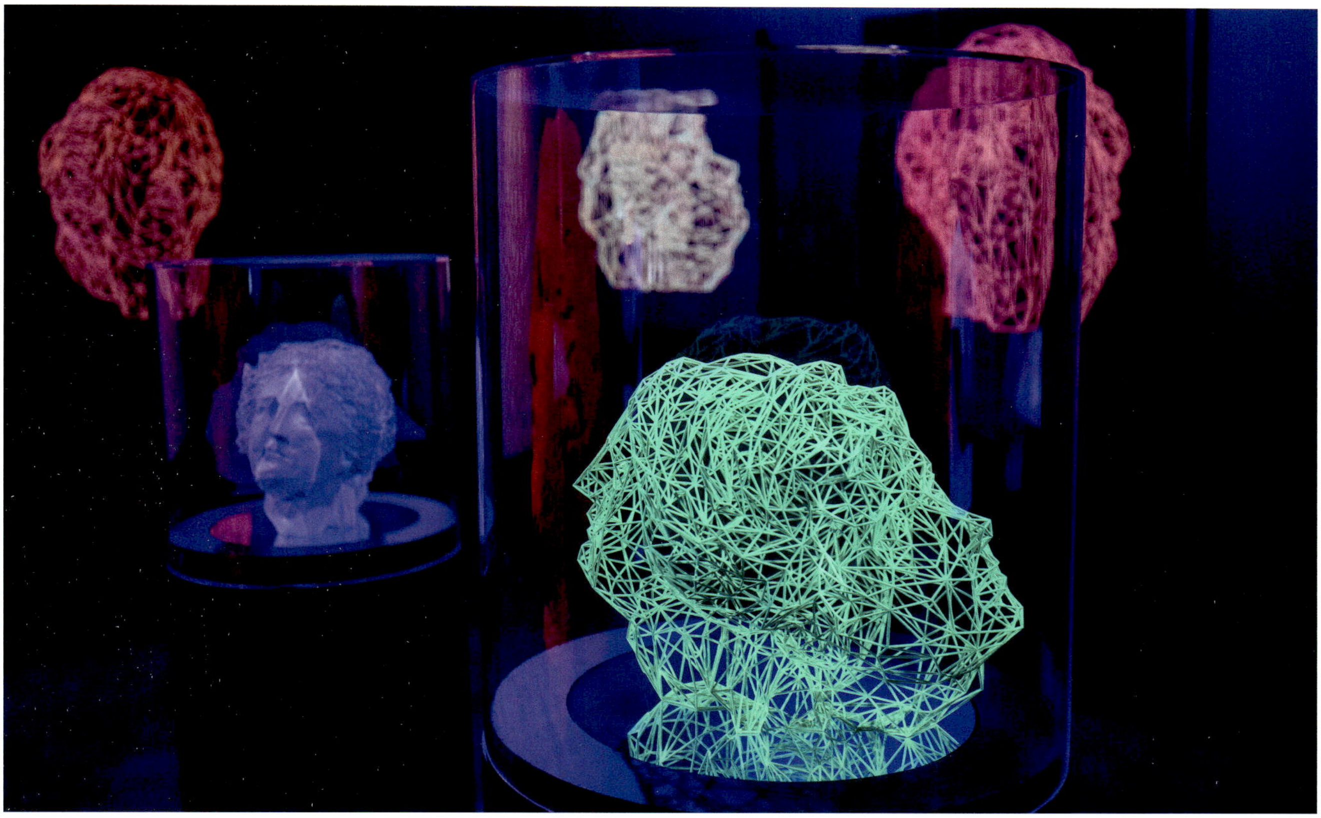

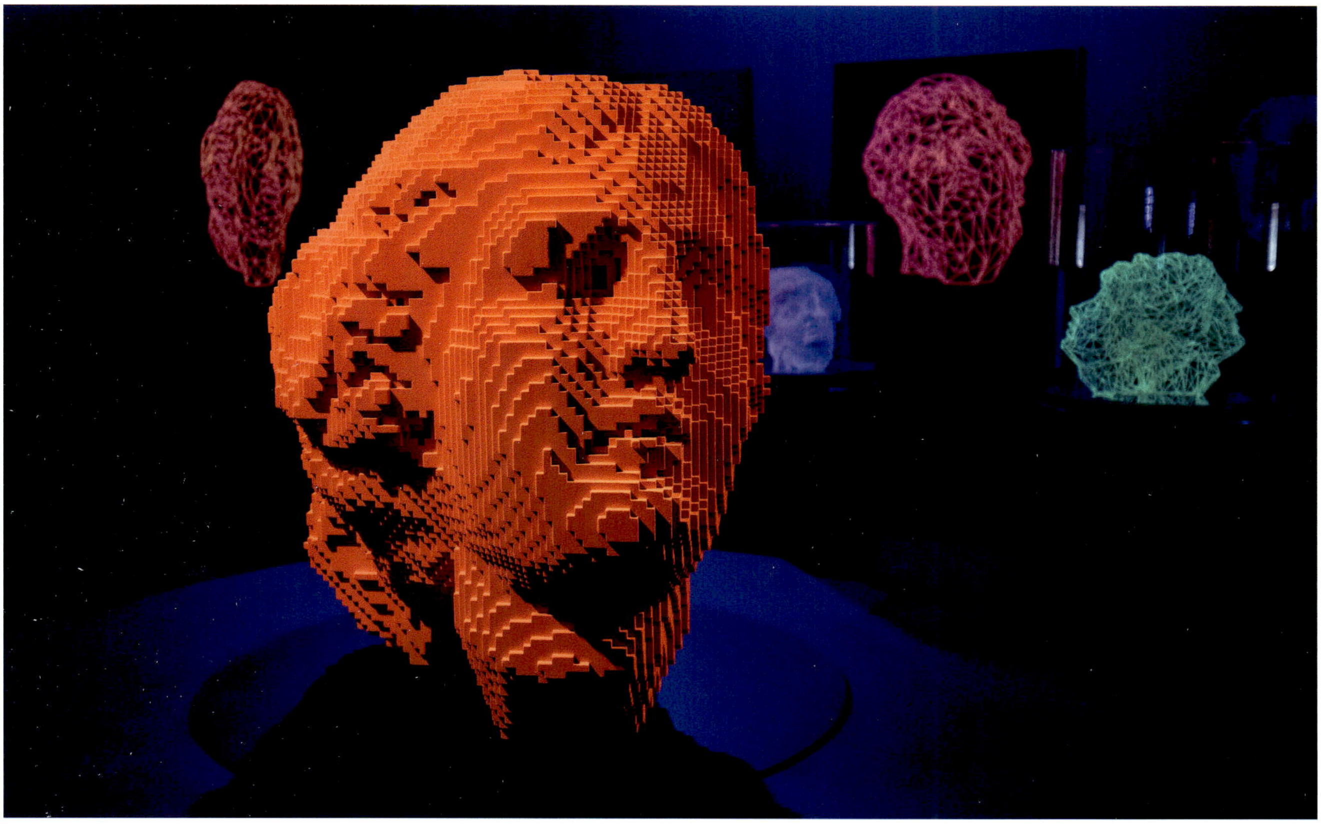

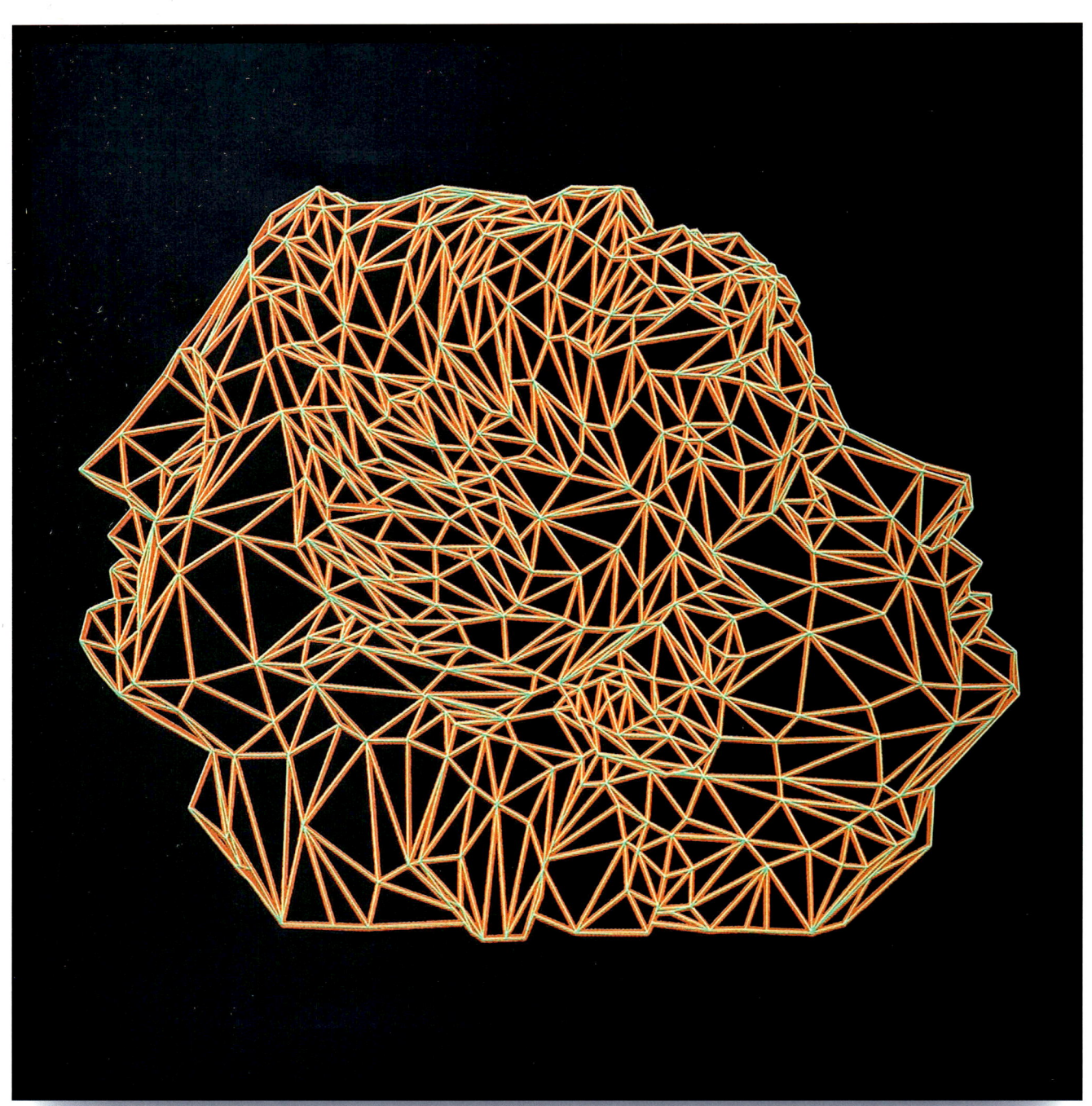

EMBROIDERY

Janus 1, 2024 · Fluorescent
threads · 103 × 103 cm
(40 1/2 × 40 1/2 in.) ·
Left: total view · Right: details

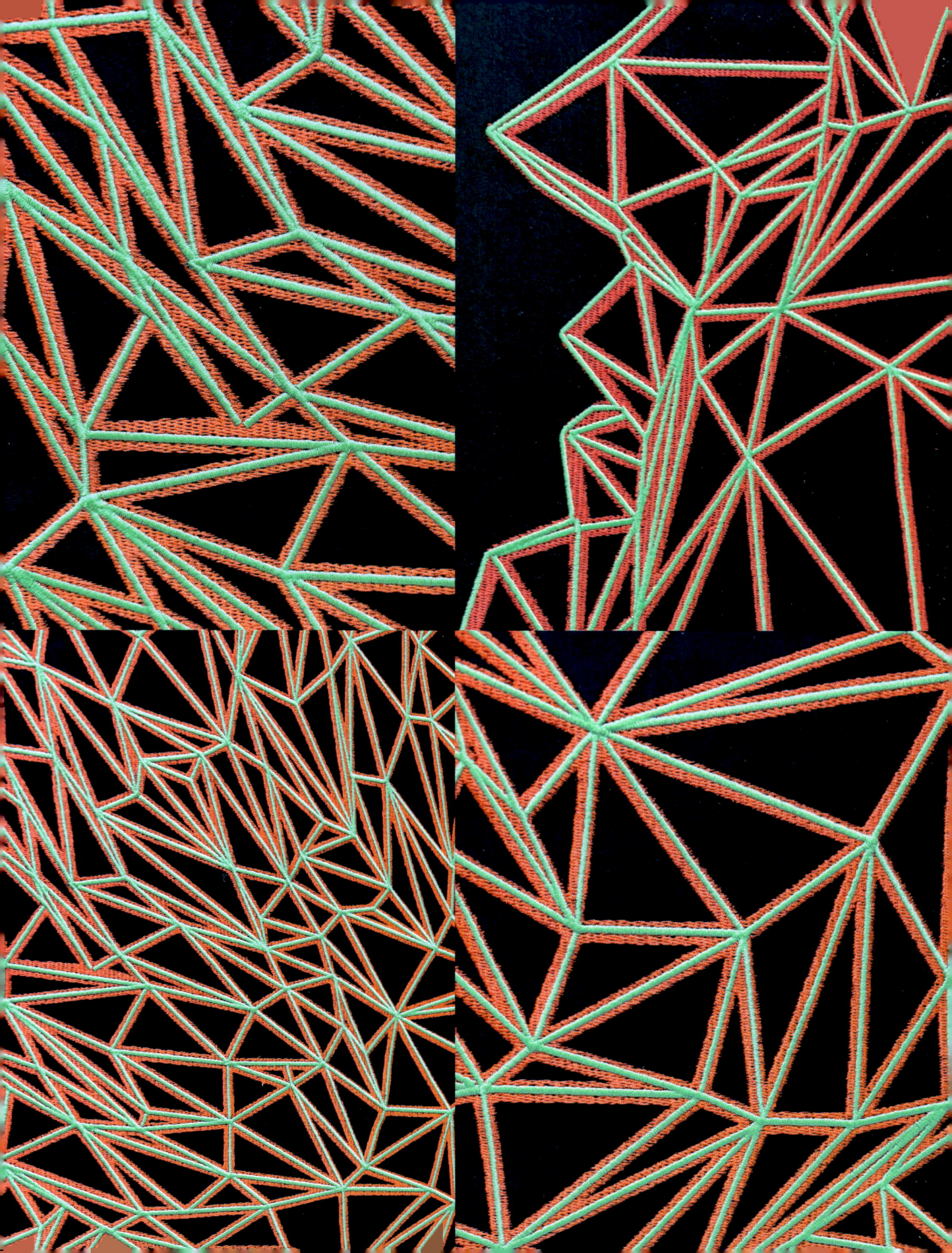

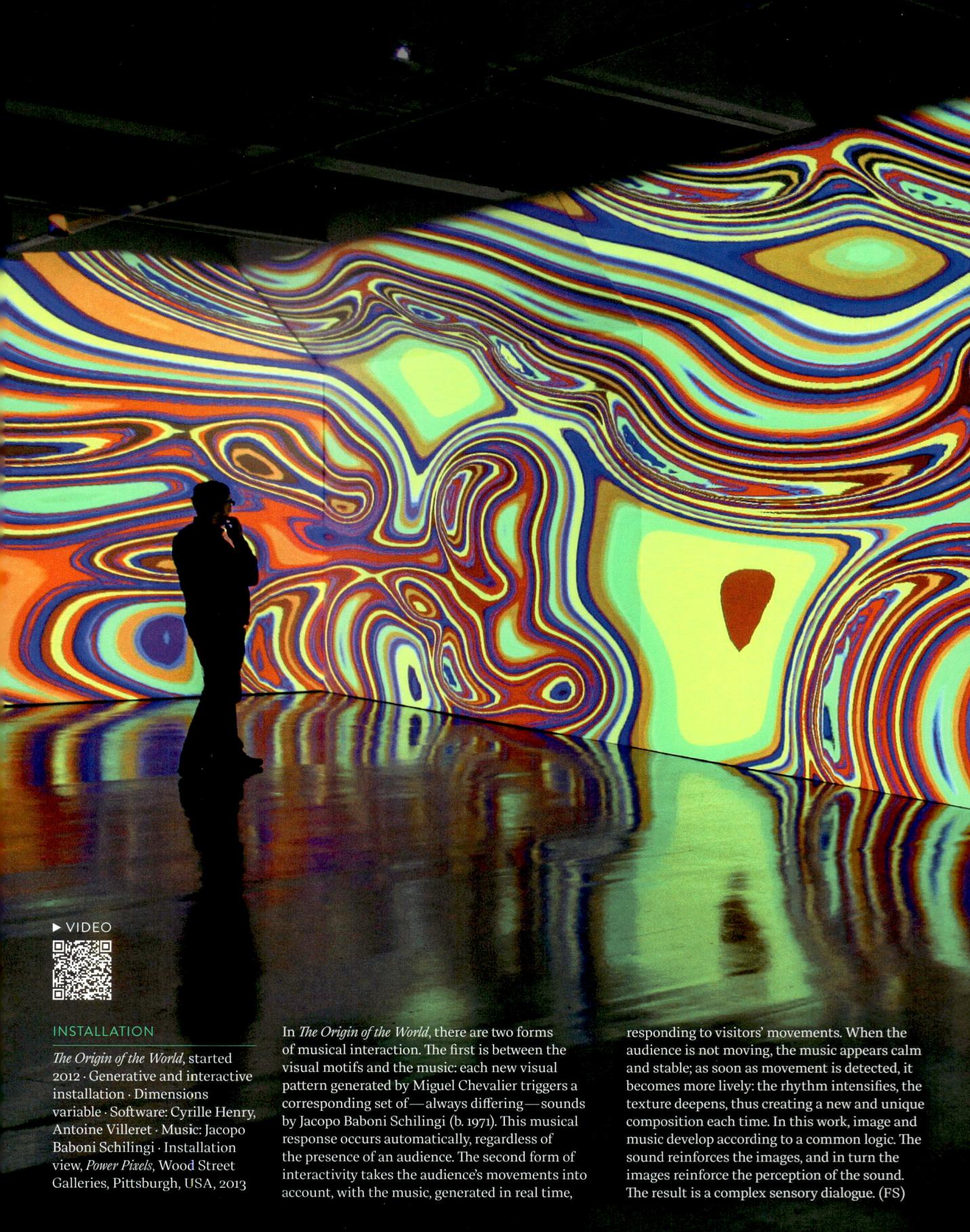

▶ VIDEO

INSTALLATION

The Origin of the World, started
2012 · Generative and interactive
installation · Dimensions
variable · Software: Cyrille Henry,
Antoine Villeret · Music: Jacopo
Baboni Schilingi · Installation
view, *Power Pixels*, Wood Street
Galleries, Pittsburgh, USA, 2013

In *The Origin of the World*, there are two forms
of musical interaction. The first is between the
visual motifs and the music: each new visual
pattern generated by Miguel Chevalier triggers a
corresponding set of—always differing—sounds
by Jacopo Baboni Schilingi (b. 1971). This musical
response occurs automatically, regardless of
the presence of an audience. The second form of
interactivity takes the audience's movements into
account, with the music, generated in real time,

responding to visitors' movements. When the
audience is not moving, the music appears calm
and stable; as soon as movement is detected, it
becomes more lively: the rhythm intensifies, the
texture deepens, thus creating a new and unique
composition each time. In this work, image and
music develop according to a common logic. The
sound reinforces the images, and in turn the
images reinforce the perception of the sound.
The result is a complex sensory dialogue. (FS)

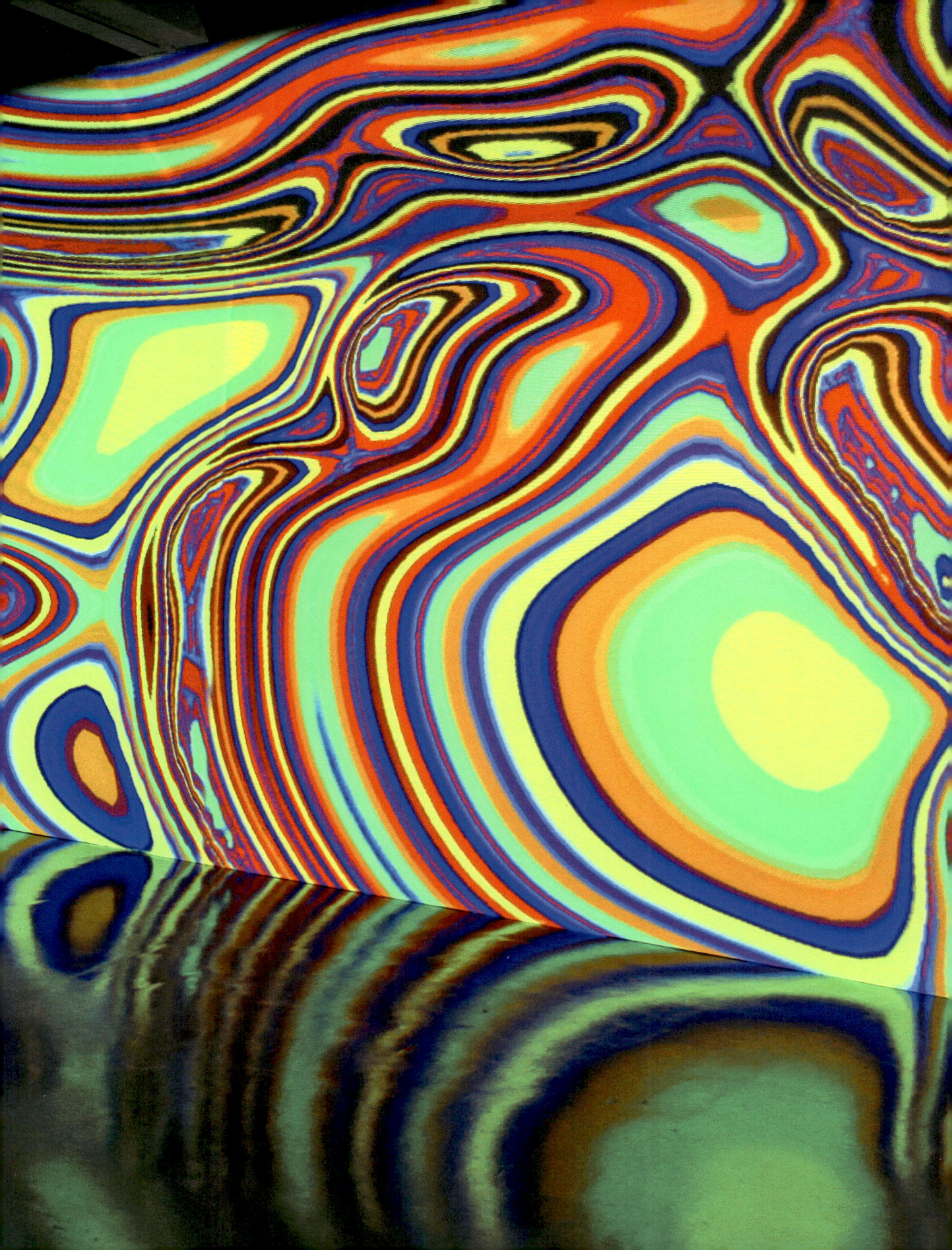

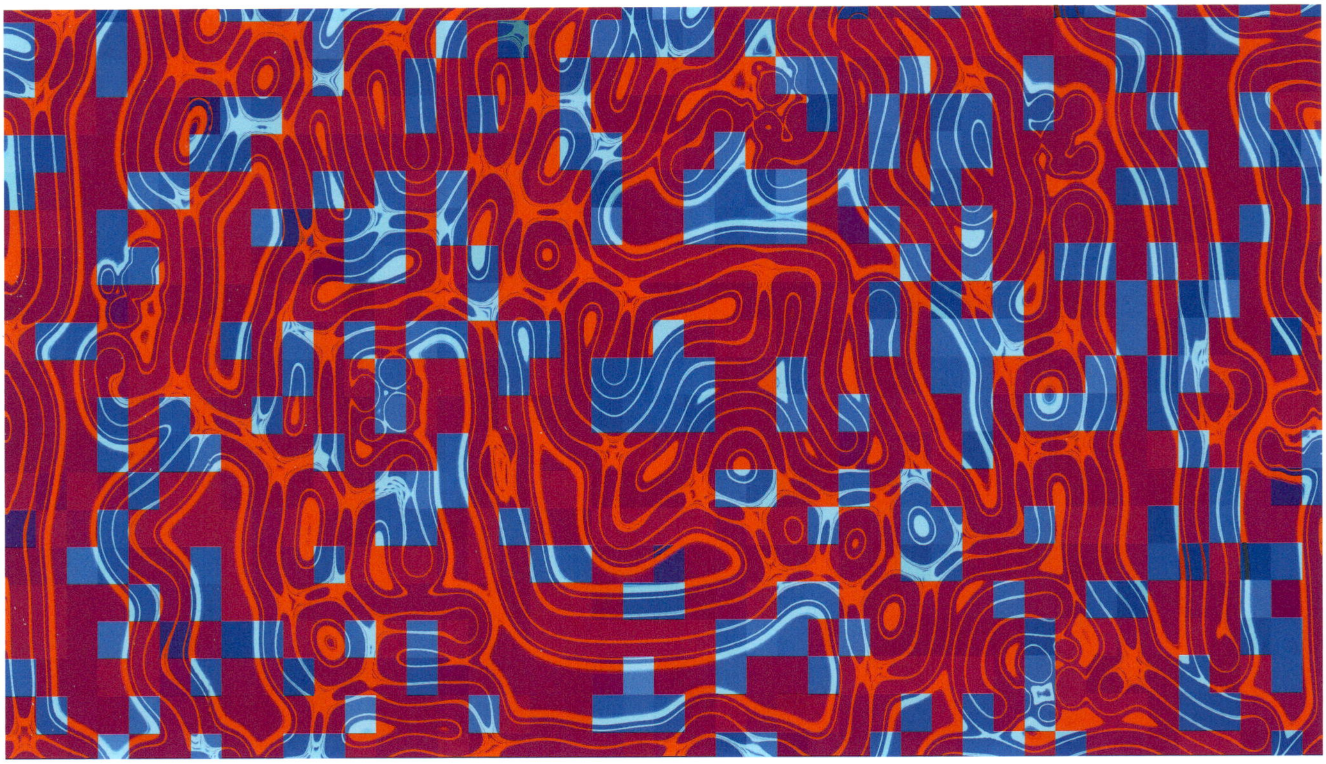

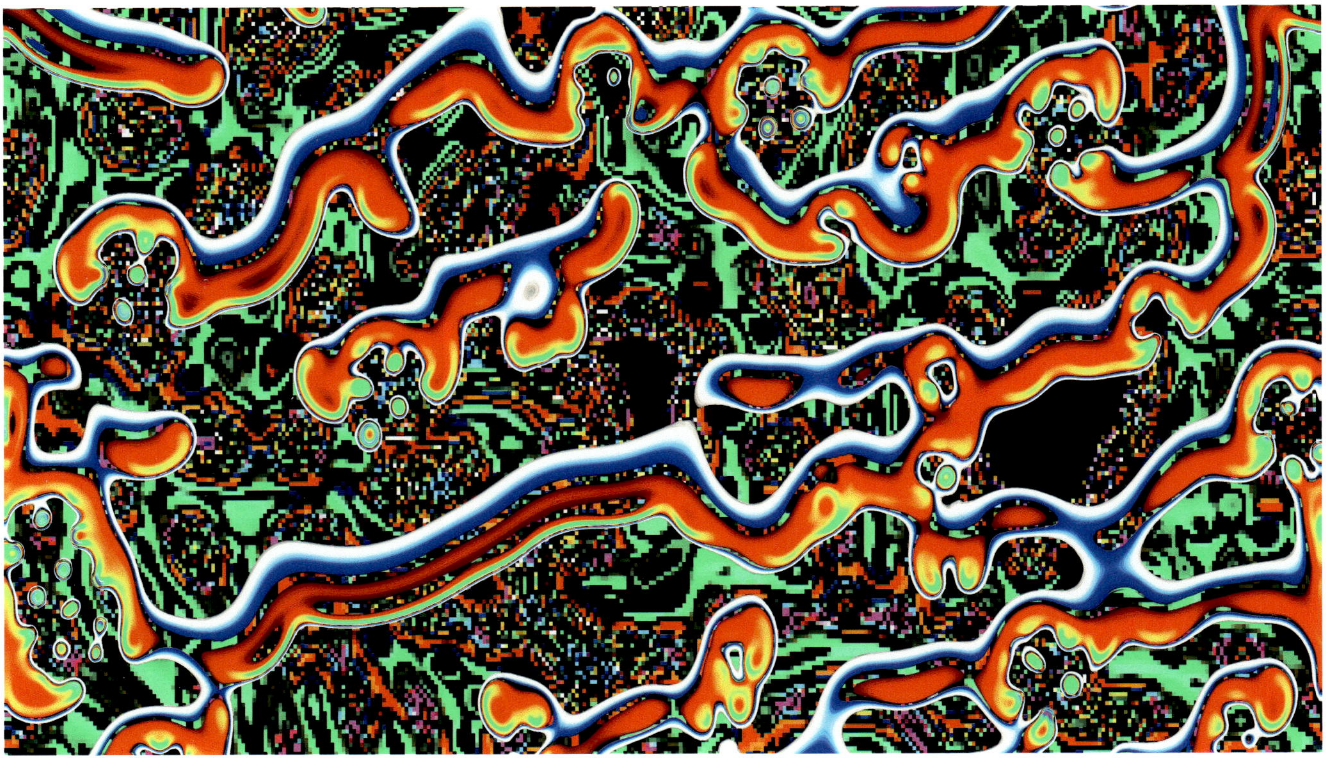

PATTERNS

The Origin of the World, started 2012

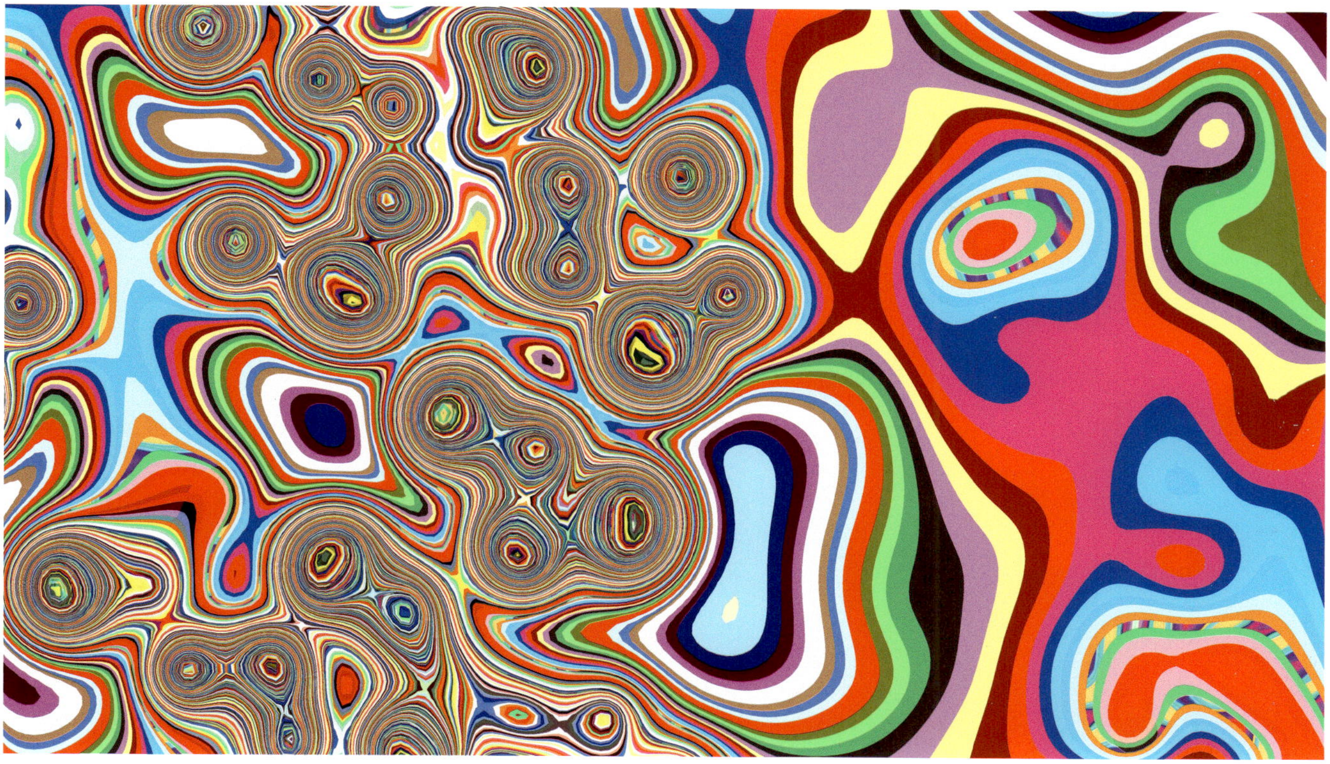

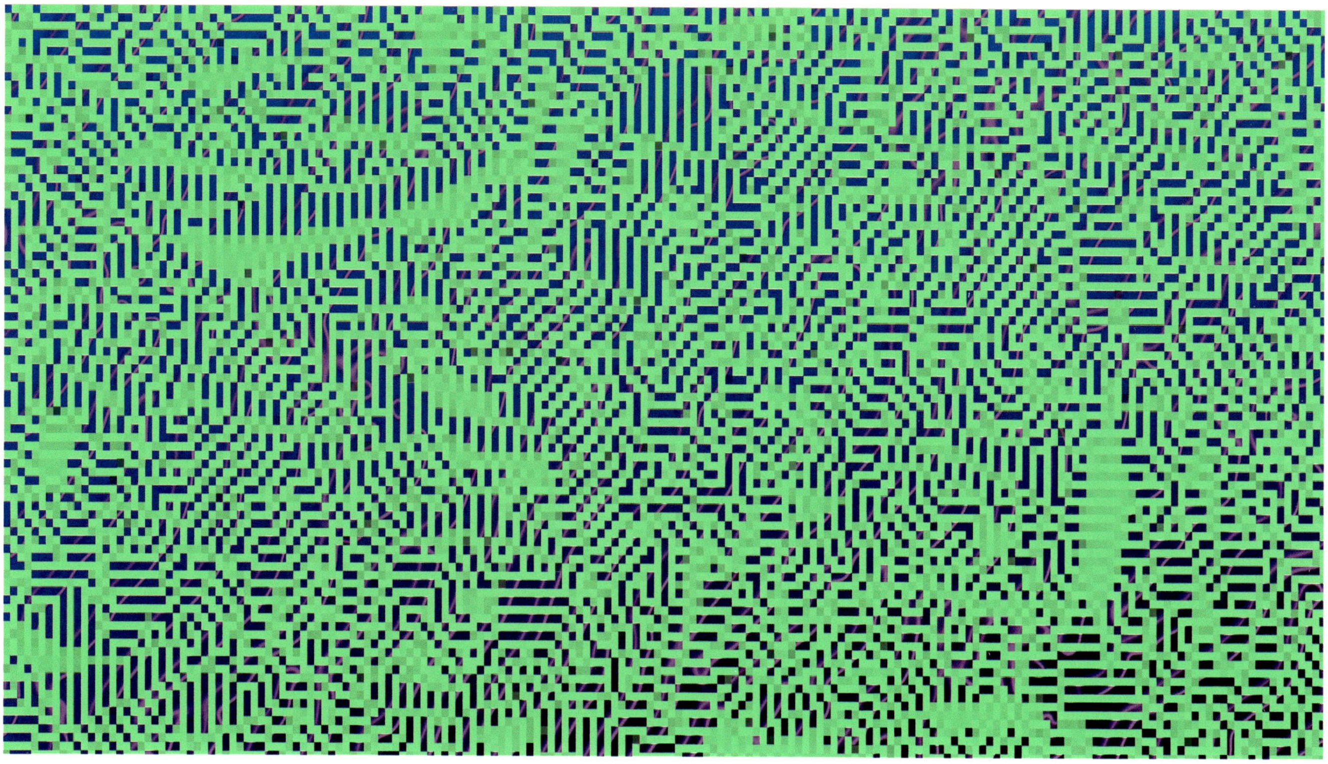

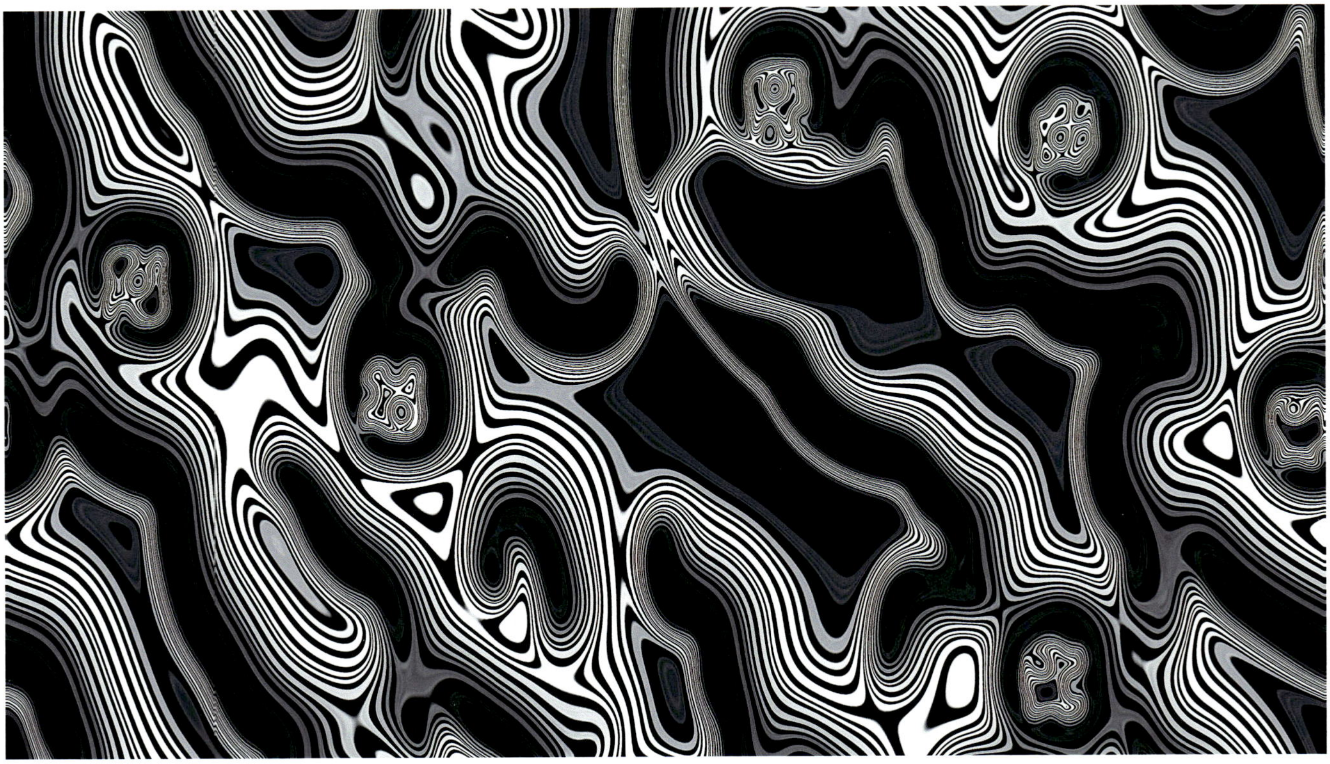

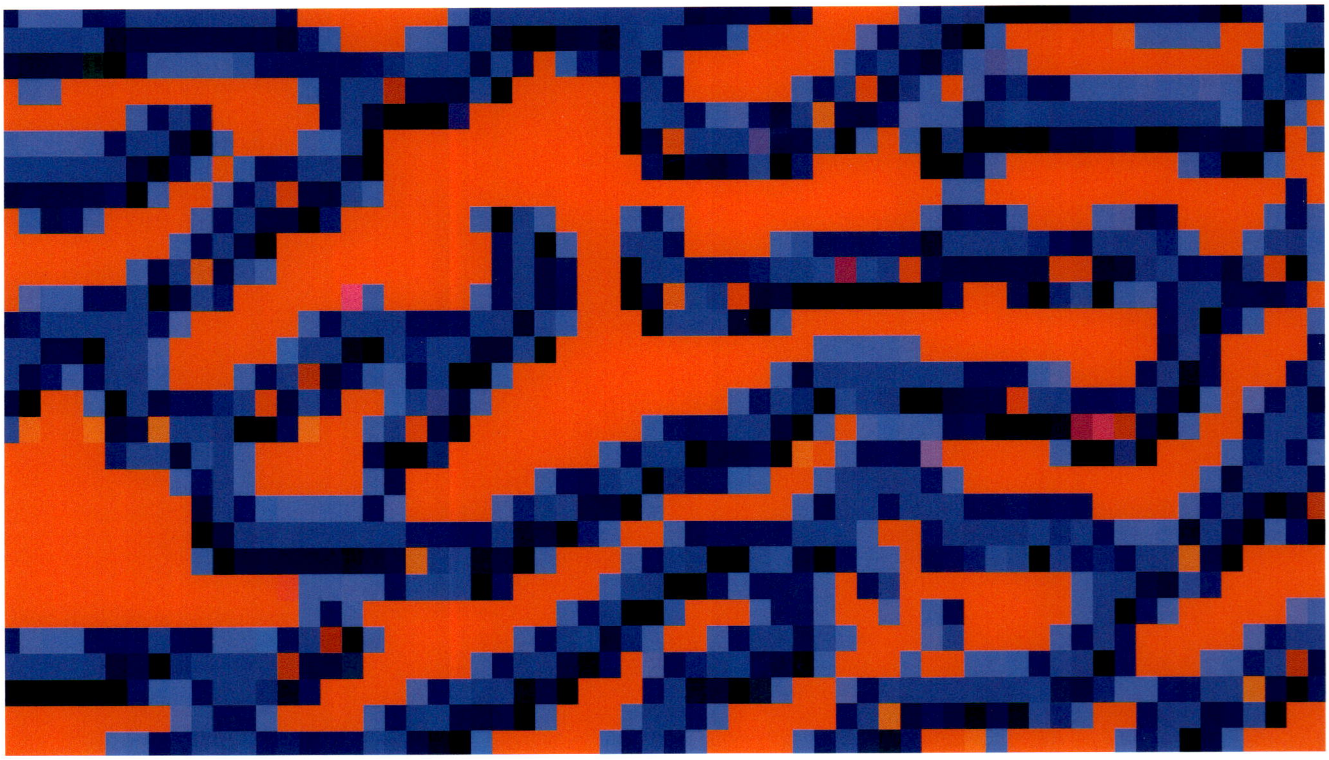

PATTERNS

The Origin of the World, started 2012

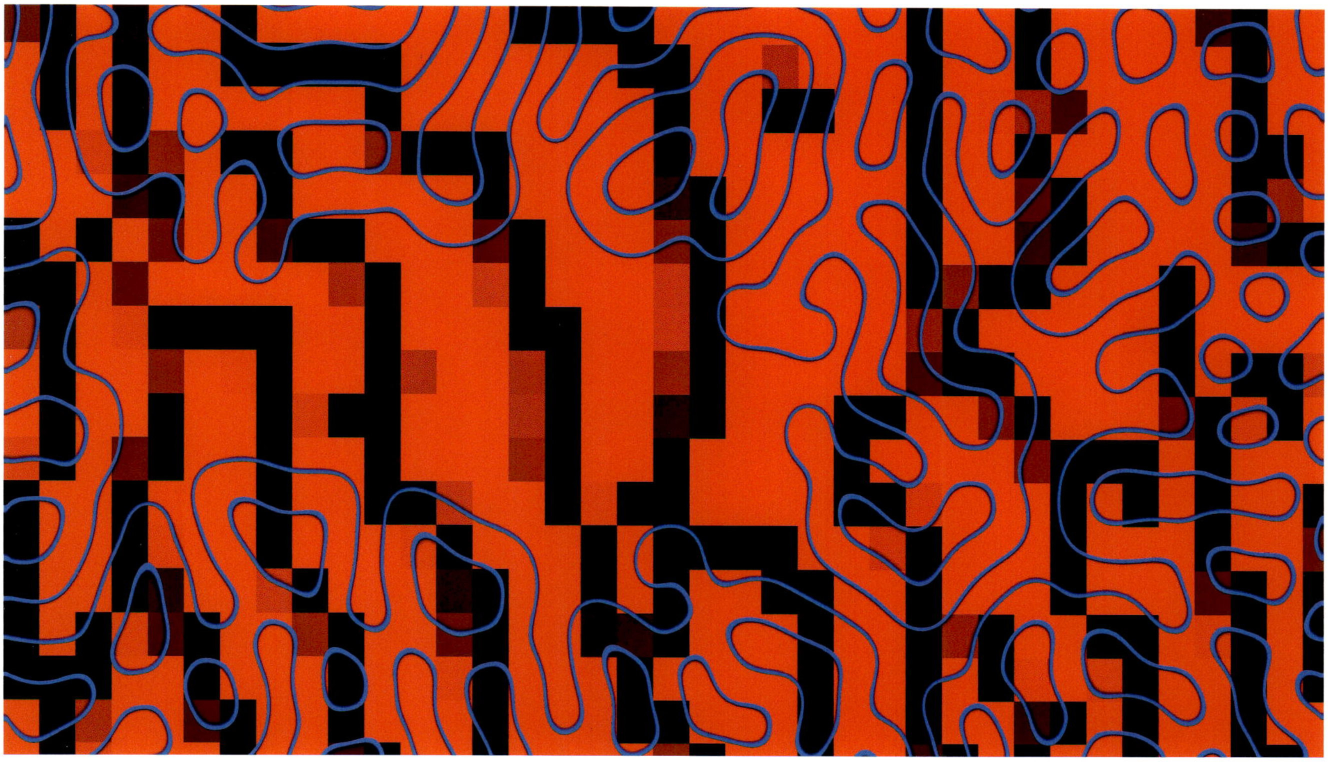

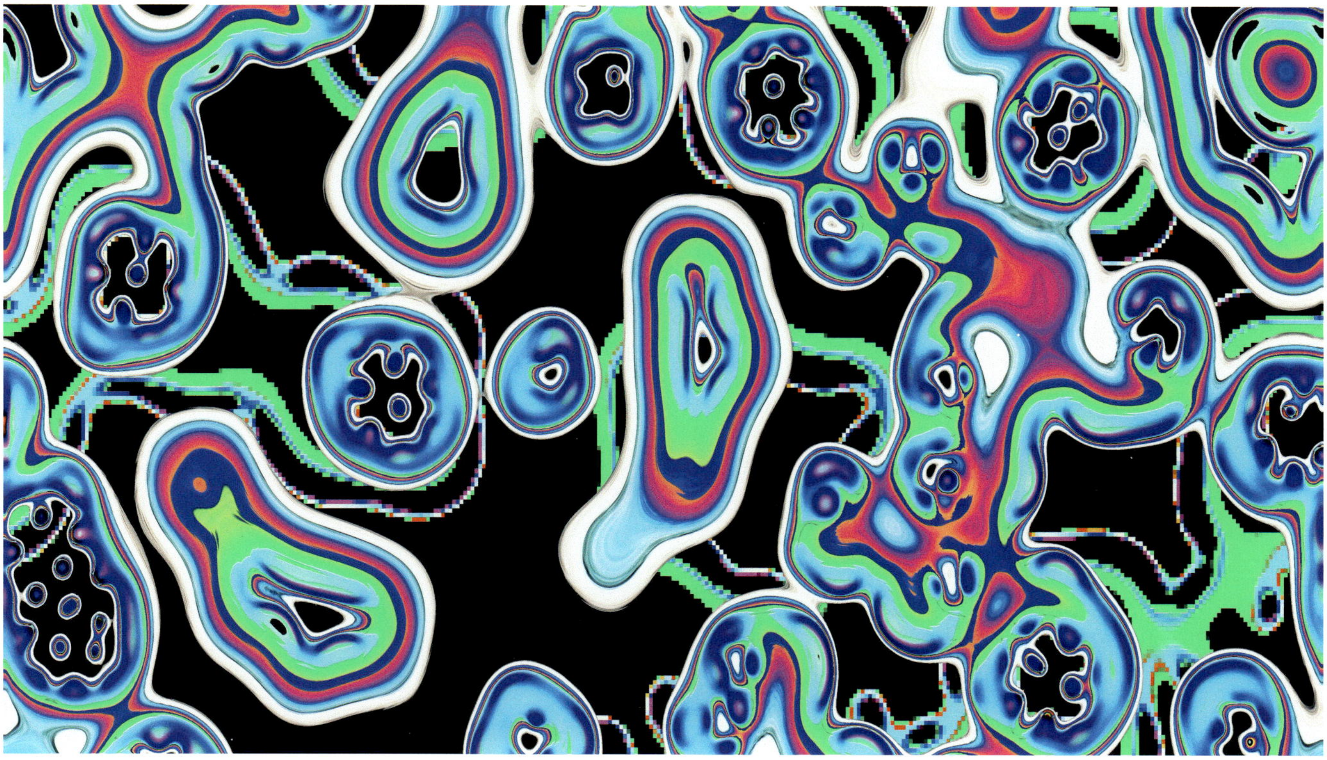

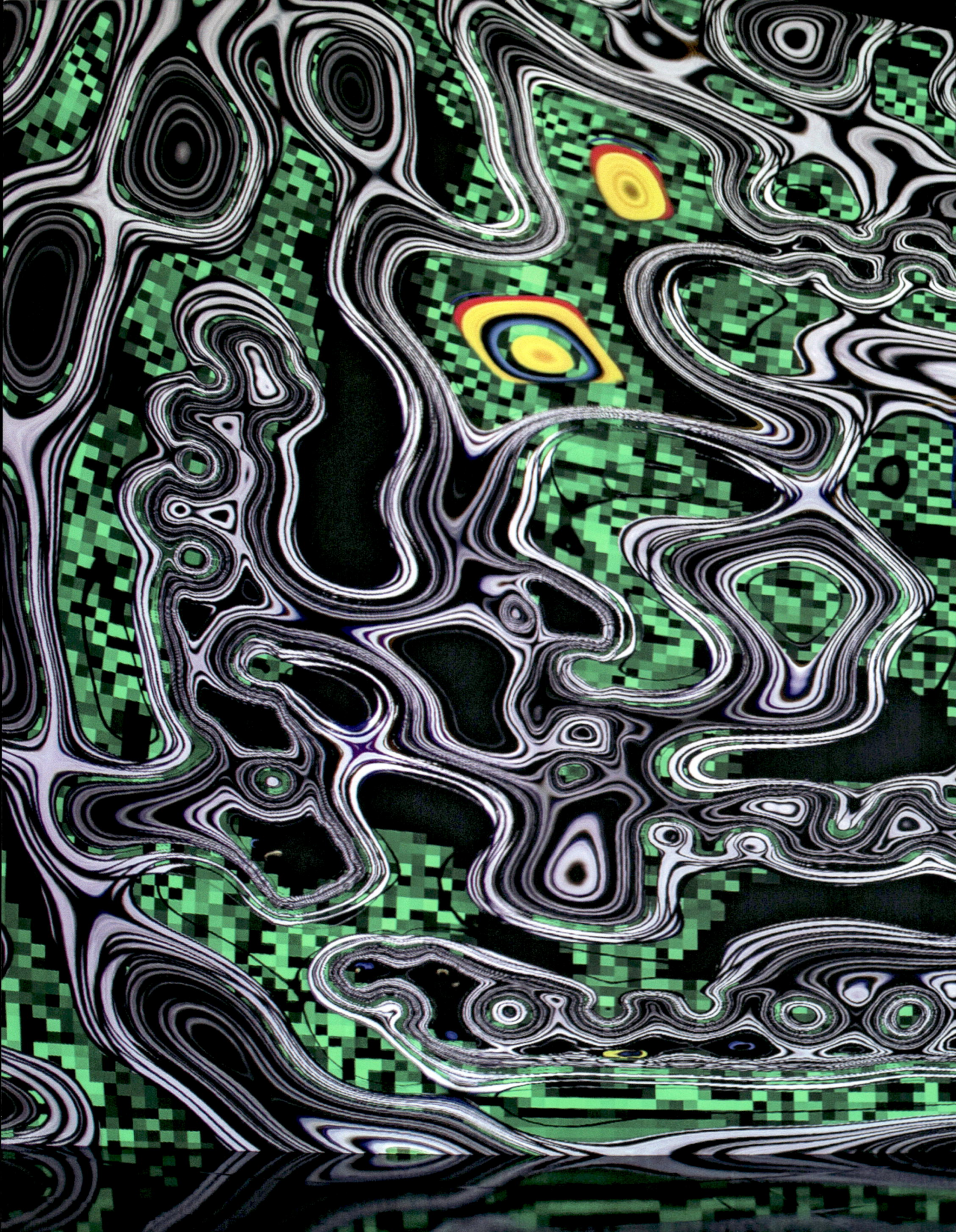

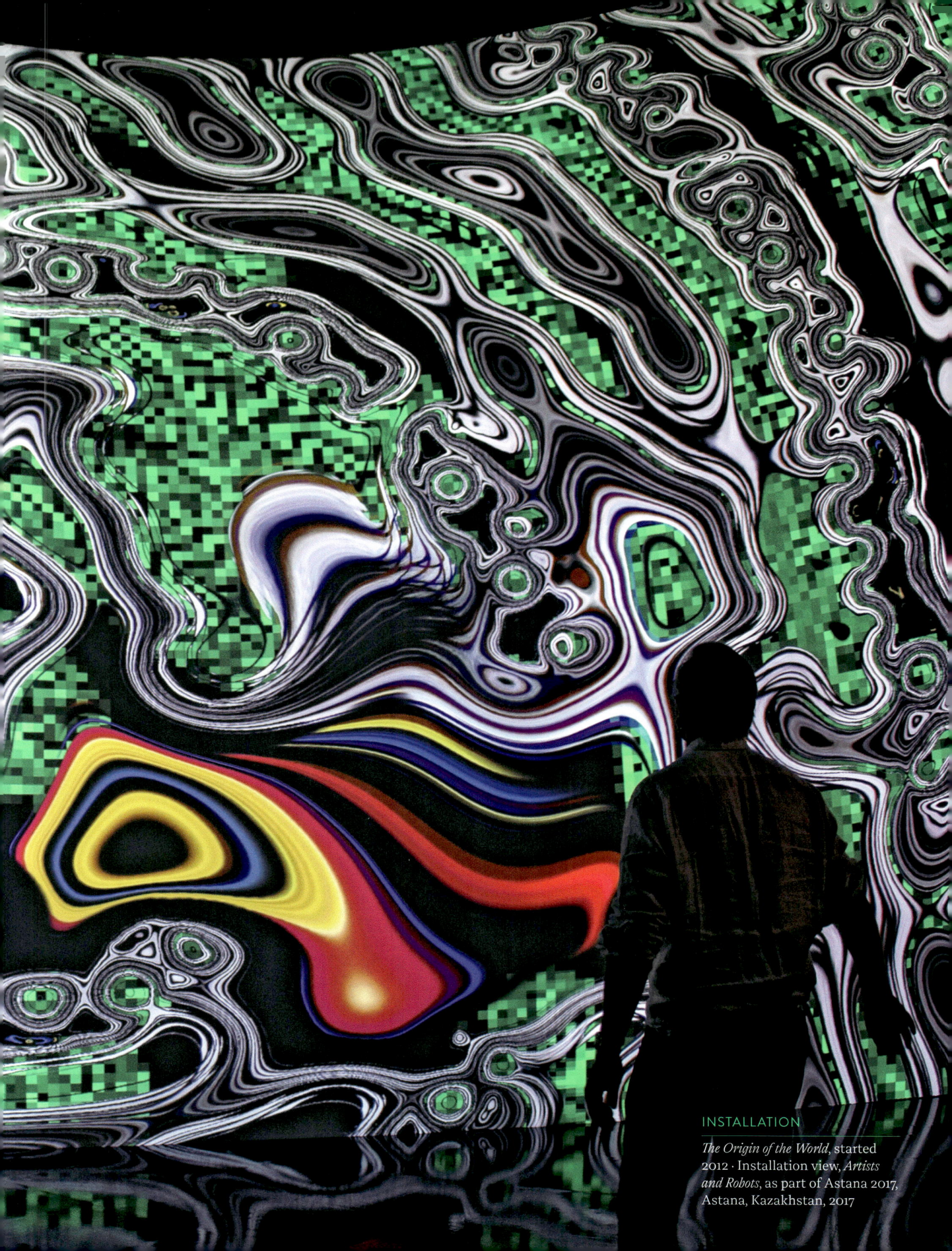

INSTALLATION

The Origin of the World, started
2012 · Installation view, *Artists
and Robots*, as part of Astana 2017,
Astana, Kazakhstan, 2017

TOOLS OF THE DIGITAL WORLD

Infinite Pixels (White), 2010 ·
Silkscreen on mirror, neon
lighting, metal box · 80×80×
15 cm (31 1/2×31 1/2×5 15/16 in.) ·
Detail from p. 76

↓ PATTERN

Pixel Wave, started 2011 ·
Generative and interactive
installation · Dimensions
variable · Software: Cyrille Henry,
Antoine Villeret · See also
pp. 78–81

● Since the 1980s, Miguel Chevalier has been creating art with the help of the computer. From the beginning he has regarded it not merely as a tool but as a partner in dialogue throughout the artistic process (see also p. 10). His early works are characterized by an examination of the central elements that enable computer graphics: for example, the ▸binary system (p. 26), which is the basic language in computing, consisting of only two digits. Chevalier also uses ▸pixels (p. 28), the smallest unit of a digital image, or ▸voxels (p. 29), the three-dimensional counterparts to pixels, as fundamental motifs in his physical artworks. Through his prints, objects, and videos, he has opened up a connection between analog and digital reality—a theme that continues to define his art to this day. His works visualize what cannot be seen by the naked eye: generative processes and ▸algorithms (p. 26) which create the virtual world. (JG)

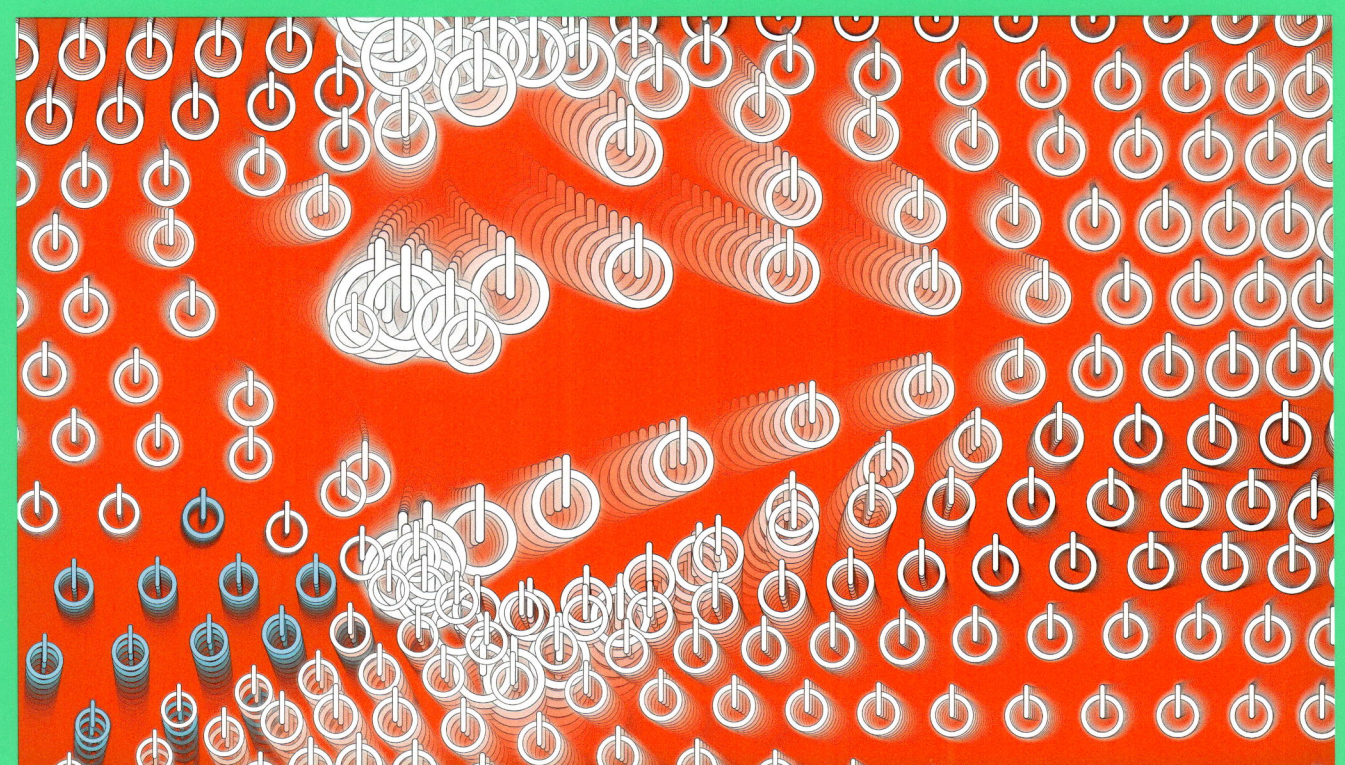

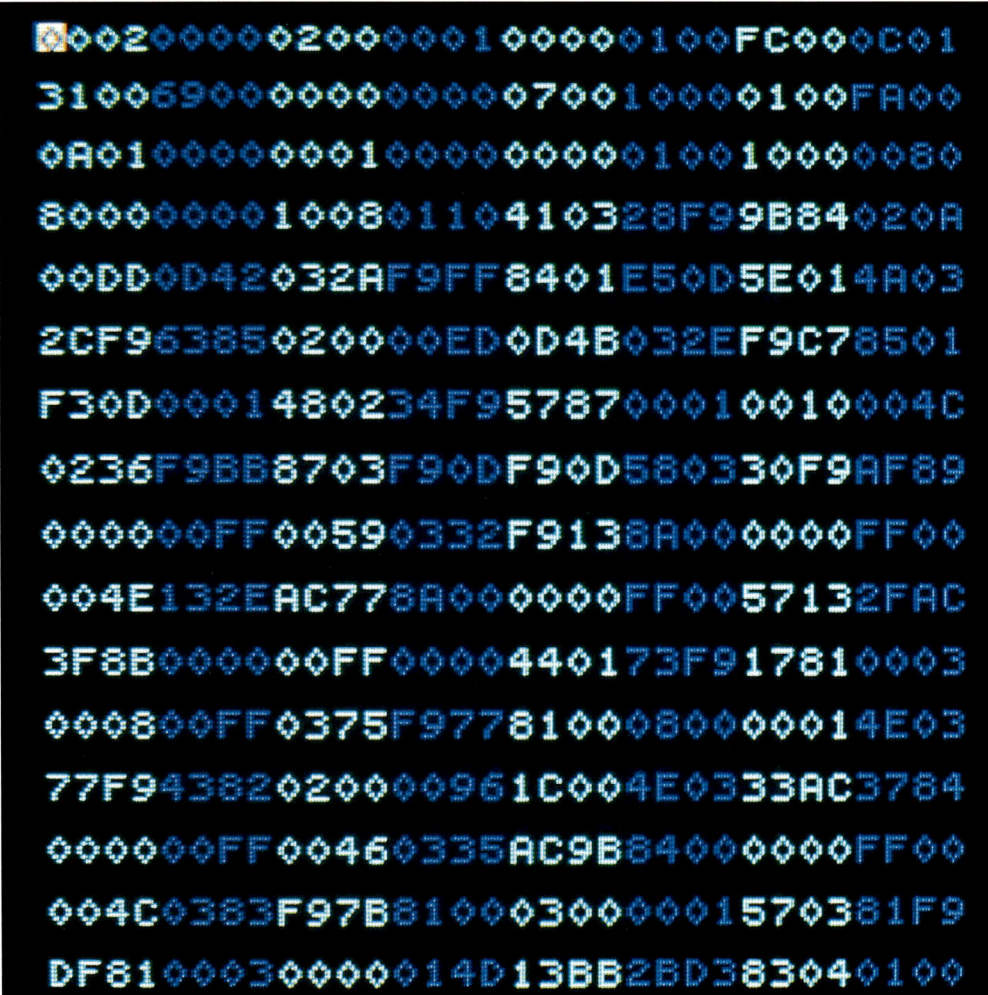

← PRINT

Flip Flop, 1987 · Varnished print mounted on wood · 82×77 cm (32 1/4×30 5/16 in.)

↑ OBJECT

Hexadecimal Memory Window, 1988 · Cibachrome, Plexiglas · 51.5×51.5×10 cm (20 1/4×20 1/4× 3 15/16 in.)

Flip Flop is made up of the two digits found in the ▸ binary system (p. 26). In this sense, the computing language's signs form the work's basic motif. Although it is a print, it represents the moment of a change of state; even the title suggests the flicking of a switch. The numbers 0 and 1 symbolize precisely this shift from on or off, true or false, positive or negative. The repetition of the two motifs creates a dynamic ornament suggesting depth. The work is one of the artist's first attempts to visualize the abstract mechanism of digital calculation in a sensory way. It was created with LightWave 3D, one of the first publicly available 3D software programs for the Amiga computer (p. 73). (JG)

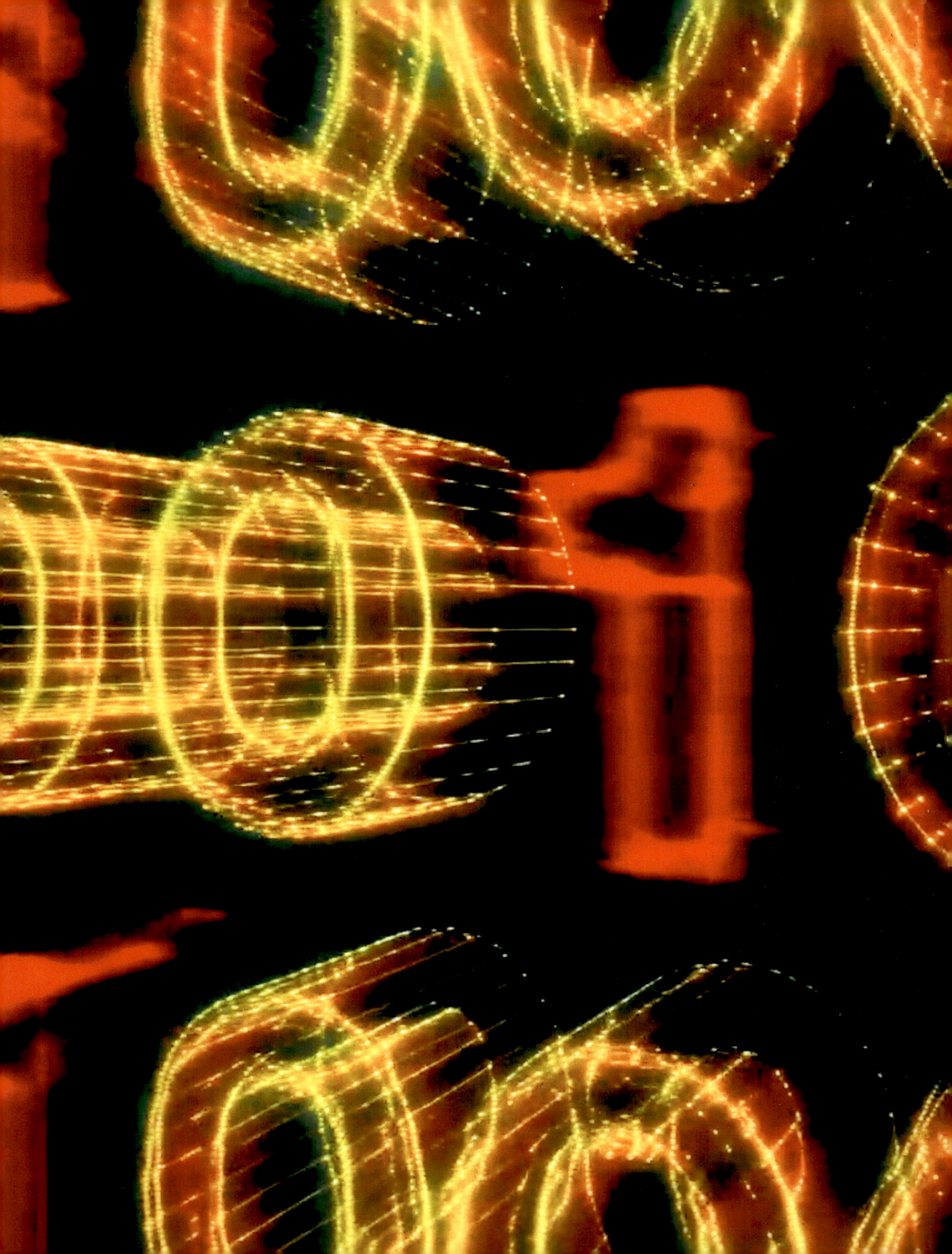

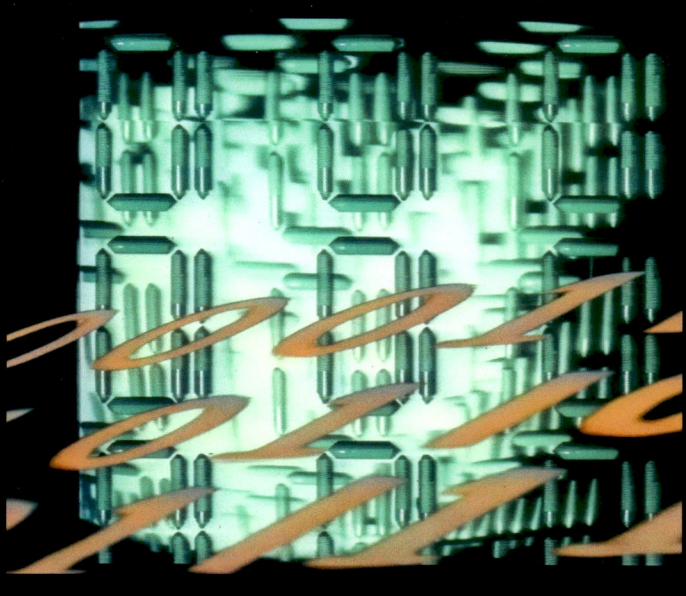

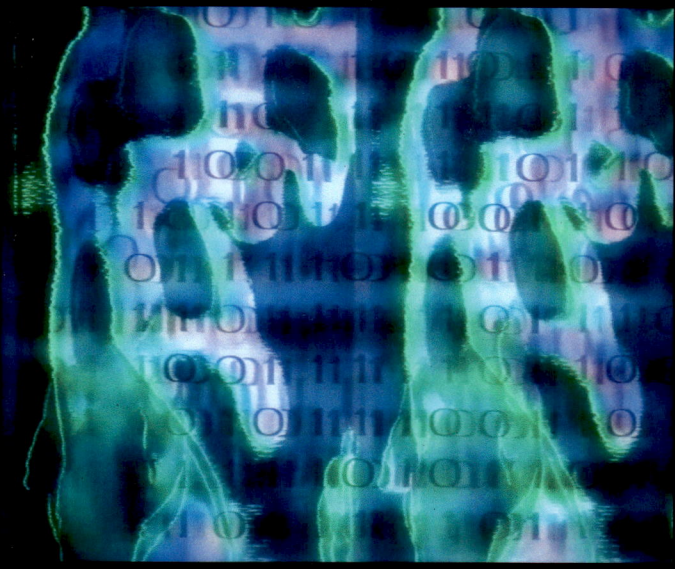

Binary State, 1990–91 · Video, color, sound, 5 min. · Music: Fred Wallich, production: Grand Canal, CICV Montbéliard Belfort

The ▸ binary system (p. 26), one of the most important computation systems, consists of only two digits: 0 and 1. Depending on their sequence and combination, it can represent all numbers and thus also an infinite pool of data that can be used to generate images, sounds, and more. Binary code is used in our daily lives, from bar codes to stock market transactions and telecommunications. Miguel Chevalier created *Binary State* with his first computer, an Amiga 1000. The work dates back to the time before the internet was generally accessible and global networks in the digital space were only just emerging. Chevalier thus visualizes a system that is now an indispensable foundation of our modern life. (FS)

▸ VIDEO

TECHNICAL REFERENCE

Commodore International · Amiga 1000 with monitor and keyboard, 1985 · In total ca. 46.1 × 50 × 55 cm (18 1/8 × 19 11 /16 × 21 5/8 in.)

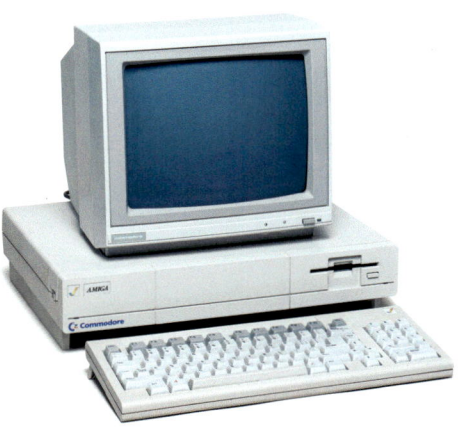

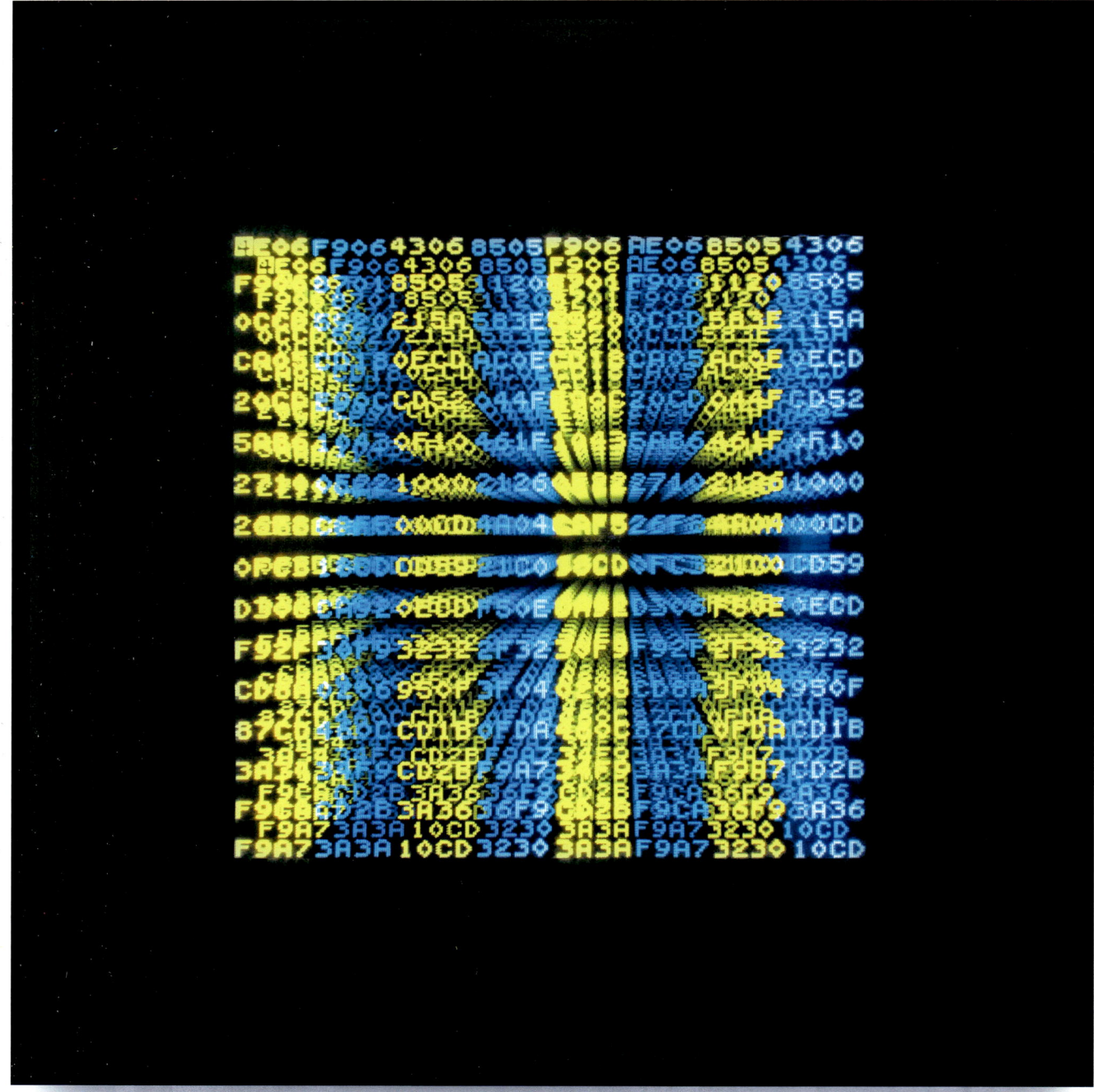

Infinite Hexadecimal Memory Window, 1992 · Silkscreen on mirror, neon lighting, metal box · 100 × 100 × 15 cm (39 3/8 × 39 3/8 × 5 15/16 in.)

While in painting the window traditionally opens to a view of the exterior, Miguel Chevalier offers a view into the interior of the computer, the depths of machine memory, so to speak. In his early works, he made the fundamentals of digital technology the subject of his oeuvre, though such technology increasingly found its way into the visual arts beginning in the early 1990s. In this work, he focuses on the ▸ hexadecimal system (p. 28), which consists of the digits 0 to 9 and the letters A to F. In computer science, this system is used to represent large numbers with fewer digits through a conversion process, so they can be written faster and read more easily. The artist uses the mirroring surface to create transparency but also a seemingly infinite reflection that corresponds to the idea of an unlimited digital universe in which data is constantly circulating. (FS)

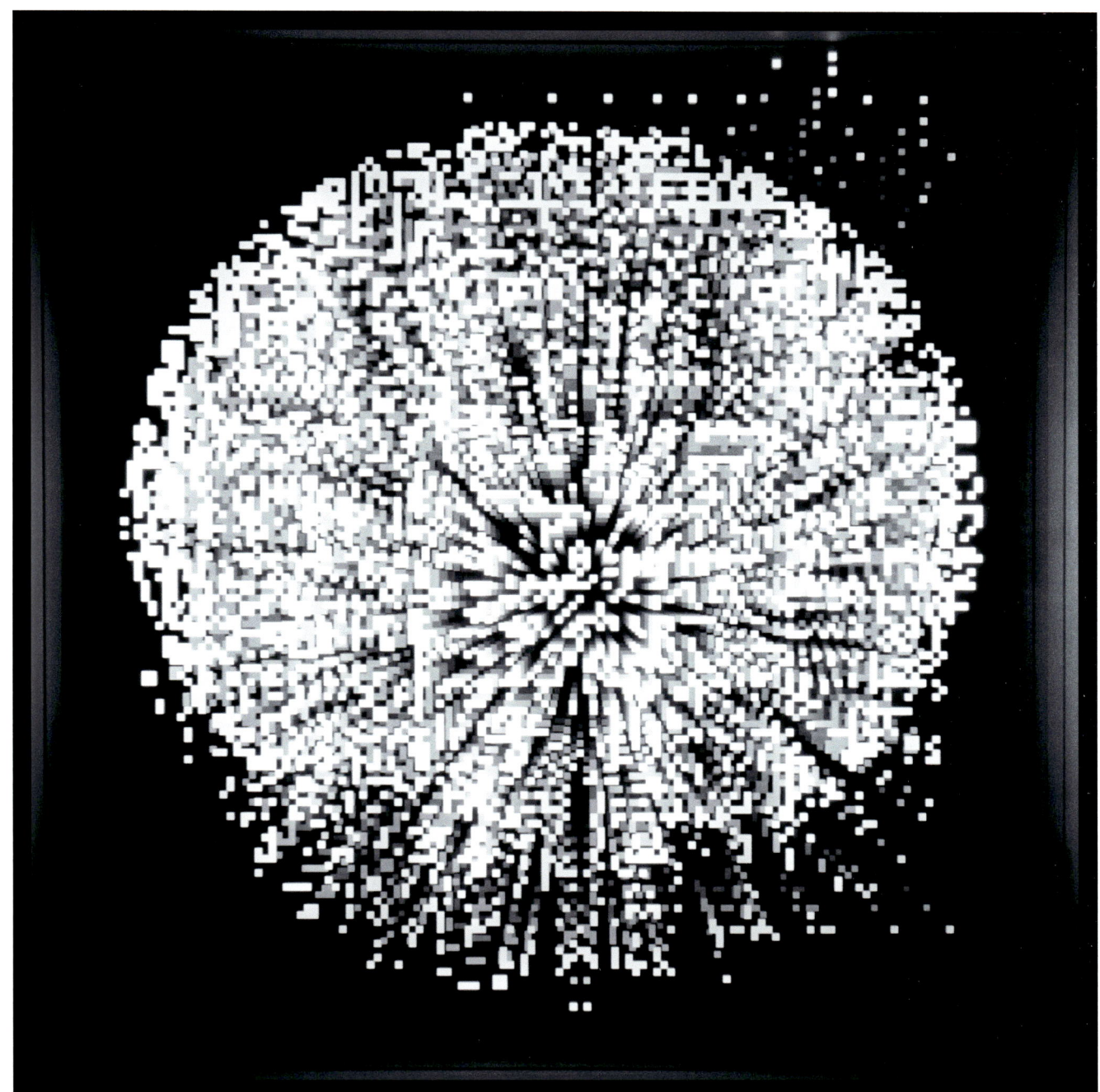

Infinite Pixels (Circular White),
2011 · Silkscreen on mirror,
neon lighting, metal box ·
80 × 80 × 15 cm (31 1/2 × 31 1/2 ×
5 15/16 in.)

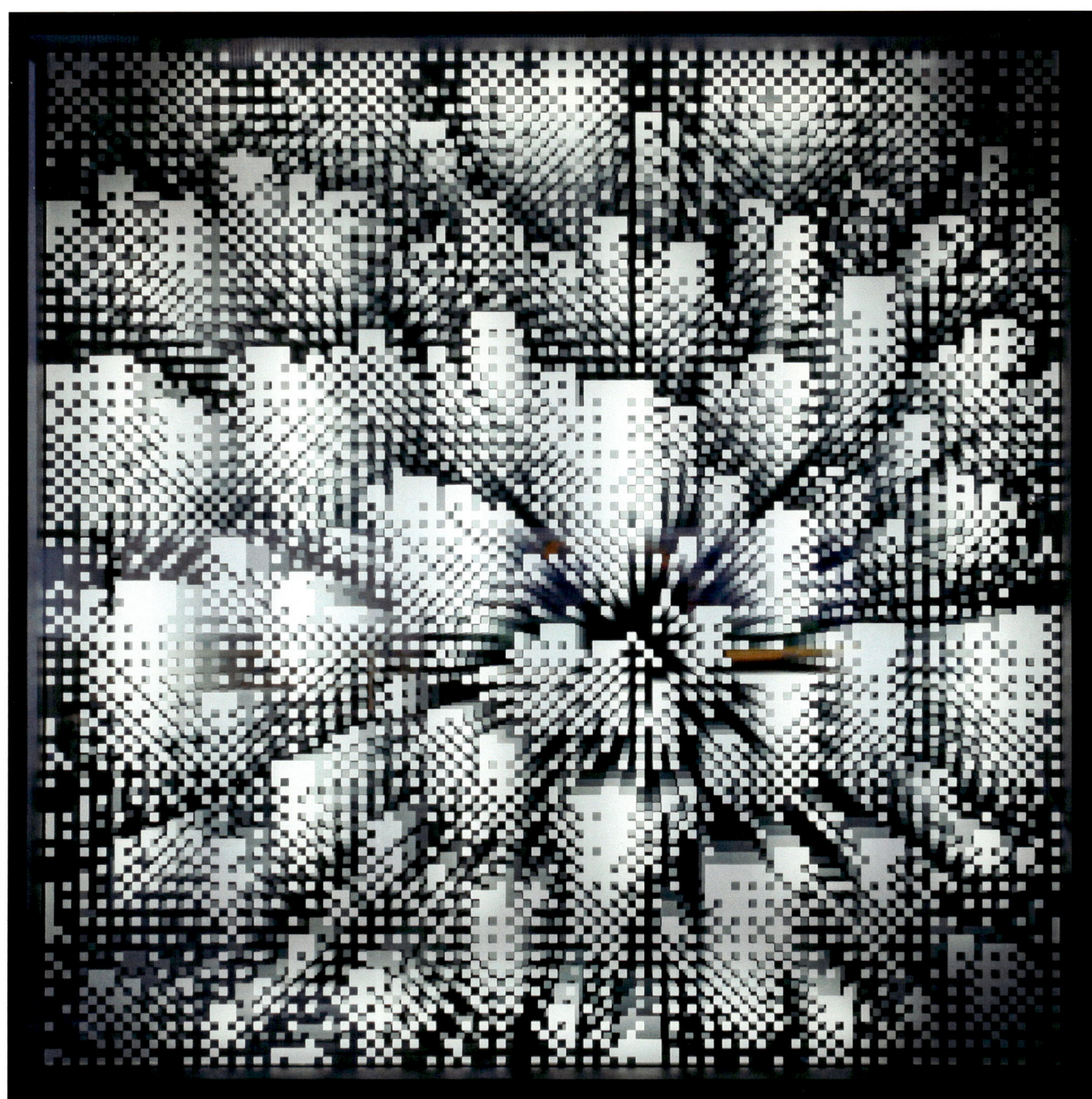

Infinite Pixels (White),
2010 · Silkscreen on
mirror, neon lighting,
metal box · 80×80×15 cm
(31 1/2 × 31 1/2 × 5 15/16 in.)

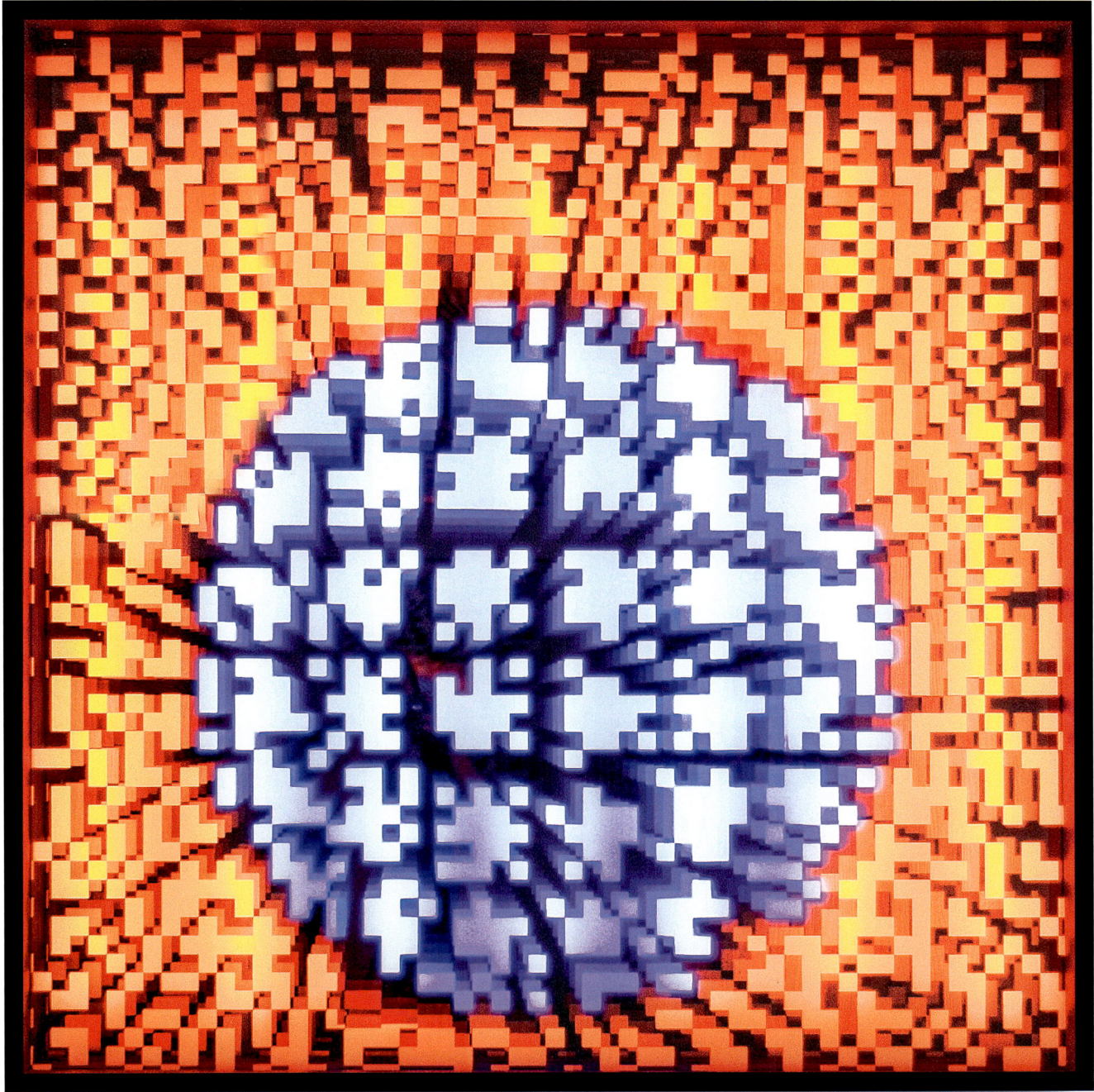

Infinite Op Art Pixels (Purple and Red), 2012 · Silkscreen on mirror, neon lighting, metal box · 100 × 100 × 15 cm (39 3/8 × 39 3/8 × 5 15/16 in.)

With the *Infinite Pixels* series, Miguel Chevalier refers to Pop and Op Art as well as Nouveau Réalisme. Artists such as Roy Lichtenstein (1923–1997) or Alain Jacquet (1939–2008) worked with enlarged Ben-Day dots, rendering the tiny dots that characterize offset printing clearly visible. In this group of works, Chevalier engages with the ▸ pixel (p. 28) as the digital image's smallest element. Analogous to the dots, the pixels now serve him as motif, material, and concept all at once. The mirrored objects each suggest an illusionistic depth that evokes the notion of virtual infinity, that is, the potentially endless continuation of these forms in digital space. *Infinite Op Art Pixels (Purple and Red)* obviously refers to Victor Vasarely (1906–1997), in particular to his works from the Vega period, which often create trompe l'oeil effects — much like this sphere of pixels, which appears to protrude from the picture. (JG)

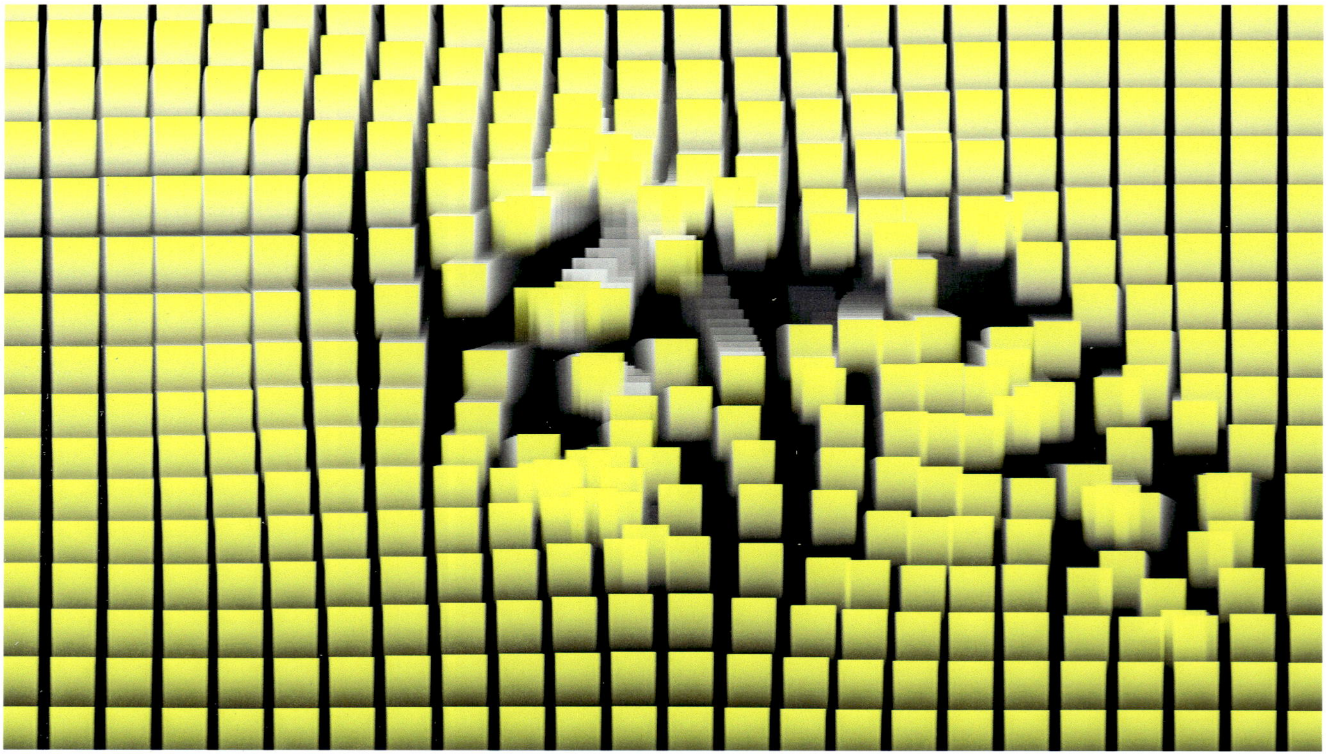

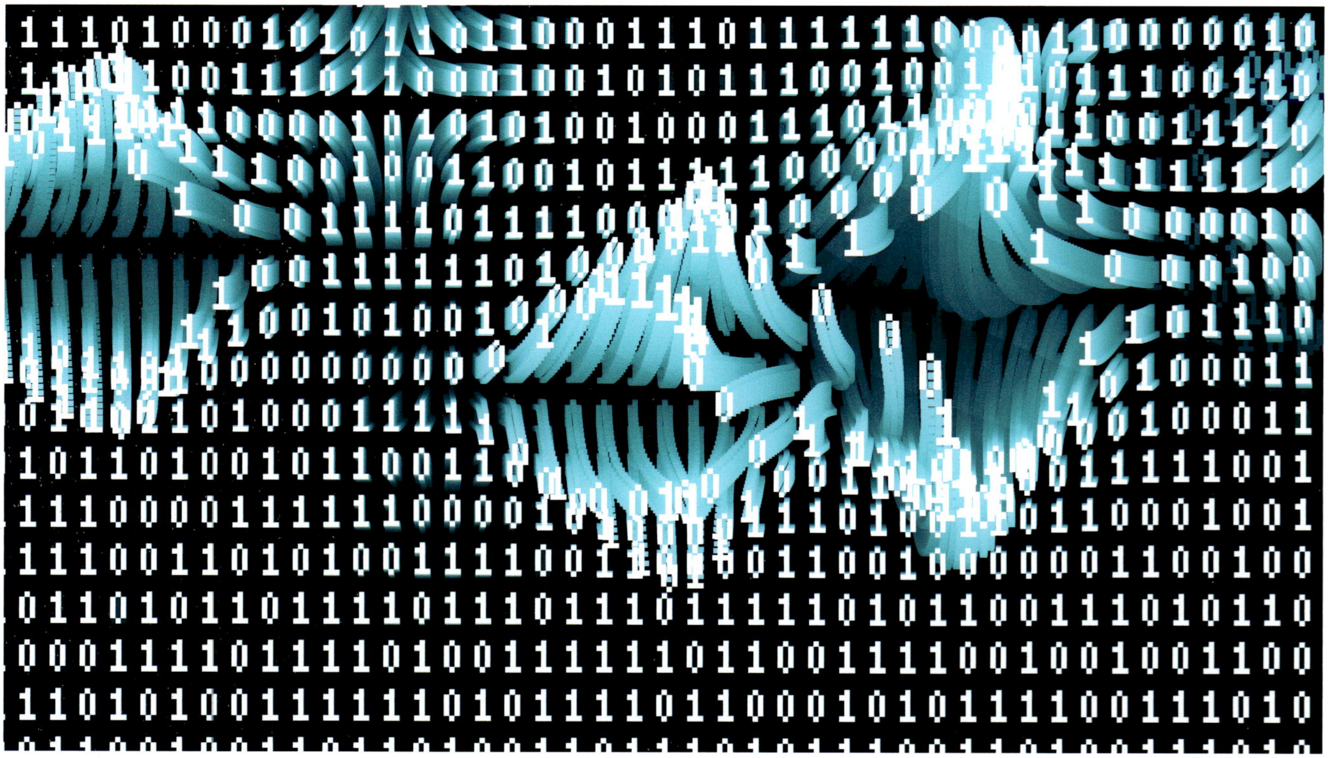

PATTERNS

Pixel Wave, started 2011

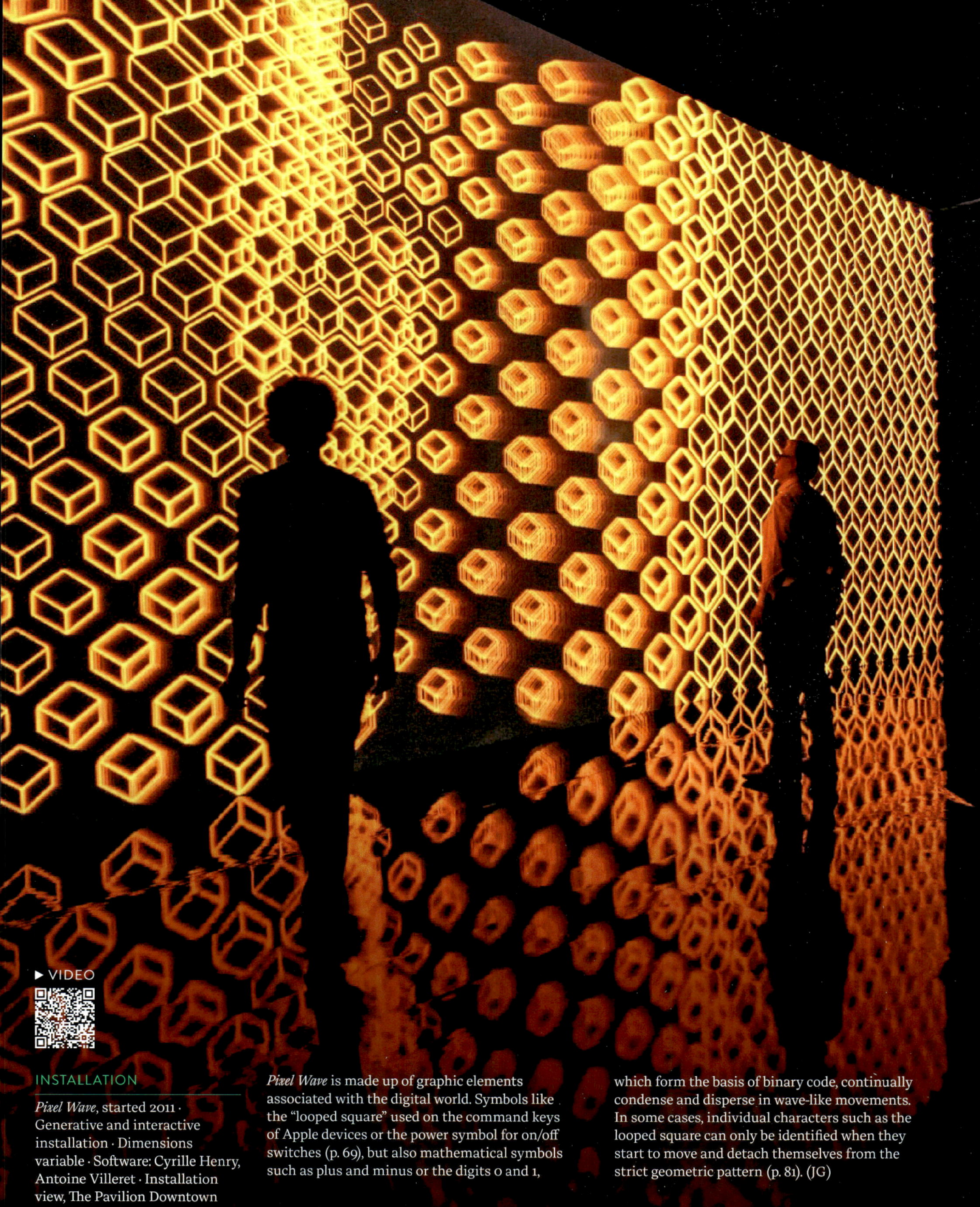

▶ VIDEO

INSTALLATION

Pixel Wave, started 2011 ·
Generative and interactive
installation · Dimensions
variable · Software: Cyrille Henry,
Antoine Villeret · Installation
view, The Pavilion Downtown
Dubai, United Arab Emirates.

Pixel Wave is made up of graphic elements
associated with the digital world. Symbols like
the "looped square" used on the command keys
of Apple devices or the power symbol for on/off
switches (p. 69), but also mathematical symbols
such as plus and minus or the digits 0 and 1,
which form the basis of binary code, continually
condense and disperse in wave-like movements.
In some cases, individual characters such as the
looped square can only be identified when they
start to move and detach themselves from the
strict geometric pattern (p. 81). (JG)

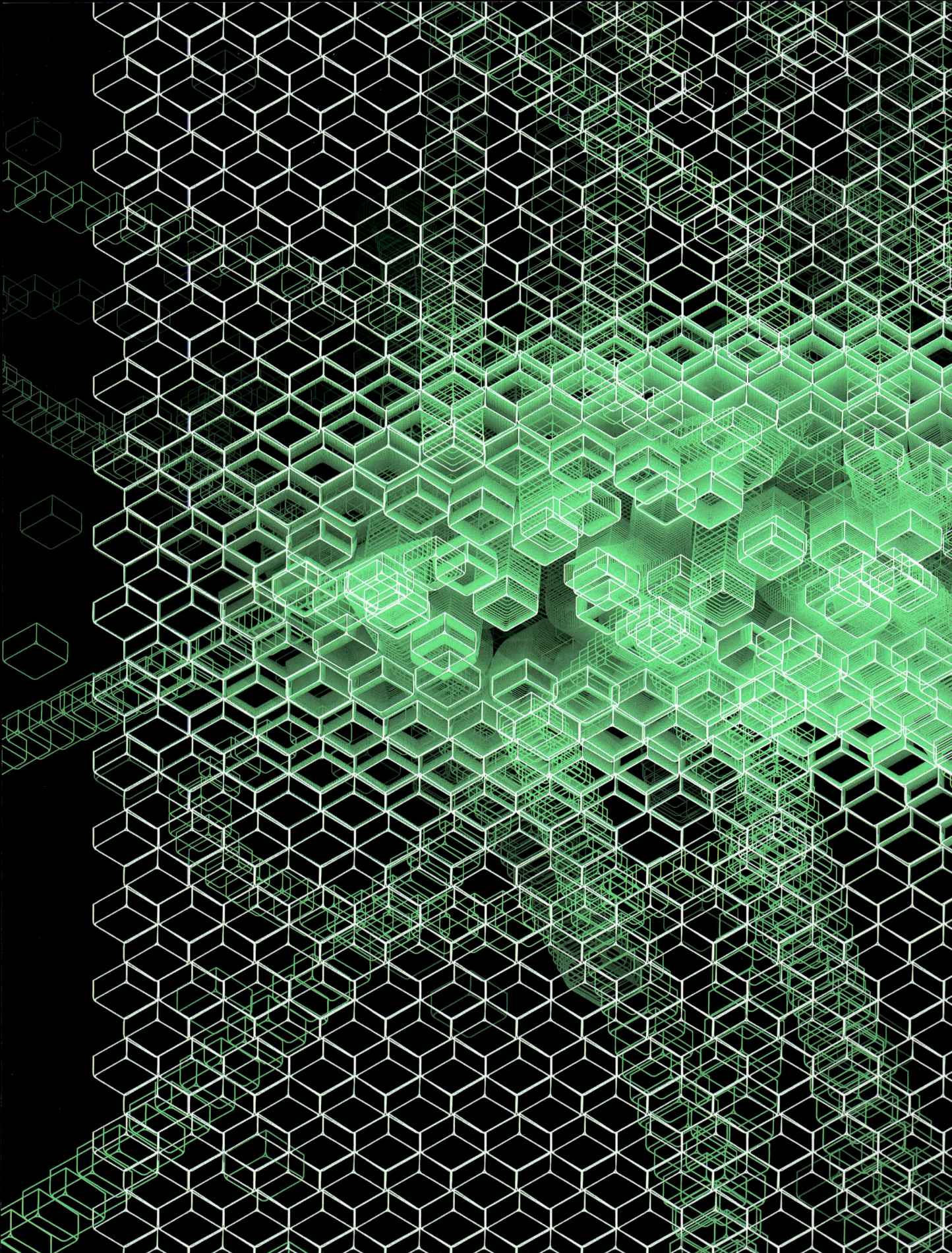

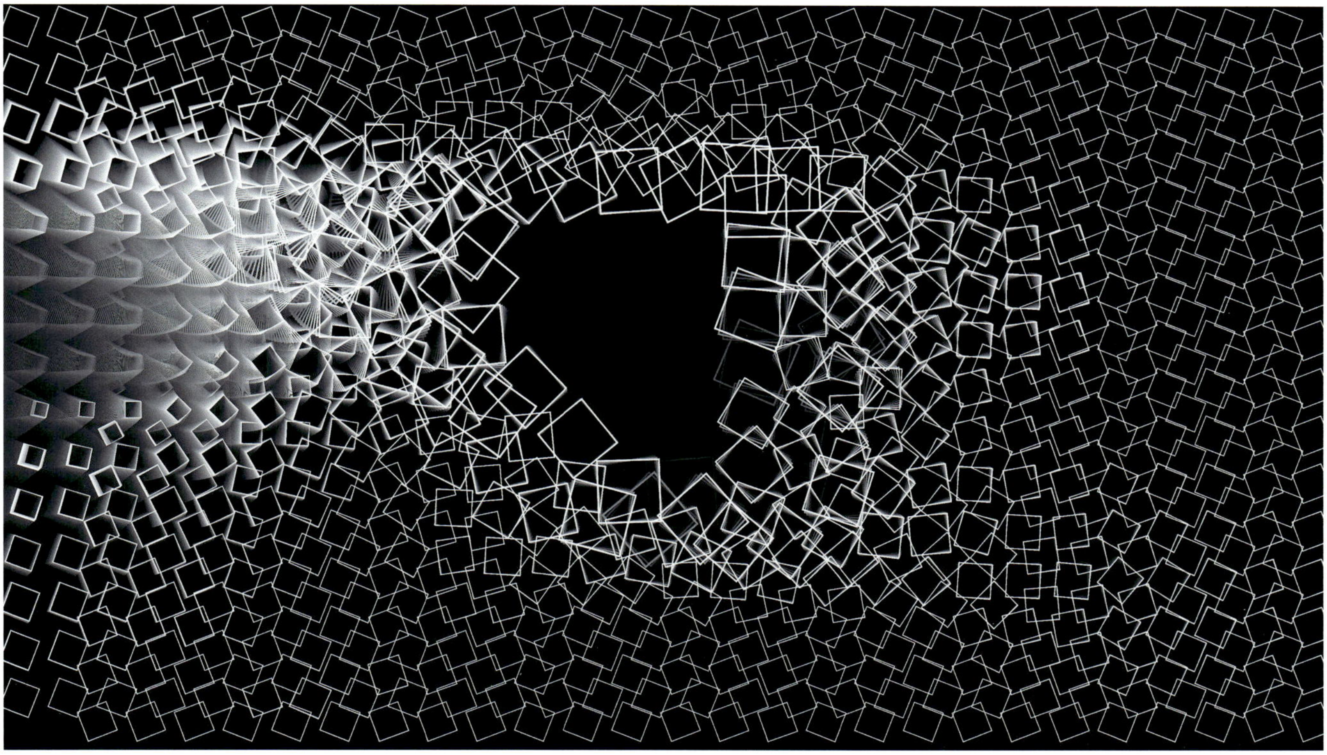

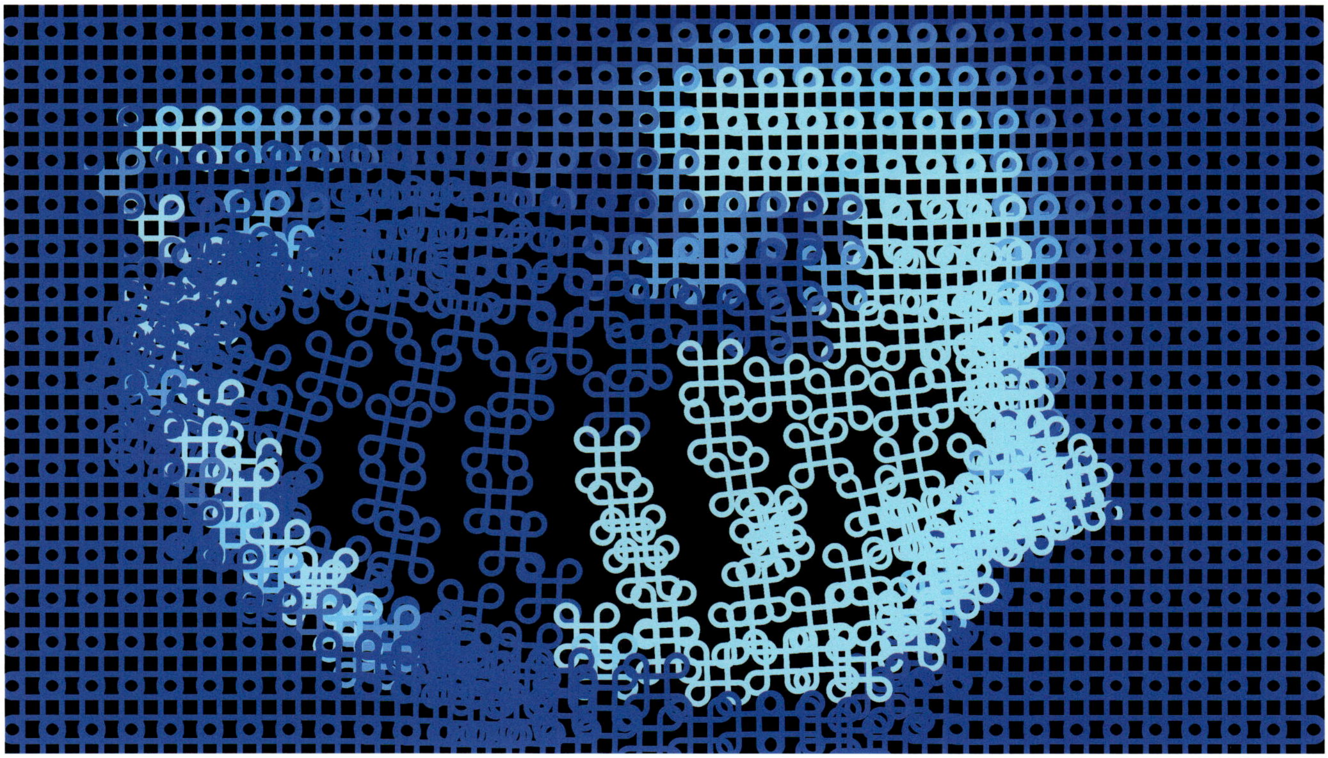

PATTERNS

Pixel Wave, started 2011

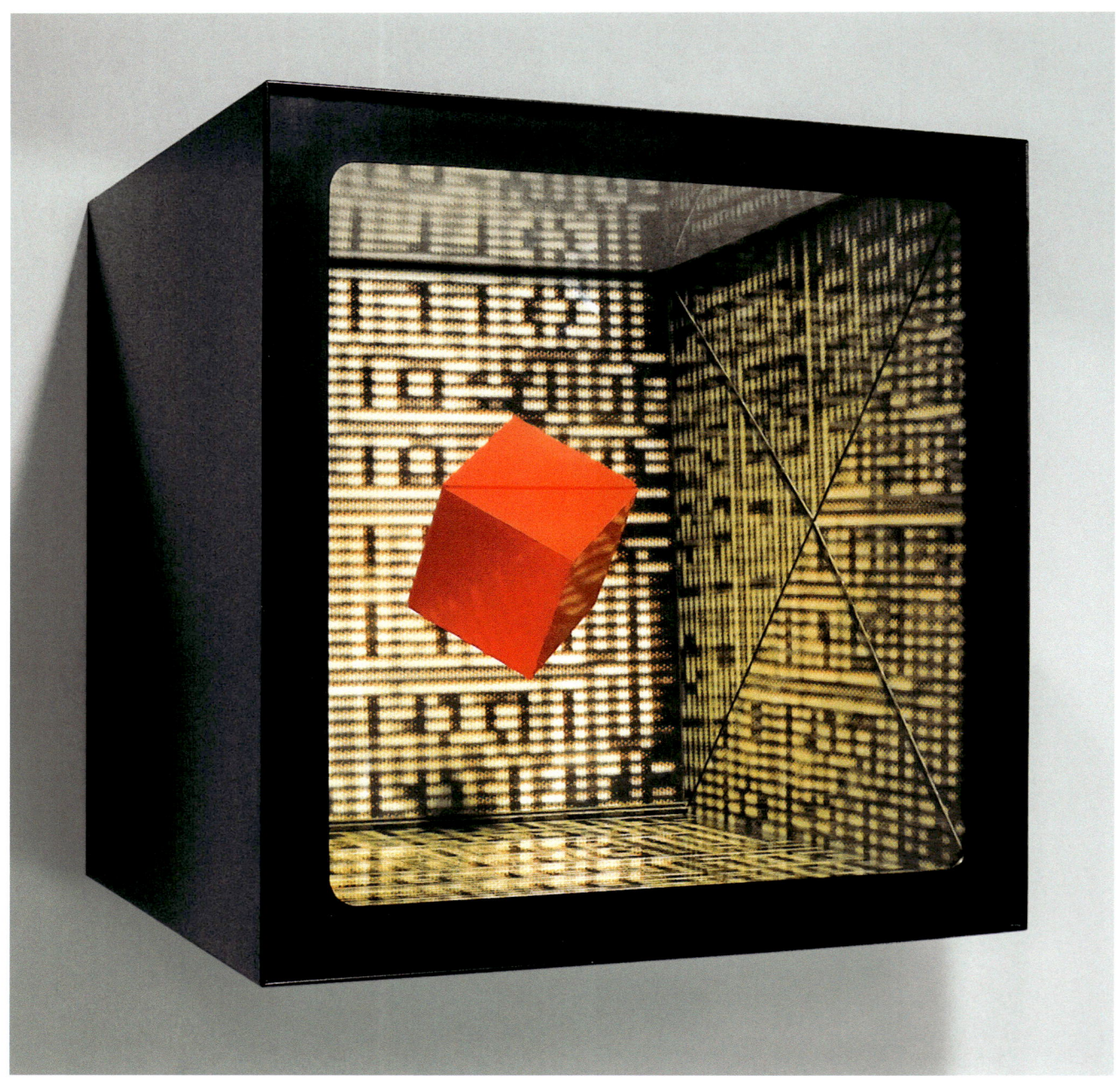

OBJECT

1m3, 1992 · Cibachrome, Plexiglas, mirror, steel · 100×100×100 cm (39 3/8×39 3/8×39 3/8 in.)

In this early work, Miguel Chevalier is already engaged with the theme of materializing the digital. A red cube appears to float in a box. It symbolizes a ▸ voxel (p. 29), the three-dimensional ▸ pixel (p. 28). The optical illusion is created by a mirror diagonally fitted into the box. Depictions of circuits and the numbers 0 and 1 serve as background motifs. The work is reminiscent of a shrine containing a valuable or sacred object. Chevalier thus pays homage to the digital unit that enables the creation of plasticity and space. (FS)

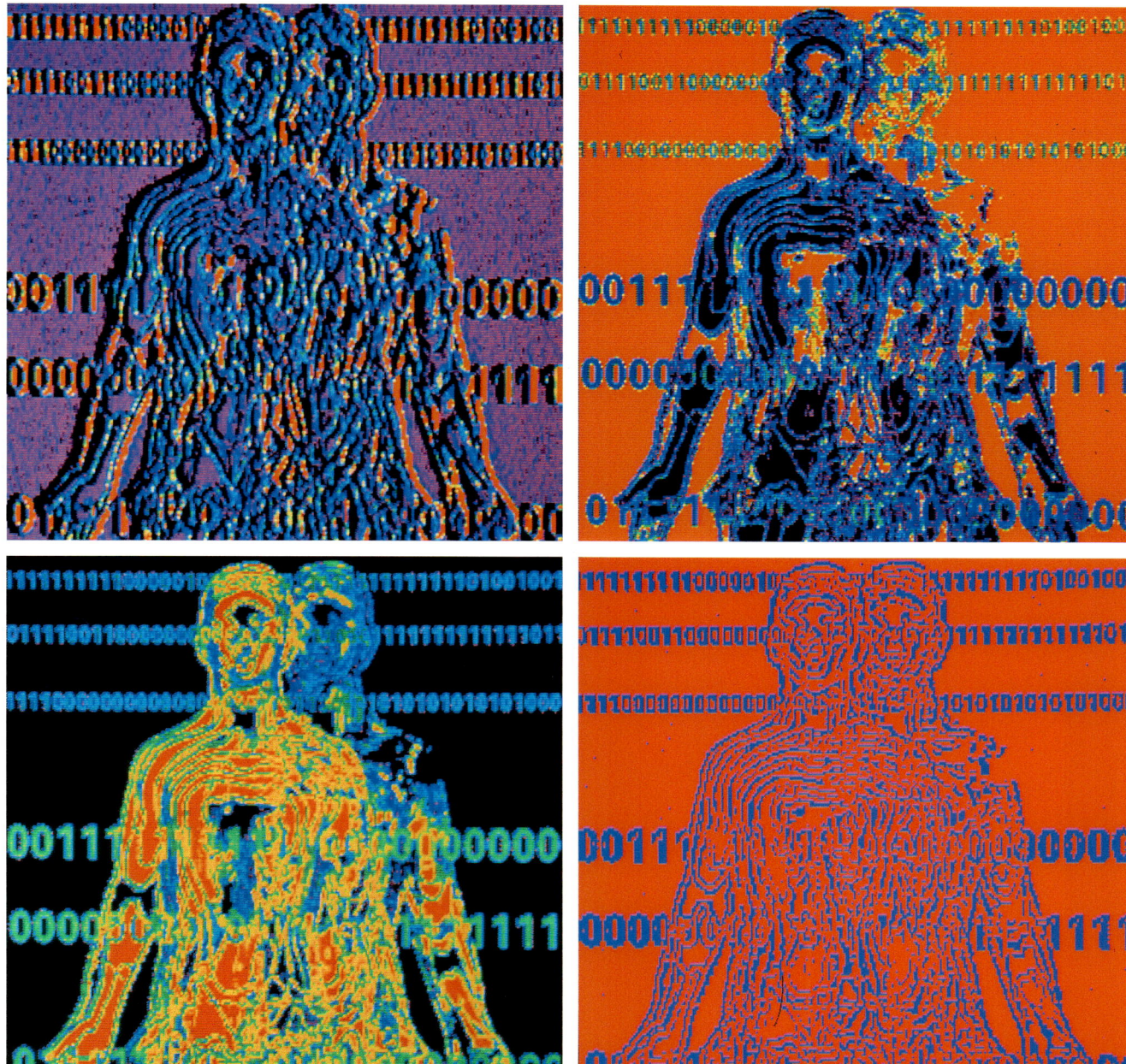

Anthropometry, 1990 · Cibachrome, Plexiglas on aluminum painted black · 4 pieces, each 53×56×15 cm (20 7/8×22×5 15/16 in.)

Anthropometry, which translates to "human measurement," alludes to Yves Klein (1928–1962), who, in his eponymous works beginning in 1958, celebrated the depiction of the female body by means of physical imprints in a performative act. Klein wanted to achieve the most direct and accurate picture of the human figure, entirely "without the psychology of the paintbrush," as he described it. Miguel Chevalier's focus is not on the body's external form, but its interior, particularly as it is rendered by magnetic resonance imaging (MRI). Whereas in Klein's work the body itself becomes the object that paints, in Chevalier's work the subject is first transformed into a kind of data set, which is then turned back into the depiction of a figure with the help of the imaging process. (FS)

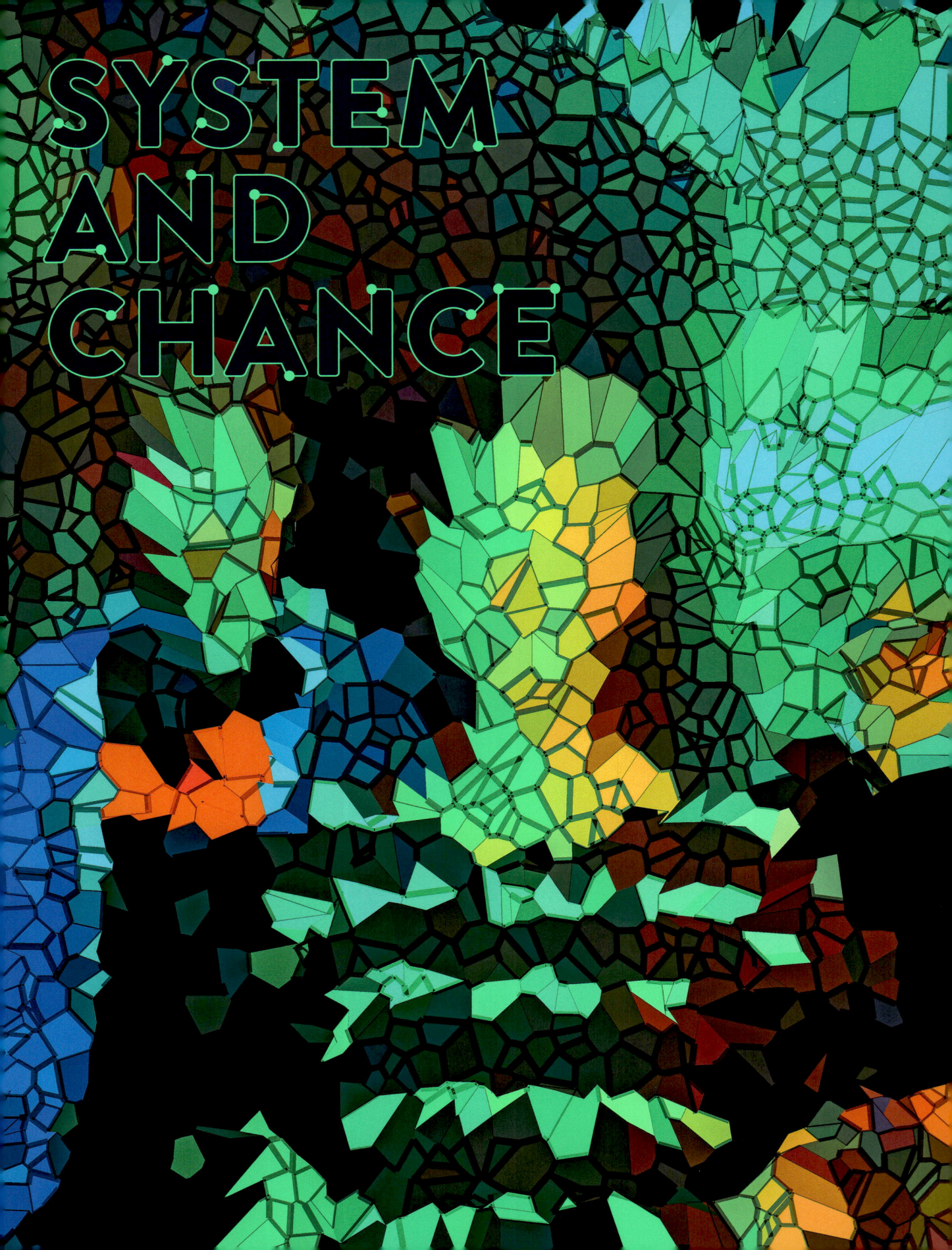

← INSTALLATION

The Eye of the Machine, started 2019 · Generative and interactive installation on a screen · Dimensions variable · Software: Claude Micheli · Detail

↓ INSTALLATION

The Eye of the Machine, started 2019 · Installation view, *Digital Beauty*, Ara Art Center, Seoul, South Korea, 2023

▶ VIDEO

● Since the early 1980s, Miguel Chevalier's art has been closely linked to the computer and thus to mechanical processes. He is often asked about his own role, as it is assumed that the computer does most of the work. However, a concrete concept and precise specifications by the artist are required to create an aesthetically and conceptually convincing work. ▸ Algorithms (p. 26) are fundamental to Chevalier's ▸ generative art (p. 27). This means that he formulates a sequence of defined, automated instructions which the computer then implements. Depending on the task, an algorithm can be simpler or more complex—with results that vary accordingly and with chance always playing an essential role.

The artist's particular fascination lies in exploring how an infinite wealth of forms and patterns can emerge from strictly and methodically organized processes, thus combining technical precision with aesthetic beauty. While his works with moving images, such as *The Origin of the World* (started 2012; pp. 60–67) or *The Eye of the Machine* (started 2019; pp. 84–87), develop incrementally and only unfold their full effect through the visitors' participation, drawings (pp. 91–93), embroideries (p. 58), and sculptures (pp. 118, 120–21, among others) are finalized works in which he consciously determines the moment of completion. These objects are also of particular importance to Chevalier in that—as opposed to the immaterial and ephemeral digital installations—they take up specific traditions of fine and applied arts (see also pp. 94–95) and make the sensory experience of these works, which are all based in the digital realm, tangible in a material way. (FS)

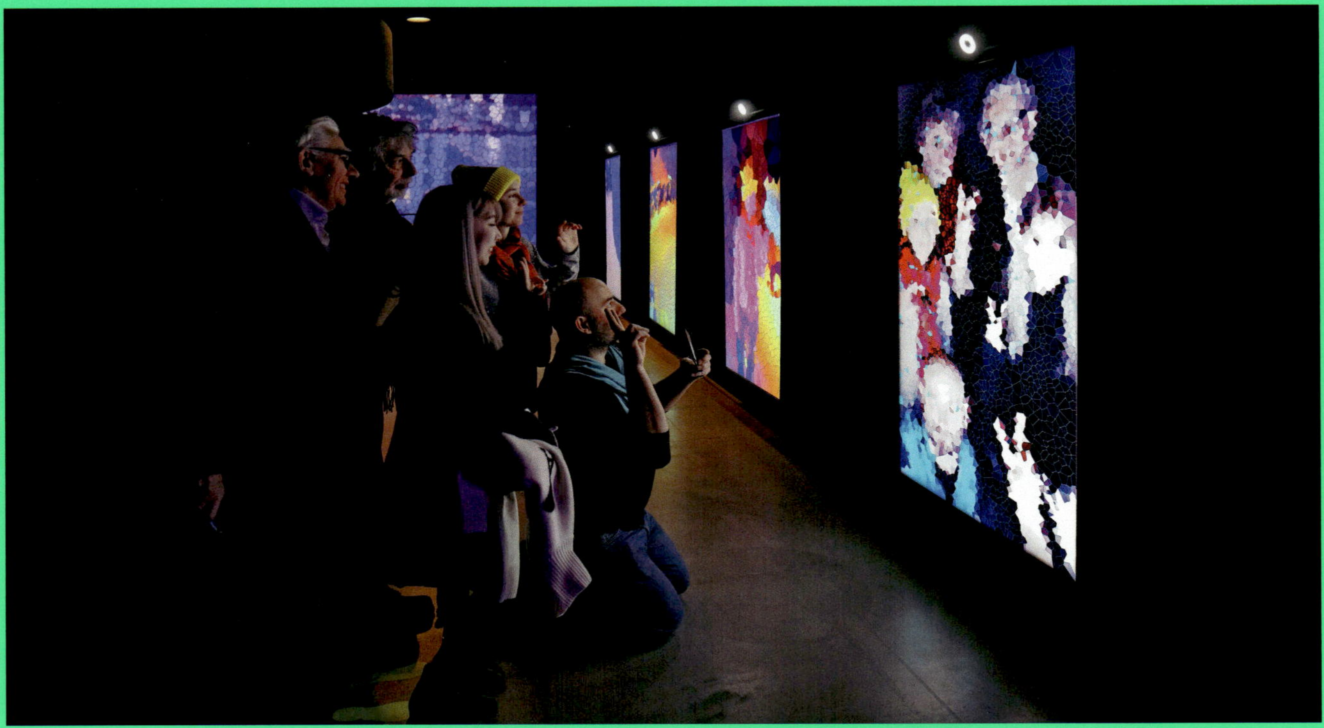

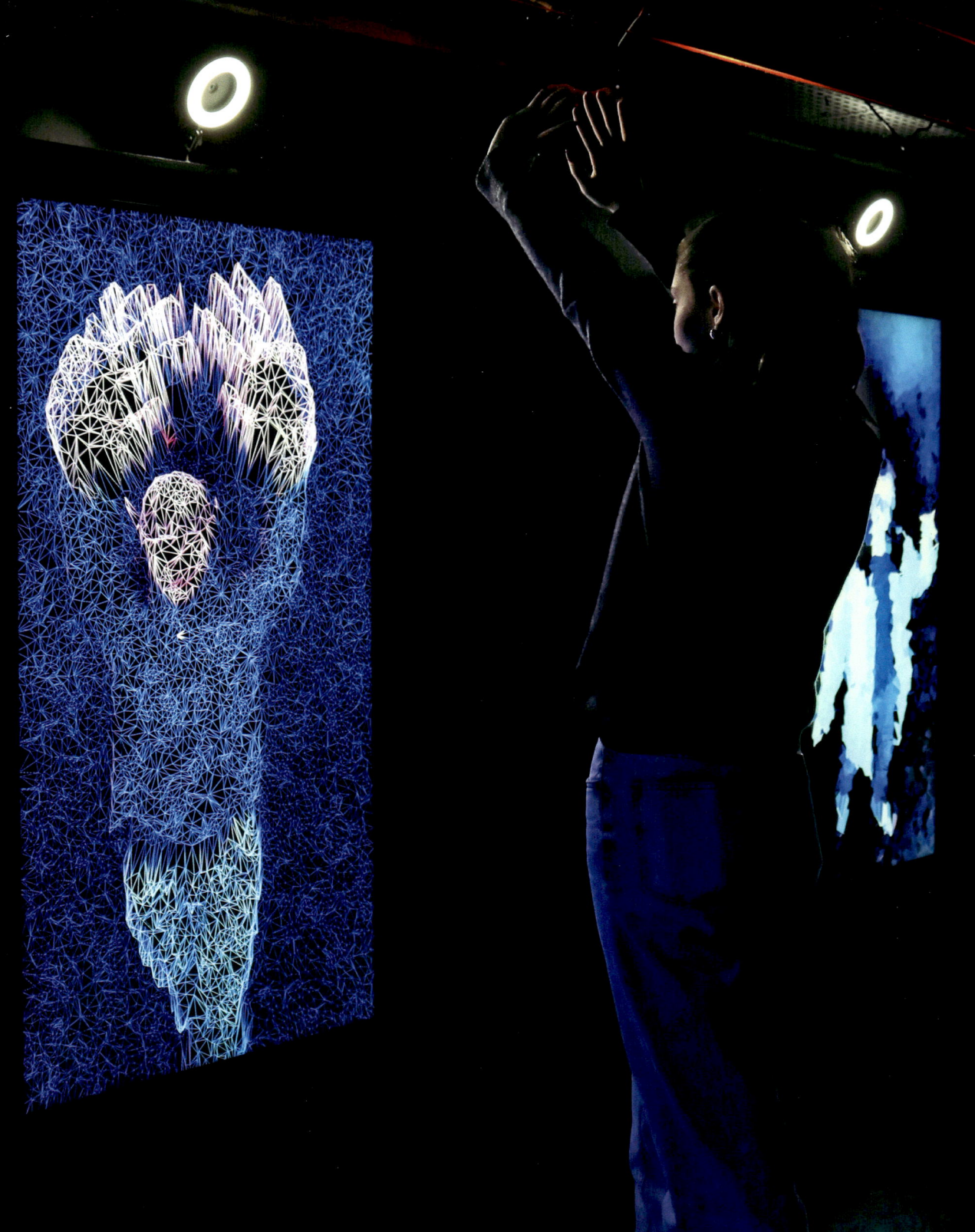

INSTALLATION

The Eye of the Machine, started
2019 · Installation view,
Pixels: Miguel Chevalier,
Grand Palais Immersif,
Paris, 2024

From figures in cave paintings to selfies, the depiction of people has always been a central theme in visual art. *The Eye of the Machine* picks up on this by creating moving portraits of visitors in real time, through a camera that captures the people standing in front of the monitor. A computer converts the images into various geometric patterns such as ▸ pixels (p. 28) or net-like structures, thus generating fragmented portraits. While this work certainly has a playful character, Miguel Chevalier also addresses the surveillance of our surroundings by cameras as well as the way we handle personal data, which we often carelessly share on the internet. (JG)

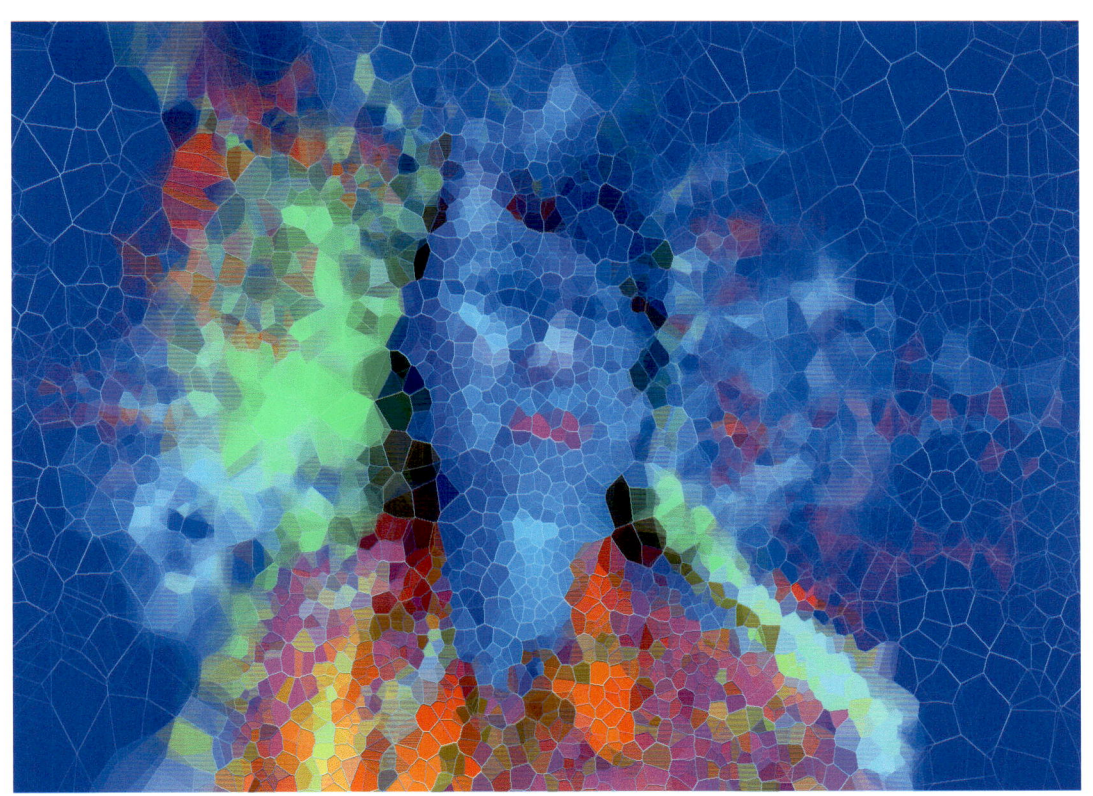

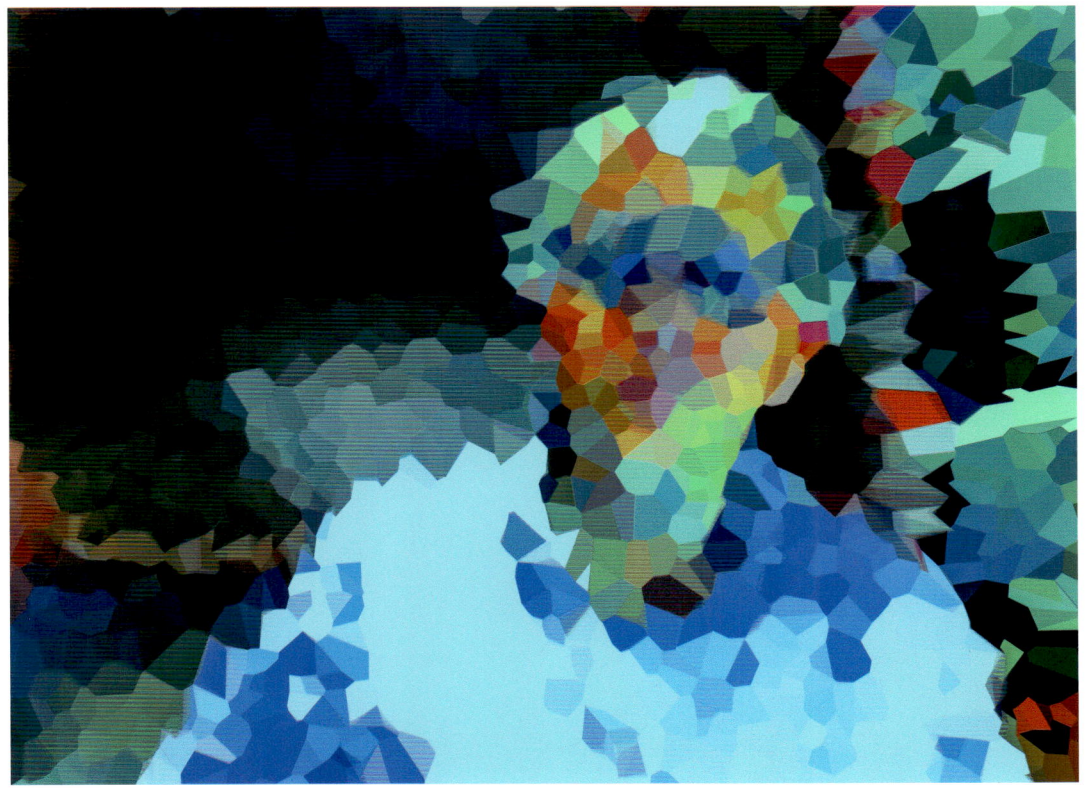

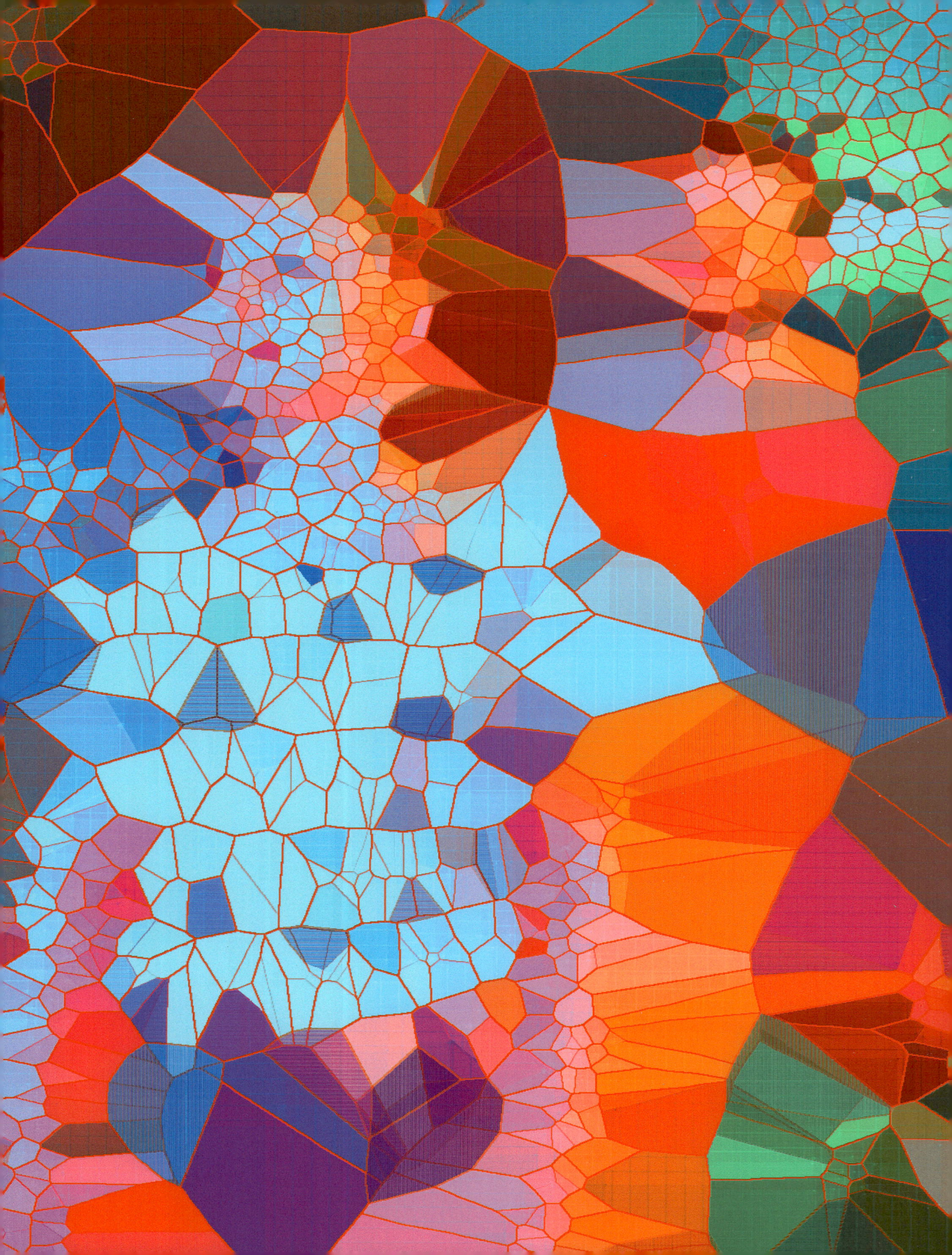

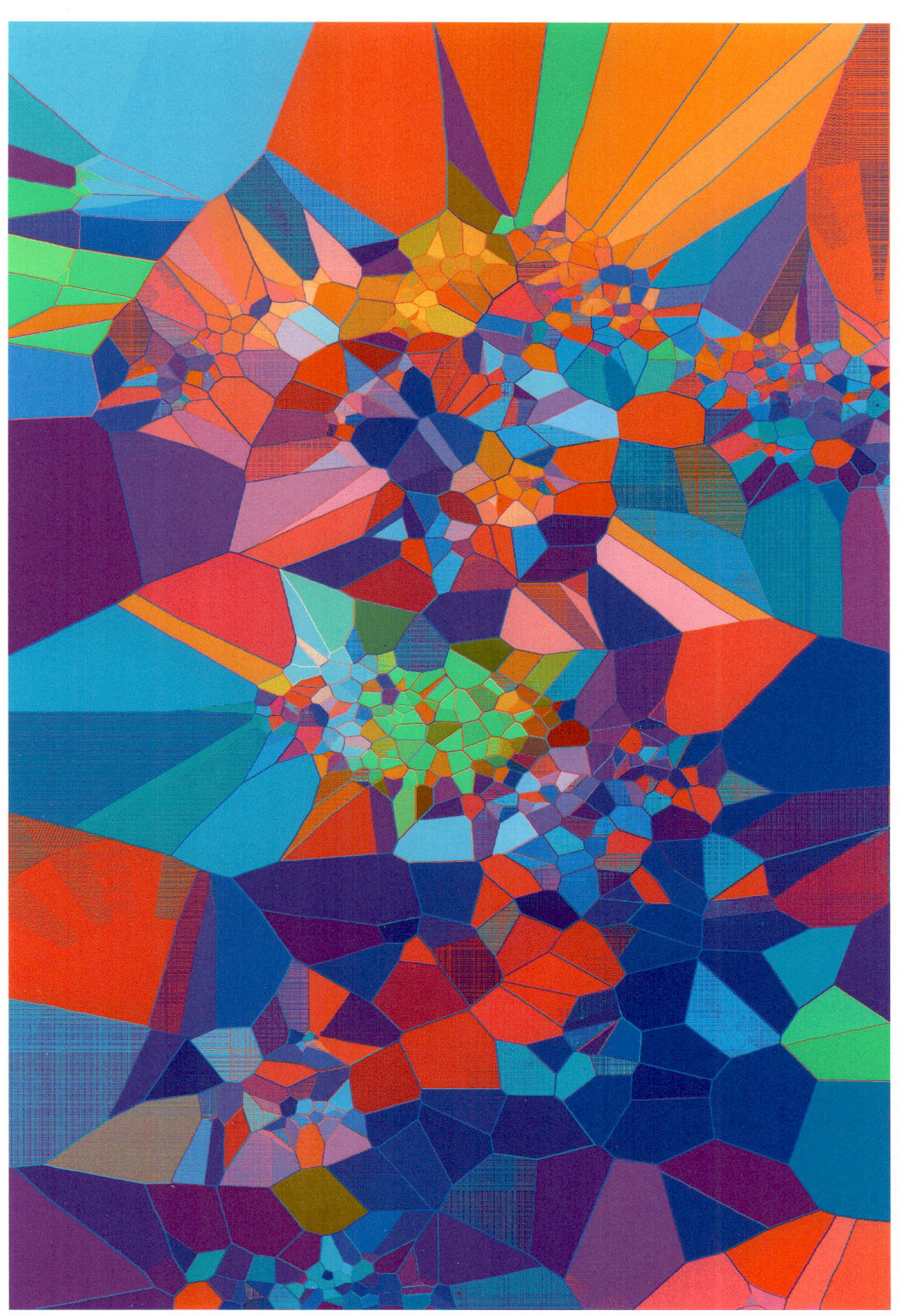

Left: *Multicolored Cells 1*, 2019 · Digital
print on Dibond with spot varnish ·
131.7 × 92 cm (51 7/8 × 36 1/4 in.) · Detail ·
Right: *Multicolored Cells 3*, 2025 · Digital print
on Dibond with spot varnish · 132.5 × 92.5 cm
(52 3/16 × 36 7/16 in)

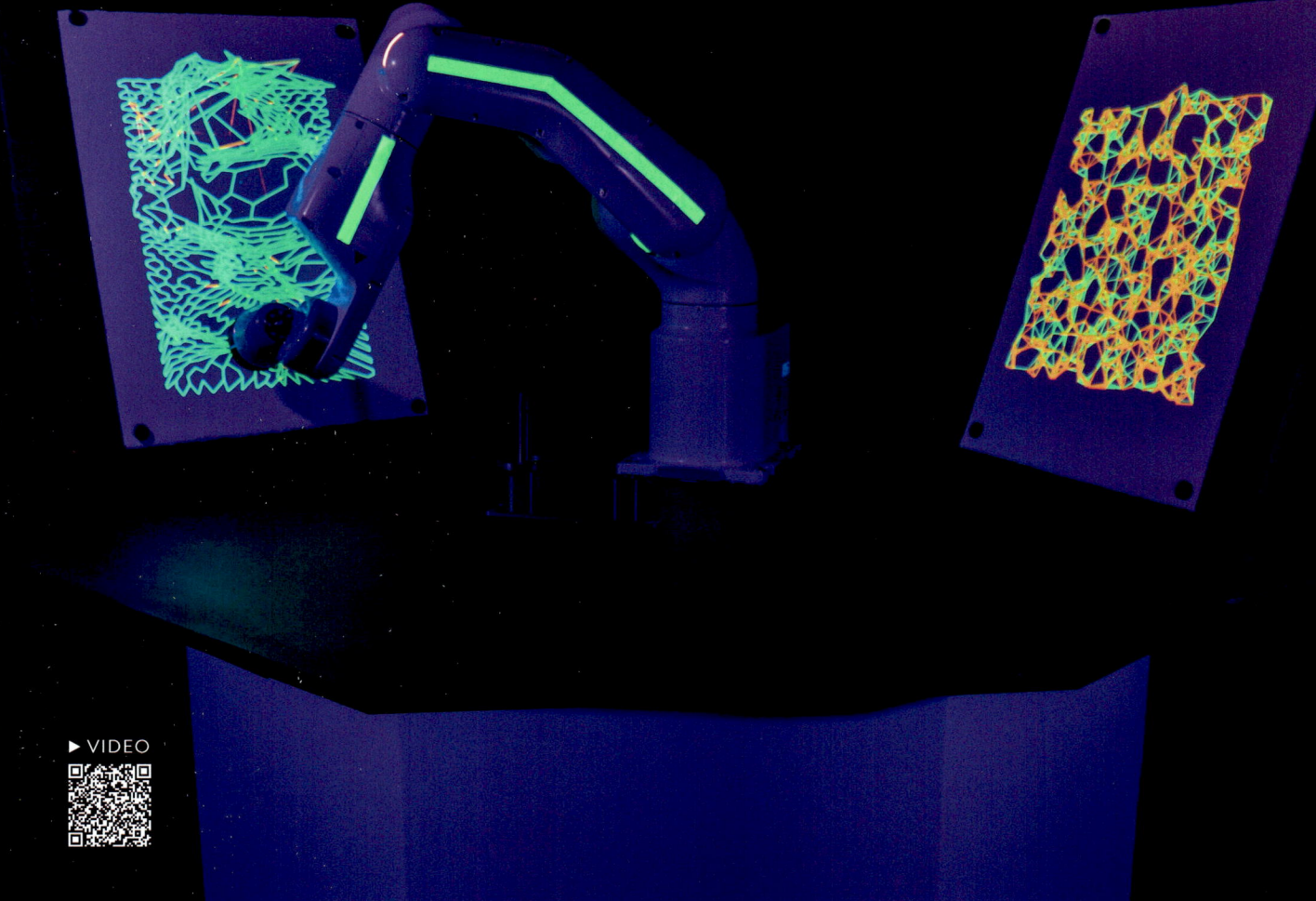

▶ VIDEO

INSTALLATION ↑

Complex Meshes Robot Drawings,
2025 · Generative robot
performance · Industrial robot,
felt-tip pen, paper · Software:
Ludovic Mallégol · Installation
view, La Fabrika Studio,
Ivry-sur-Seine, France, 2025

DRAWINGS →

Top: *Complex Meshes 1* · Bottom:
Complex Meshes 3 · Both 2022 ·
Felt-tip pen on paper, drawn by
a robot · Each 50 × 65 cm
(19 11/16 × 25 9/16 in.)

These drawings were created by a six-axis robot.
The motifs, based on snapshots from the generative
and interactive installation *Complex Meshes* (started
2015; pp. 96, 98–105), are fed into a database.
Miguel Chevalier selects the paper and pencil
and instructs the robot to draw these motifs. The
process, however, would be impossible without
human programming beforehand, as this robot
was designed for simple and repetitive tasks
such as packing or loading and unloading. Artist
and machine thus collaborate to create unique
pieces whose drawing gestures are reminiscent
of the human hand rather than automated
technology. (FS)

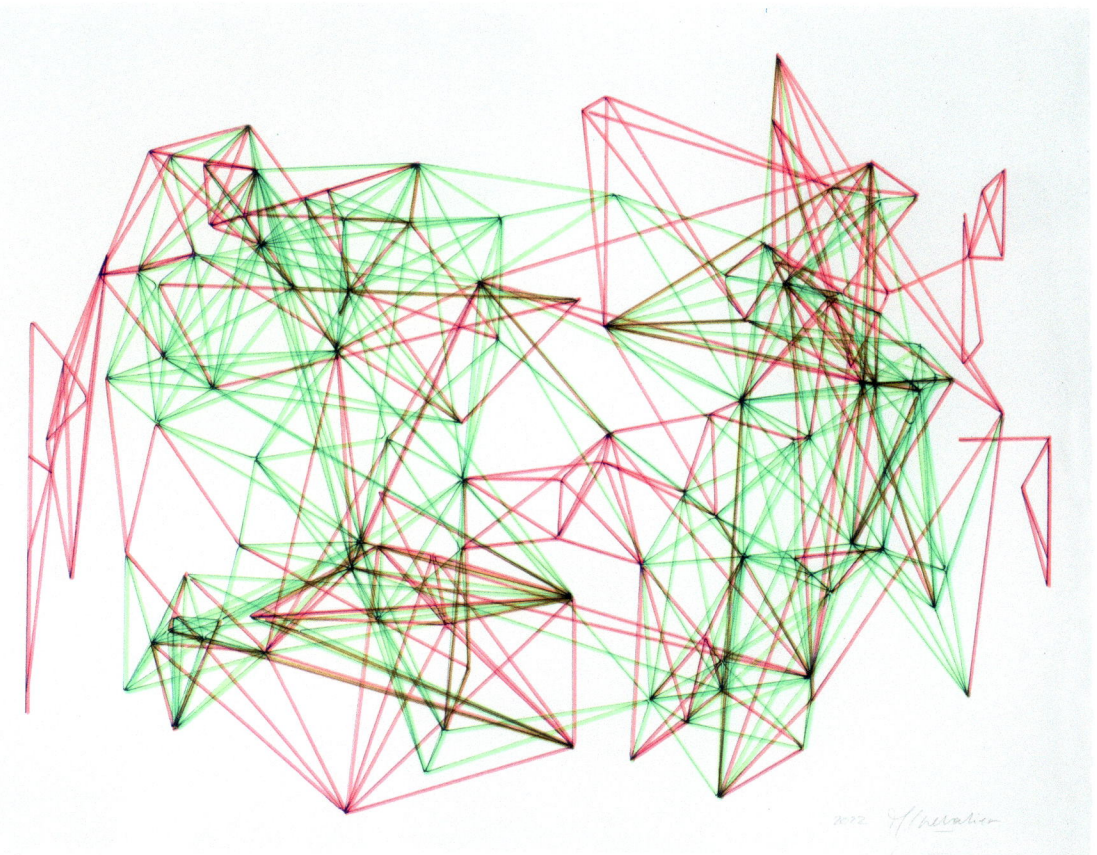

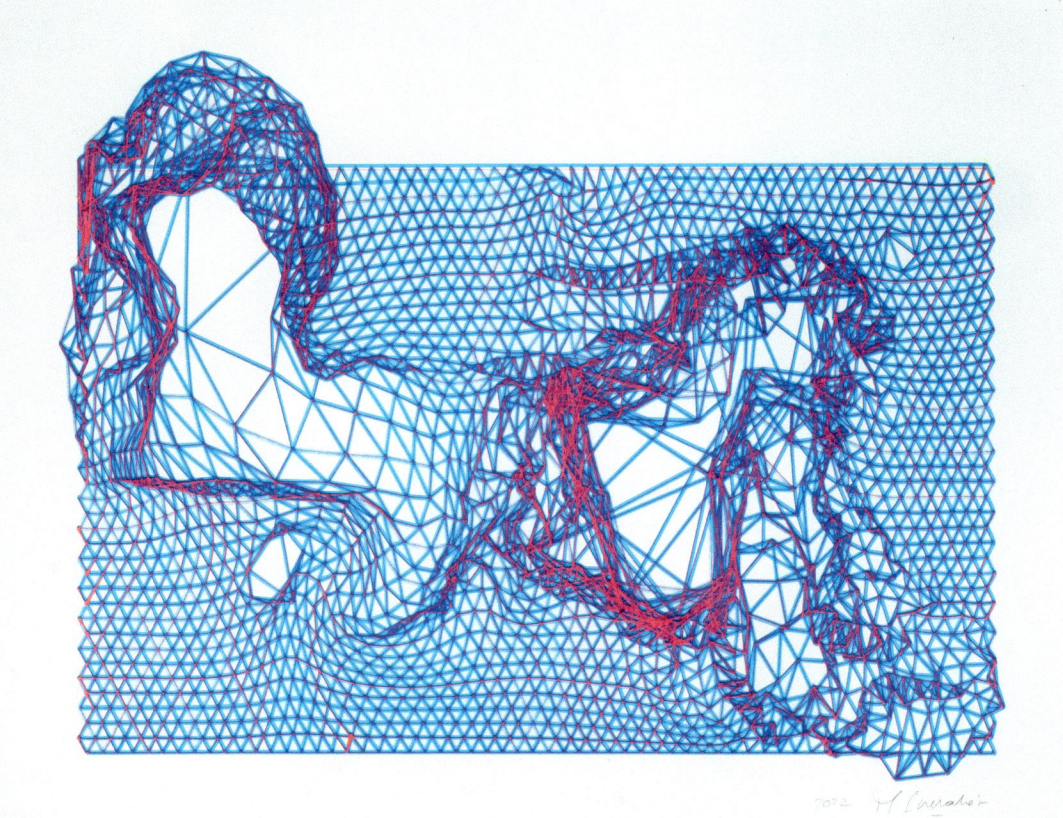

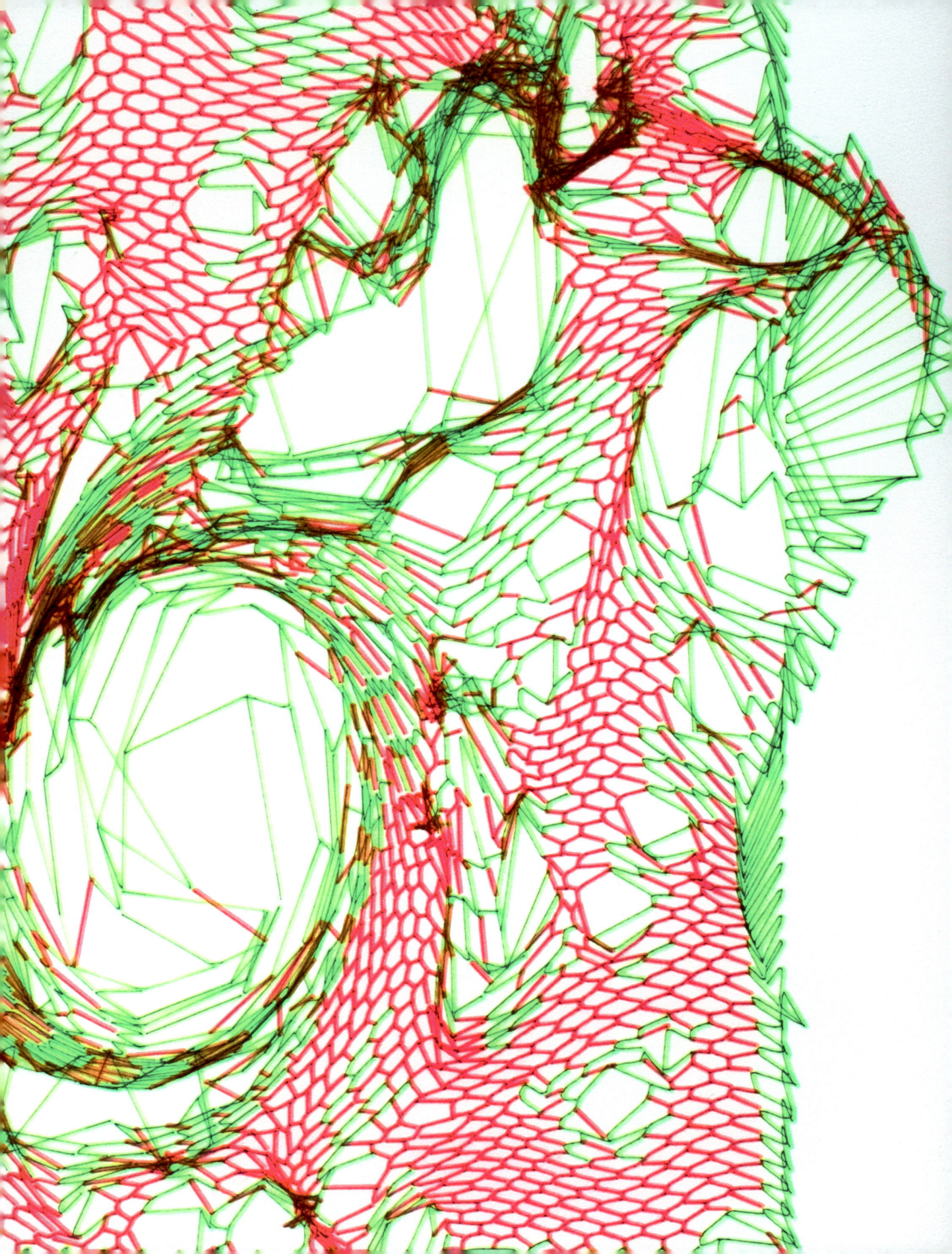

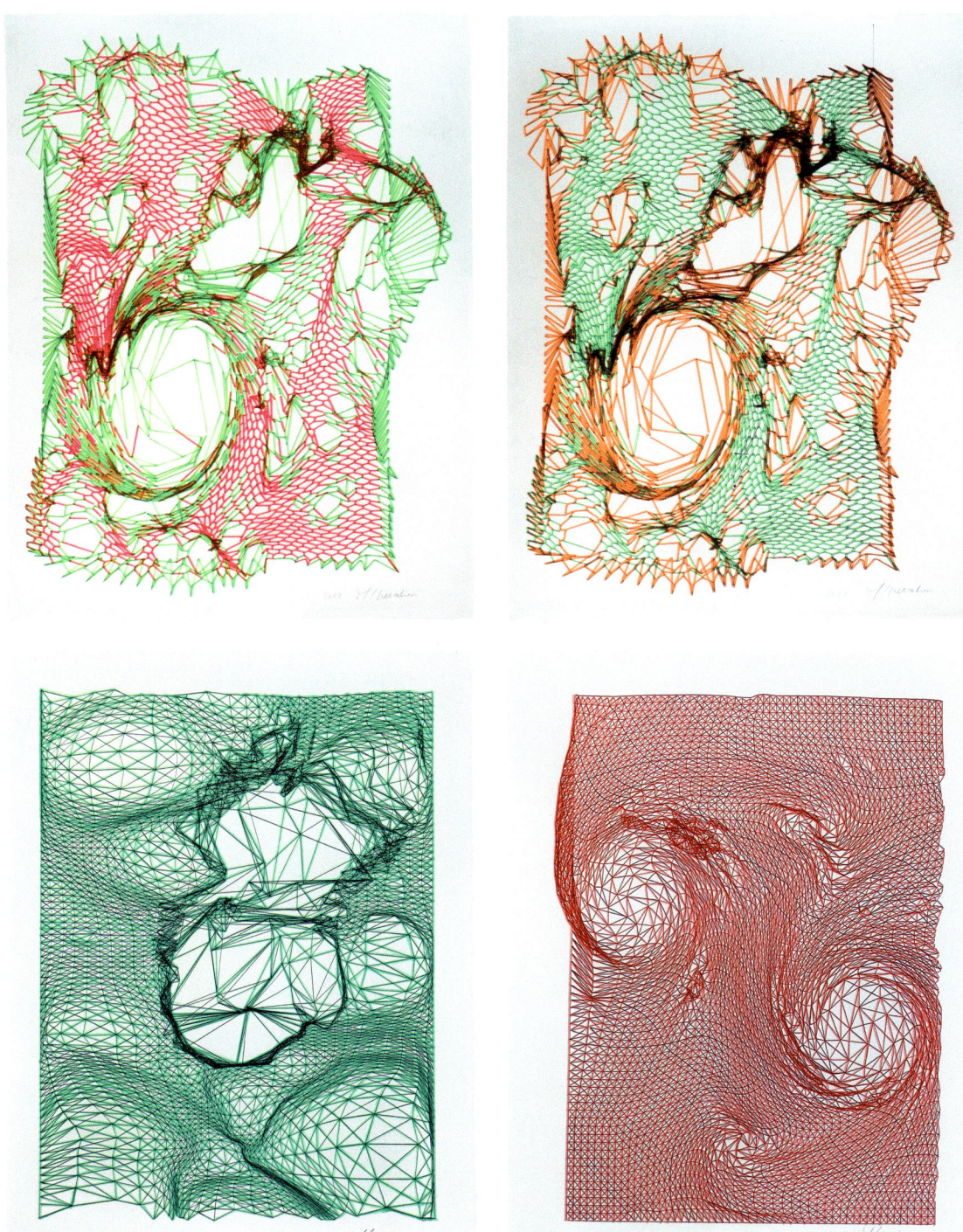

← DRAWING

Complex Meshes 12, 2022 · Detail
from p. 93 top left

↑ DRAWINGS

Top left: *Complex Meshes 12* · Top right: *Complex Meshes 13* · Bottom left:
Complex Meshes 14 · Bottom right: *Complex Meshes 15* · All 2022 · Felt-tip
pen on paper, drawn by a robot · Each 65×50 cm (25 9/16 × 19 11/16 in.)

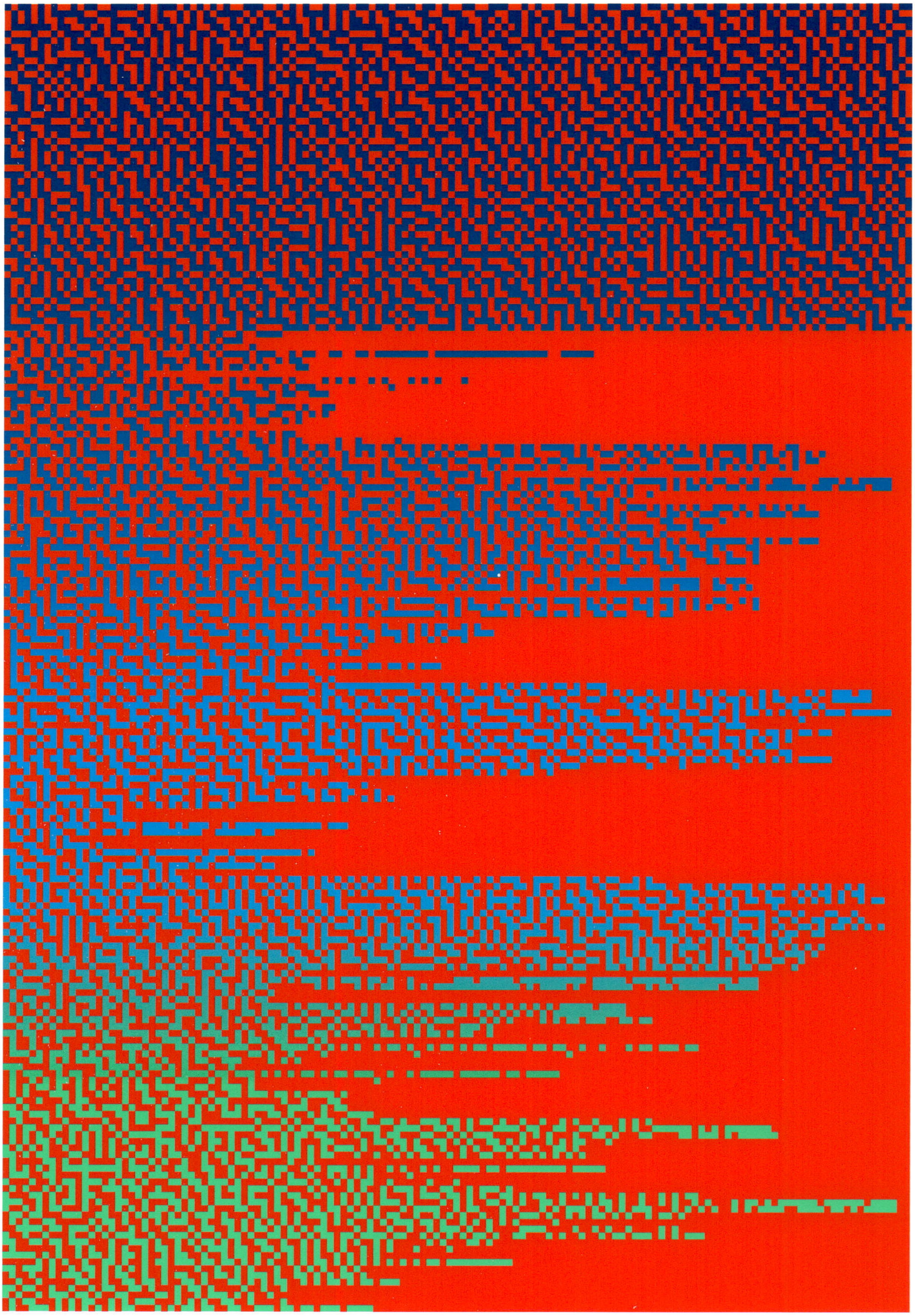

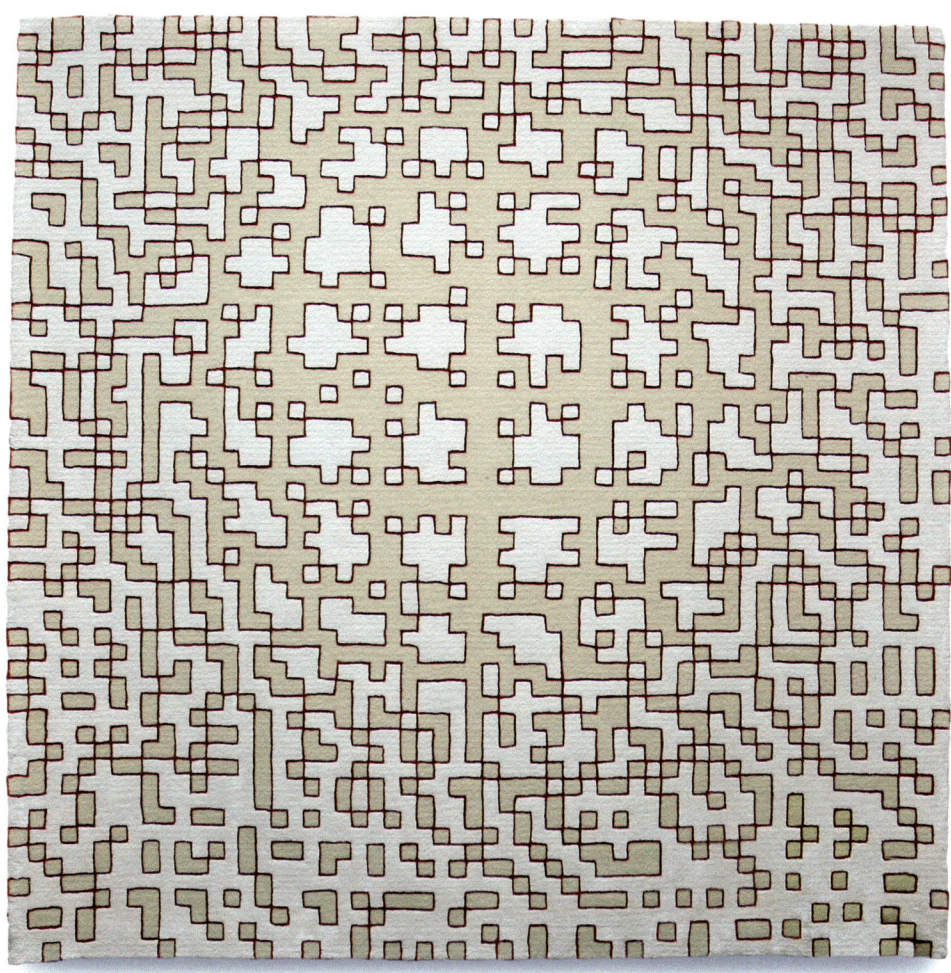

Pixels Op Art, 2011 · Silk threads, bamboo fiber · 200×200 cm (78 3/4×78 3/4 in.)

Pixel Brush (RGB), 2016 · Digital print on neon Dacryl synthetic resin · 200×125 cm (78 3/4×49 3/16 in.) · Courtesy Lélia Mordoch Gallery

With *Pixel Brush (RGB)* and *Pixels Op Art*, Miguel Chevalier takes up more traditional techniques from the visual and decorative arts: *Pixel Brush* relates to the analog brushstroke while reproducing it through digitally printed ▸ pixels (p. 28). *Pixels Op Art* is a tapestry based on a digital drawing by the artist, with a motif that references compositions by Victor Vasarely (1906–1997; see also pp. 37, 77). The tapestry was handmade by working yarn into a textile grid using a tufting gun. Both works also provoke reflection on the relationship between the creation of analog and digital images: like a brushstroke, the pixels come together to form lines, and just as the tapestry is based on a grid, so too is the digital image. (FS)

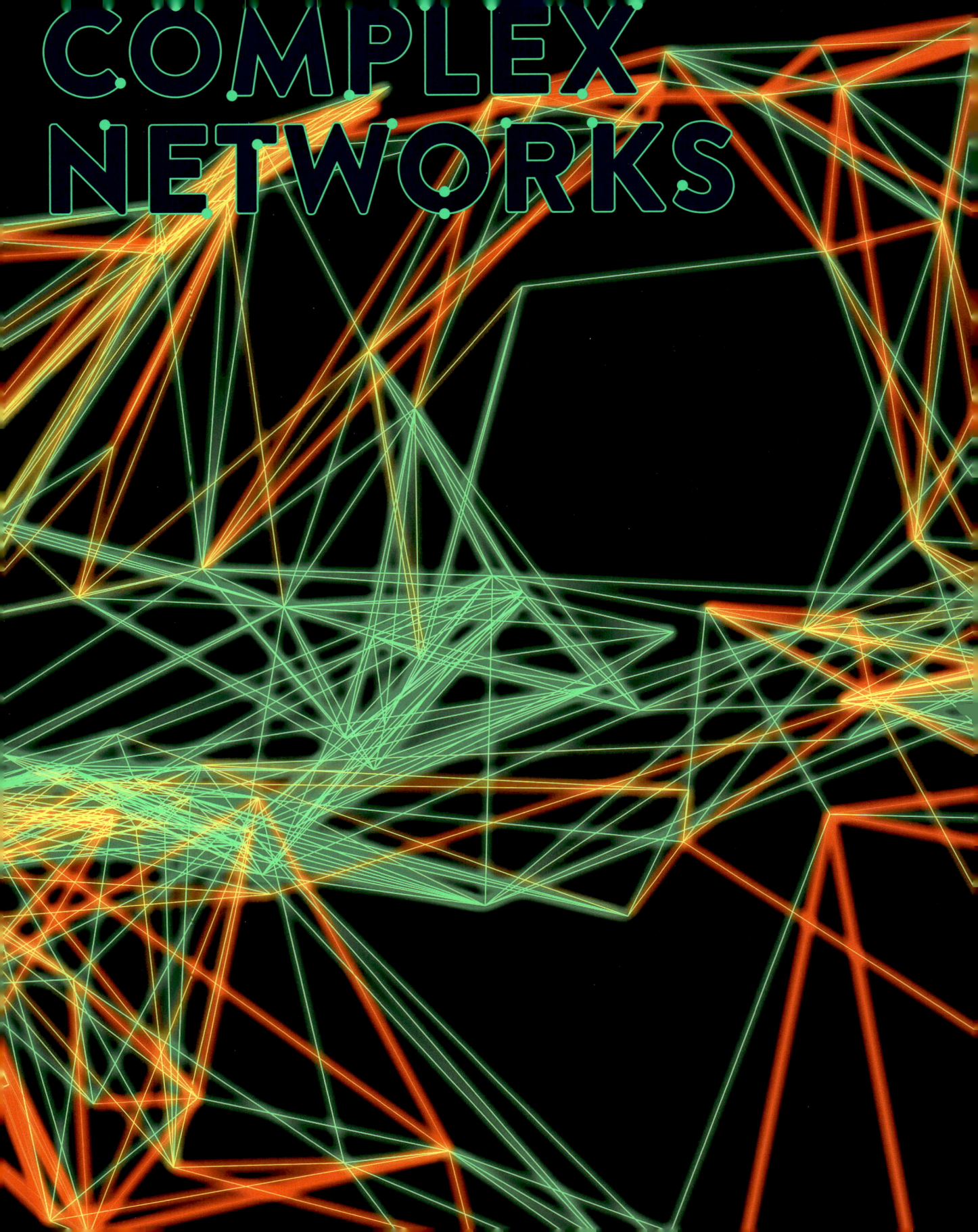

Complex Meshes, started 2015 ·
Generative and interactive
installation · Dimensions
variable · Software: Cyrille Henry,
Antoine Villeret

● Miguel Chevalier often explores the processes of flows and networks, which are inherently hard to perceive but play an essential role in our society — seeing that all elements of our world are increasingly connected through ever expanding data streams. The positive effects of these complex, global interrelations are productive exchanges, such as the sharing of scientific knowledge or artistic collaborations. However, increasing surveillance, the potential misuse of data, and spiraling energy consumption are among the negative consequences of this development. The two works *Complex Meshes* (started 2015; pp. 96, 98–105) and *Rhizomatic* (started 2005; pp. 106–7) visualize and materialize the theme of interconnection.

Besides signifying fabrics or nets, the term "mesh" can also refer to a three-dimensional, polygonal structure consisting of vertices, edges, and faces, for example in building models or architecture. In data processing, the term "network" describes the connection of different electronic devices and information systems, but it also stands for sociological relationships within groups of people with common interests or characteristics. For *Complex Meshes*, Miguel Chevalier has so far developed over thirty-three individual pattern templates with differently colored, polygonal grids, which alternate in the presentation and can be interactively set in motion by the visitors. Single elements are attracted to or repelled by each other. The motifs represent virtual network structures but are also a symbol of our interaction in the digital realm — and therefore in our analog lives as well.

The title *Rhizomatic* refers to the biological rhizome, a root system found for example in bamboo, from which new shoots grow in different places. However, it also pays homage to the philosopher Gilles Deleuze (1925–1995) and the psychoanalyst Félix Guattari (1930–1992), who used the terms "rhizome" and "rhizomatic" as metaphors for a postmodern model of knowledge organization in which each element is linked to every other one. They formulated this to contrast older models that employed the tree metaphor to describe hierarchically organized structures. Chevalier's work translates this theme into a geometric mesh of metal braces that fluoresce when exposed to UV light. The installation is reassembled by the artist for every exhibition according to the size and nature of the space it is presented in, and may also be shown with ribbons as a relief on a wall. While visitors can stroll through the installation and face the wall piece head-on, they can only view the connections as a whole from the outside. (JG)

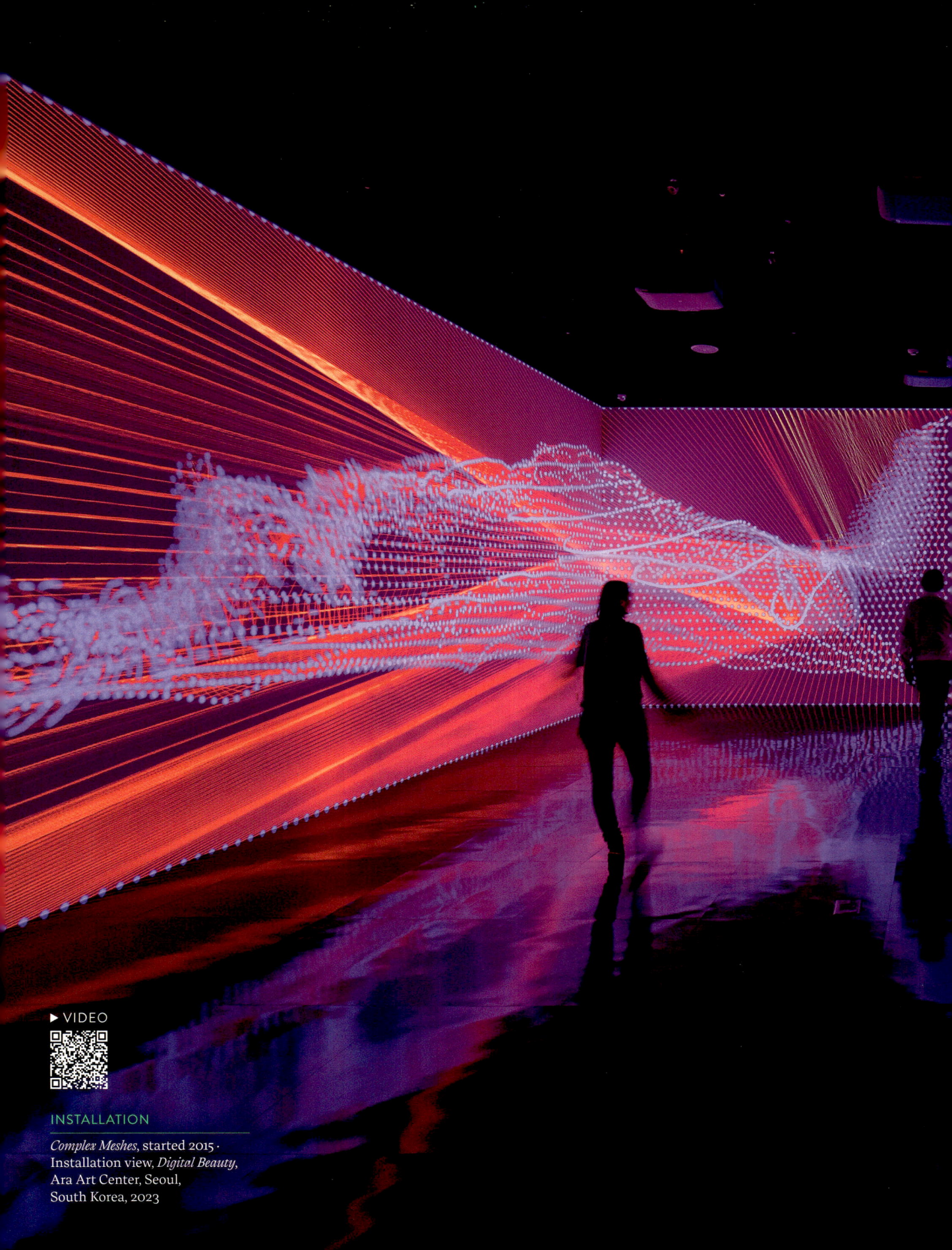

▶ VIDEO

INSTALLATION

Complex Meshes, started 2015 ·
Installation view, *Digital Beauty*,
Ara Art Center, Seoul,
South Korea, 2023

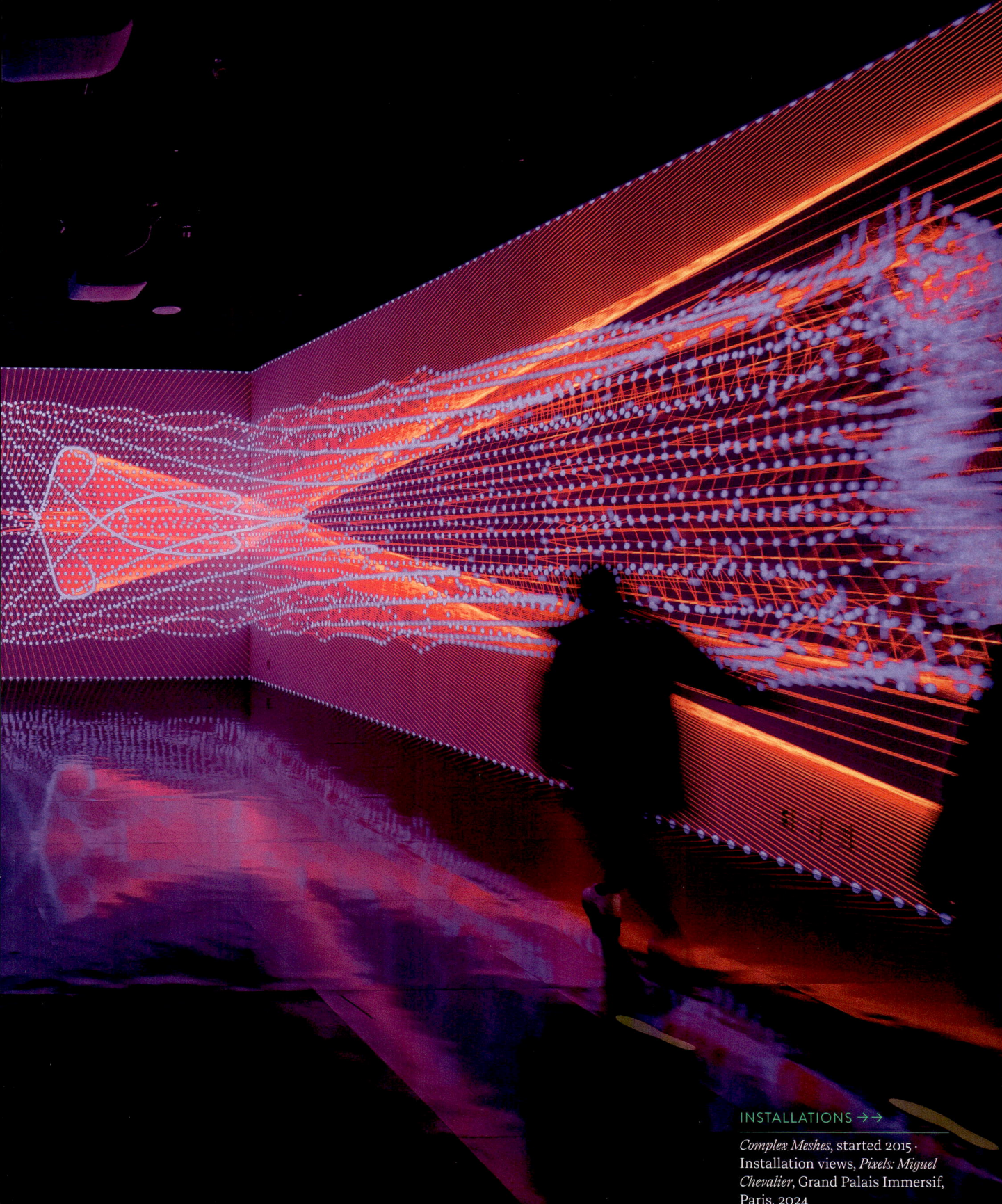

INSTALLATIONS → →

Complex Meshes, started 2015 ·
Installation views, *Pixels: Miguel
Chevalier,* Grand Palais Immersif,
Paris, 2024

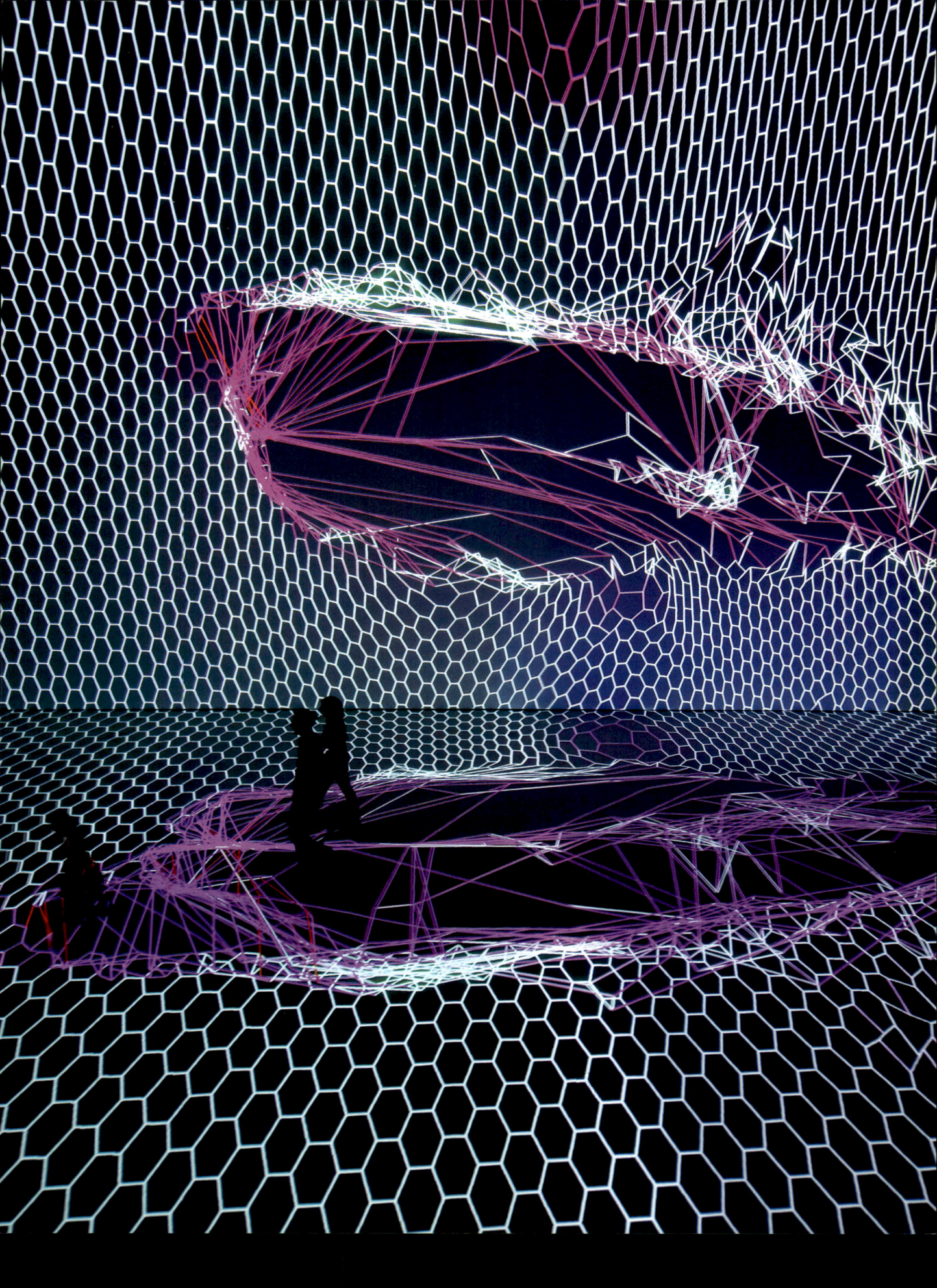

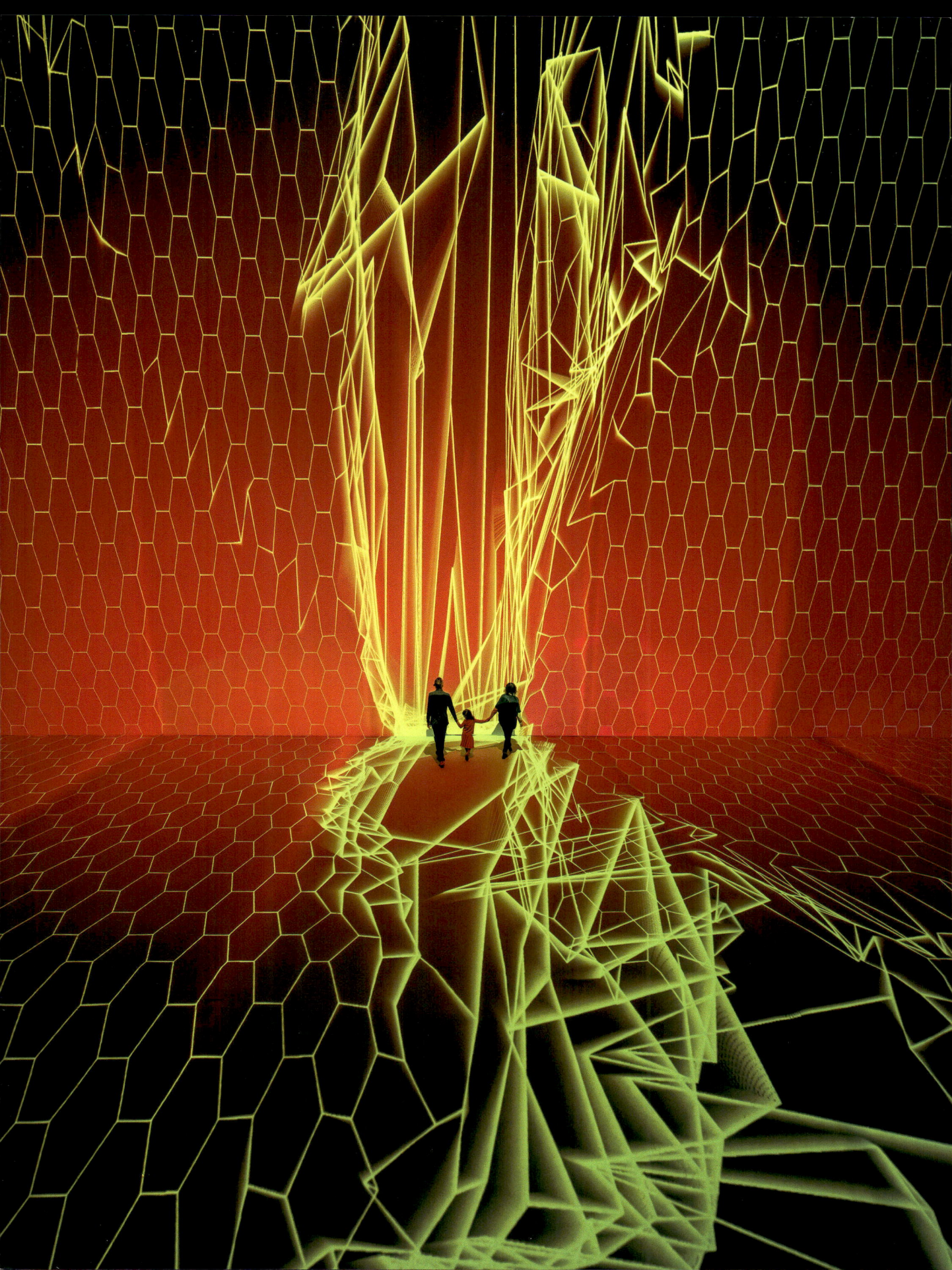

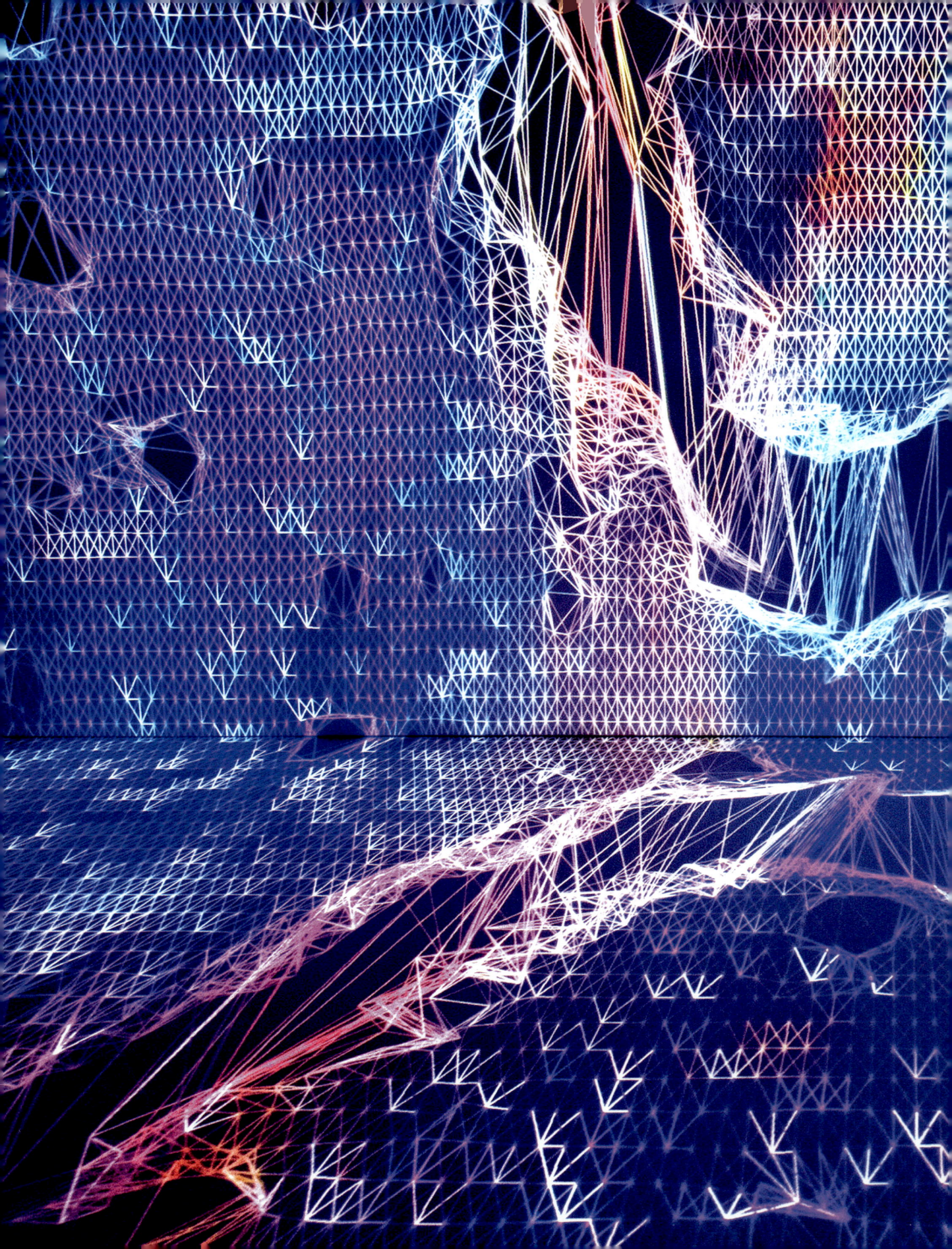

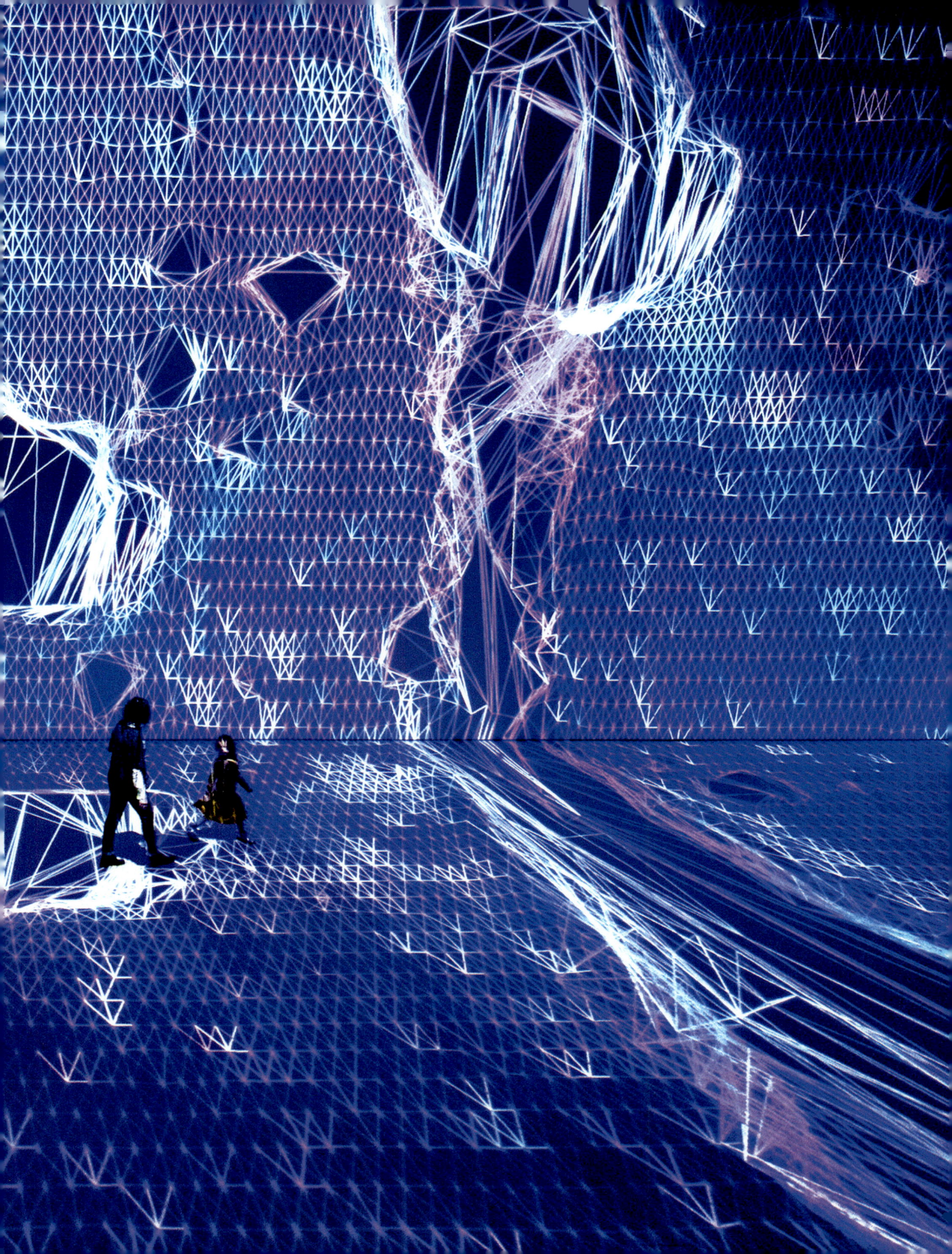

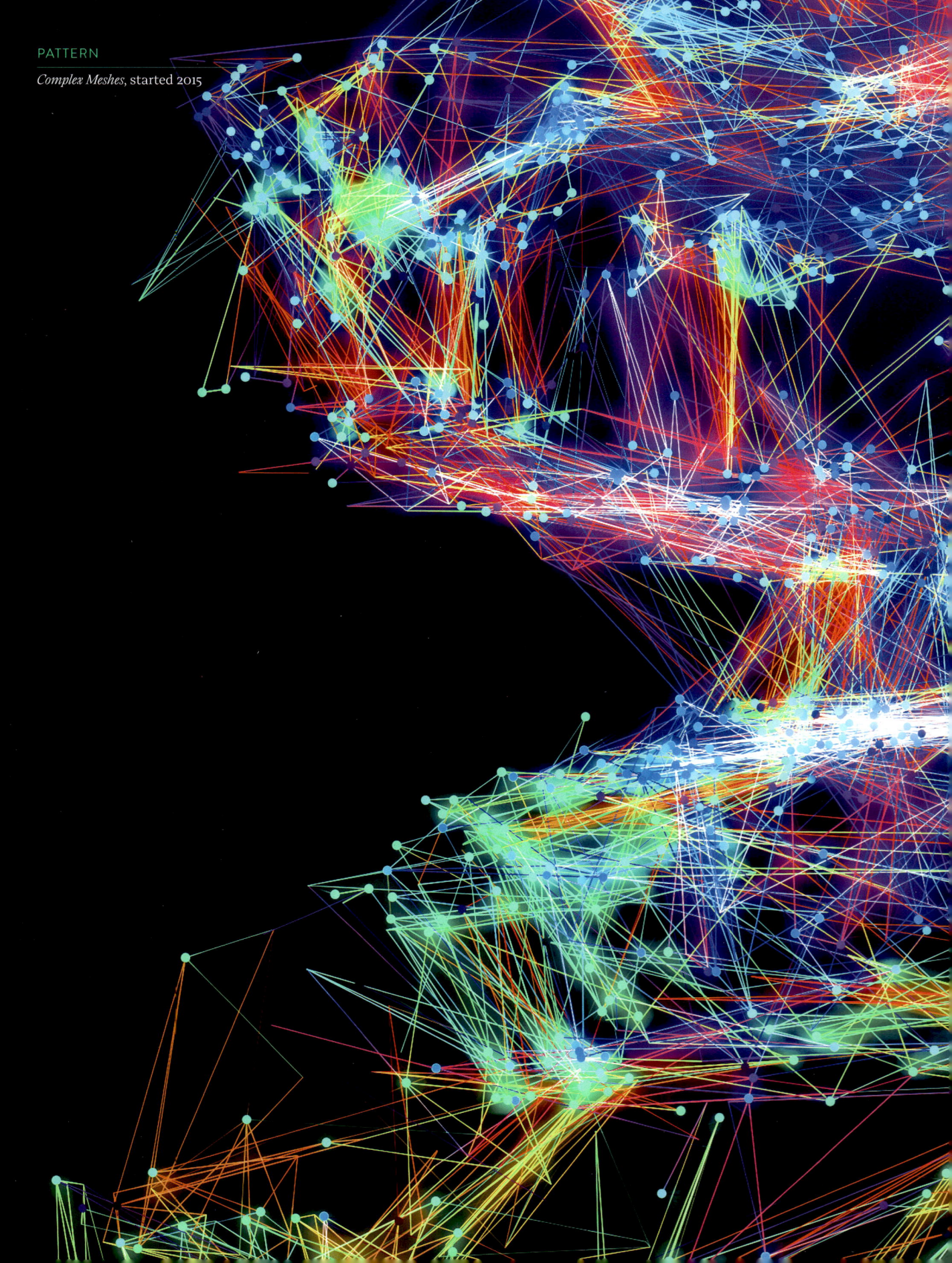

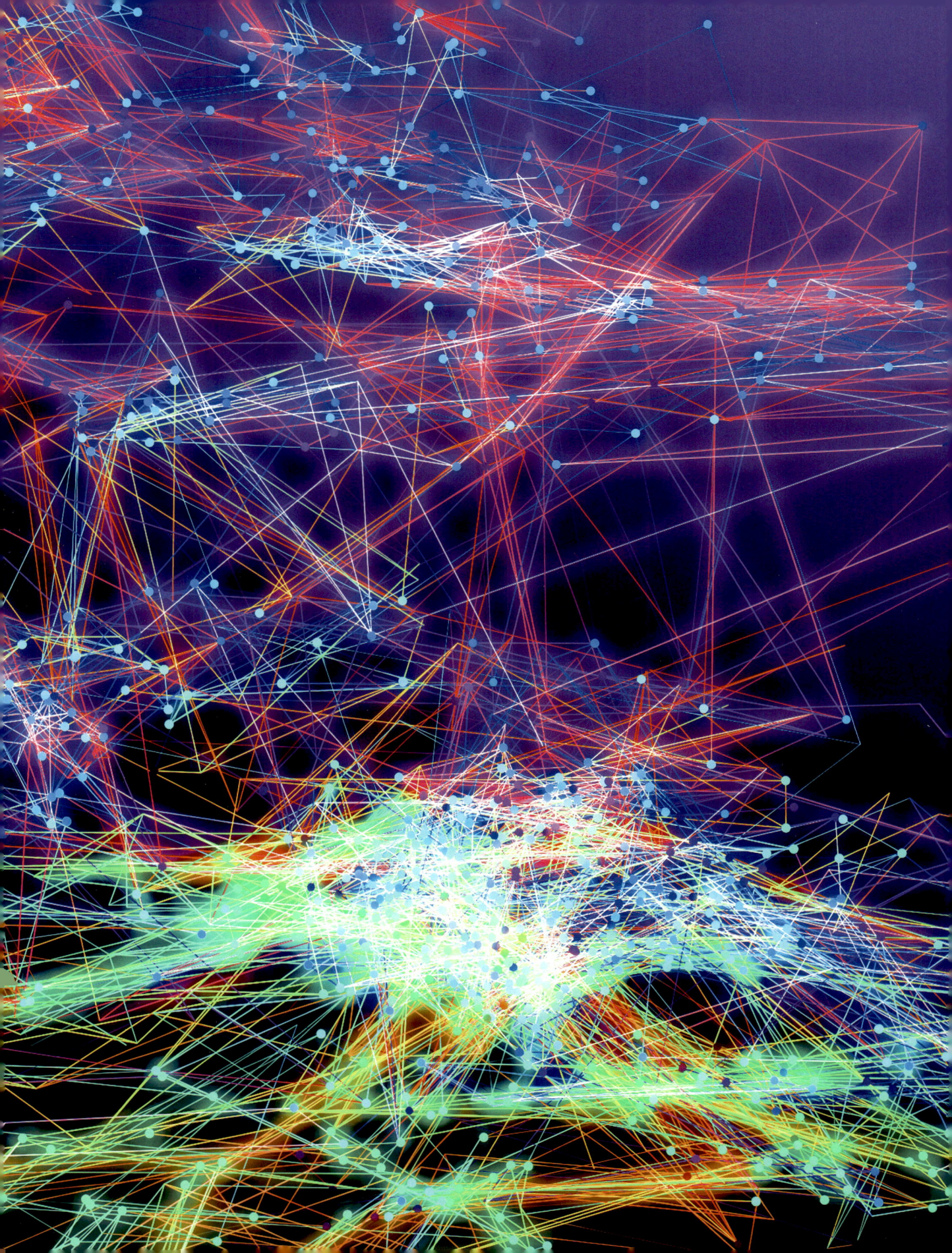

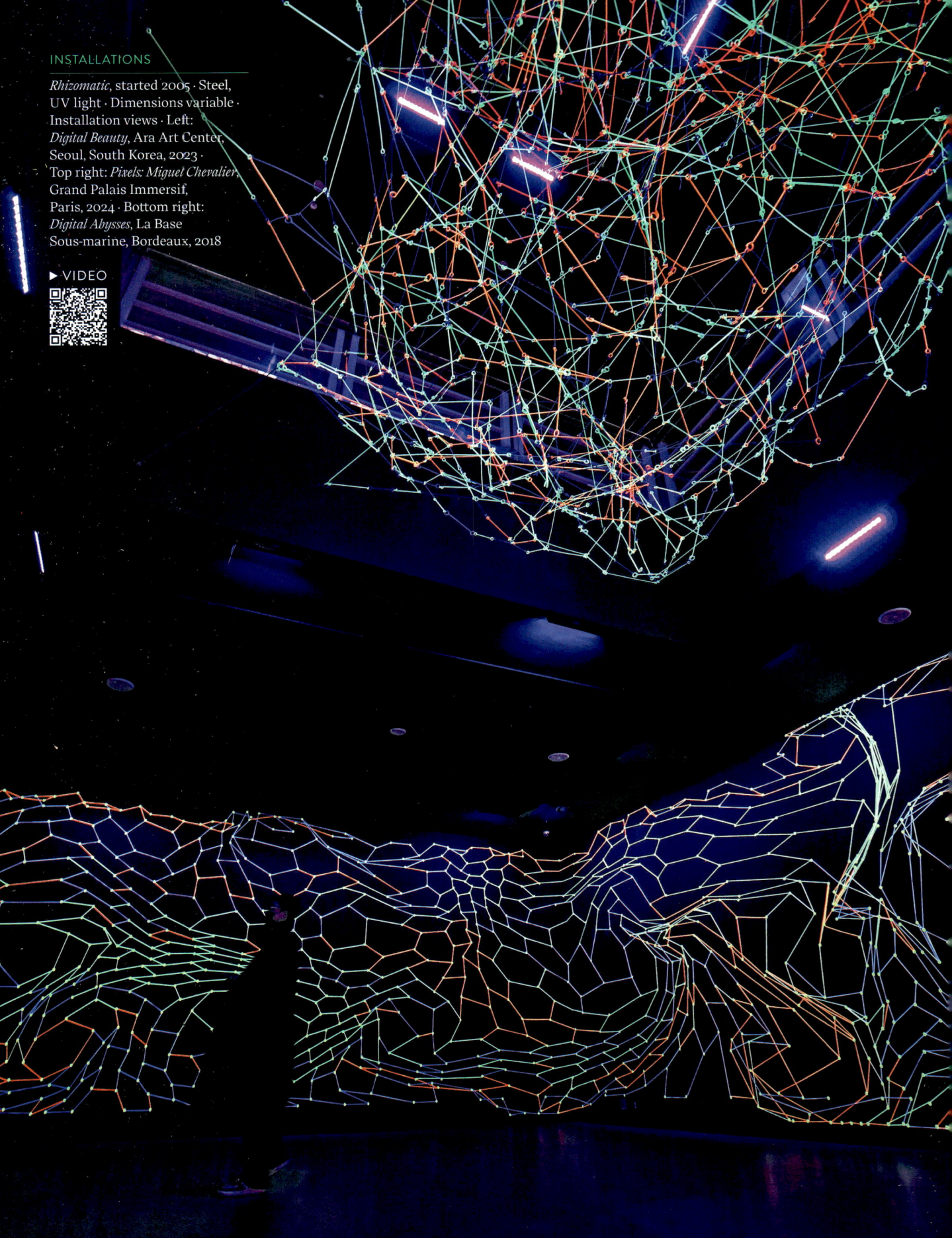

INSTALLATIONS

Rhizomatic, started 2005 · Steel,
UV light · Dimensions variable ·
Installation views · Left:
Digital Beauty, Ara Art Center,
Seoul, South Korea, 2023 ·
Top right: *Pixels: Miguel Chevalier*,
Grand Palais Immersif,
Paris, 2024 · Bottom right:
Digital Abysses, La Base
Sous-marine, Bordeaux, 2018

▶ VIDEO

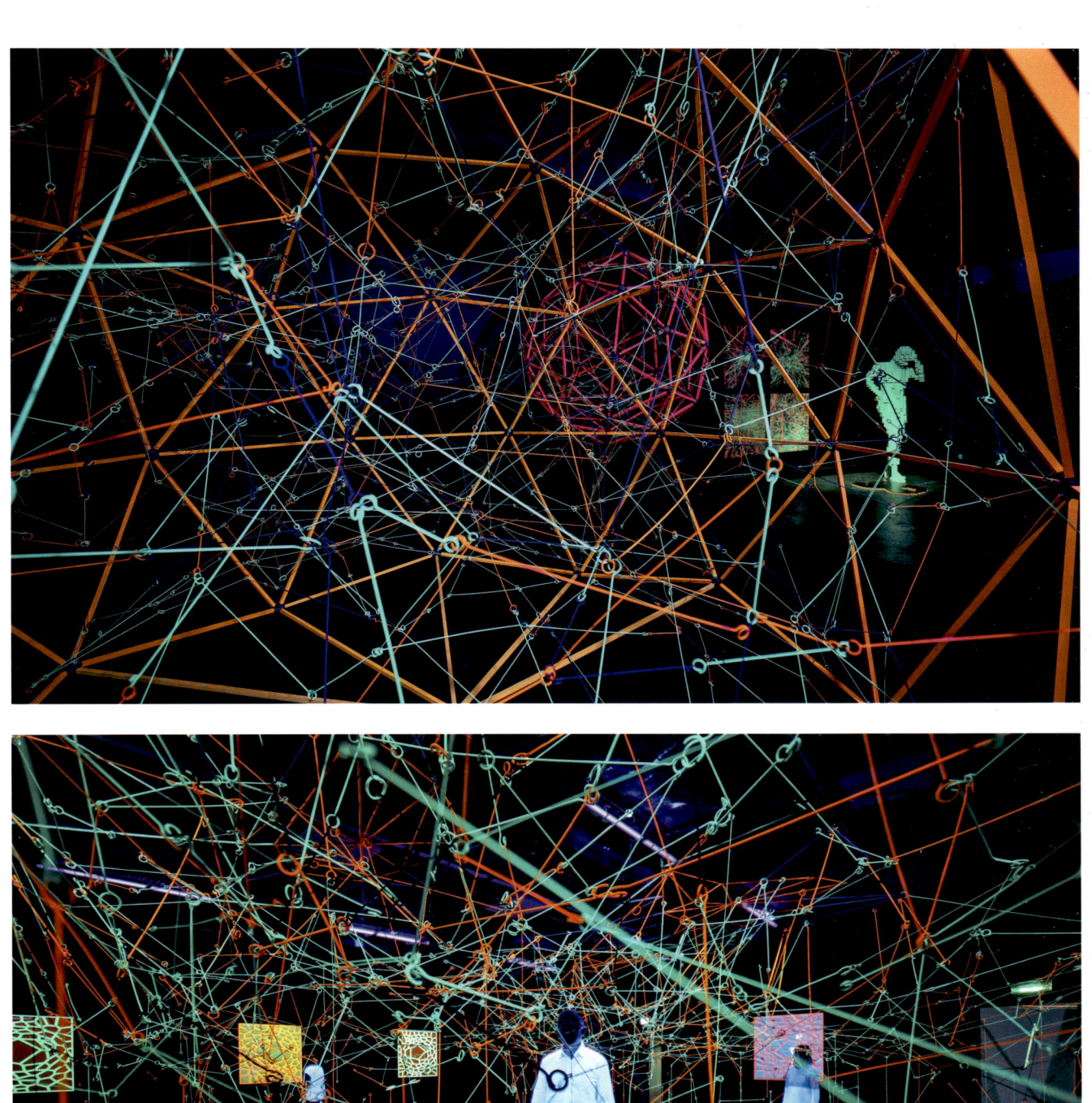

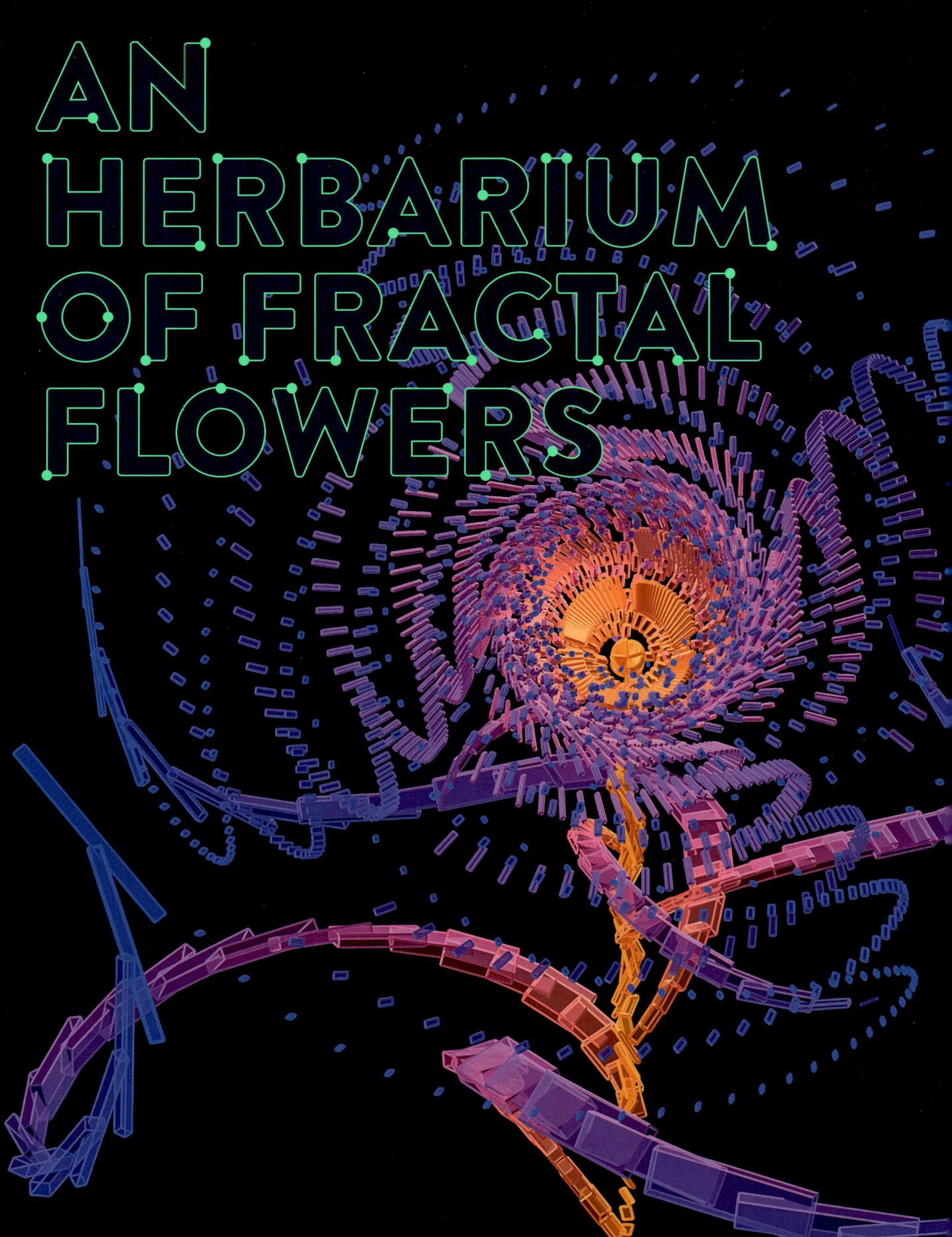

AN HERBARIUM
OF FRACTAL
FLOWERS

Cosmos Newtonia, 2008 · From the series *Fractal Flowers* · Software: Cyrille Henry

● *Fractal Flowers*, which the artist has been developing continuously since 2008, is one of the largest groups of works in Miguel Chevalier's oeuvre. It includes sculptures, drawings, holograms, but also videos presented on screens (pp. 108, 110–21) and large-scale interactive installations presented either indoors or outdoors. The project started in 2004 with *Ultra-Nature*, for which the artist first created a kind of ▸ herbarium (p. 27) with eighteen digital seeds that become flowers on a monitor, continually blossoming and fading in different ways by means of generative processes. This marked the beginning of Chevalier's deep engagement with nature and the virtual garden (see also p. 161). The titles of the individual flowers were invented by the artist and combine cultural and scientific history. They are hybrids made up of Latin plant names and references to writers such as Edgar Allan Poe (1809–1849), scientists such as Charles Darwin (1809–1882), musicians such as John Lennon (1940–1980), and philosophers such as Aristotle (384–322 BCE).

Fractal Flowers immediately evokes associations with the floral world, yet the geometric and angular shapes emphasize their deliberately artificial character. At the same time, they are an indication that Chevalier finds his inspiration not only in plants, but also in ▸ crystals (p. 26). The ▸ fractal (p. 27) represents a link between the two realms: the term, coined in 1975 by mathematician Benoît Mandelbrot (1924–2010), is derived from the Latin *fractus* ("broken") or *frangere* ("to break into pieces"). It is used to describe structures in nature, but also in mathematics, which are infinitely repeated in the same way at different scales. Examples to be found in nature are the branches of trees, waves, snowflakes, ferns, and even romanesco broccoli, whose individual florets reflect the vegetable's larger shape.

Digital data serves as the source material for all of Chevalier's works. This applies to the drawings, which are created with the help of a drawing robot; the sculptures, which are produced in a 3D-printing process; and the moving image works. Many experimental steps are required before a drawing or sculpture is considered successful and complete by the artist. This process may involve the robot drawing incorrectly because the instructions were not clear enough, or the sculpture turning out to be insufficiently stable.

In the *Fractal Flowers* interactive installations, the flowers follow the visitors by moving along with them. Sensors track people's movements and pass this information on to the computer, which operates the flowers in real time. Compared to flowers in nature, the representations in Chevalier's projections are oversized. Directed by an ▸ algorithm (p. 26), they grow randomly in different places on the wall in a variety of shapes. They blossom and fade, and sometimes they even mutate and hybridize with each other. Even if they do not always fulfill the common cultural-historical notion of symbols of beauty, they remind us, like other floral representations in art history, of transience—not least of human mortality. The artificial paradise the artist transports us into awakens our inner playful instinct to interact with the flowers and to influence the work of art with our own body. At the same time, Chevalier points to the imbalance between humans and nature—invoking the thoroughly dystopian vision that our future could end in a virtual garden if we do not change our behavior in caring for and preserving the environment. (FS)

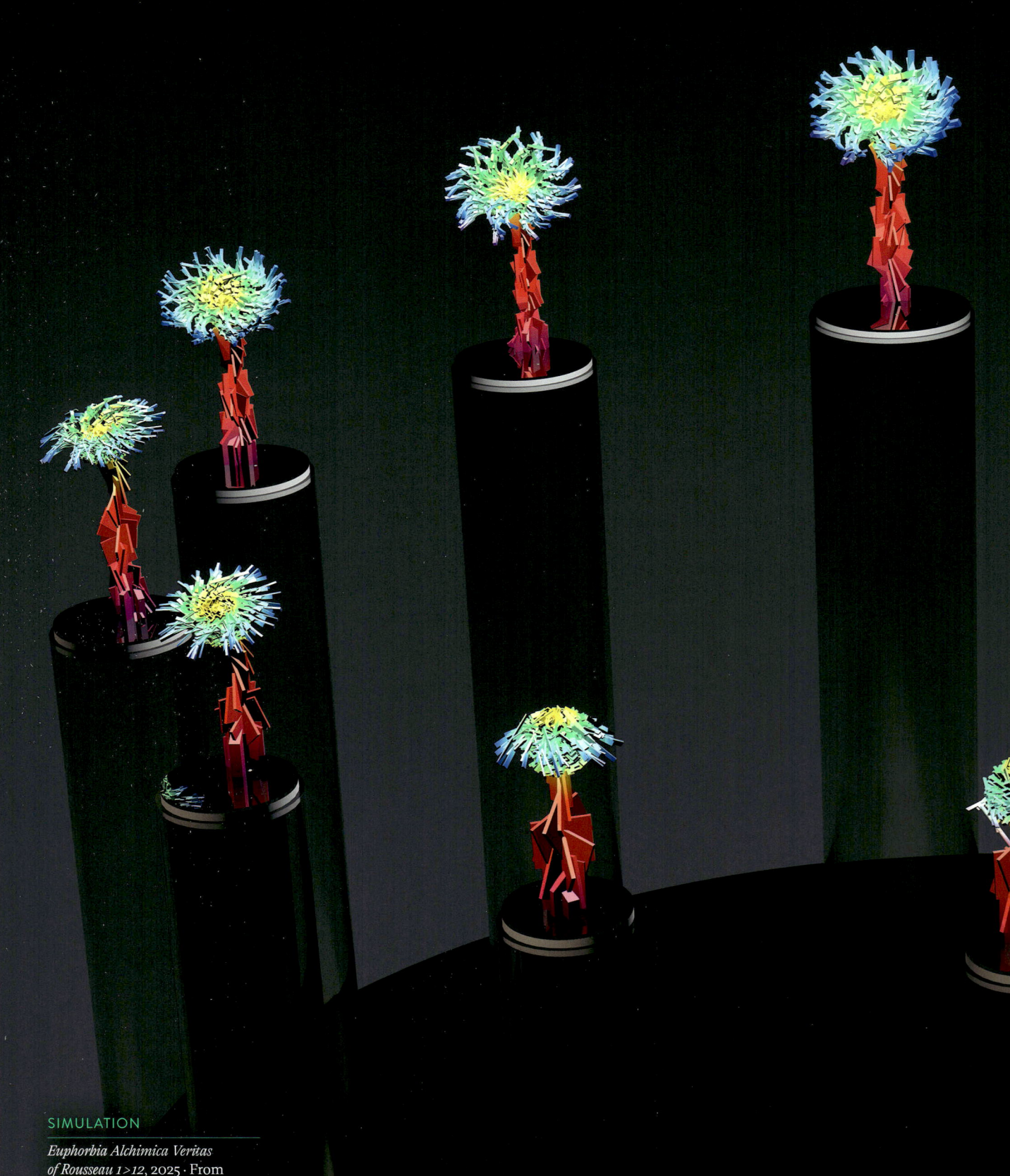

SIMULATION

*Euphorbia Alchimica Veritas
of Rousseau 1 > 12*, 2025 · From
the series *Fractal Flowers* ·
12 3D-printed sculptures,
synthetic resin · Diam. 190 cm
(74 13/16 in.)

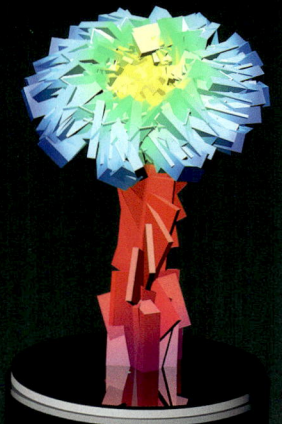
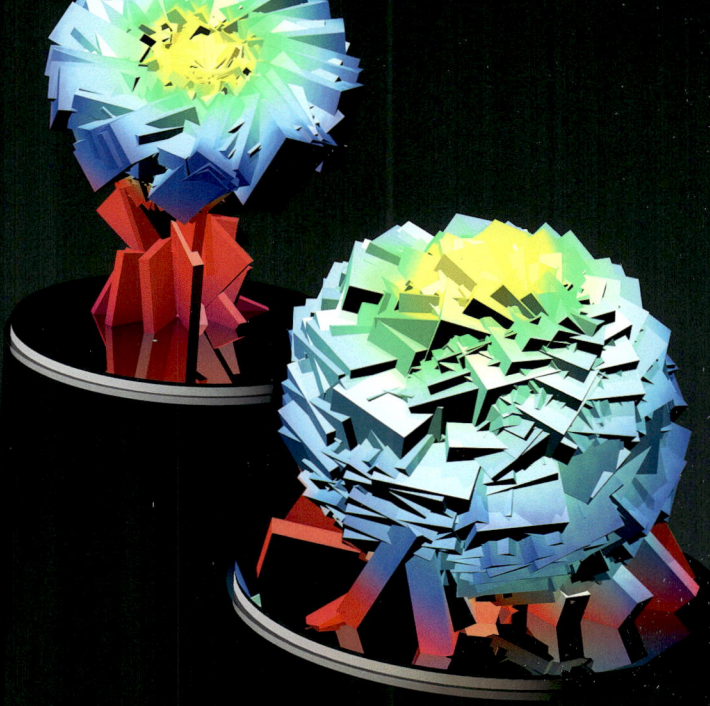
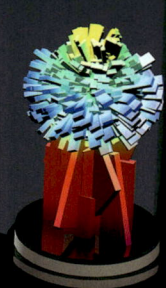
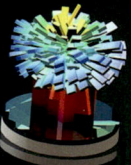

PRINTS →

Chronography 1 > 6, 2009 ·
From the series *Fractal Flowers* ·
6 Diasec digital prints · Each
20 × 200 cm (7 7/8 × 78 3/4 in.) ·
Private collection

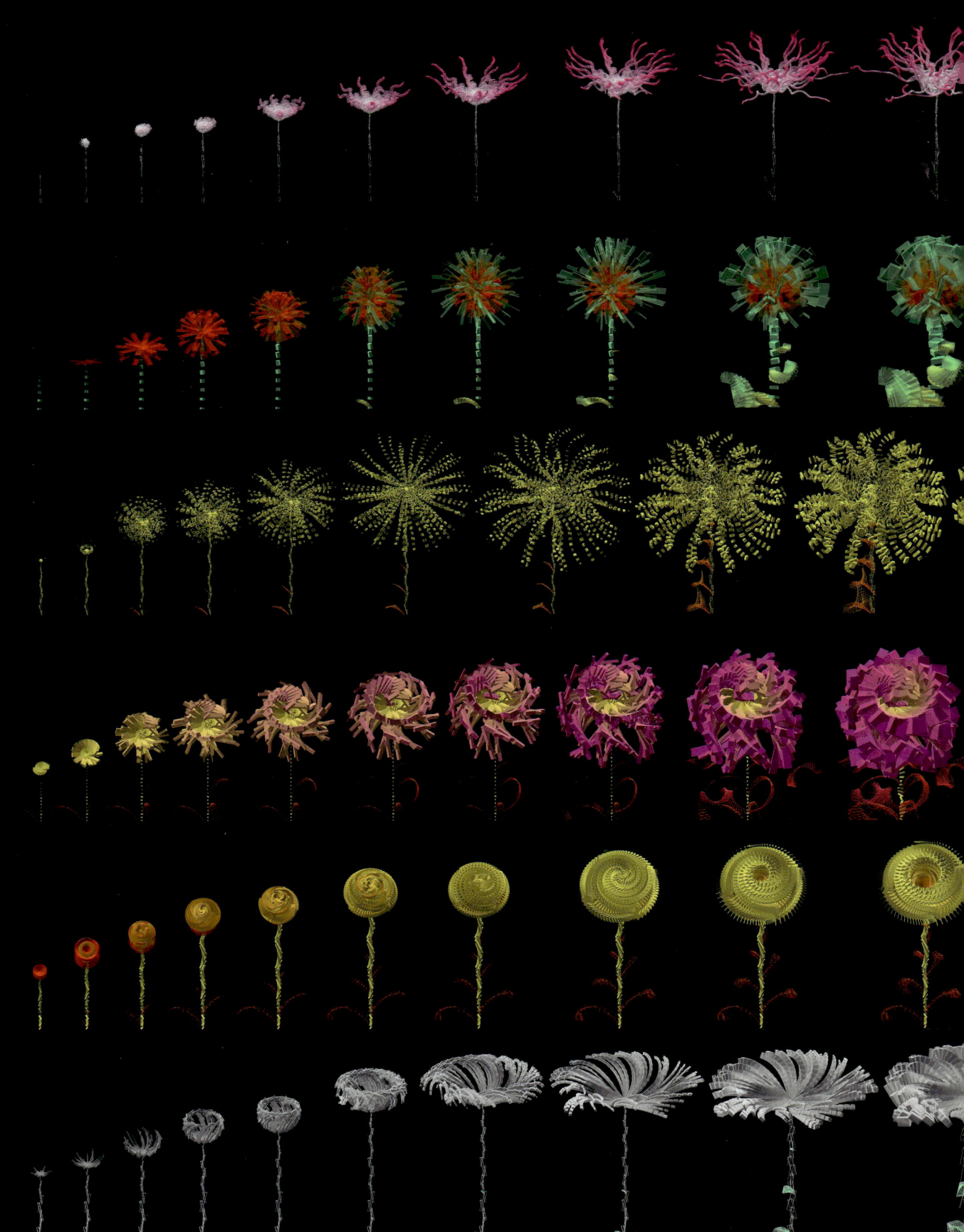

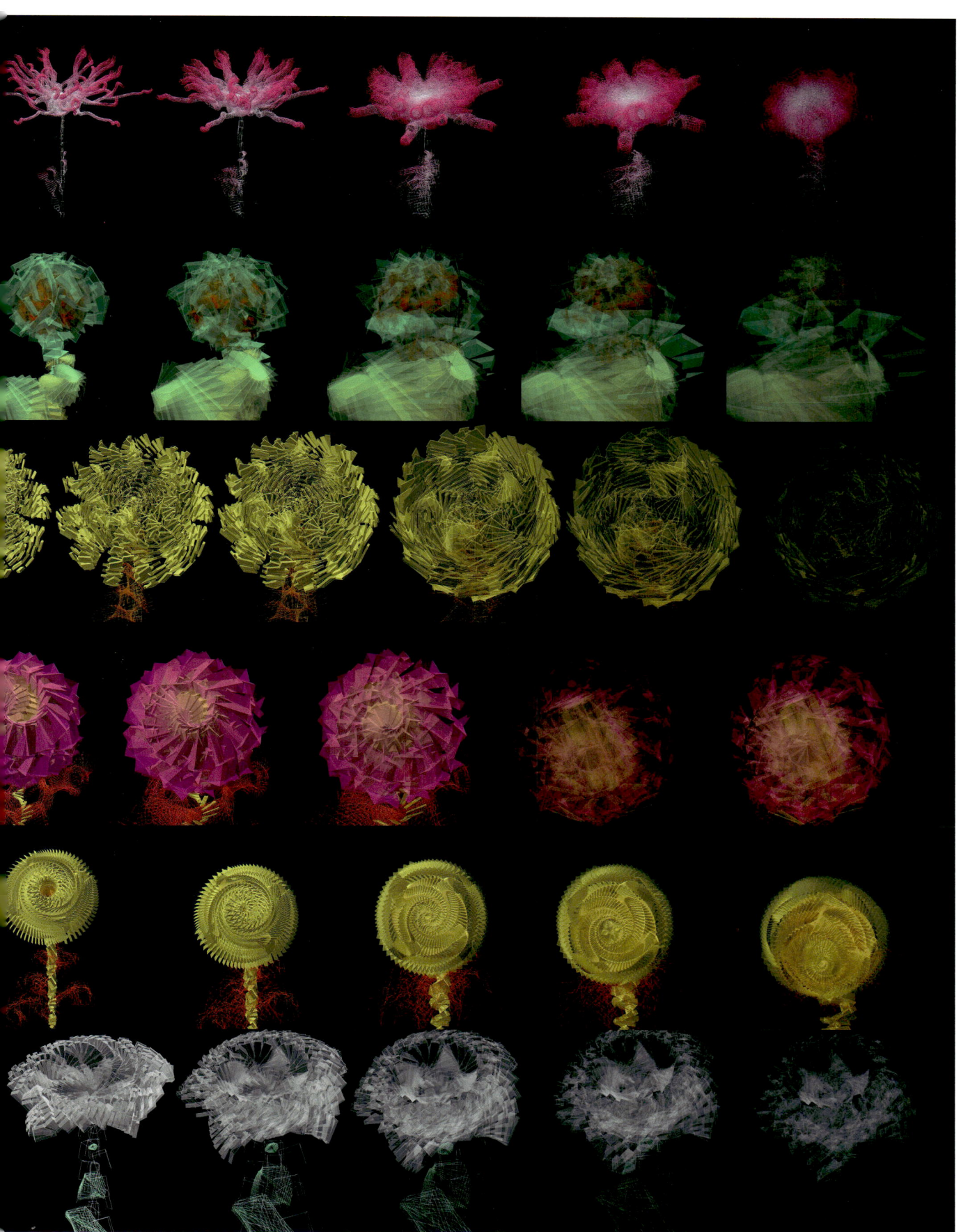

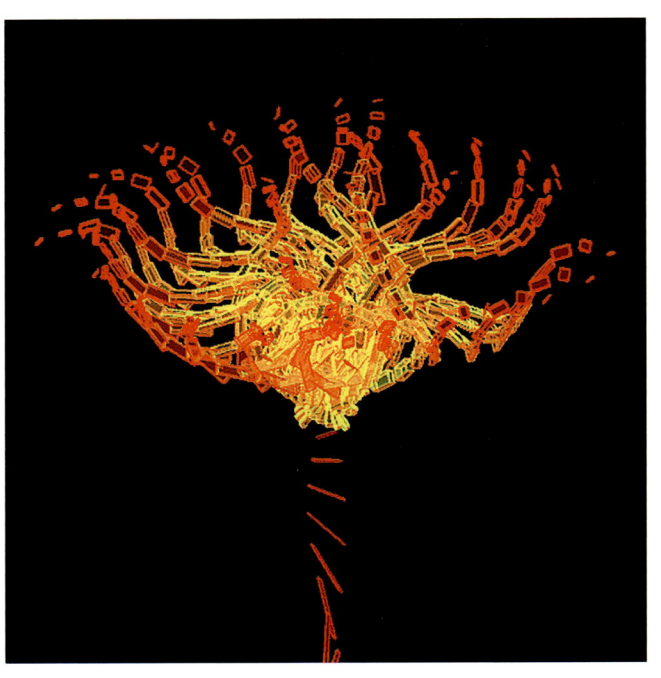
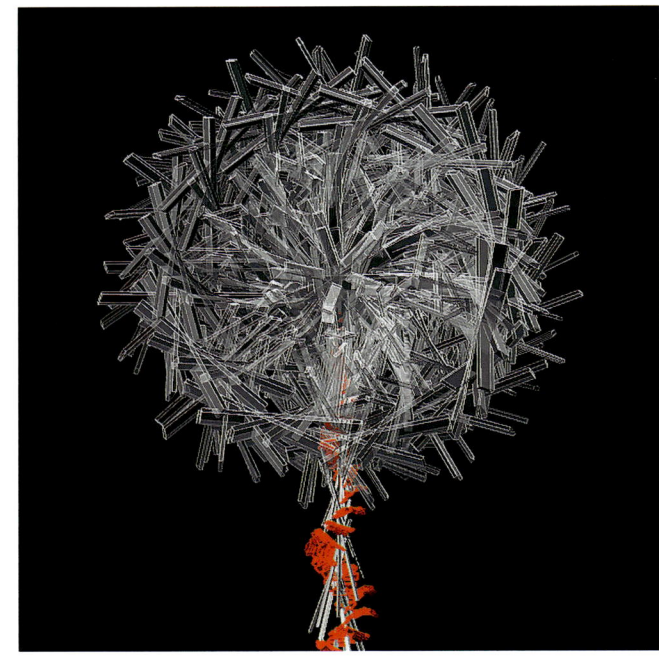
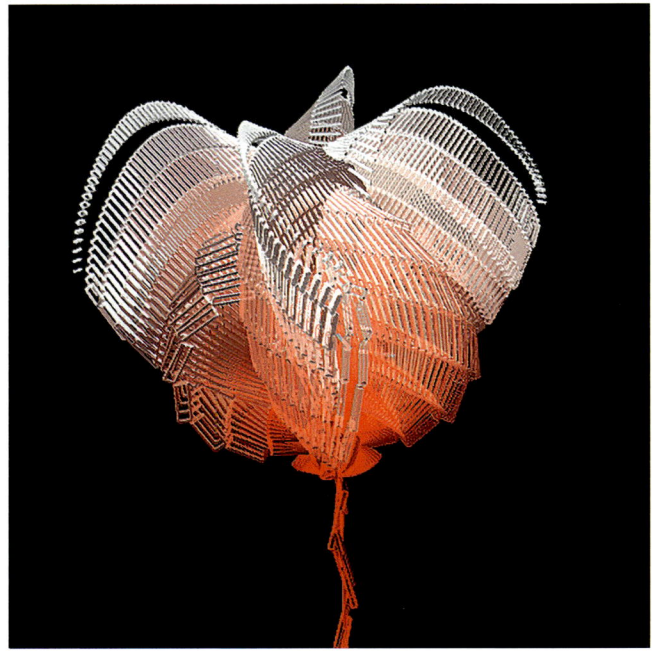
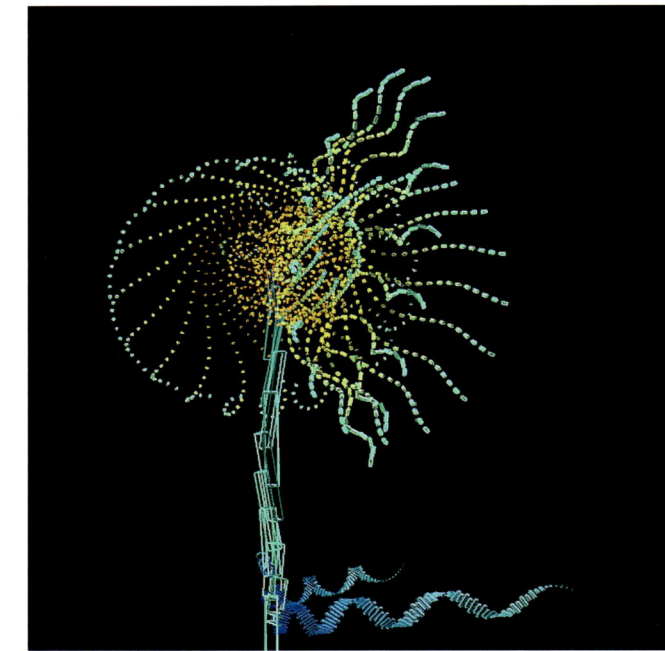

DIGITAL FILES

Top left: *Ayahuasca Neurologica Emersoniana* · Top right: *Coronae Digitalis* ·
Bottom left: *Psychotria hypnagogica Ken Kesey* · Bottom right:
Lophophora Williamsii Shakespeare · All 2008 · From the series
Fractal Flowers

DIGITAL FILE →

Purple Haze Artifilis Femina, 2008 ·
From the series *Fractal Flowers*

▶ VIDEO

114 (AN HERBARIUM OF FRACTAL FLOWERS)

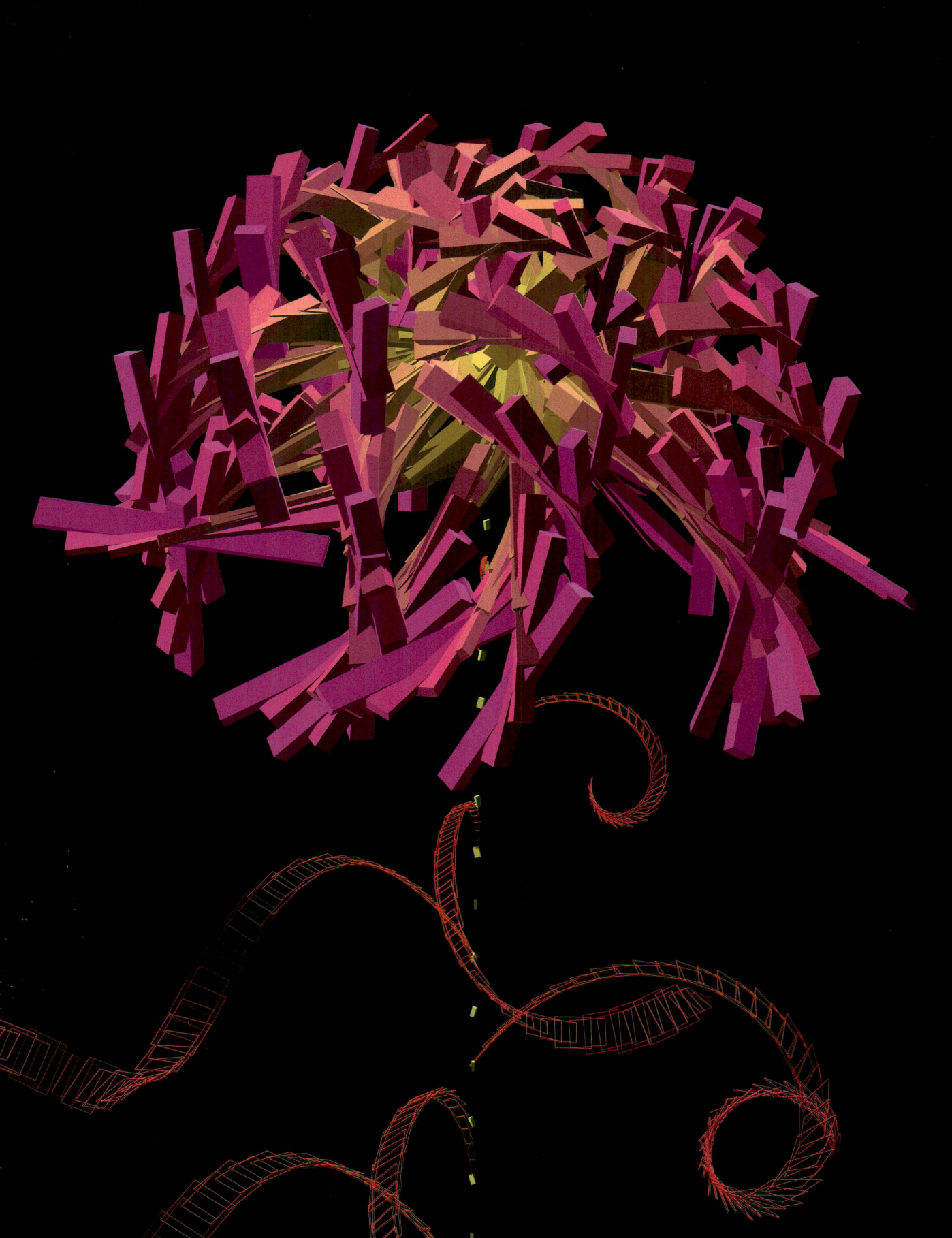

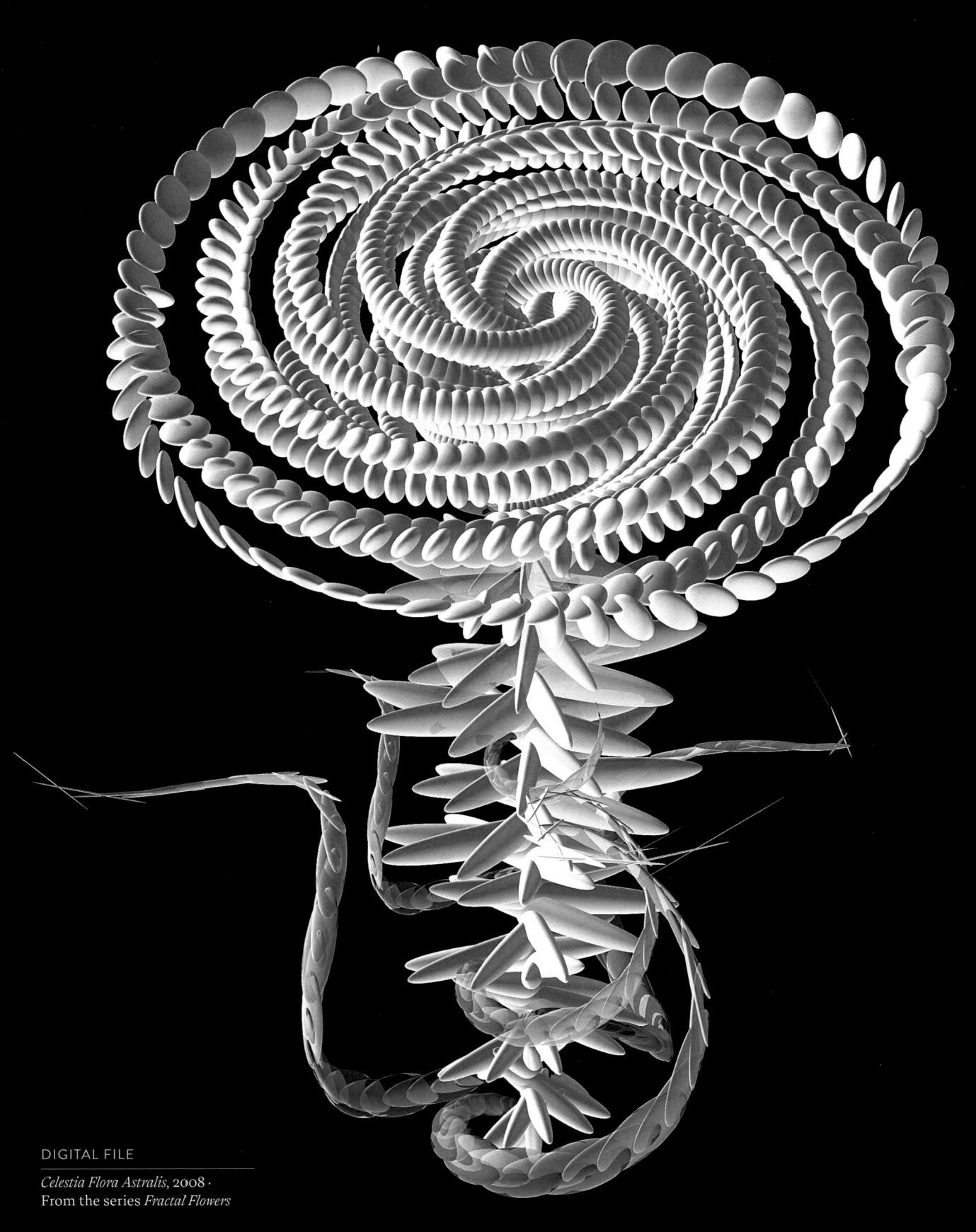

DIGITAL FILE

Celestia Flora Astralis, 2008 ·
From the series *Fractal Flowers*

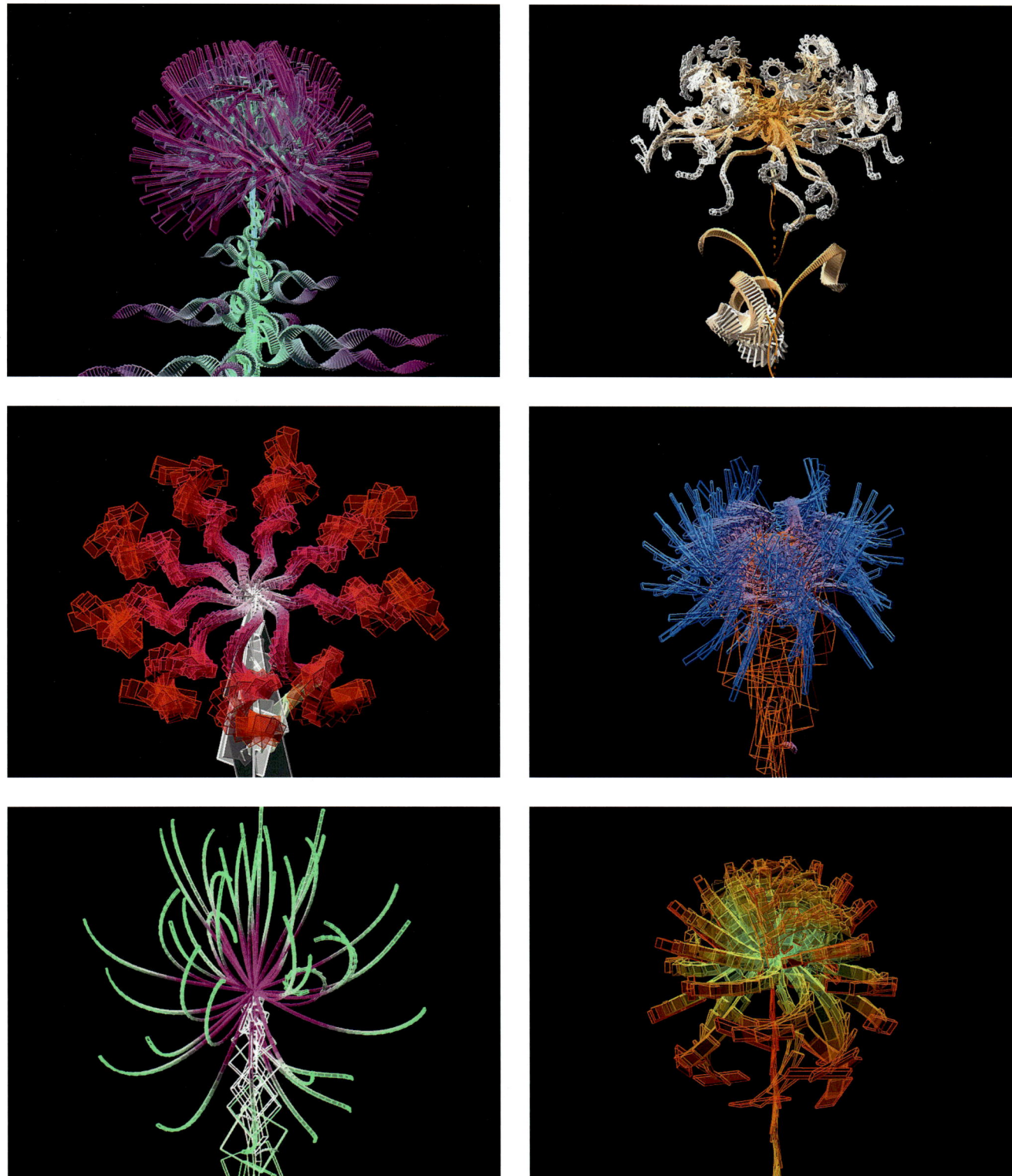

DIGITAL FILES

Top left: *Psychonautica Ornettica Hexadecimalis* · Top right: *Nymphaea Hybrida Darwin* · Middle left: *Cannabis Sativa of Edgar Poe* · Middle right: *Acidum Ordinatri Owsley* · Bottom left: *Adonis Aestivalis Hitchcock* · Bottom right: *Lennon NicoTiana Tabacum* ·

All 2008 · From the series *Fractal Flowers*

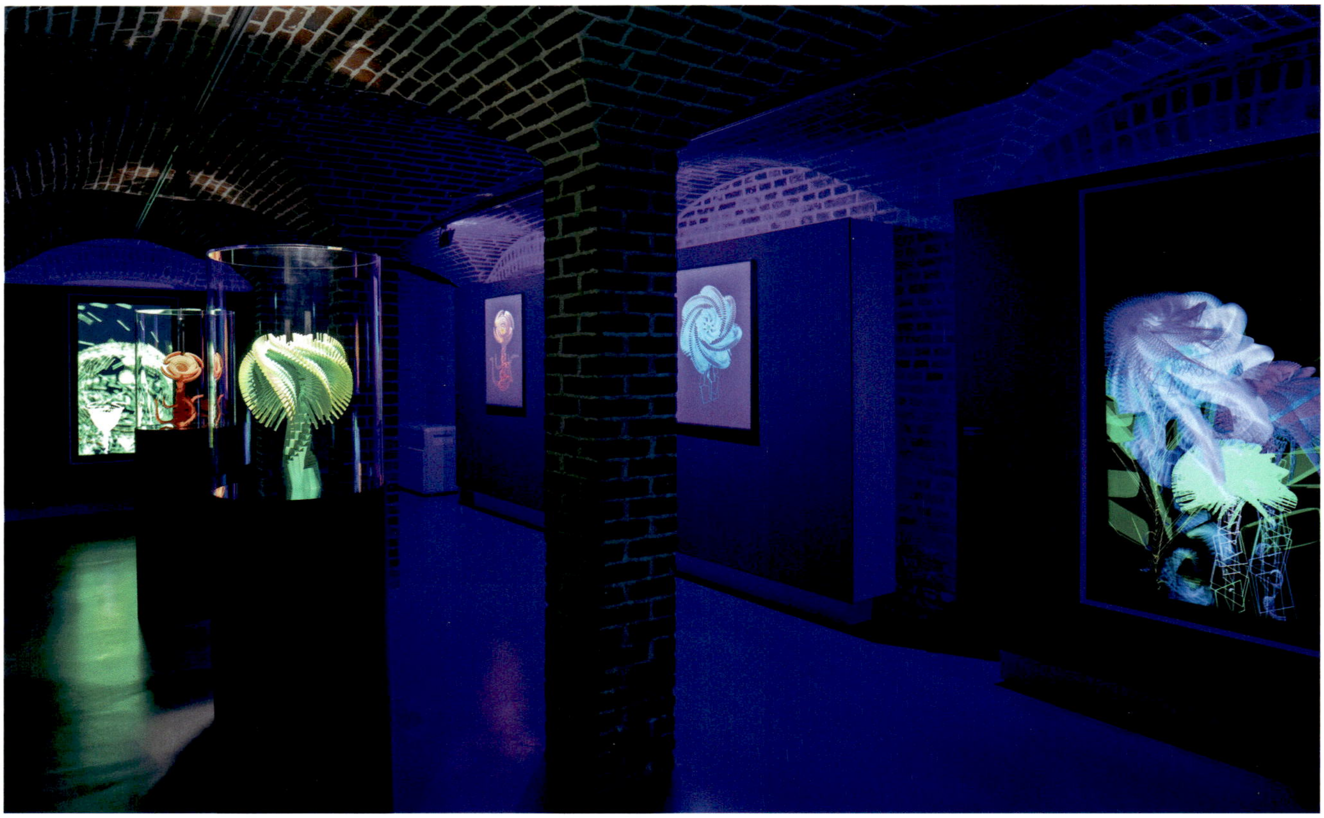

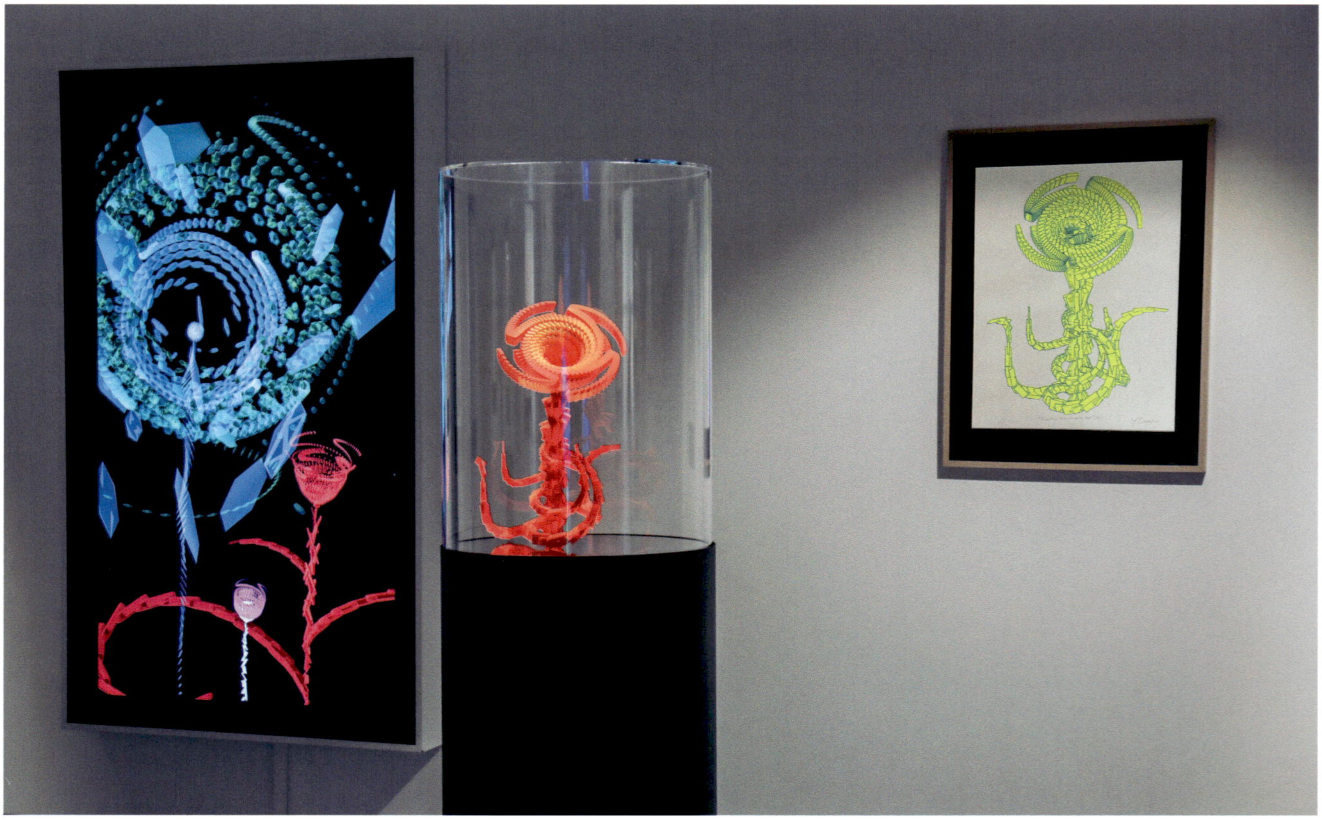

AN HERBARIUM OF FRACTAL FLOWERS

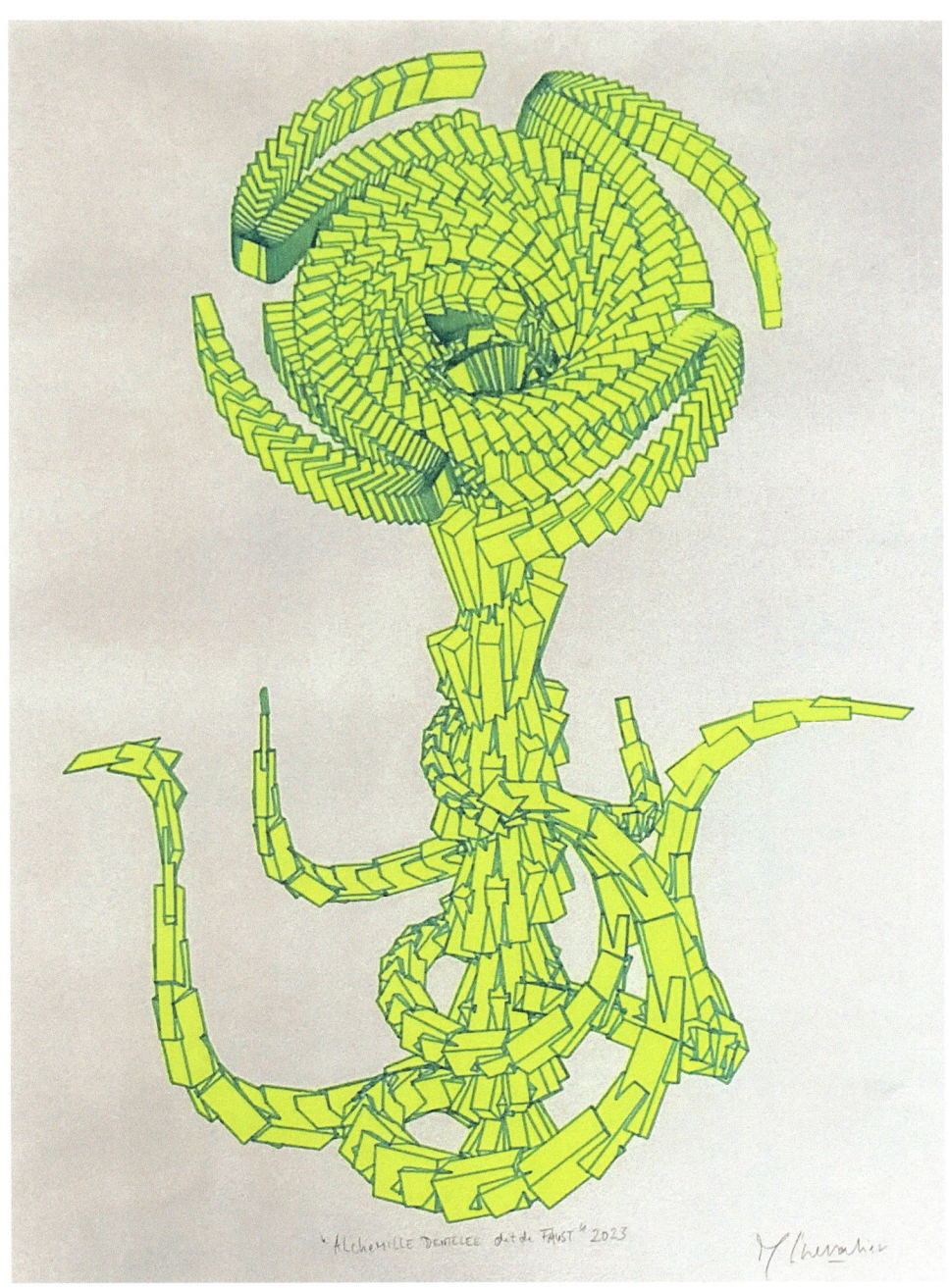

"Alchemille Dentelée dit de Faust" 2023   M Chevalier

↖ OBJECT

Lilus Arythmeticus named by Euclid, 2023 ·
From the series *Fractal Flowers* · 3D-printed
sculpture, synthetic resin · 46 × 37 × 28 cm
(18 1/8 × 14 9/16 × 11 in.) · Installation view,
Pixels Botaniques, Matmut pour les Arts,
Saint-Pierre-de-Varengeville, France, 2024

← OBJECT

Alchemille Dentelée named by Faust (Evolution),
2023 · From the series *Fractal Flowers* ·
3D-printed sculpture, synthetic resin ·
46 × 32 × 27 cm (18 1/8 × 12 5/8 × 10 5/8 in.) ·
Installation view, *Fractal Flowers*, Centre d'Art
de Mougins, France, 2024

↑ DRAWING

Alchemille Dentelée named by Faust, 2023 ·
From the series *Fractal Flowers* · Felt-tip
pen on paper, drawn by a robot · 65 × 50 cm
(25 9/16 × 19 11/16 in.)

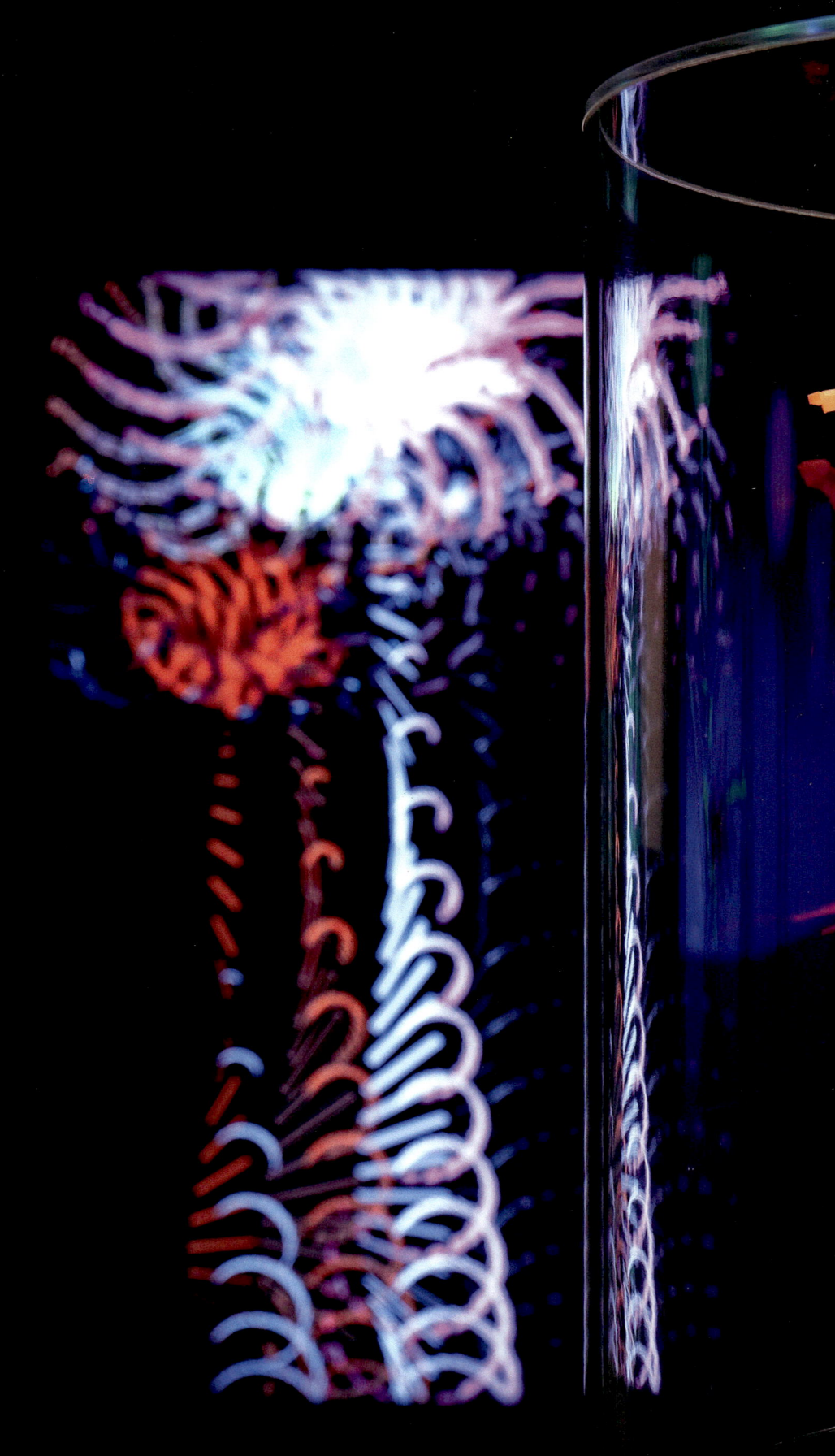

INSTALLATION

Ayahuasca Neurologica, 2022 ·
From the series *Fractal Flowers* ·
3D-printed sculpture,
synthetic resin · 40×25×25 cm
(15 3/4 × 9 13/16 × 9 13/16 in.) ·
Installation view, *Fractal Flowers*,
Ara Art Center, Seoul,
South Korea, 2023

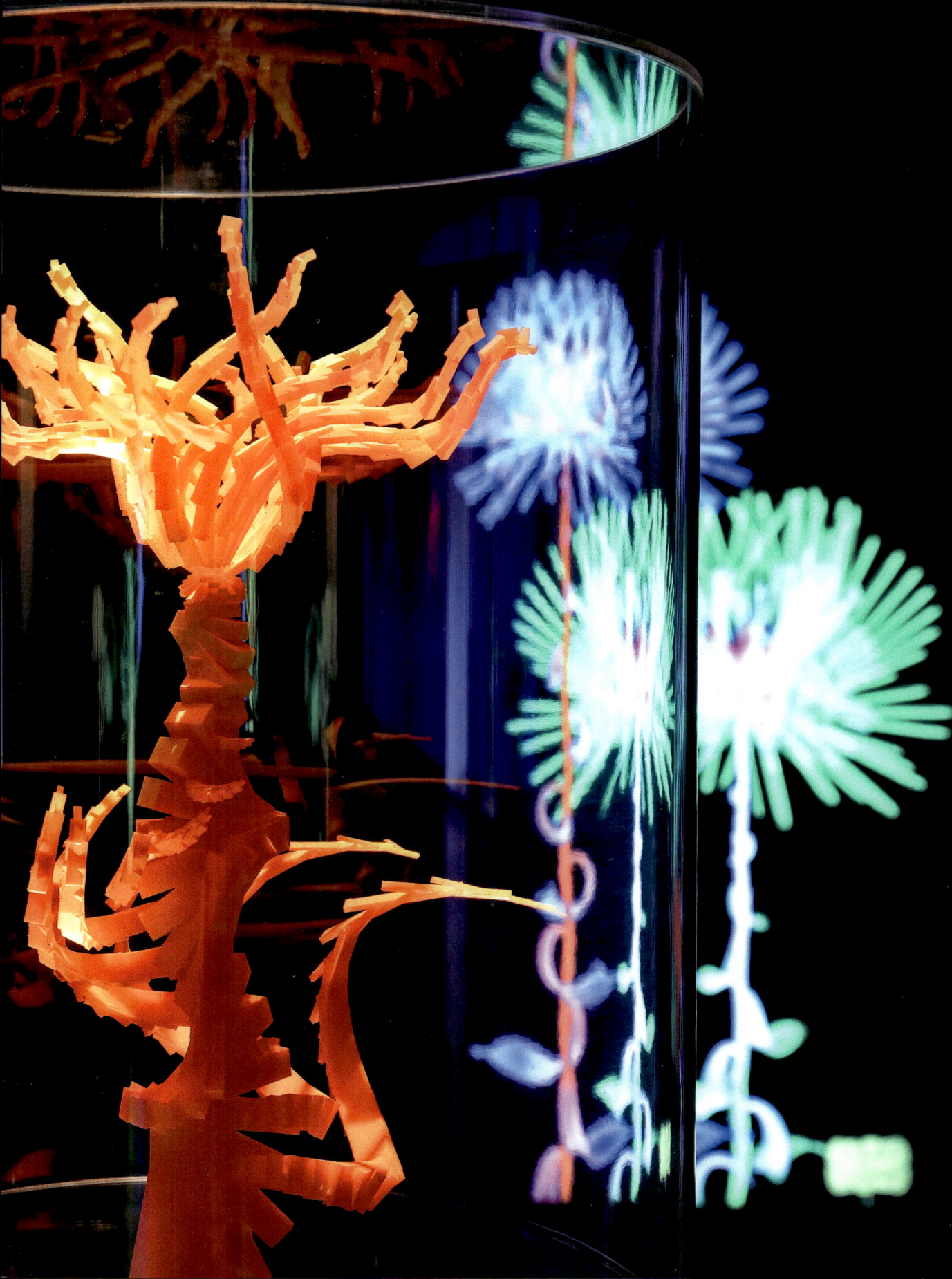

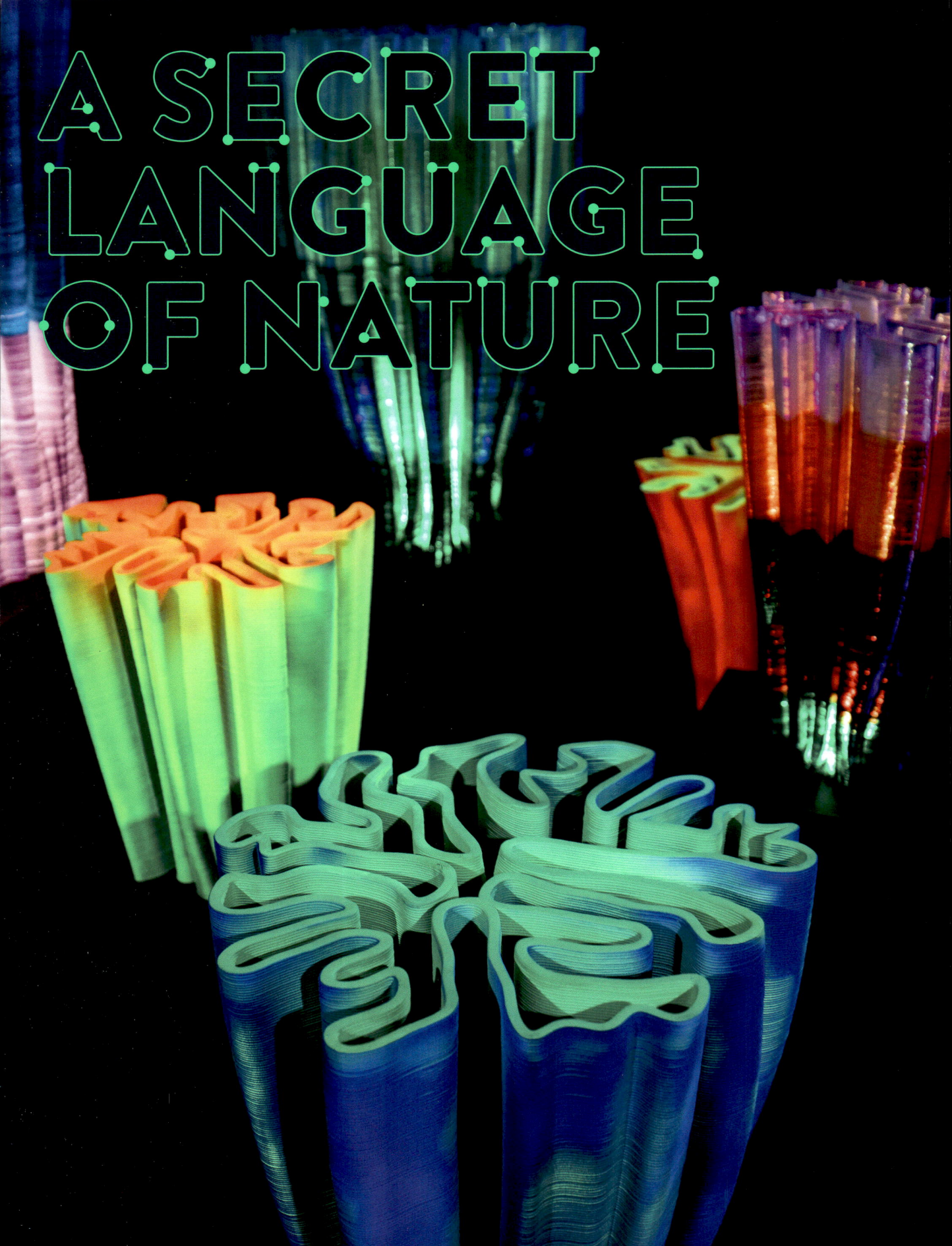

A SECRET LANGUAGE OF NATURE

Digital Abysses, started 2018 ·
3D-printed sculptures, synthetic
resin, ceramic, recycled plastic ·
Dimensions variable · Installation
view, *Digital Abysses*, Château d'If,
Marseille, 2024

● Since the mid-2000s, nature has become an increasingly important point of reference in Miguel Chevalier's oeuvre. On the one hand, he is interested in the enormous richness of our planet's flora and fauna. On the other, he wants to raise awareness about the fragility of nature's beauty and diversity.

Chevalier's preoccupation with the ▸ fractal (p. 27) is not limited to the floral world or his group of works *Fractal Flowers* (started 2008; pp. 108, 110–21). The term "fractal" was coined in 1975 by mathematician Benoît Mandelbrot (1924–2010) and is derived from the Latin *fractus* ("broken") or *frangere* ("to break into pieces"). The fractal generally refers to a geometric shape infinitely repeated in the same way at different scales, resulting in complex structures. While this process can be continued indefinitely in mathematical calculations, it generally remains limited in nature. Nevertheless, the fractal could be described as a kind of hidden developmental principle of nature, as it determines the growth of many living things. In this context, scientists use the term "statistical self-similarity," meaning that the forms do not rigidly repeat themselves, with slight variations being possible.

Chevalier created three further groups of works with nature and the fractal at their core, specifically, they deal with crystalline structures (*Digital Crystals*, started 2018; pp. 134–39), creatures of the underwater world (*Digital Abysses*, started 2018; pp. 122, 124–31), and the so-called Lichtenberg figure, which appears during high-voltage electrical discharges, such as lightning strikes, and also features fractal structures (*Fractal Arborescence*, started 2023; pp. 144–51).

Even if at first glance these works appear to have a very different aesthetic from Chevalier's earlier works, which aimed at a pictorial expression of elements of the digital sphere (see also pp. 70–74), they are united by the fact that the artist devotes himself to structures that are fundamental in both the digital and analog worlds and that are not always visible to the naked eye (see also p. 16). What they have in common is an infinite wealth of possibilities for creating complex forms through an ongoing generative system. (FS)

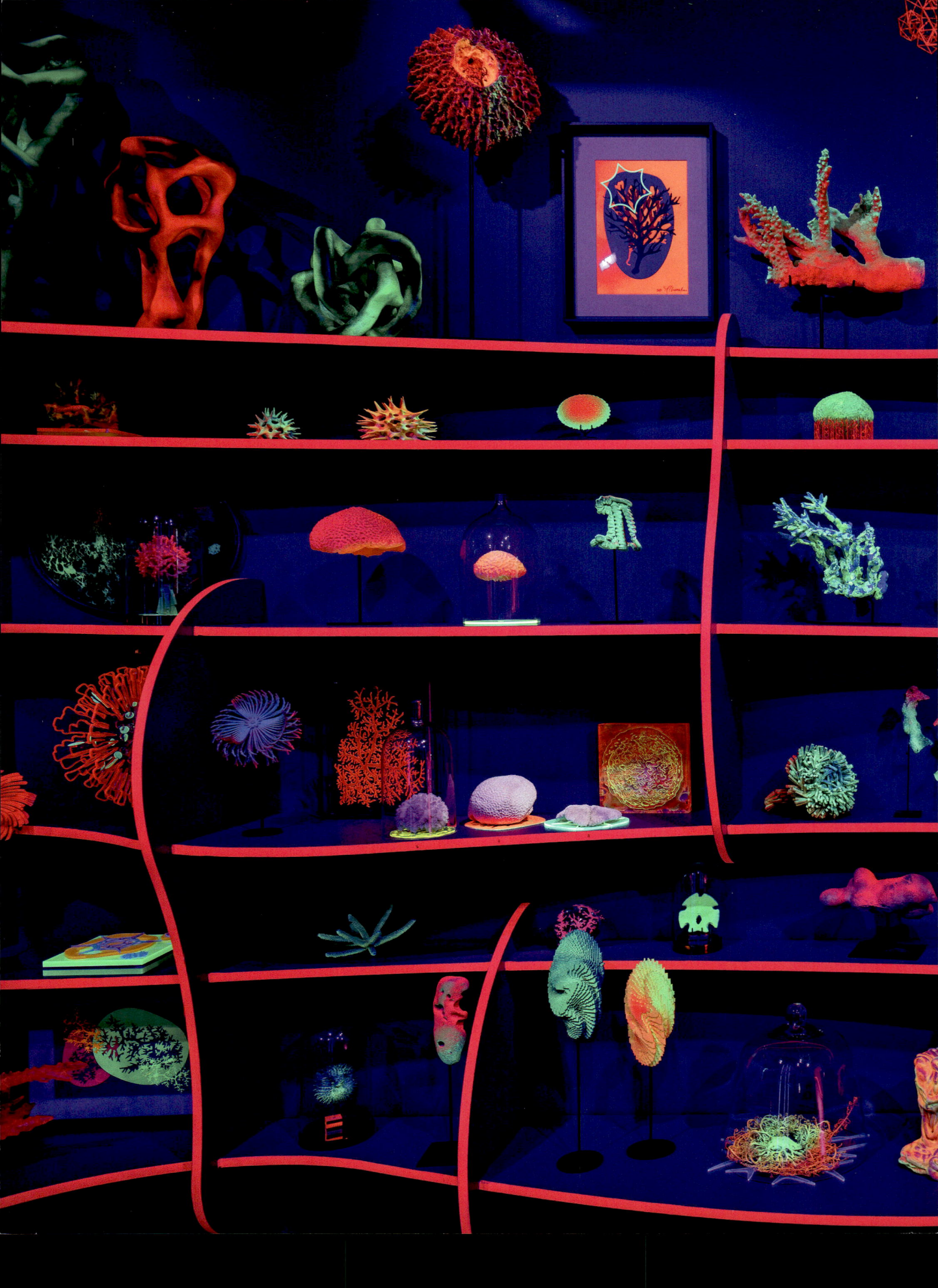

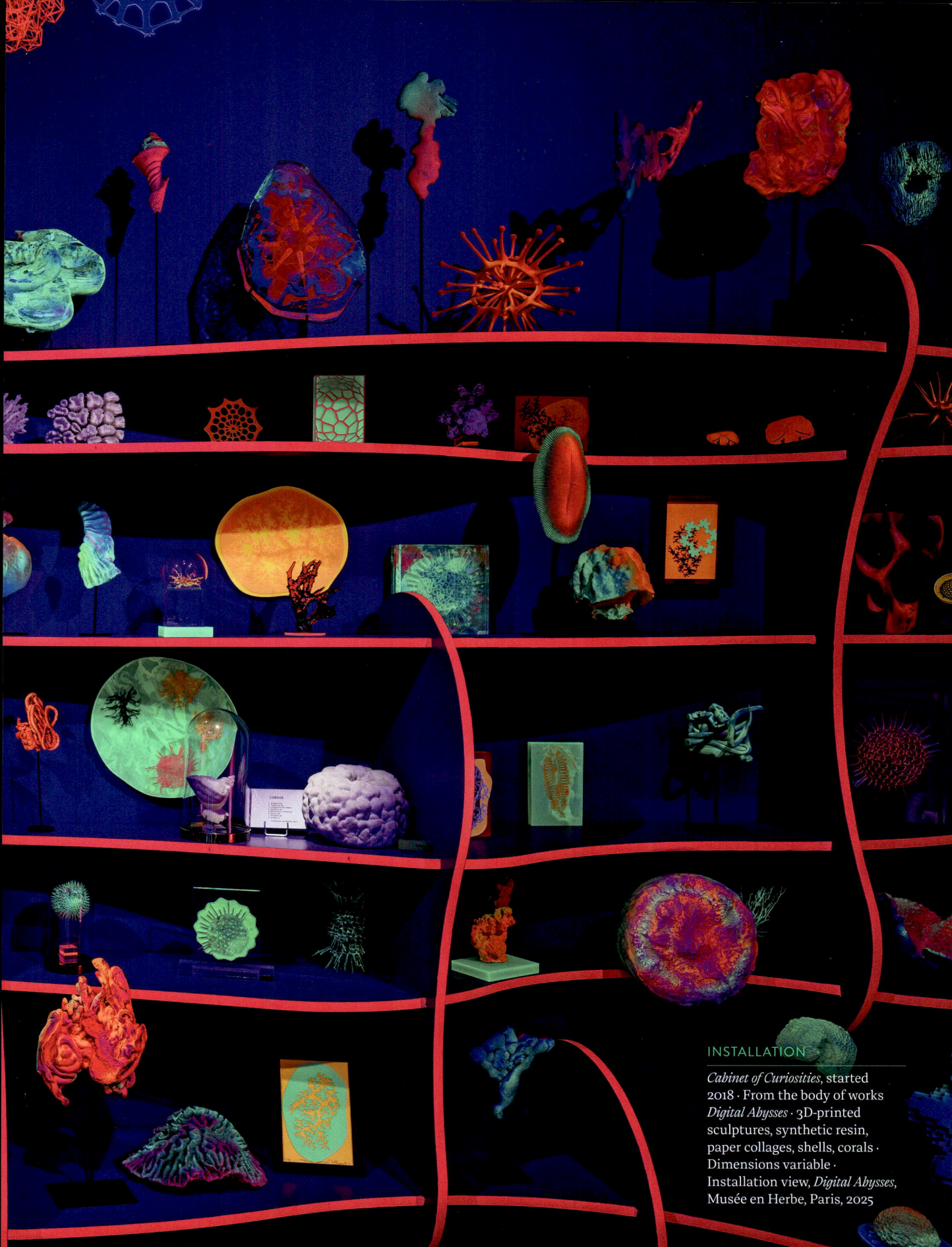

INSTALLATION

Cabinet of Curiosities, started 2018 · From the body of works *Digital Abysses* · 3D-printed sculptures, synthetic resin, paper collages, shells, corals · Dimensions variable · Installation view, *Digital Abysses*, Musée en Herbe, Paris, 2025

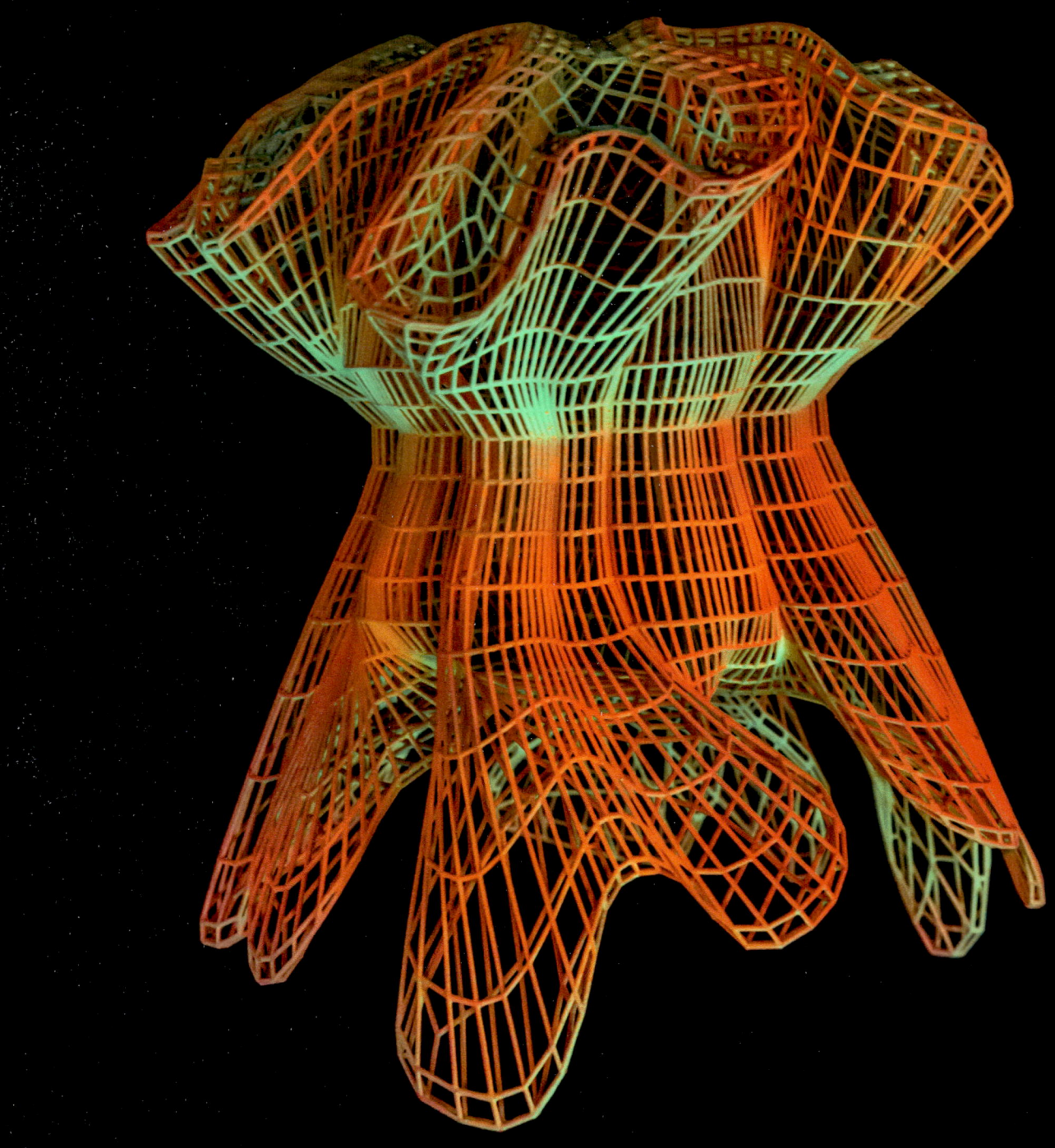

OBJECT

Aurelia, 2012 · From the body
of works *Digital Abysses* ·
3D-printed sculpture,
synthetic resin, fluorescent
pigments · 30×30×28 cm
(11 13/16×11 13/16×11 in.)

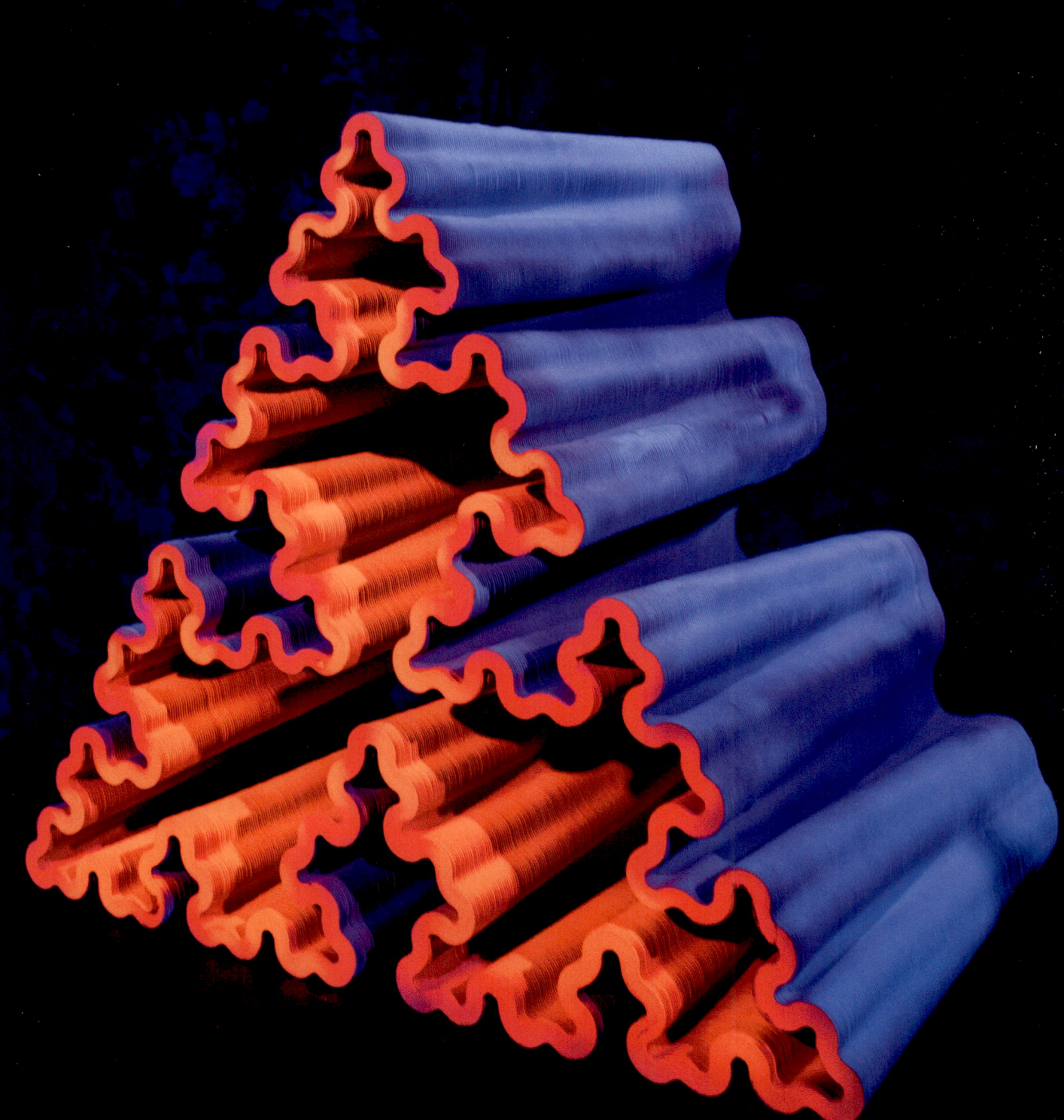

OBJECT

Fractal Stratigraphy 1, 2024 ·
From the body of works *Digital
Abysses* · 3D-printed sculpture,
ceramic · 54×615×425 cm
(21 1/4×24 3/16×16 3/4 in.)

The depths of the ocean still remain largely unexplored. With his *Digital Abysses* (started 2018; pp. 122, 124–31), Miguel Chevalier renders the underwater world visible: his sculptures are reminiscent of corals, anemones, and other cnidarians, and some have fractal structures. The objects, which glow when exposed to UV light, and sometimes are translucent, were produced with the help of a 3D printer.

Inspired by marine shapes, the works all refer to the artist's central theme: the tension between nature and technology. While earlier sculptures were made of ceramic, an earthy substance, more recently Chevalier has also been using fishing nets or recycled plastic. In this respect, his choice of material draws attention to environmental pollution and the challenge of preserving our fragile ecosystem. (JG)

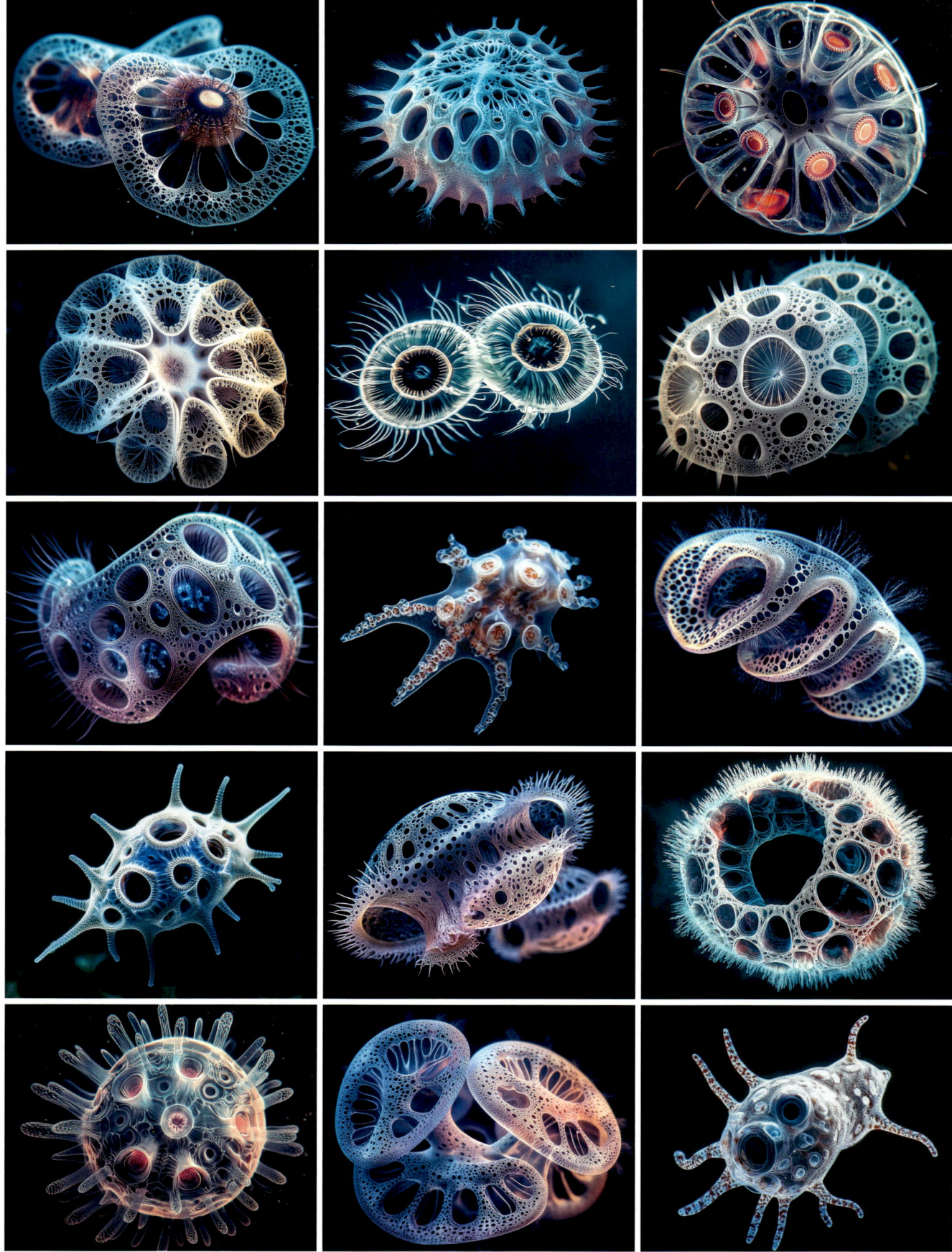

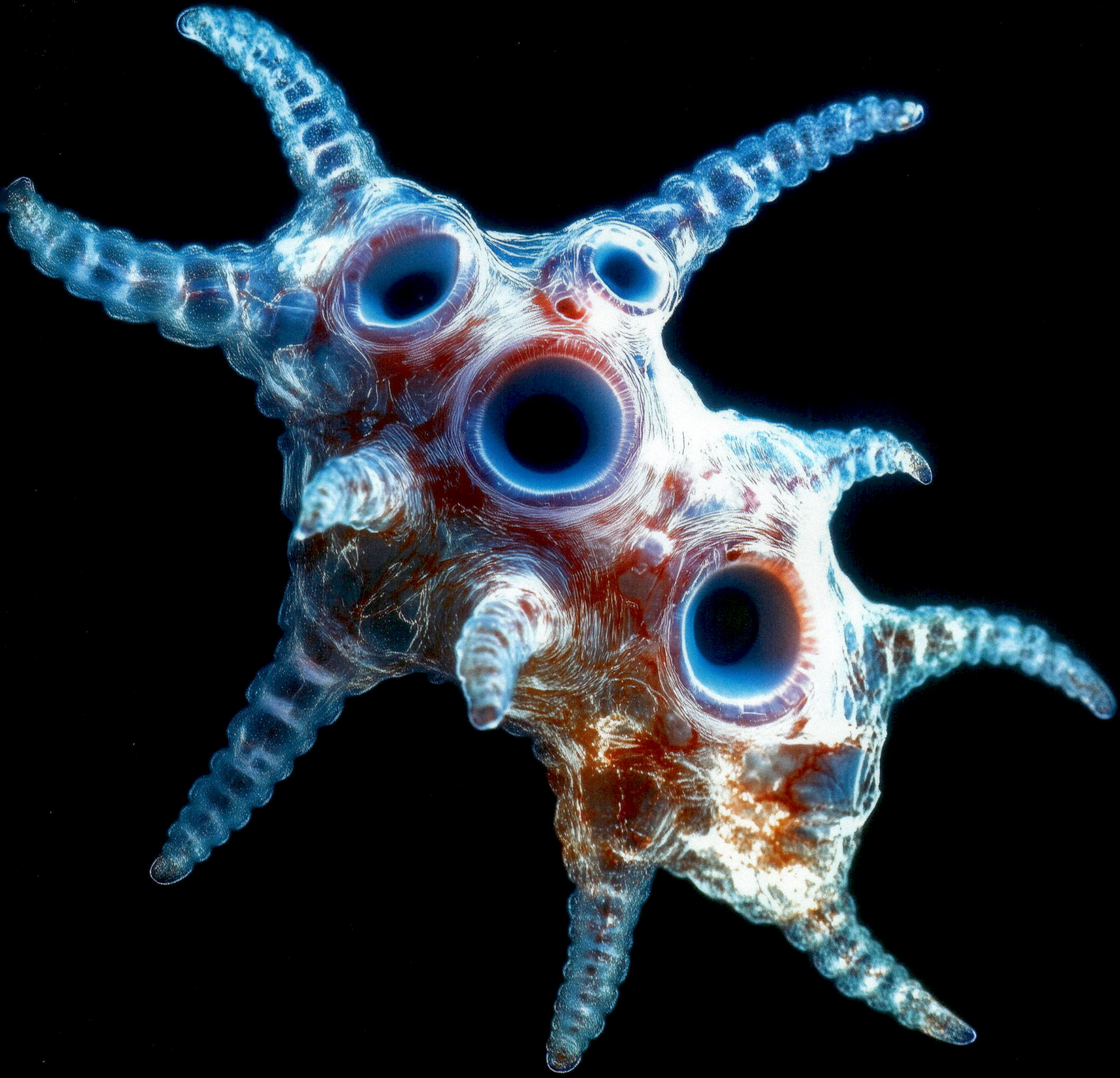

Digital Abysses AI, 2025 · Video, color, no sound, 60 min.

▶ VIDEO

Translucent moving forms that continuously take on different shapes: for this video, Miguel Chevalier compiled a large number of radiolaria images—from the famous lithographs of depictions of such creatures based on drawings by natural scientist and artist Ernst Haeckel (1834–1919; p. 157) to more recent high-resolution microscope images. The depictions of radiolaria, unicellular creatures invisible to the naked eye, are complemented by pictures of plankton, marine microorganisms that do not move on their own but drift with the current.

Based on these, Chevalier used five programs employing ▸ artificial intelligence (p. 26) to create new forms with the help of ▸ prompts (p. 29): the aim was to produce symbioses from the images provided, to change surfaces according to his ideas, to set them in motion, and to trigger the process of shapeshifting. The artist continuously intervened in this procedure by further processing promising visual results, ultimately creating this poetic metamorphosis inspired by creatures from the underwater world's infinite depths. (FS)

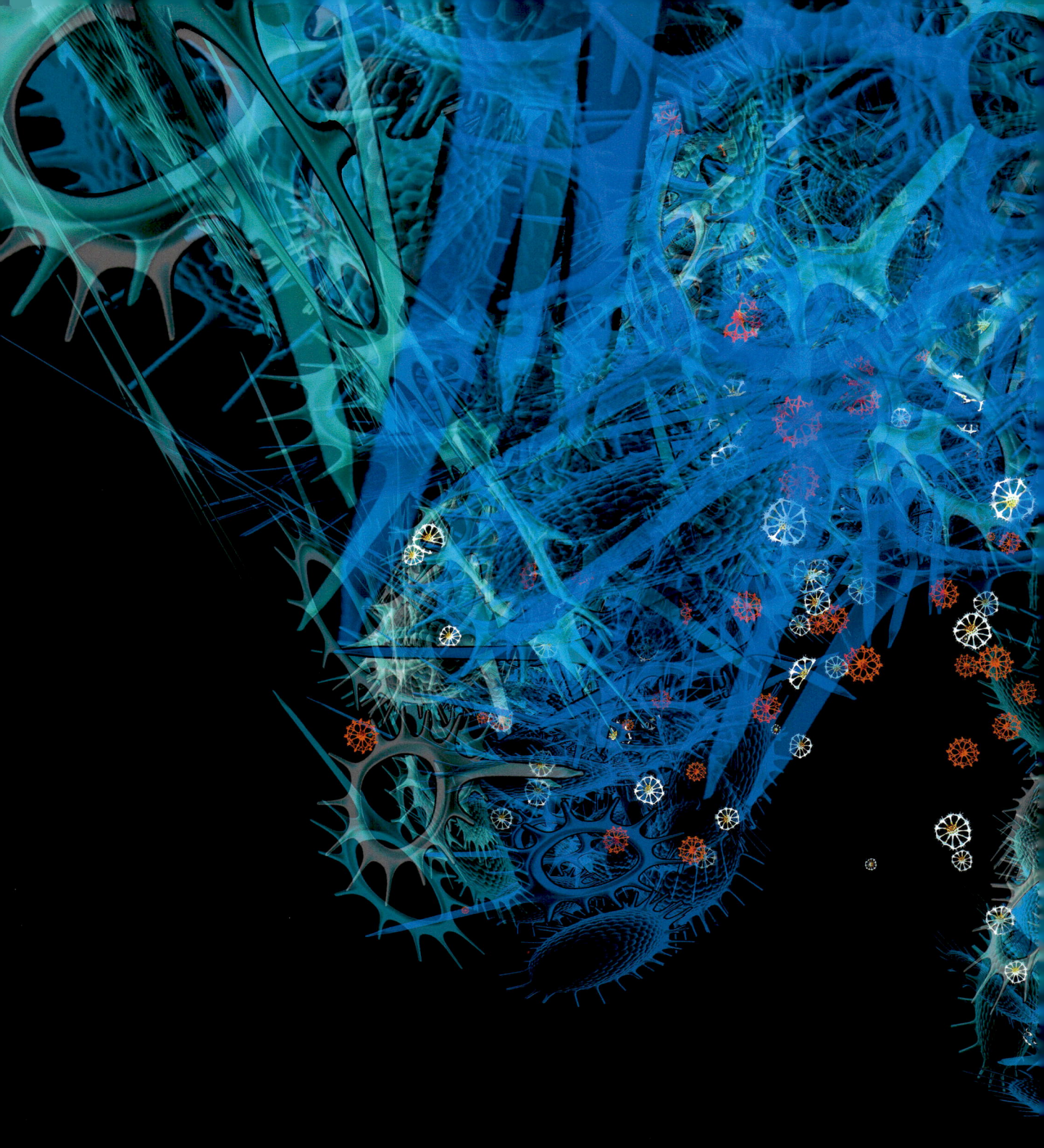

Digital Plankton, 2021 · From the
body of works *Digital Abysses* ·
Video, color, no sound, 60 min. ·
Software: Claude Micheli

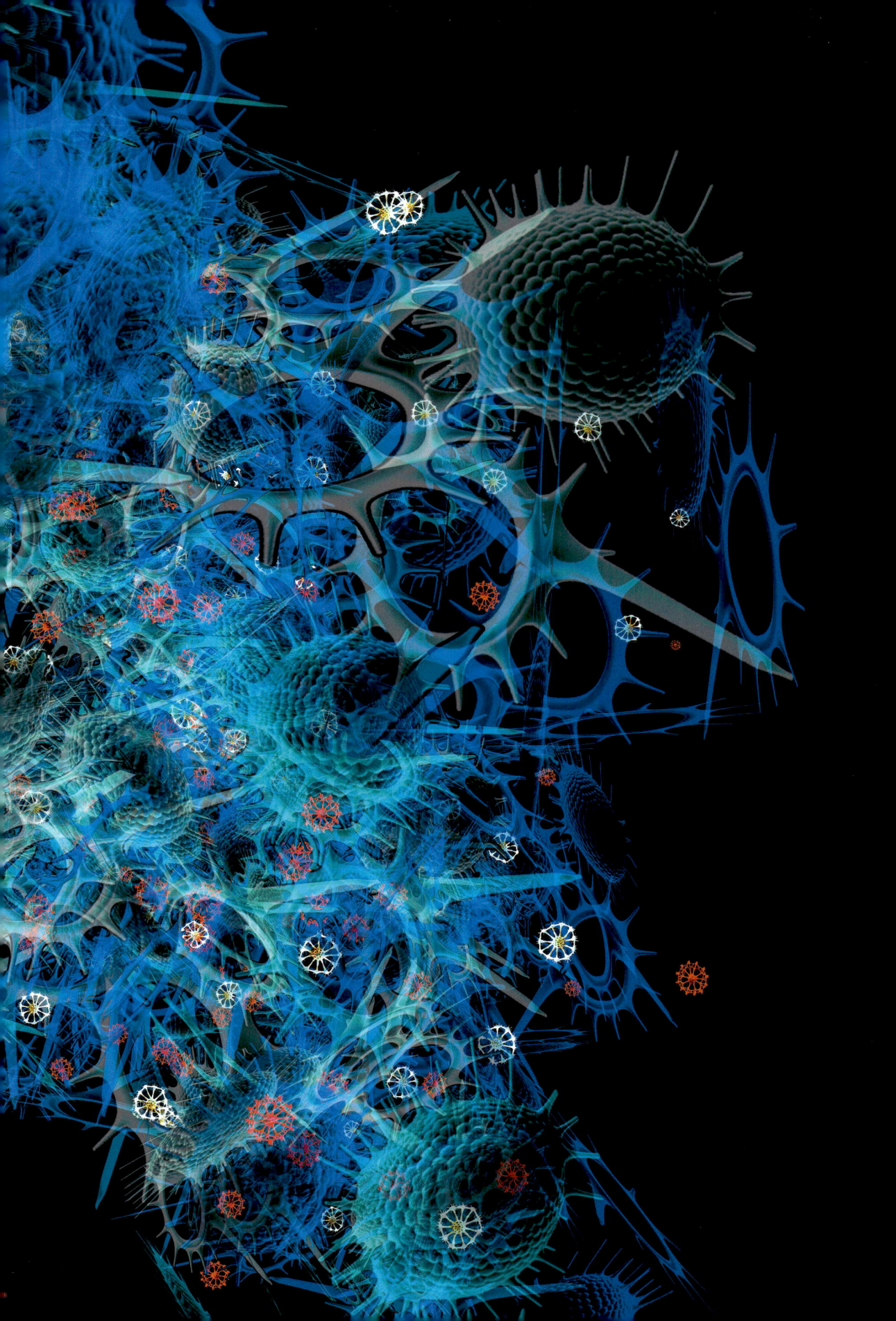

This installation is based on the so-called Koch snowflake, named after Swedish mathematician Helge von Koch (1870–1924). It is a ▸ fractal (p. 27) that presents the same shape at any magnification. Hungarian biologist Aristid Lindenmayer (1925–1989) used it to mathematically describe the development of organisms such as algae. With *Fractal Expansion*, Miguel Chevalier points out the fascinating connection between biology and geometry. (FS)

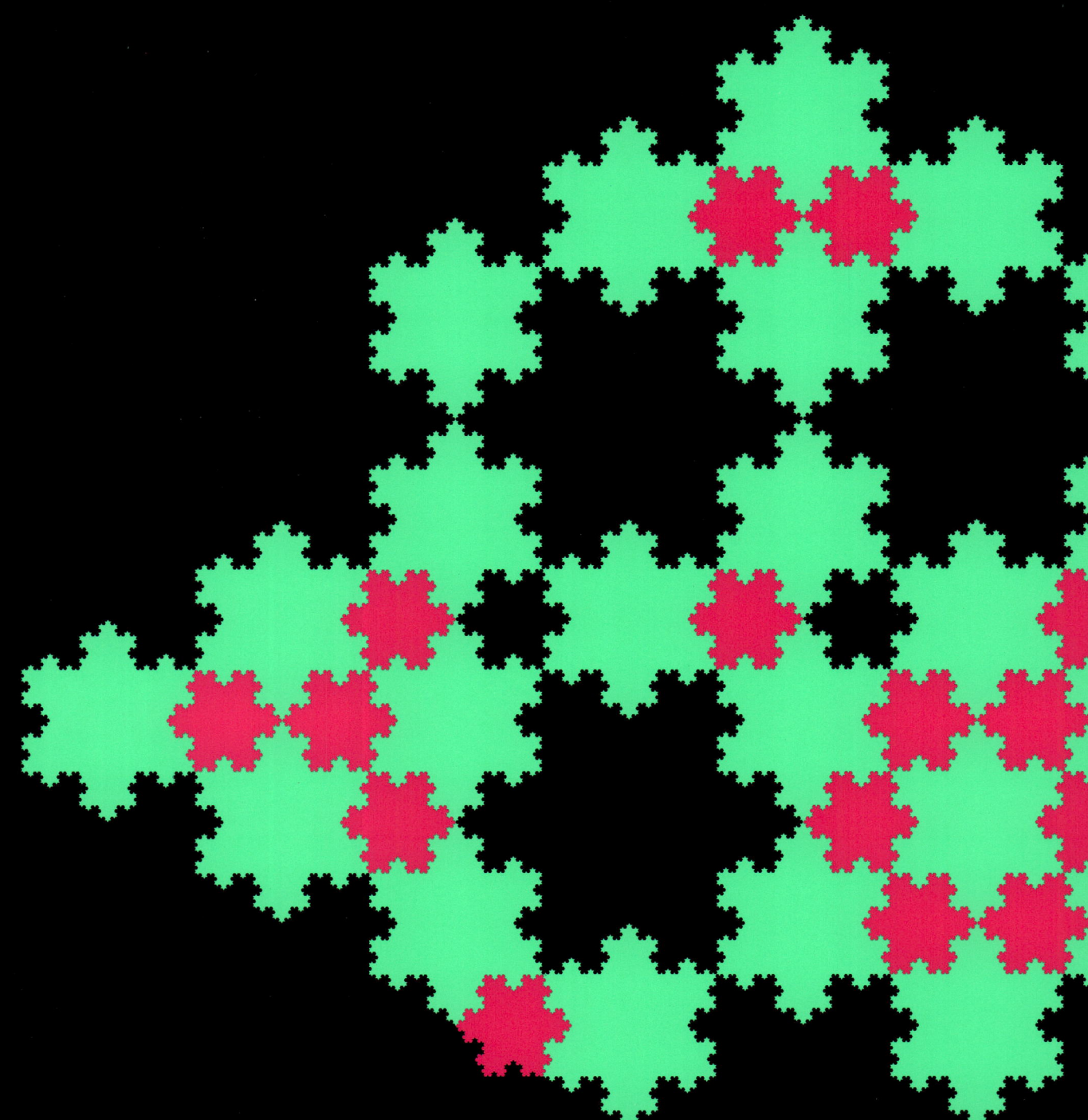

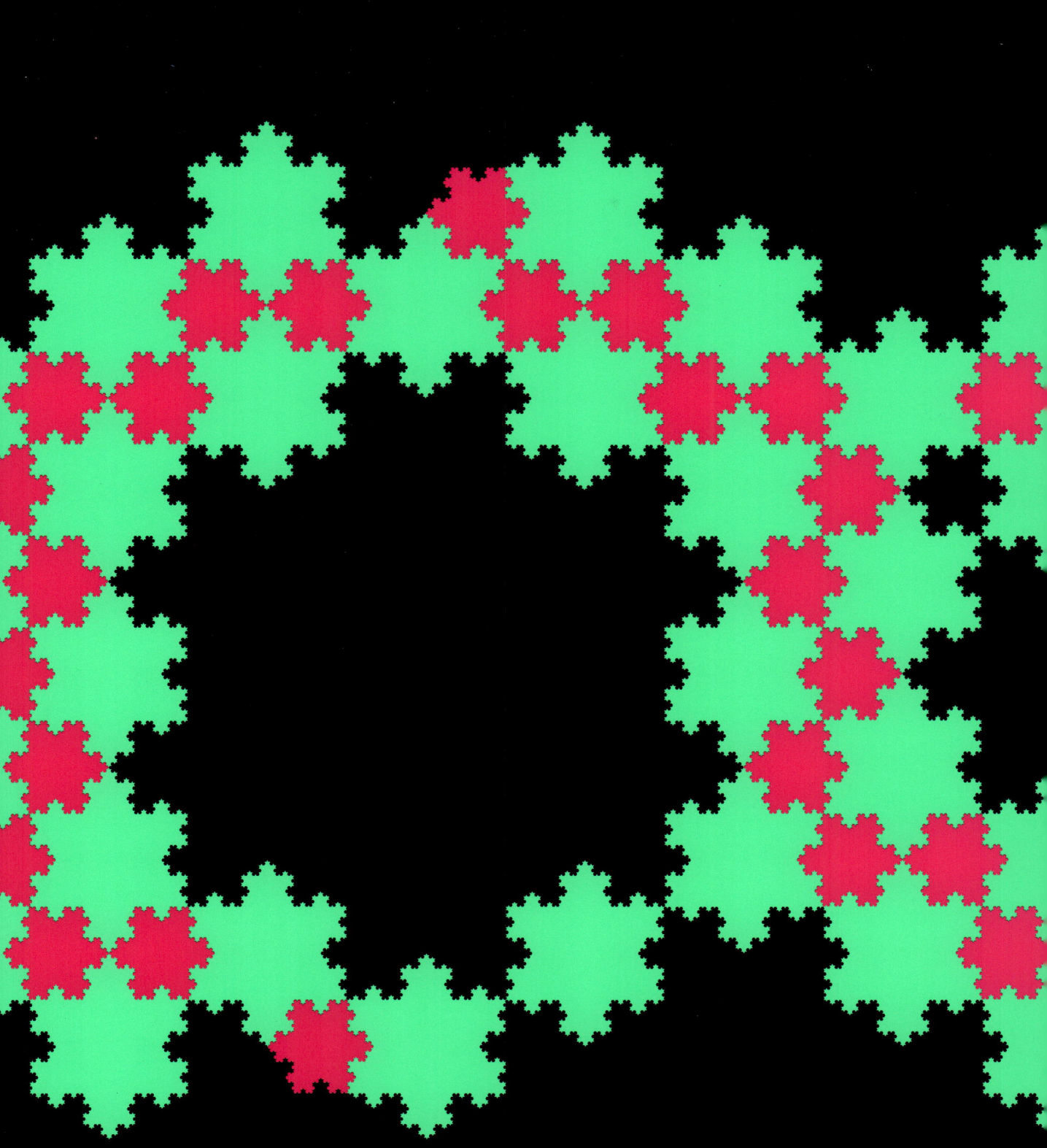

Digital Crystal (Negative), 2018 ·
Plexiglas · 30 × 30 × 30 cm
(11 13/16 × 11 13/16 × 11 13/16 in.)

Since the late 1990s, Miguel Chevalier has increasingly focused on naturally occurring forms and phenomena. These include ▸ crystals (p. 26) and snowflakes, which are both defined by geometric structures, and although they may look similar, no two designs are ever fully identical. Using a digitally controlled laser, the artist cuts out shapes from same-size Plexiglas sheets that are then mounted on top of each other, thus creating cubes that enclose hollow areas resembling frozen forms. Alternatively, the cut-out shapes can be combined to create a positive model. The sculptures are illuminated from below, emphasizing the material's transparency. (FS)

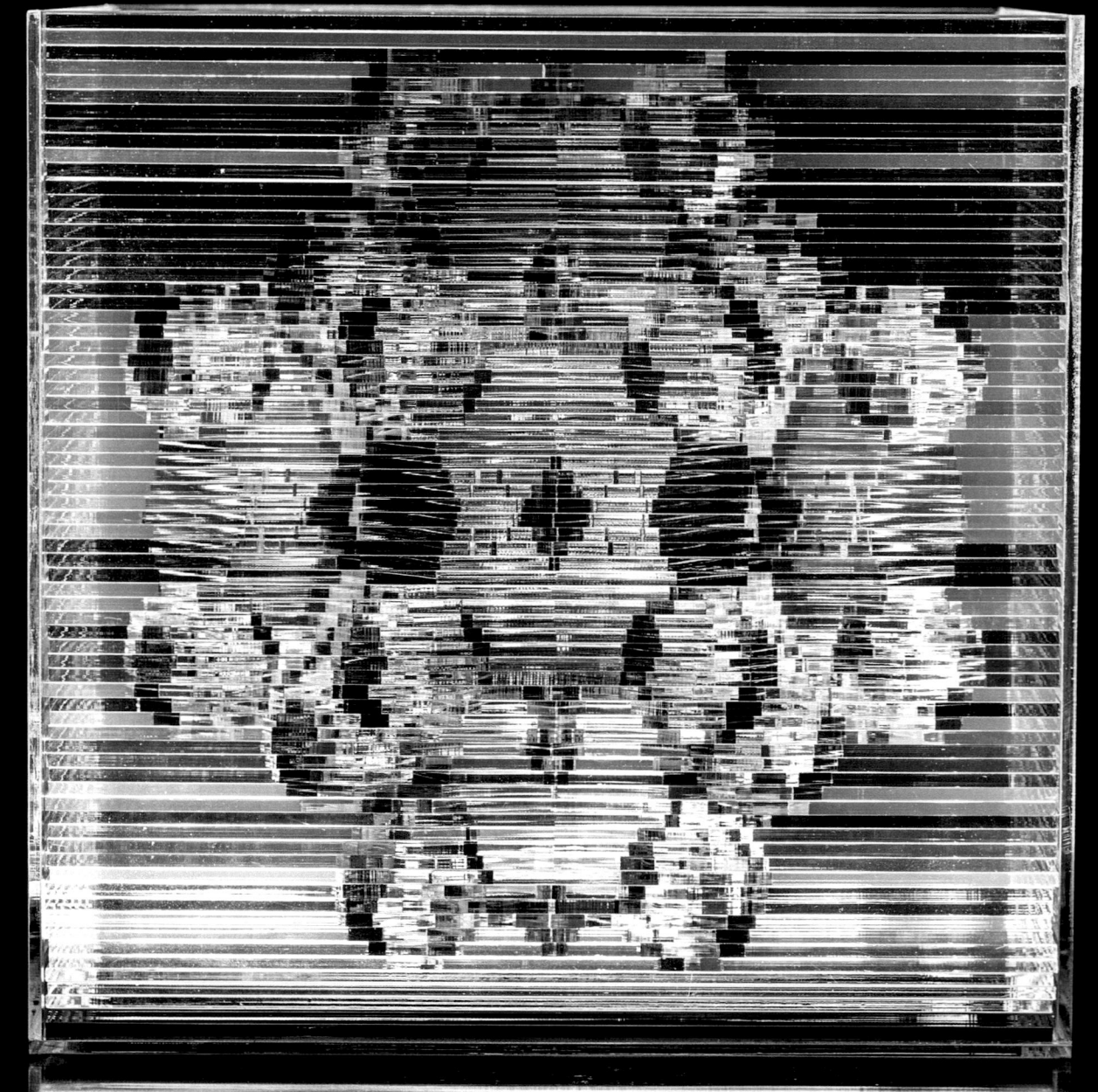

↓ OBJECT

Digital Crystal (Positive), 2018 ·
Plexiglas · 255 × 255 × 255 cm
(10 × 10 × 10 in.) · Private collection

DIGITAL FILES →

Digital Crystals AI, started 2018 ·
Software: Claude Micheli

VIDEO STILL → →

Digital Crystals AI, started 2018 ·
Video, color, no sound, 60 min. ·
Software: Claude Micheli

▶ VIDEO

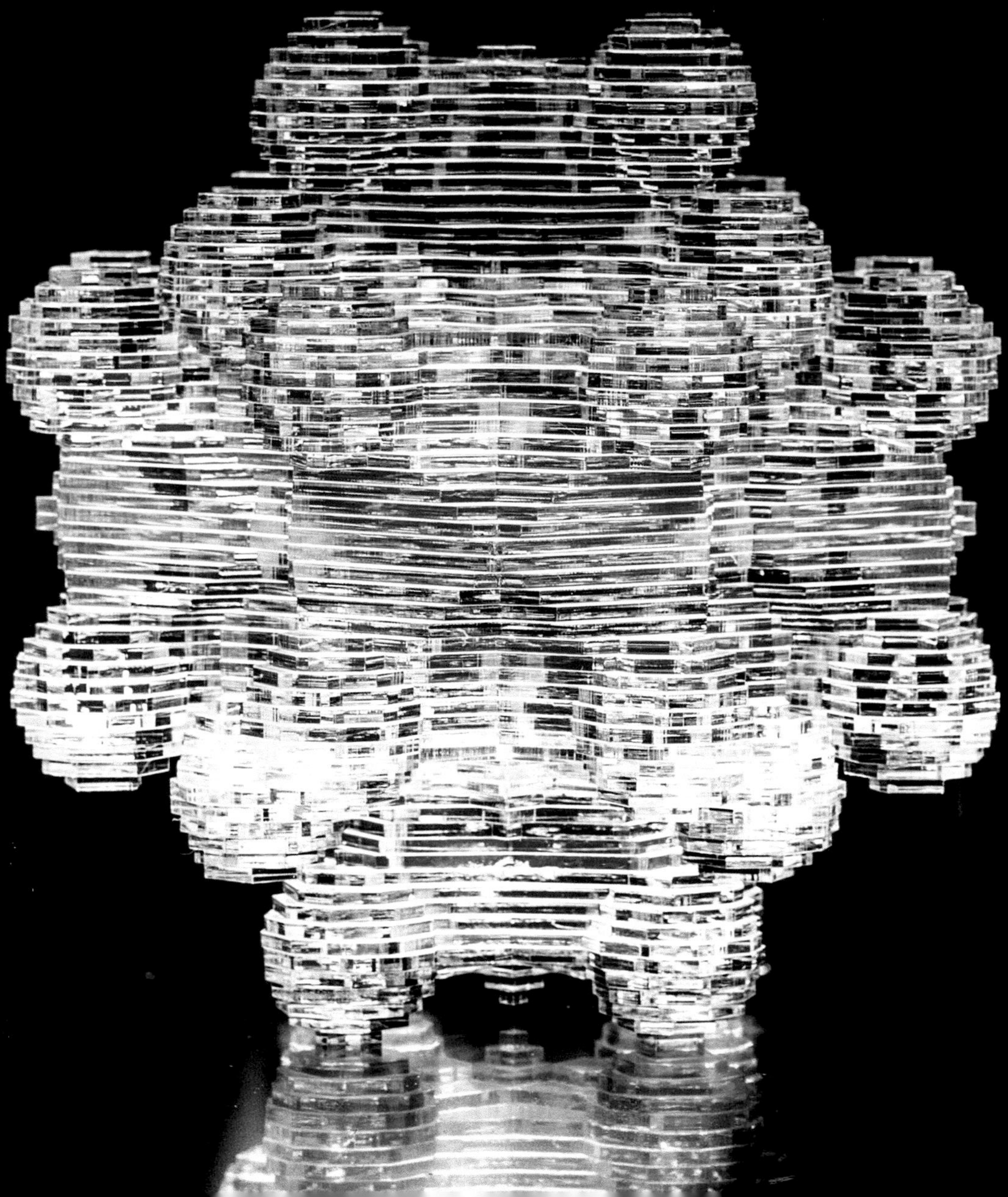

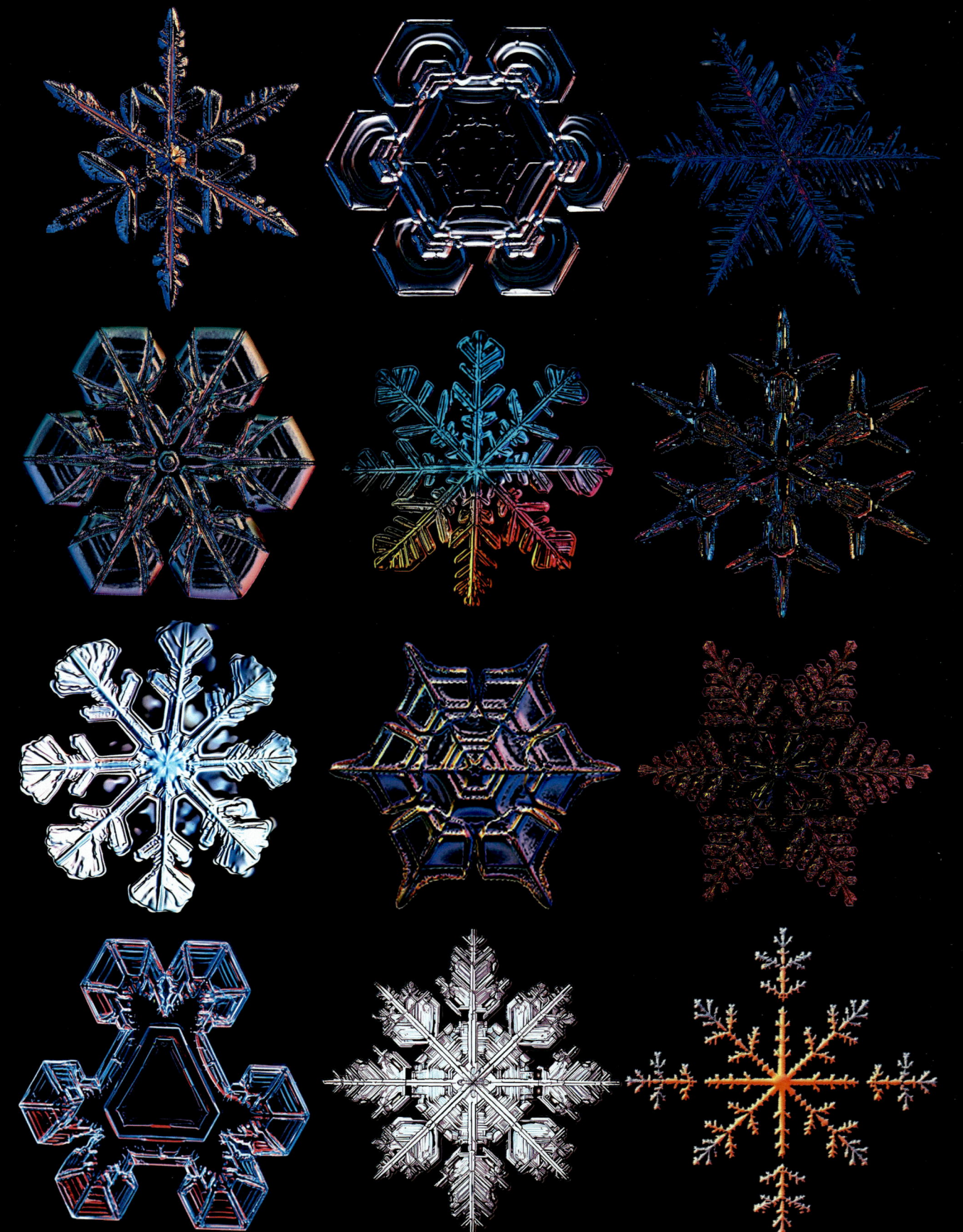

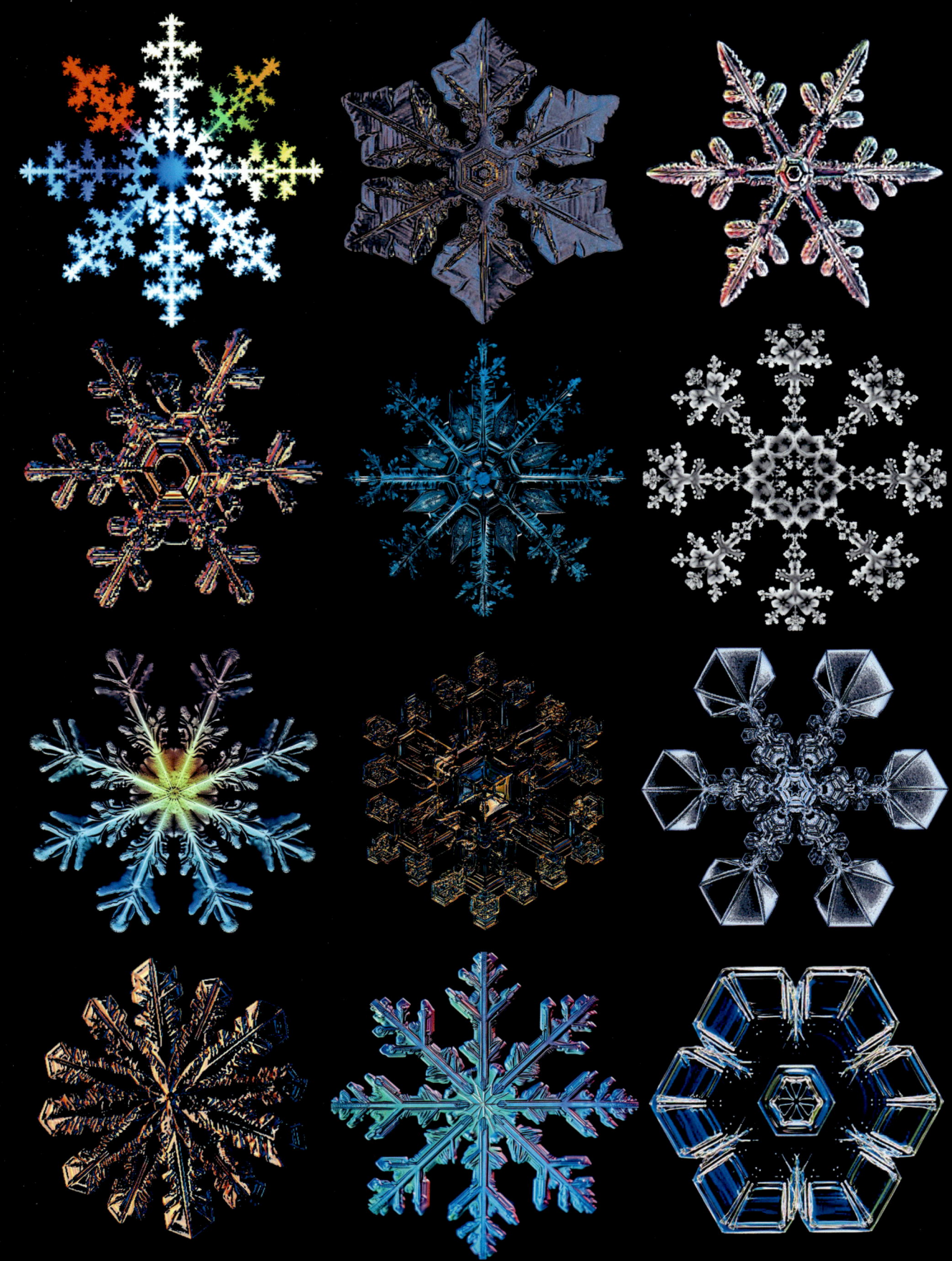

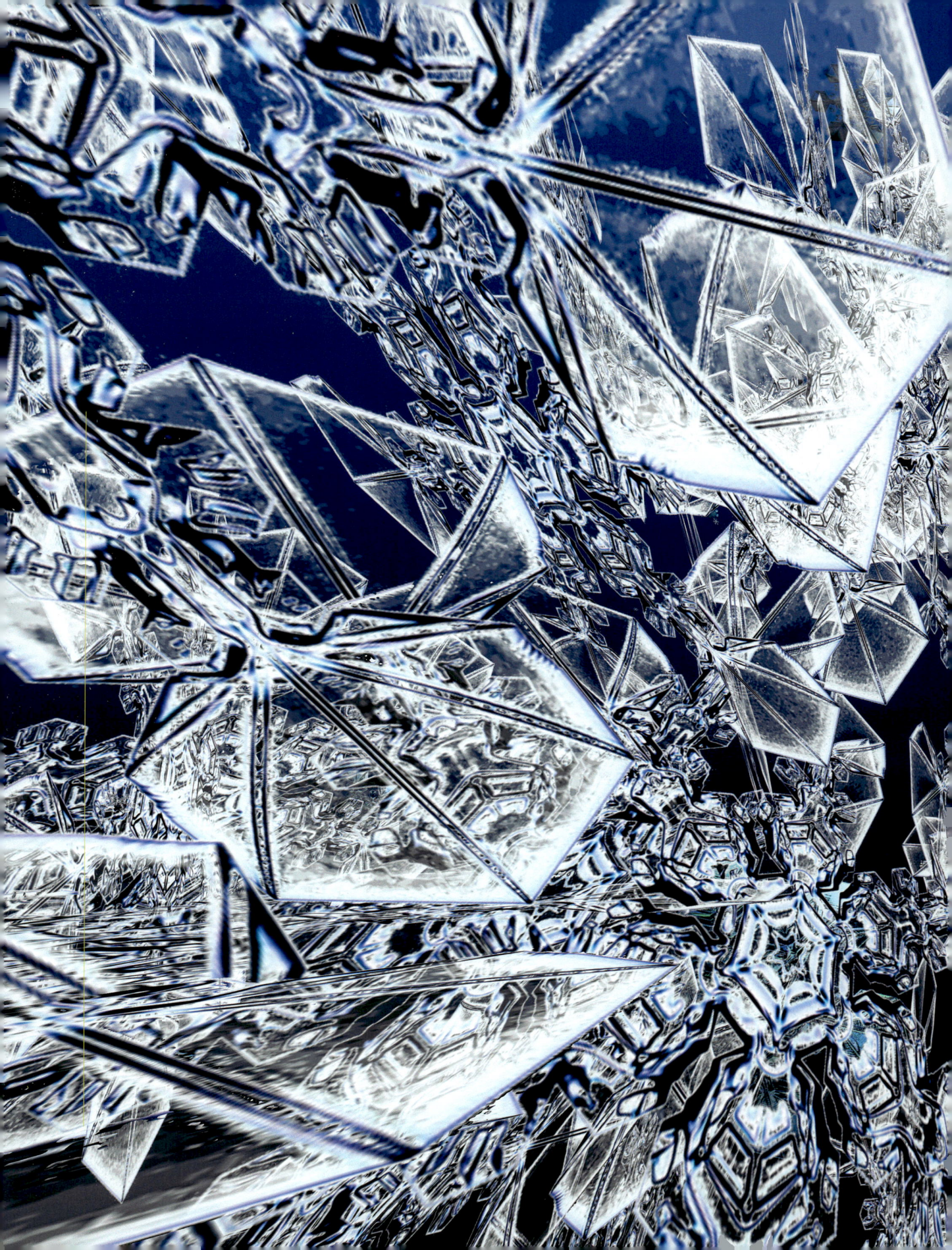

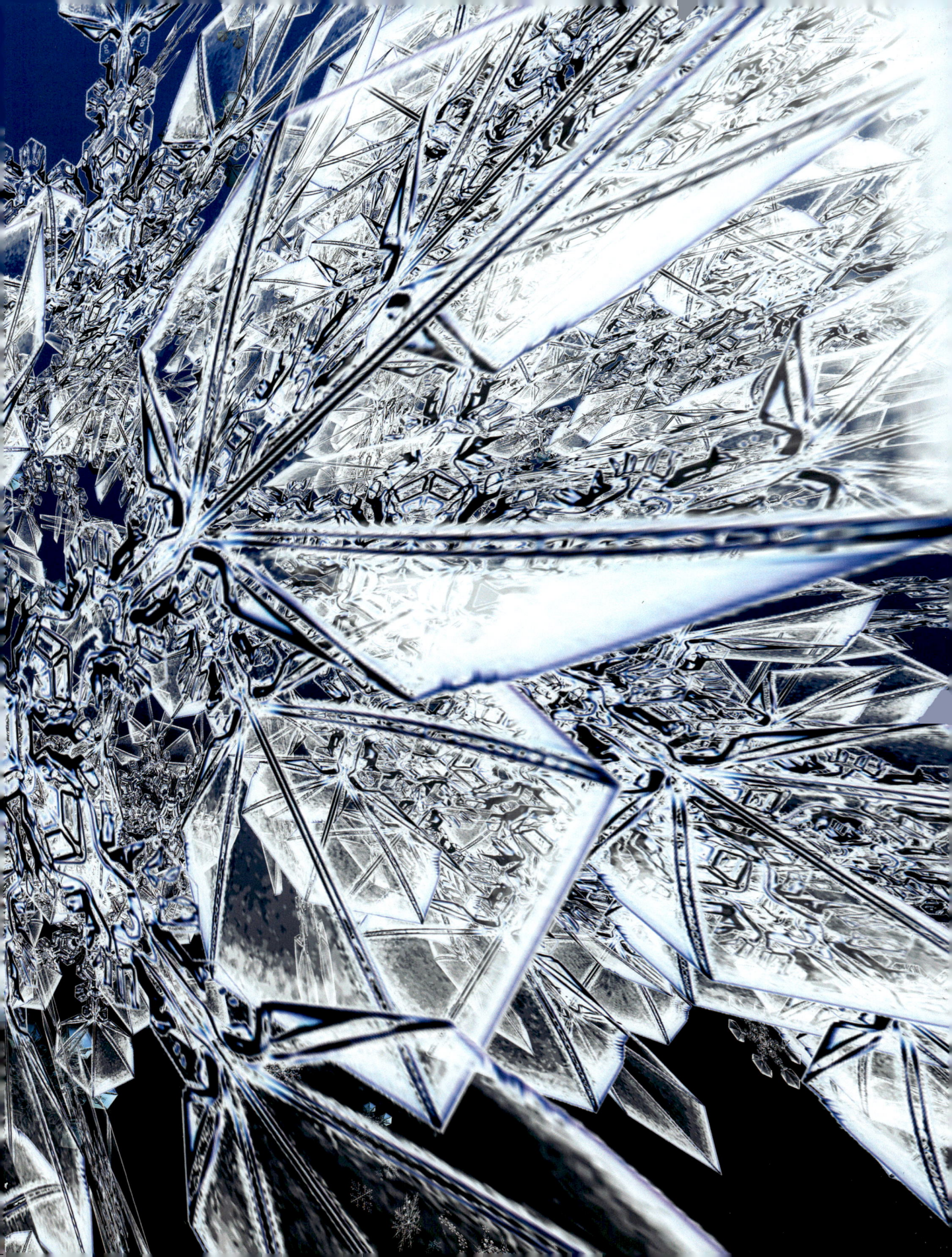

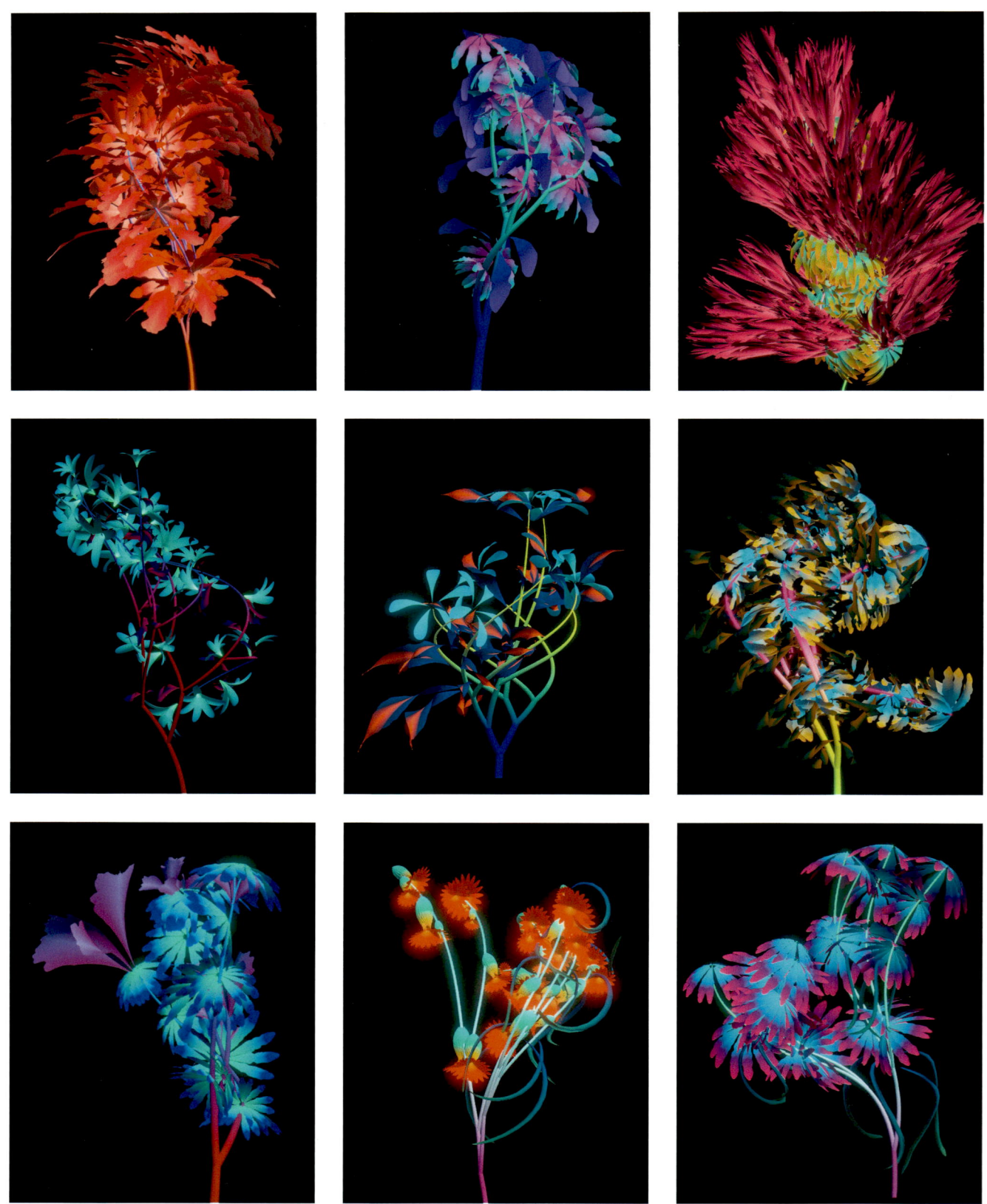

A SECRET LANGUAGE OF NATURE

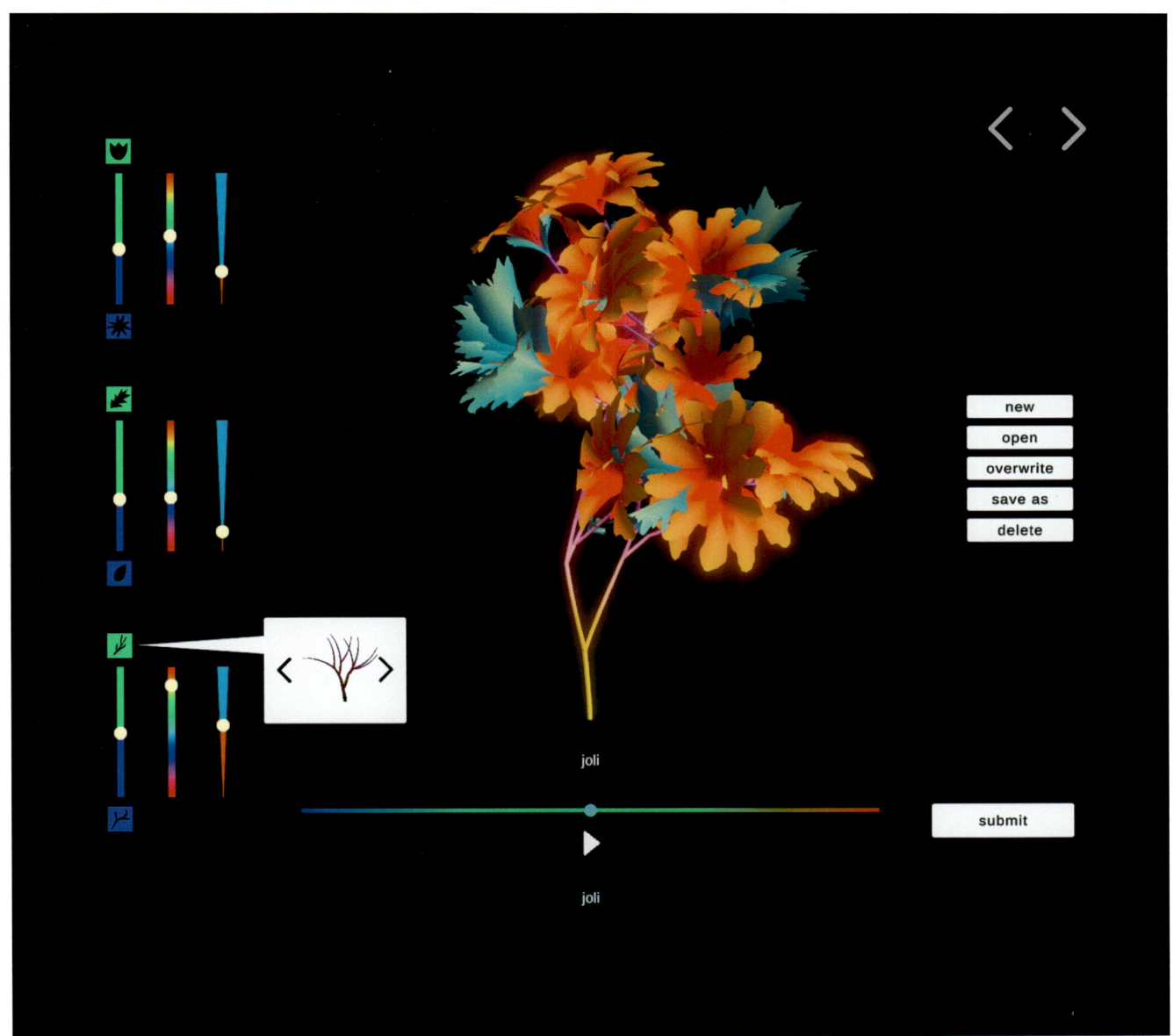

Pixel Flowers, started 2025

← DIGITAL FILES

Pixel Flowers, started 2025

WEBSITE

www.pixel-flowers.net

In Vitro Pixel Flowers is a participatory installation designed to be presented in a greenhouse. For Miguel Chevalier, the greenhouse is both an artificial space and a symbol of a controlled and protected nature. Here, it becomes a poetic laboratory of collective imagination in which the artist explores the relationship between culture, human intervention, and the manipulation of living organisms. Chevalier has long been exploring the theme of virtual gardens (see also pp. 109, 161), and with *In Vitro Pixel Flowers* he takes a new step by opening his creative process

to the public for the first time. Everyone is invited to imagine and design their own digital plants through an online interface or directly on-site at the exhibition. These individual creations are then projected within the space of the greenhouse, resulting in a collective virtual ▸ herbarium (p. 27) that forms a vast digital garden. This project goes beyond simple contemplation: it offers a shared experience of co-creation, raising questions about biodiversity, the role of humans in relation to technology, and our collective ability to invent new forms of life. (FS)

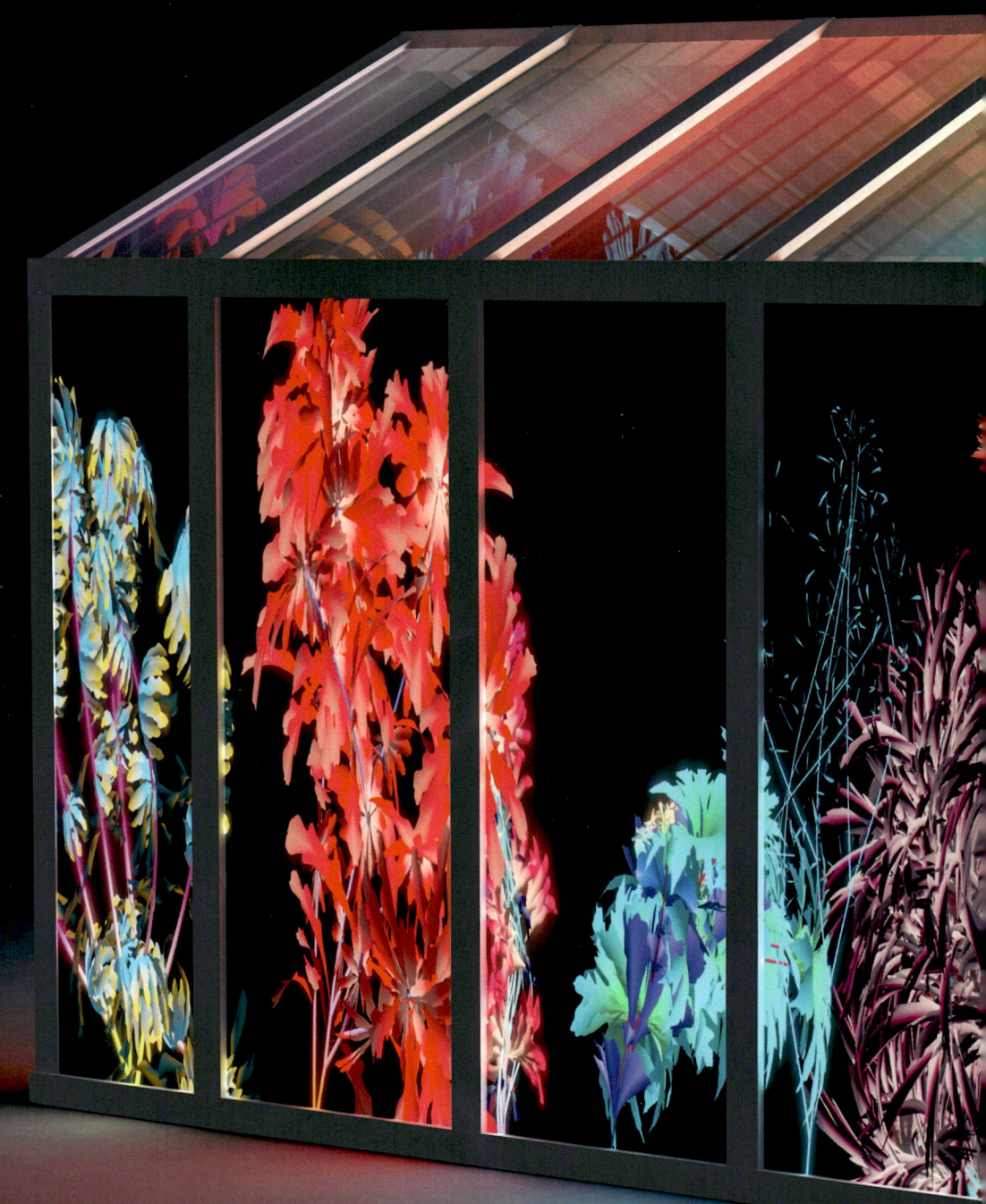

▶ VIDEO

SIMULATION

In Vitro Pixel Flowers, started 2025 ·
Generative and participative
installation in a greenhouse ·
Software: Ollie Smith,
Samuel Twidale

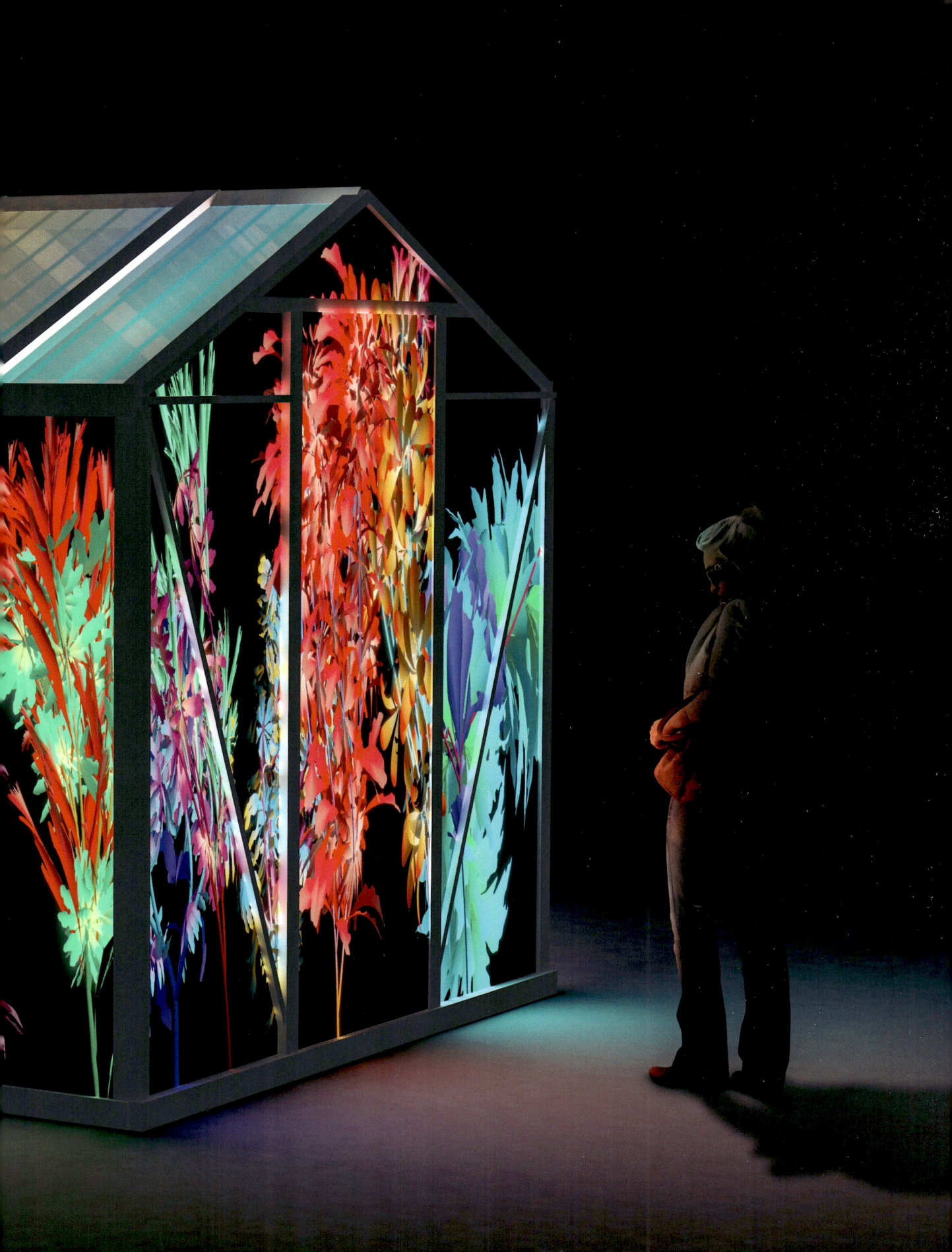

INSTALLATION

Fractal Arborescence, started 2023 · Generative and interactive installation · Dimensions variable · Software: Cyrille Henry, Antoine Villeret · Installation view, *Digital Beauty*, Ara Art Center, Seoul, South Korea, 2023

▶ VIDEO

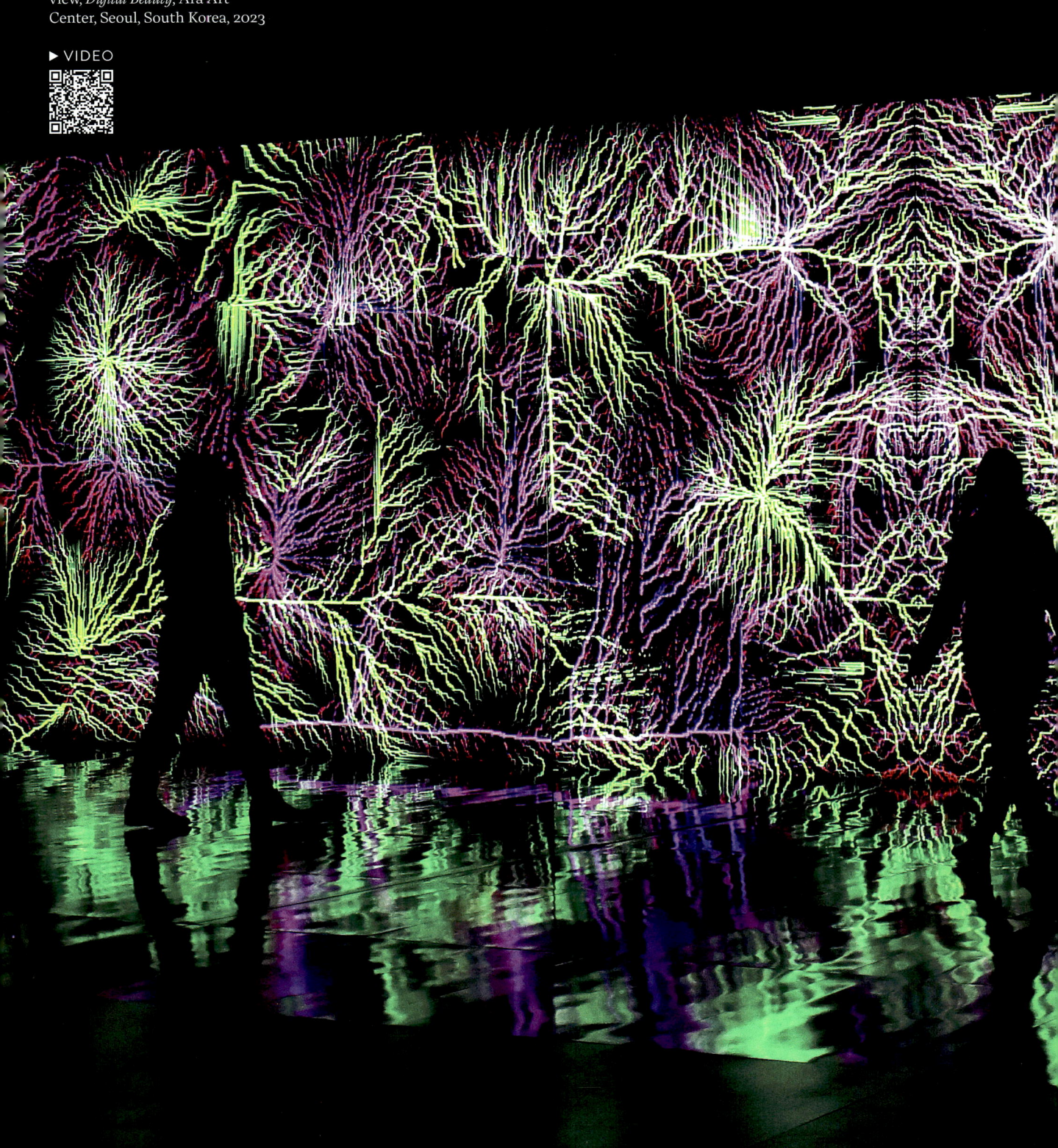

A lightning bolt is an electrostatic discharge. When it strikes wood, it leaves a burn mark whose shape can resemble trees, roots, or veins. These branching patterns caused by the flow of electrons are called Lichtenberg figures after their discoverer, physicist Georg Christoph Lichtenberg (1742–1799). Miguel Chevalier takes up this form of fractal arborescence (from the Latin *arbor*, "tree"). The installation changes randomly and reacts to the visitor's interactions—creating ever new, multicolored, luminous structures. The work visualizes the energy of these movements and thus pays homage to the natural phenomenon of lightning while also evoking the circulation of blood in living organisms. (JG)

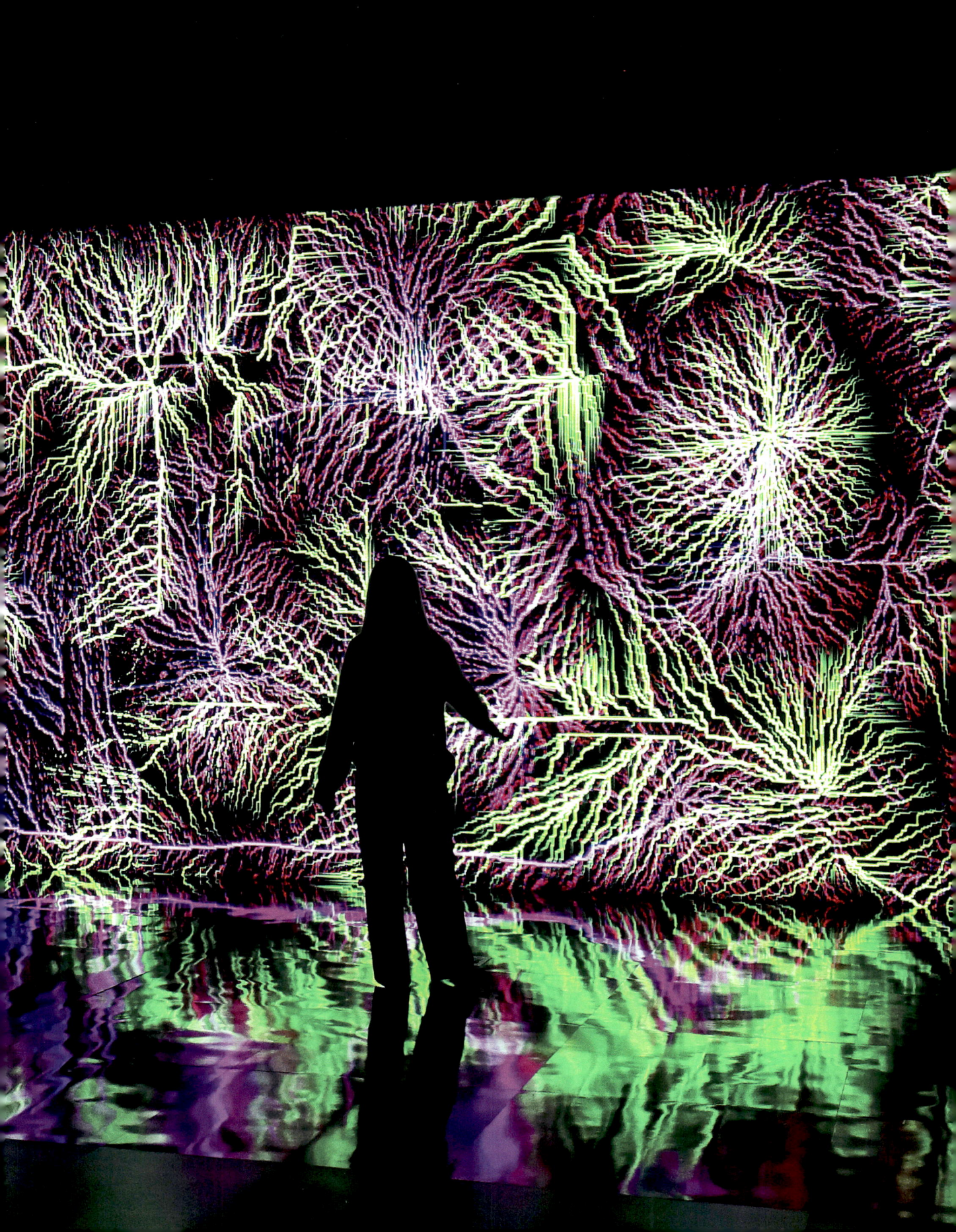

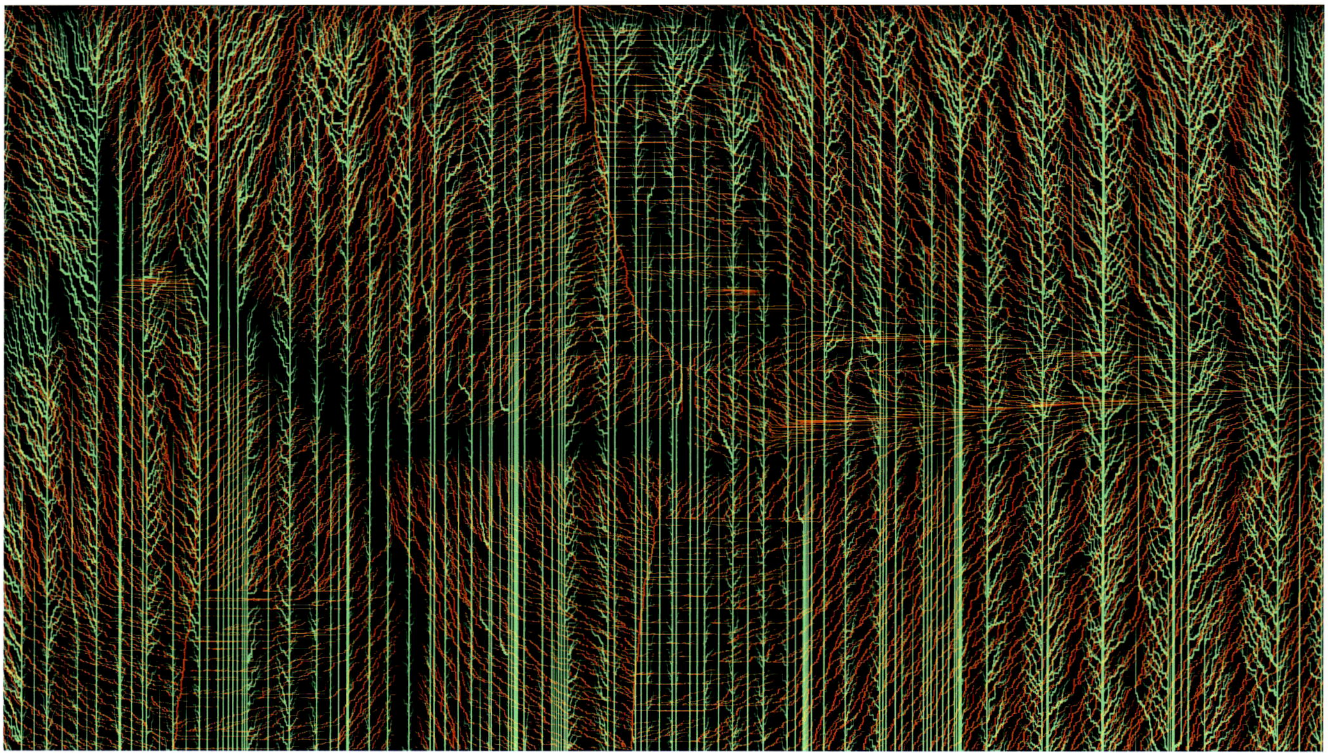

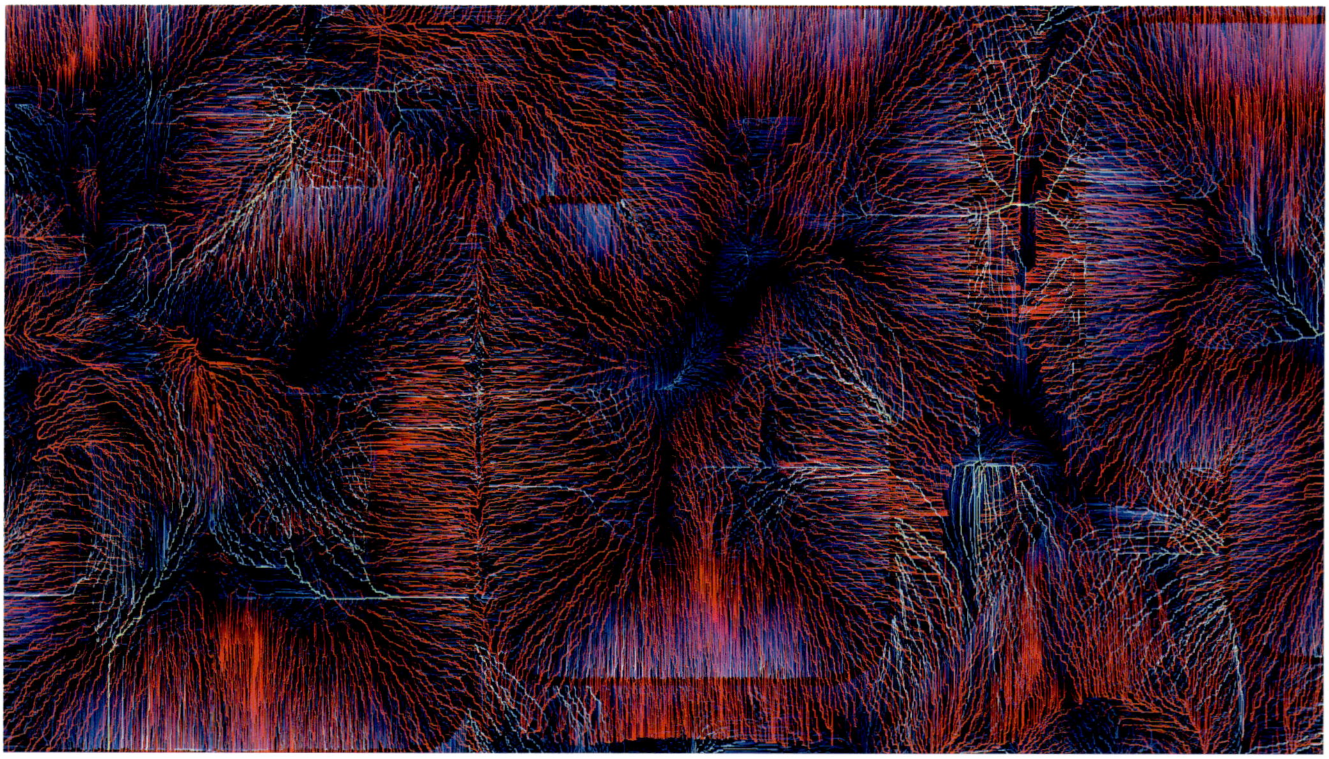

PATTERNS

Fractal Arborescence, started 2023

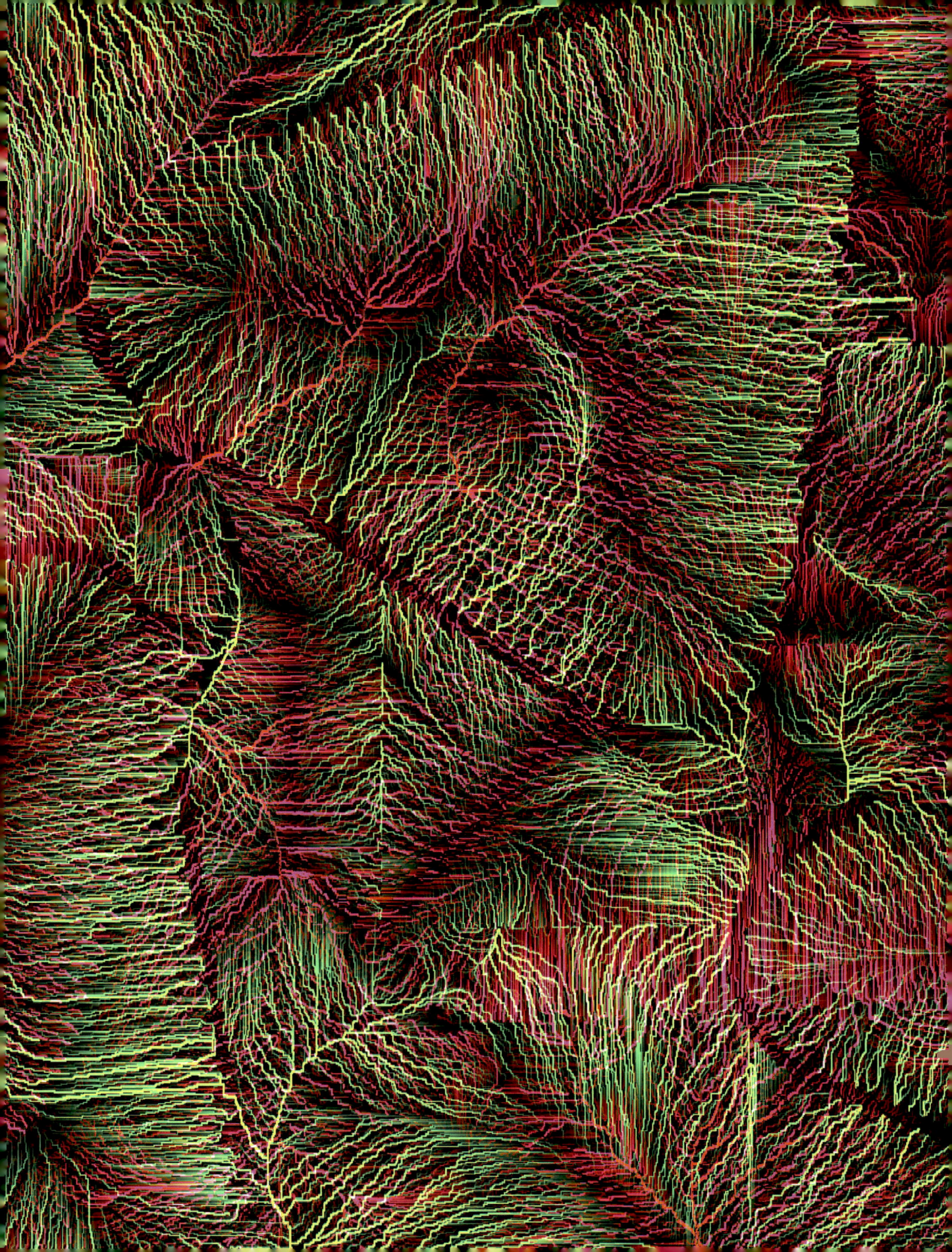

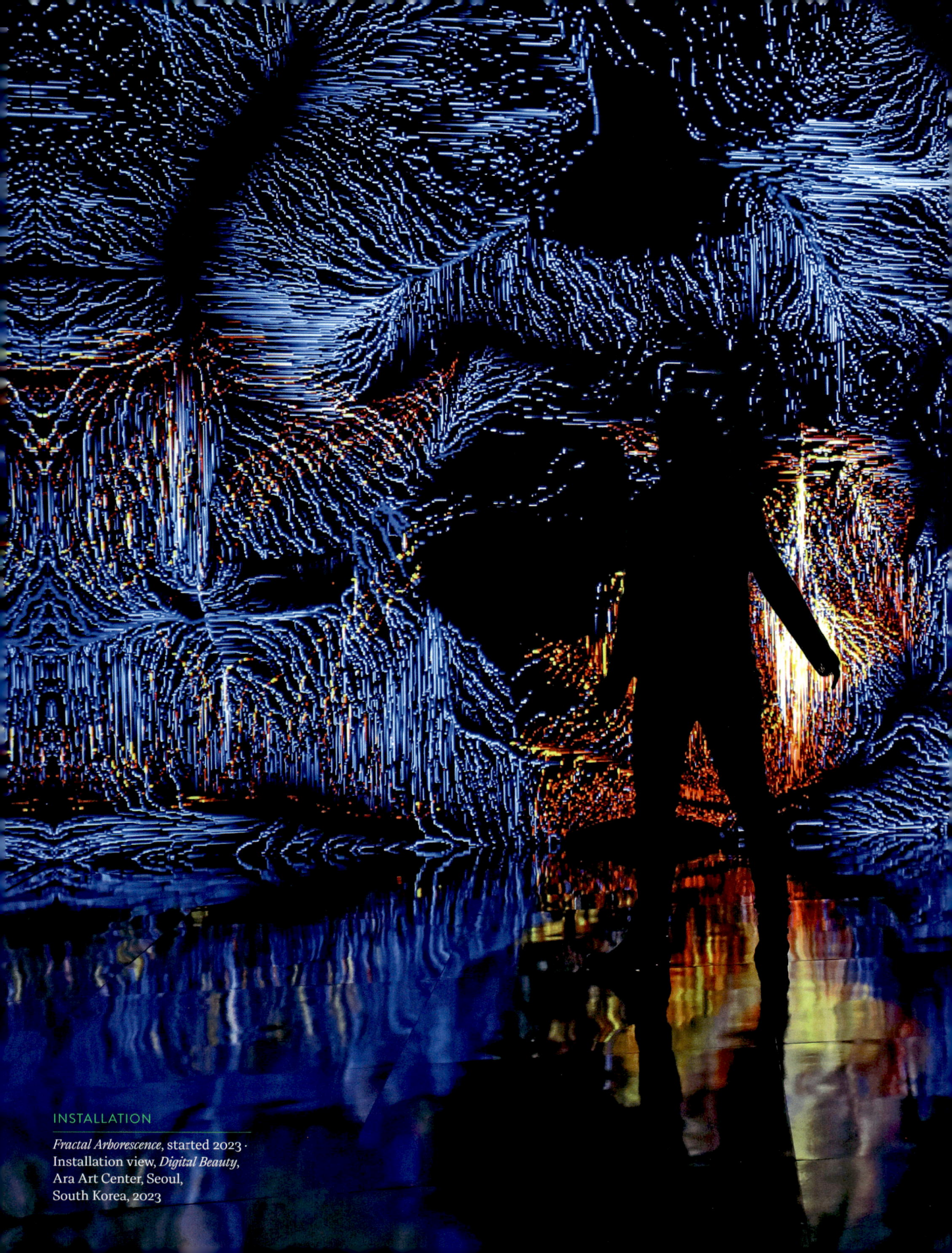

INSTALLATION

Fractal Arborescence, started 2023 ·
Installation view, *Digital Beauty*,
Ara Art Center, Seoul,
South Korea, 2023

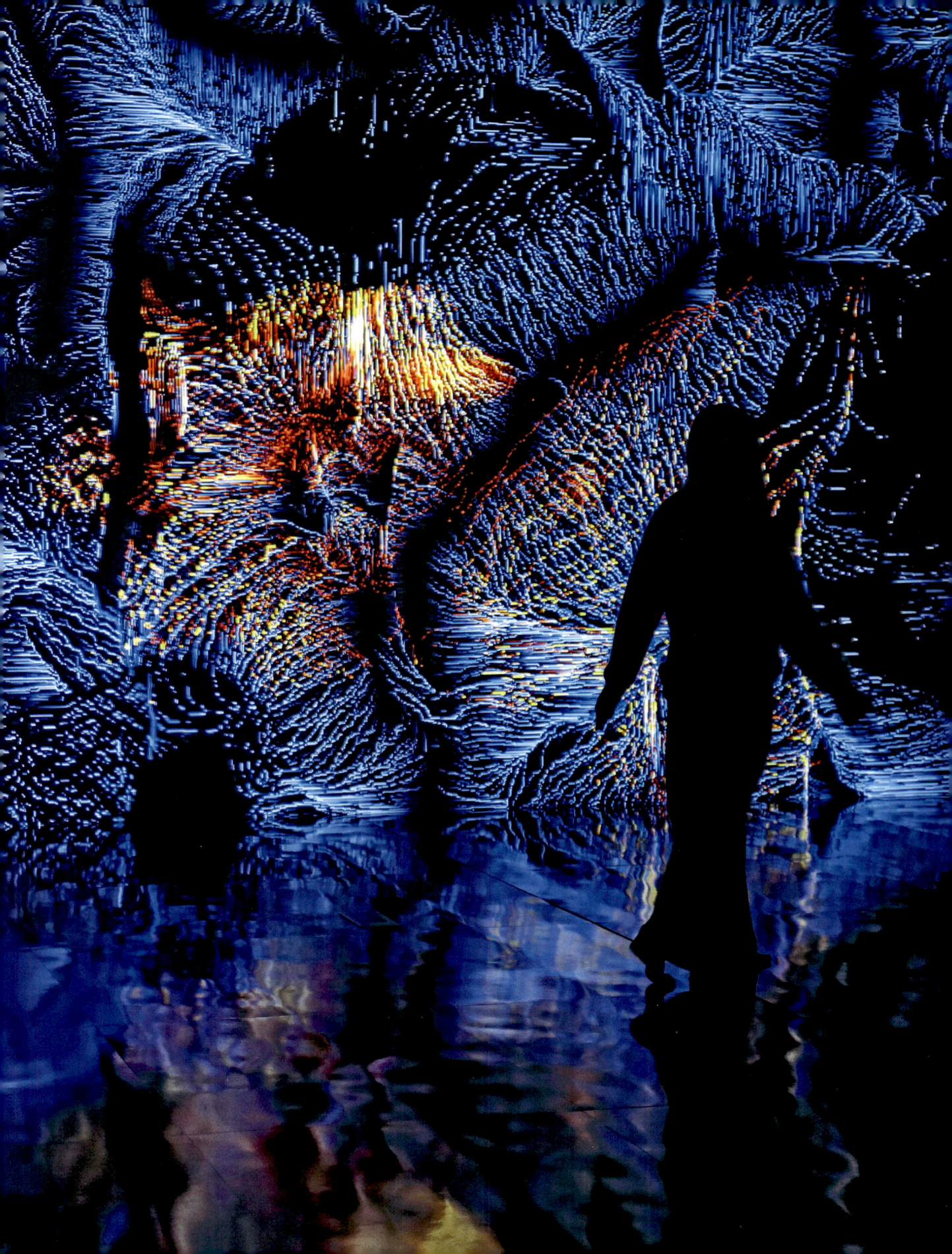

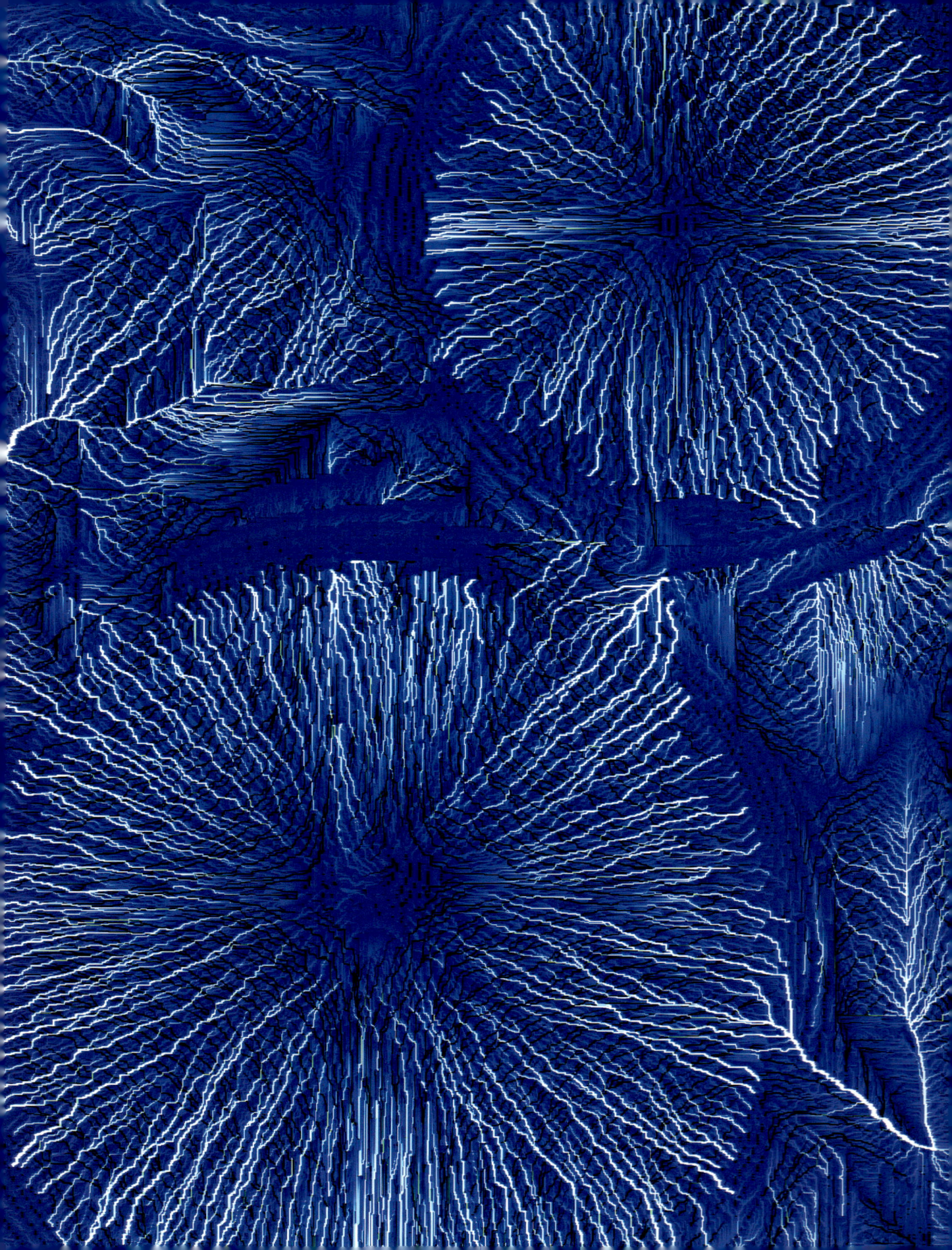

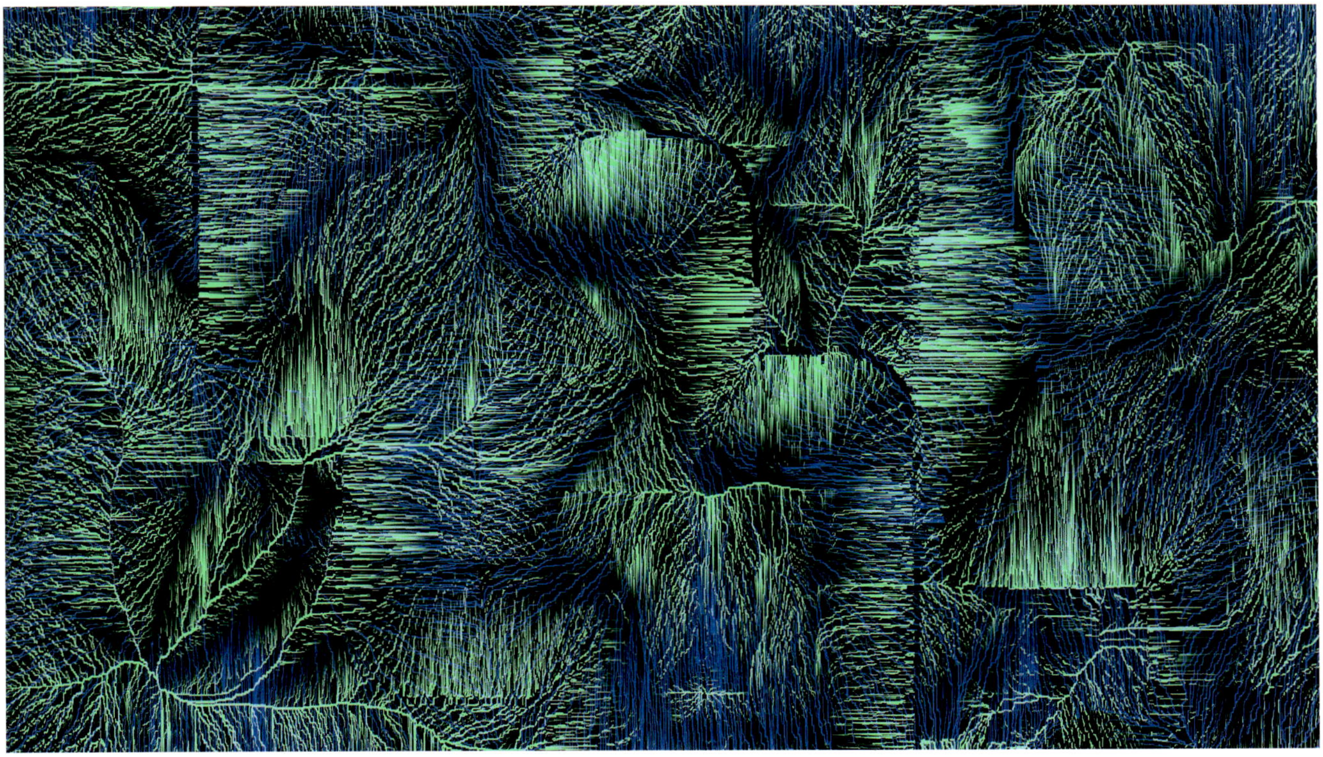

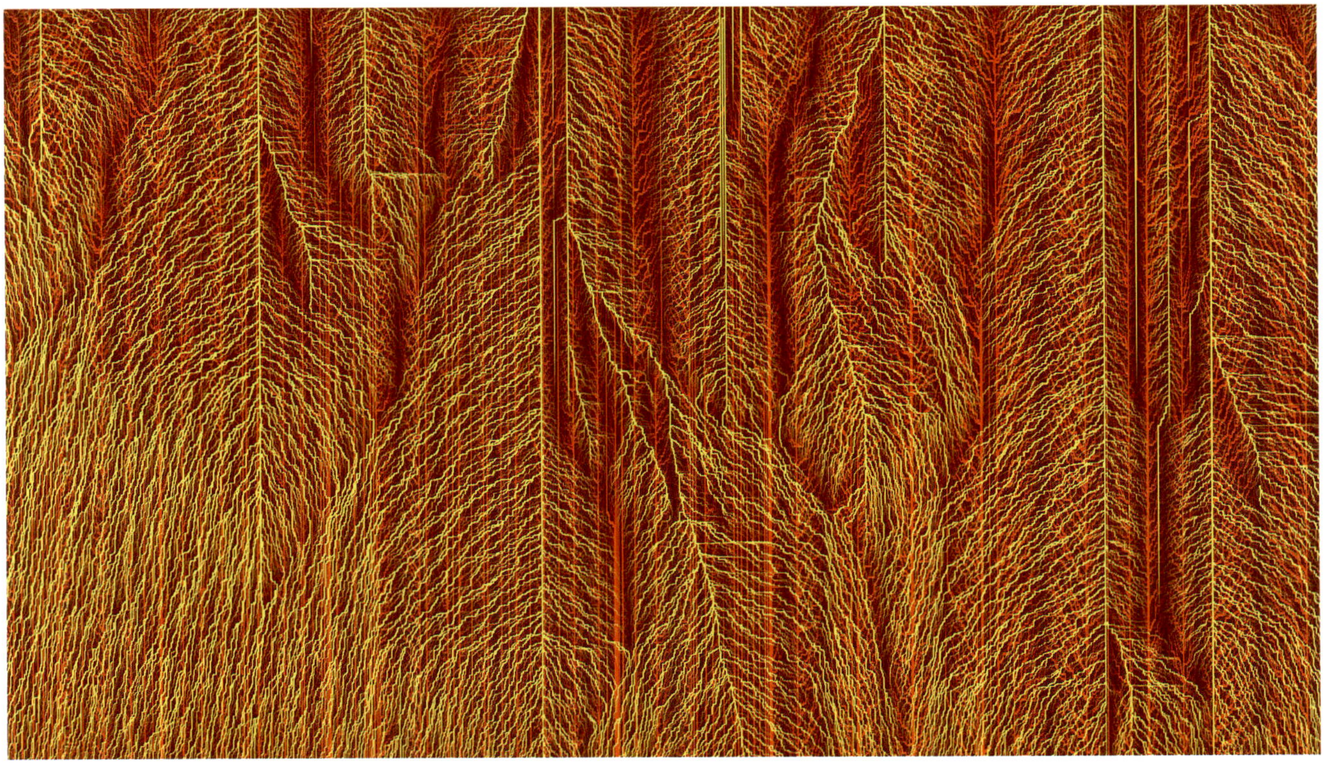

PATTERNS

Fractal Arborescence, started 2023

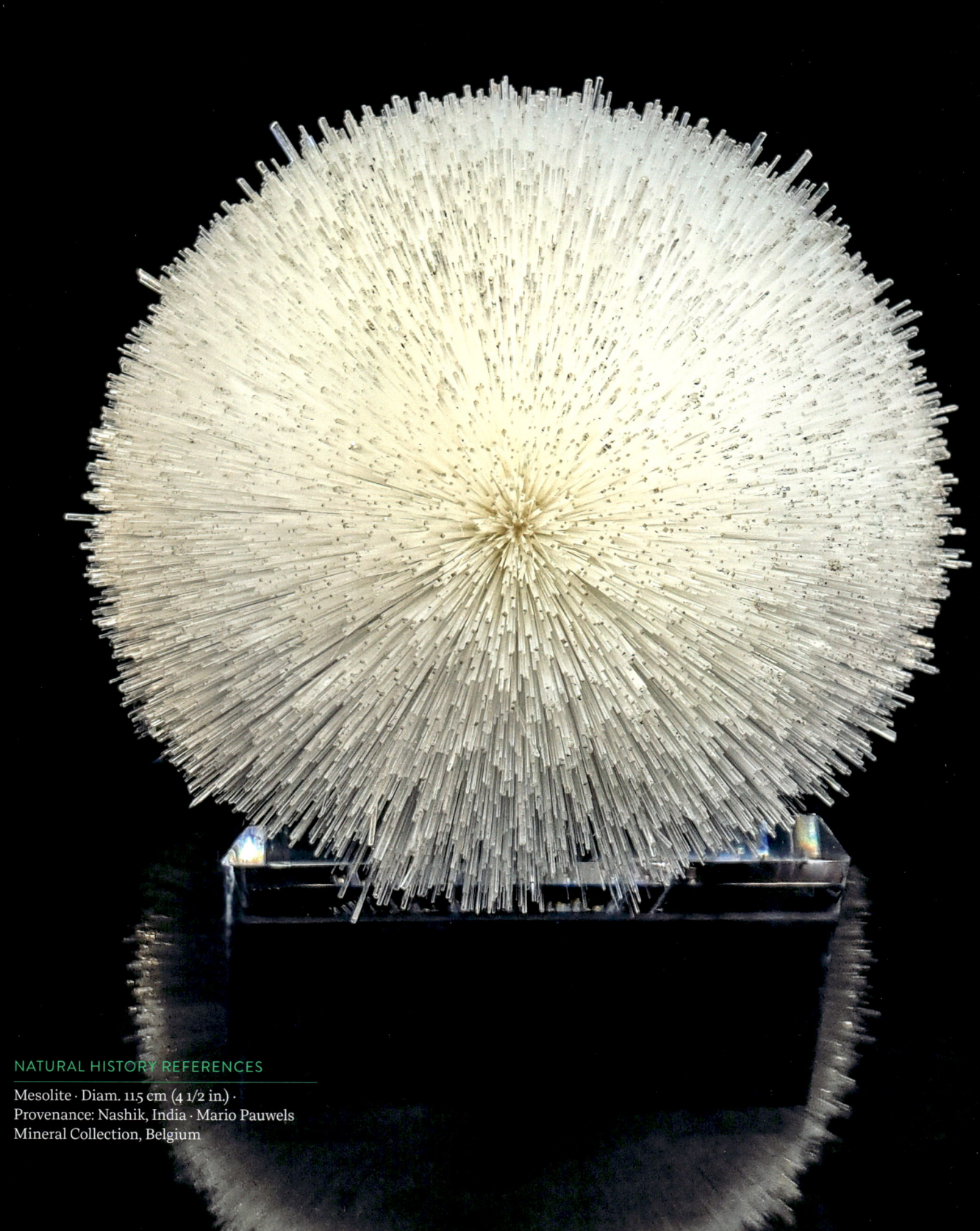

Mesolite · Diam. 11.5 cm (4 1/2 in.) ·
Provenance: Nashik, India · Mario Pauwels
Mineral Collection, Belgium

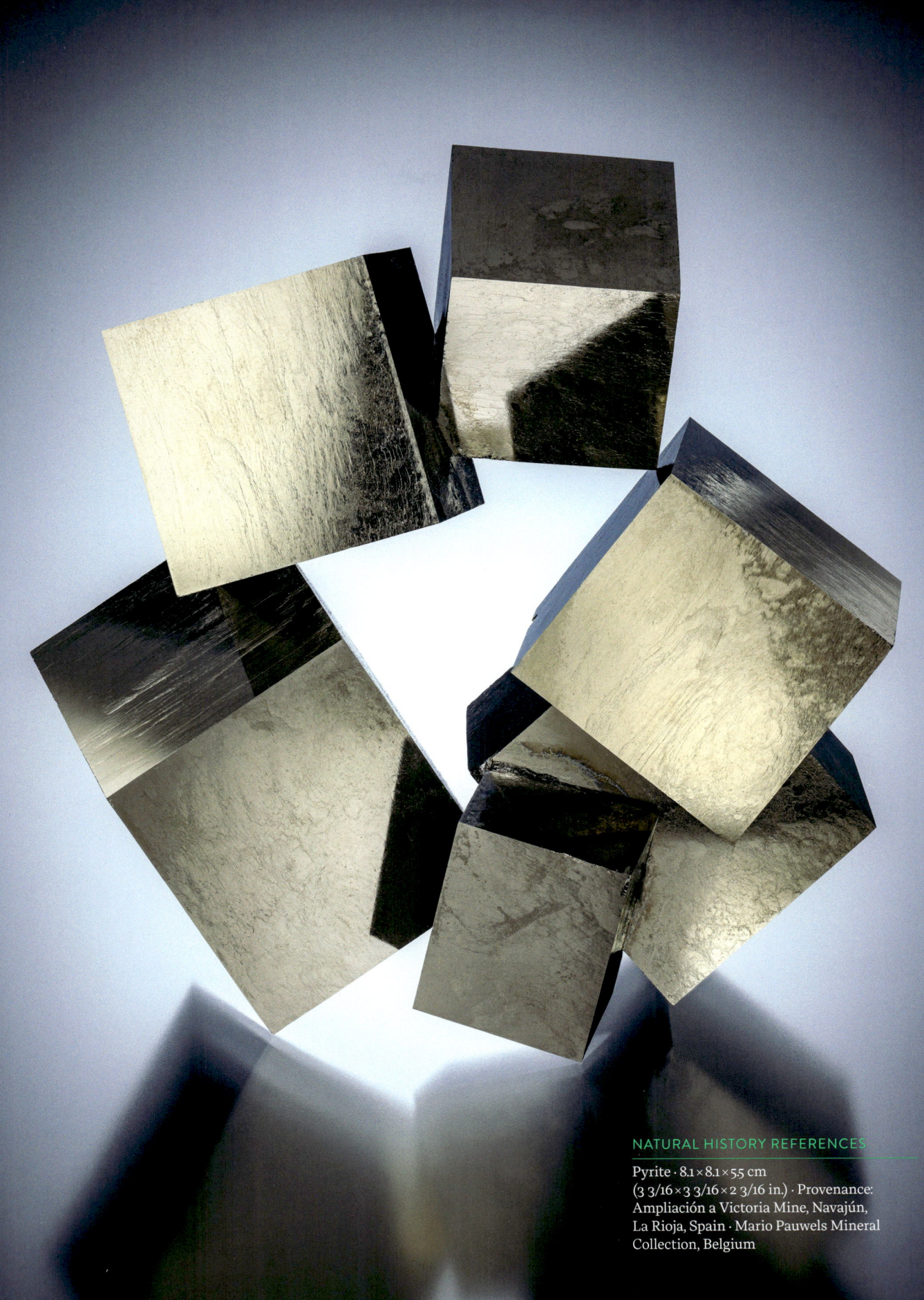

NATURAL HISTORY REFERENCES

Pyrite · 8.1 × 8.1 × 5.5 cm
(3 3/16 × 3 3/16 × 2 3/16 in.) · Provenance:
Ampliación a Victoria Mine, Navajún,
La Rioja, Spain · Mario Pauwels Mineral
Collection, Belgium

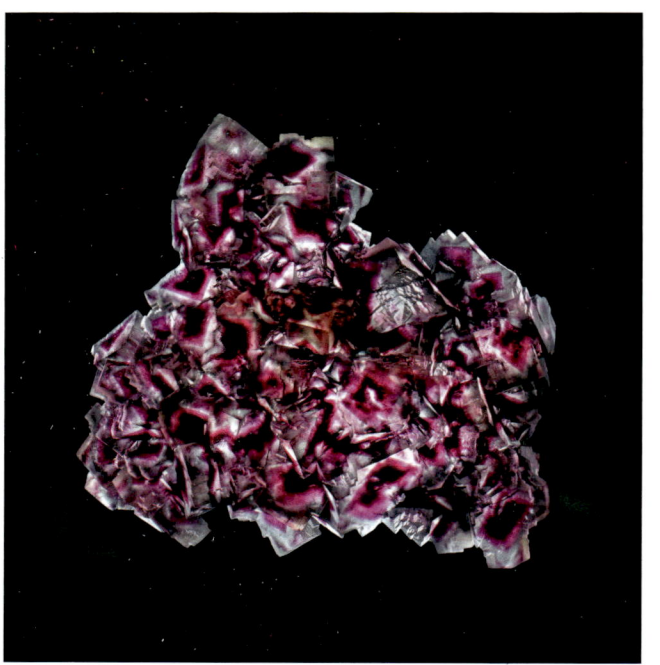

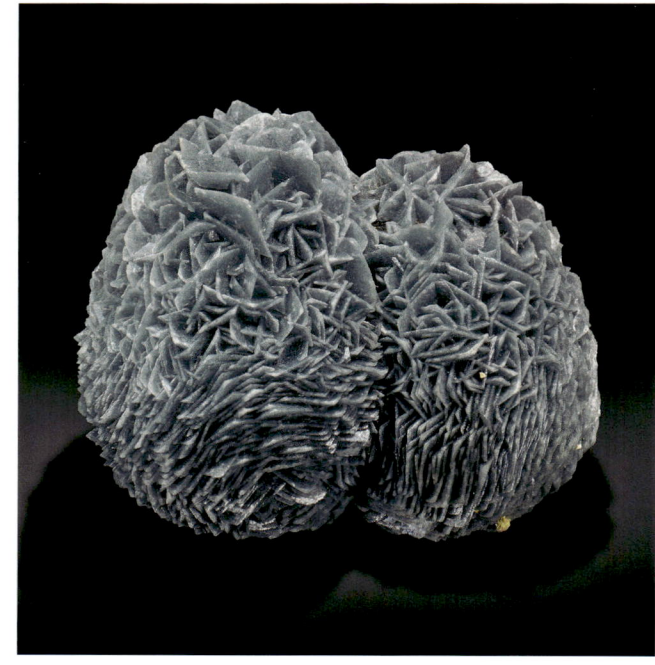

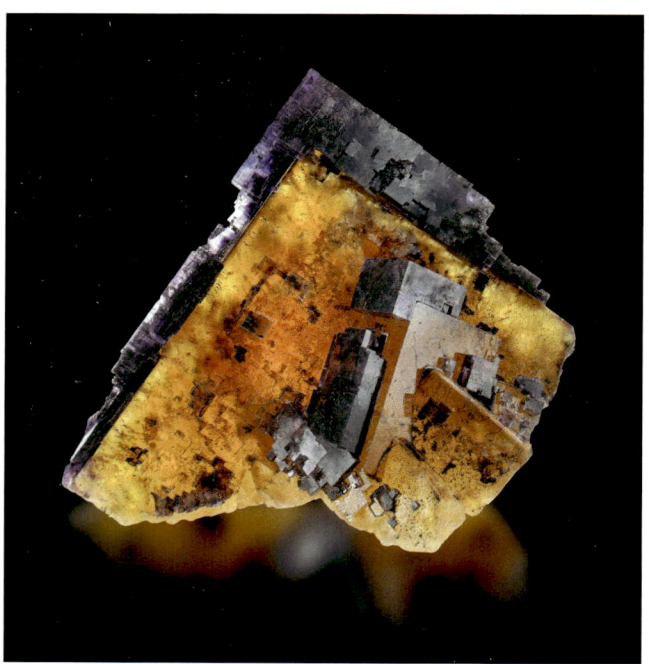

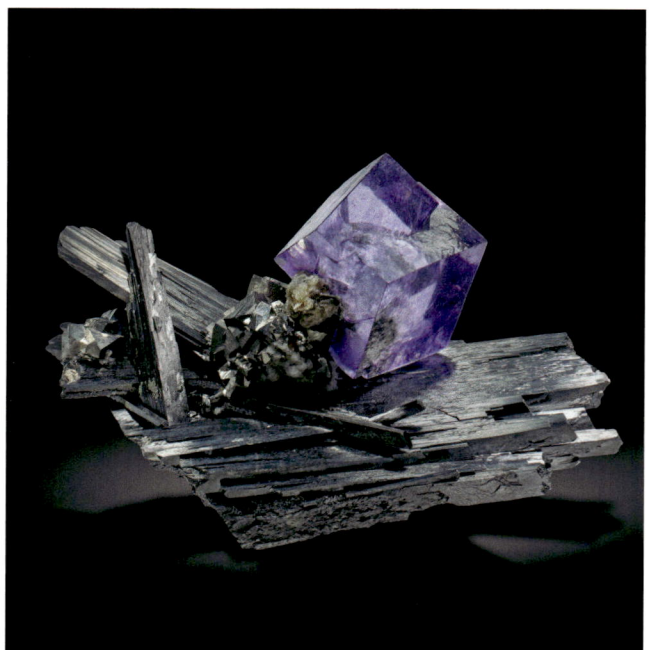

NATURAL HISTORY REFERENCES

Top: Fluorite · 23 × 20 × 16.5 cm
(9 × 7 7/8 × 6 1/2 in.) · Provenance: Okoruso
Mine, Otjiwarango District, Namibia ·
Bottom: Fluorite on Fluorite · 14 × 12 × 8 cm
(5 1/2 × 4 3/4 × 3 1/8 in.) · Provenance: Minerva
no. 1 Mine, Cave-in-Rock, Illinois, USA ·
Mario Pauwels Mineral Collection, Belgium

NATURAL HISTORY REFERENCES

Top: Calcite · 9.3 × 7.8 × 7.5 cm (3 11/16 × 3 ×
2 15/16 in.) · Provenance: Herja Mine,
Romania · Bottom: Fluorite / Wolframite /
Pyrite · 6 × 9.5 × 5 cm (2 3/8 × 3 3/4 × 2 in.) ·
Provenance: Yaogangxian Mine, Hunan,
China · Mario Pauwels Mineral Collection,
Belgium

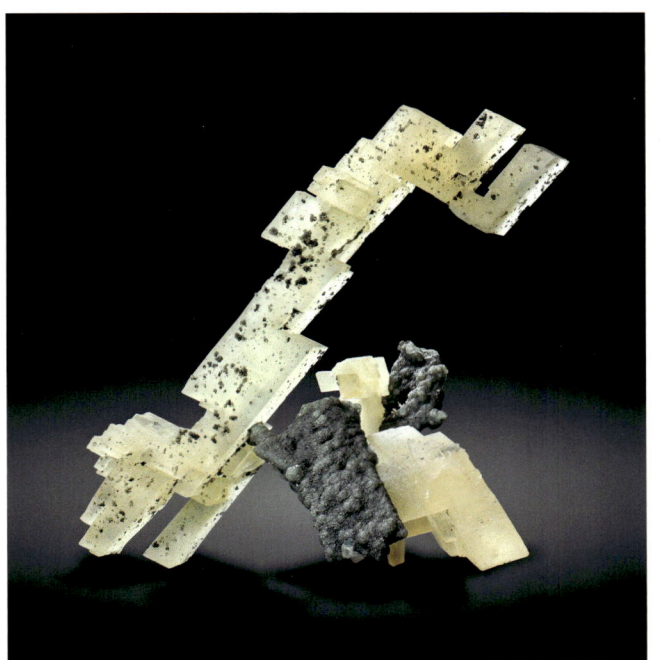

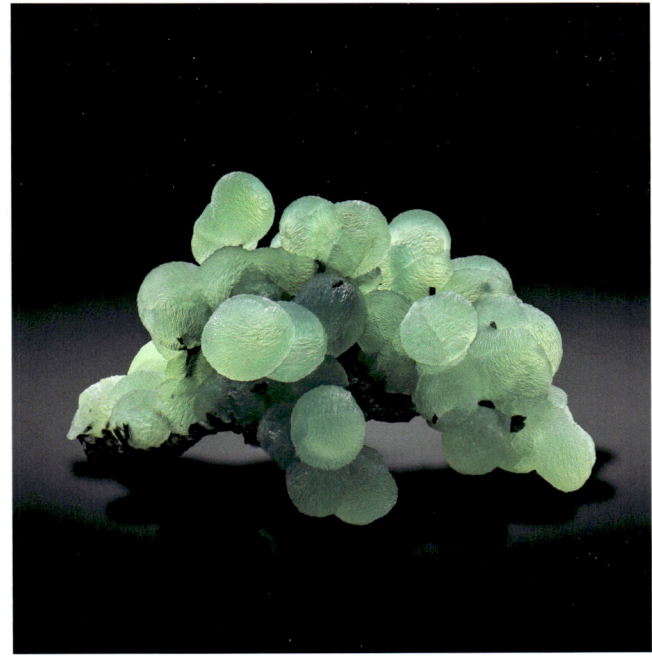

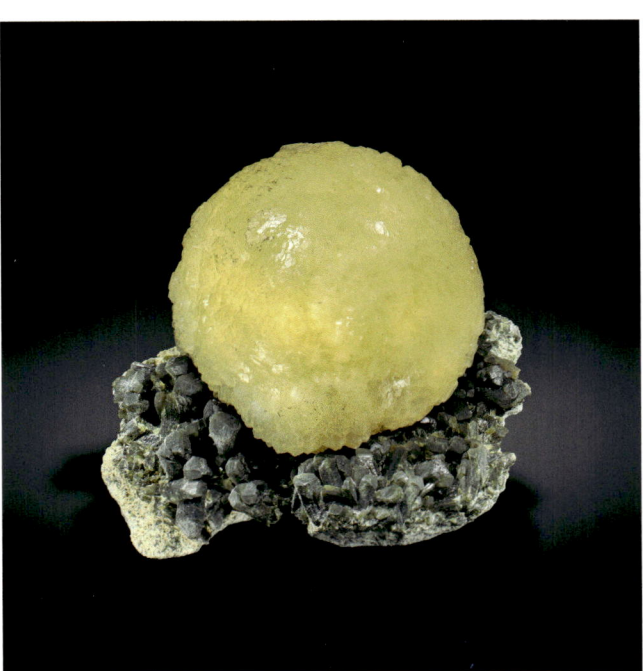

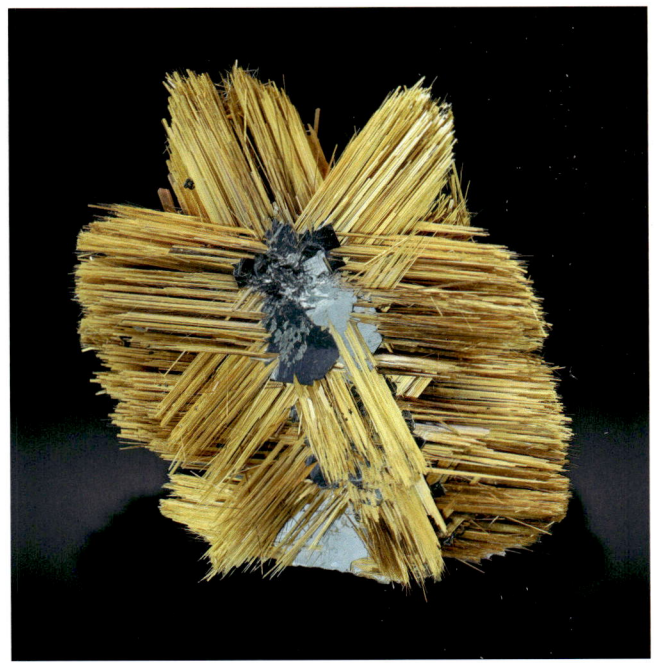

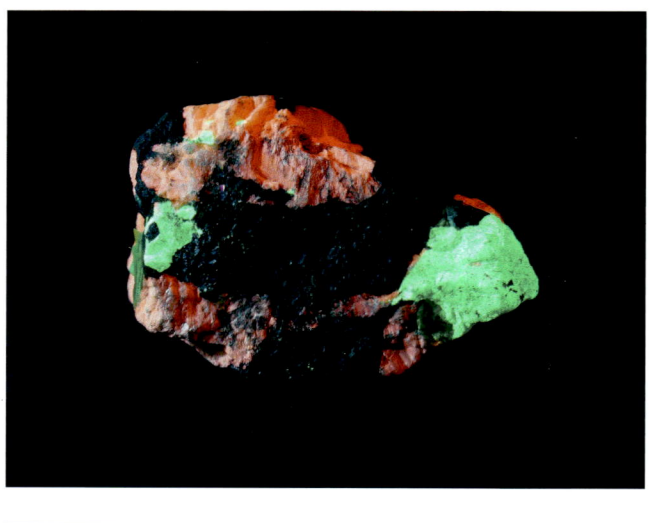 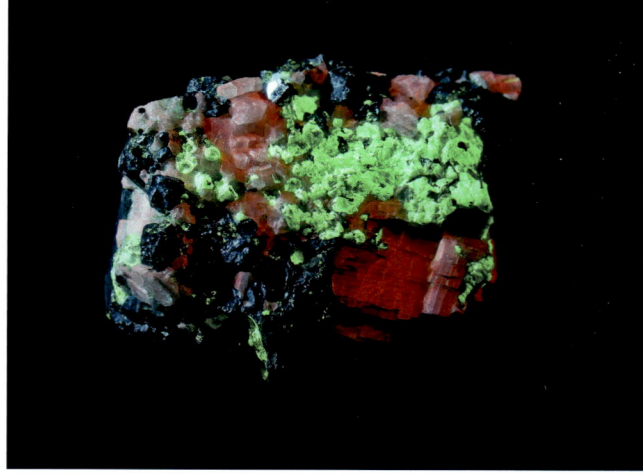

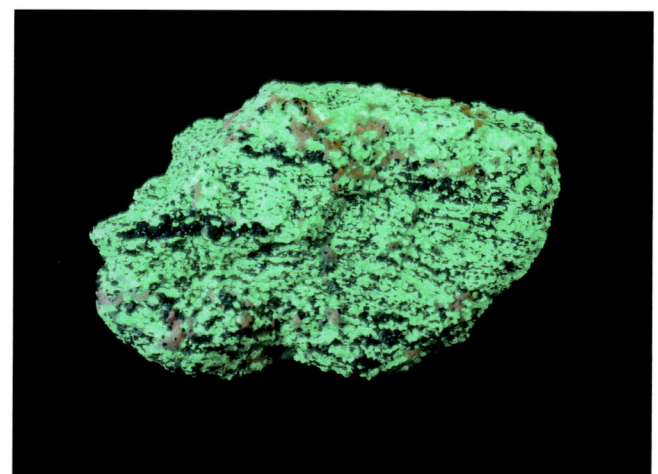 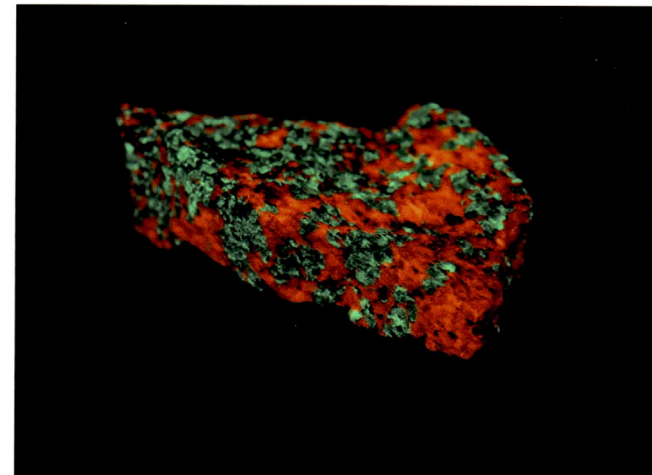

Miguel Chevalier draws upon ▸ minerals (p. 28) and ▸ crystals (p. 26) as an inexhaustible reservoir of inspiration for shapes and colors, especially in his series *Digital Crystals* (started 2018; pp. 134–39) and *Fractal Flowers* (started 2008; pp. 108, 110–21). He also has a strong interest in the effects of fluorescence, the phenomenon by which a mineral is irradiated with ultraviolet light and then re-emits the light at a different wavelength: Willemite shines in green, for example, and Calcite in red. (FS)

In 1904, natural scientist and artist Ernst Haeckel (1834–1919) published *Kunstformen der Natur (Art Forms in Nature)*, a portfolio of one hundred plates that enabled a wide audience to have a visual experience of microorganisms and other forms of marine life. The lithographs, based on Haeckel's drawings, were realized by Adolf Giltsch (1852–1911), who had collaborated with Haeckel for over four decades. In these artistic yet scientifically precise illustrations, the symmetrical and fractal structures of radiolaria, corals, algae, shells, and other ocean phenomena stand out particularly clearly. Haeckel's achievement is an important inspiration for Miguel Chevalier's works addressing the underwater world. (JG)

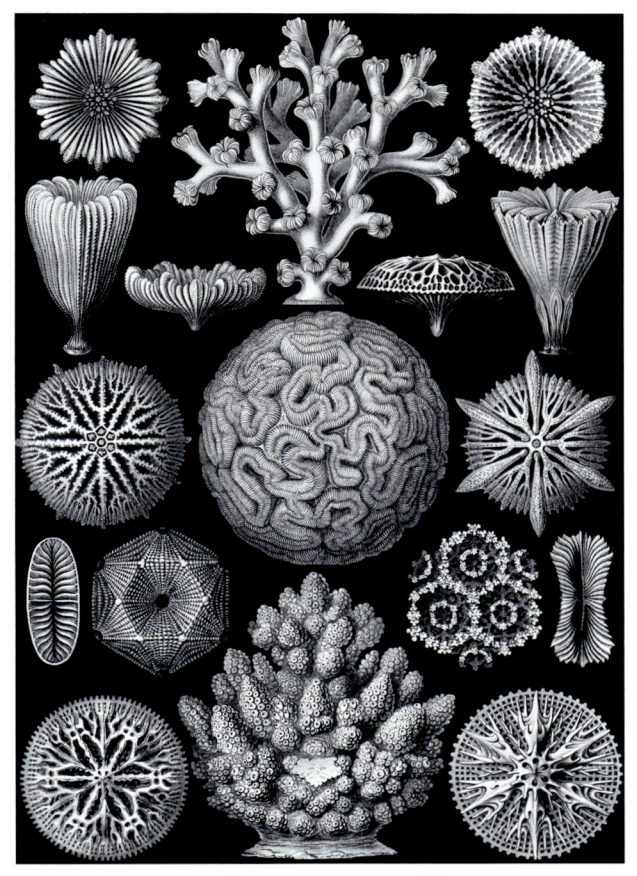

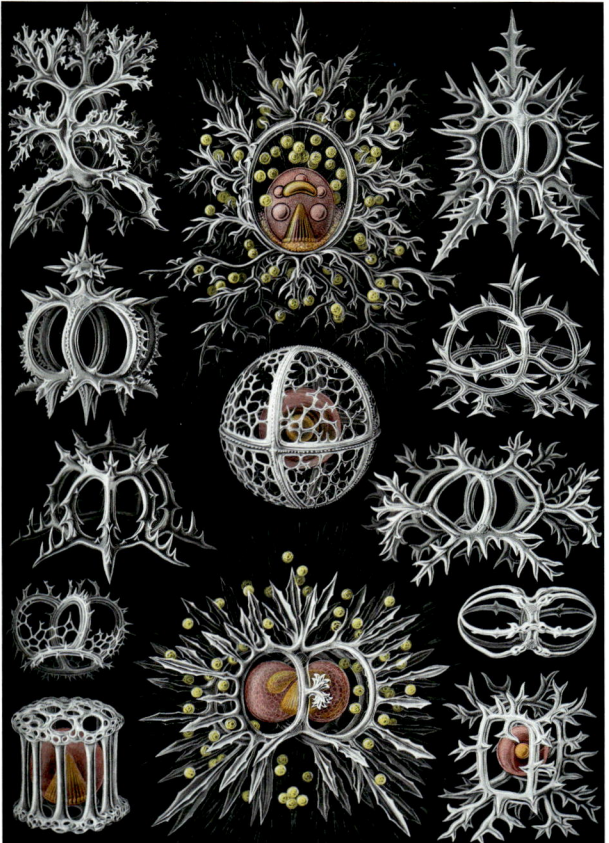

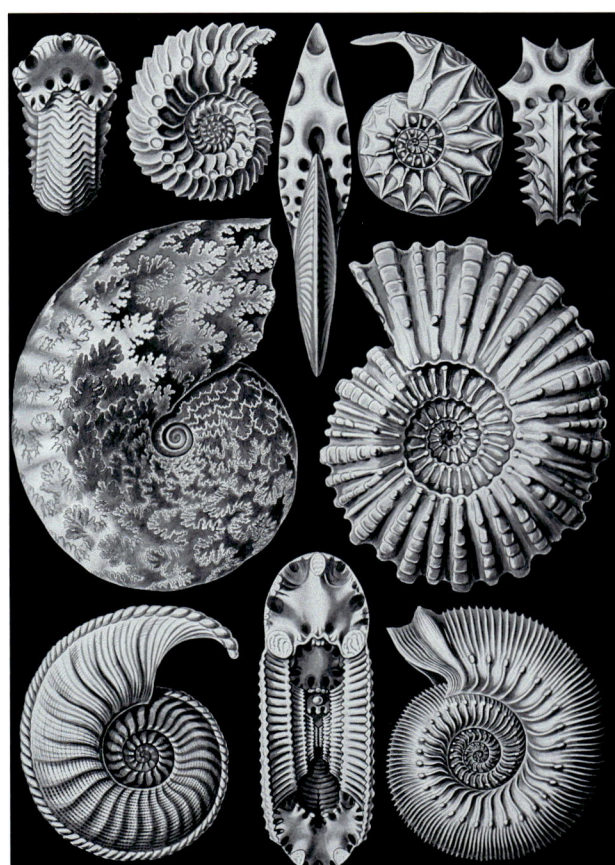

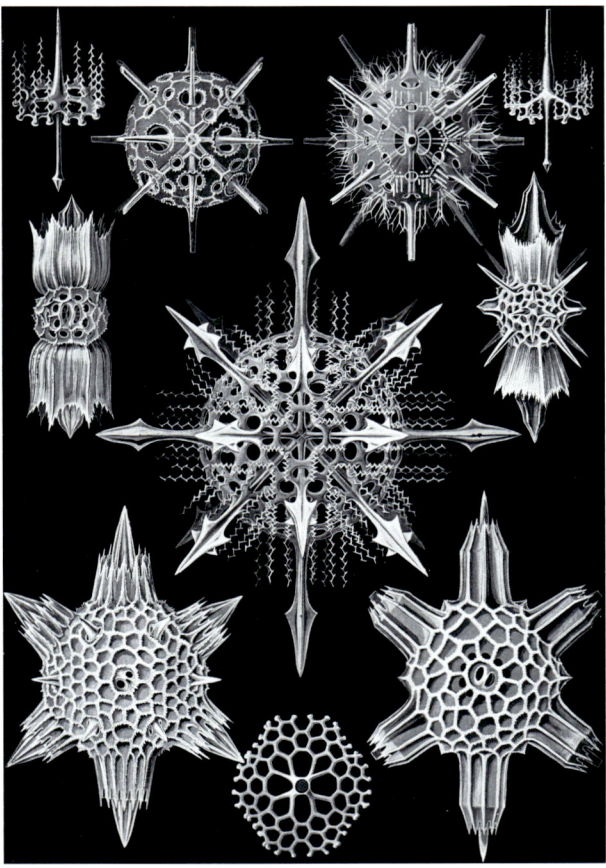

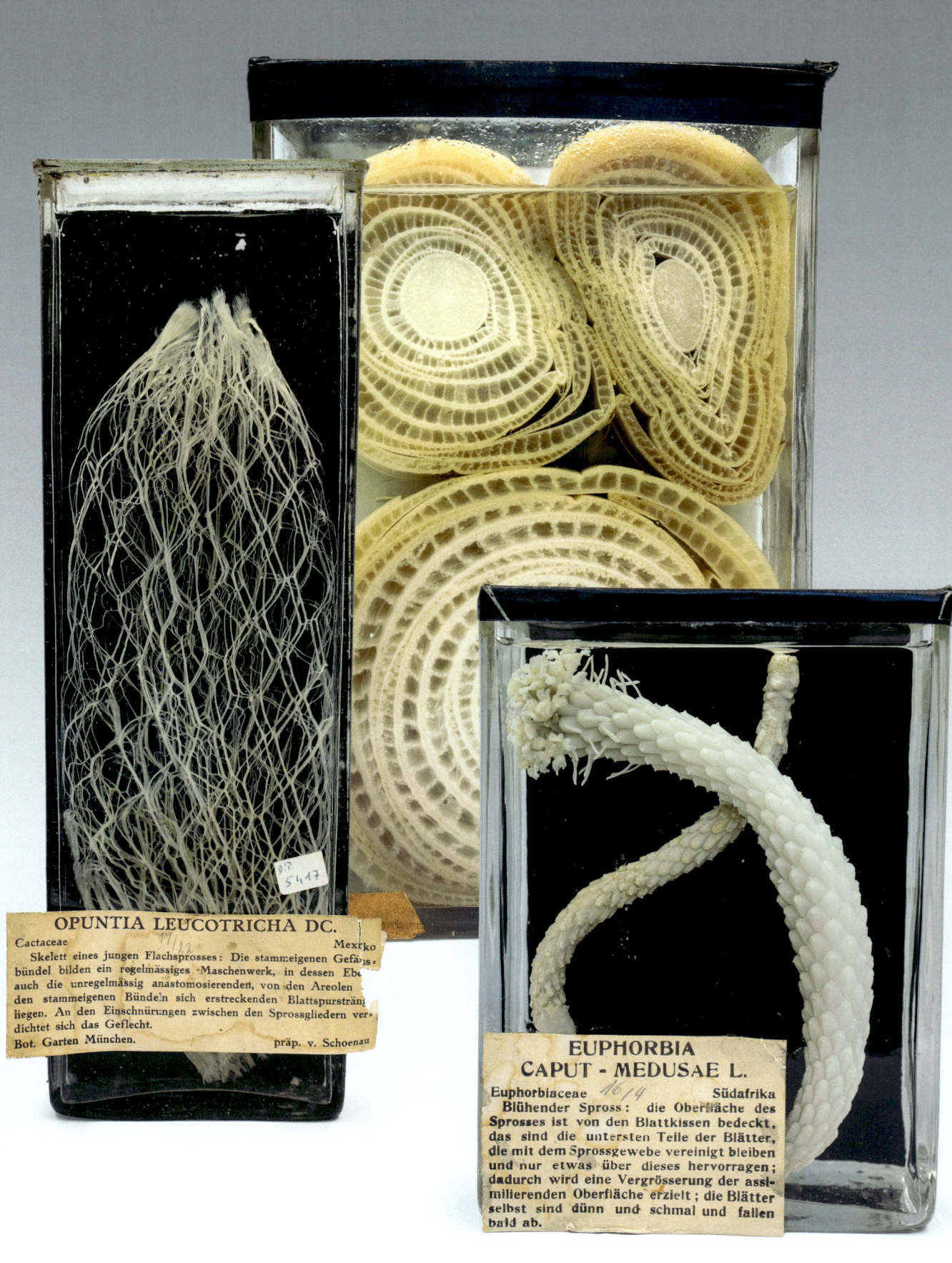

OPUNTIA LEUCOTRICHA DC.

Cactaceae   Mexriko
    Skelett eines jungen Flachsprosses: Die stammeigenen Gefäss-
bündel bilden ein regelmässiges Maschenwerk, in dessen Eber
auch die unregelmässig anastomosierenden, von den Areolen
den stammeigenen Bündeln sich erstreckenden Blattspursträng
liegen. An den Einschnürungen zwischen den Sprossgliedern ver-
dichtet sich das Geflecht.
Bot. Garten München.   präp. v. Schoenau

**EUPHORBIA
CAPUT - MEDUSAE L.**

Euphorbiaceae   16/4   Südafrika
    Blühender Spross: die Oberfläche des
Sprosses ist von den Blattkissen bedeckt,
das sind die untersten Teile der Blätter,
die mit dem Sprossgewebe vereinigt bleiben
und nur etwas über dieses hervorragen;
dadurch wird eine Vergrösserung der assi-
milierenden Oberfläche erzielt ; die Blätter
selbst sind dünn und schmal und fallen
bald ab.

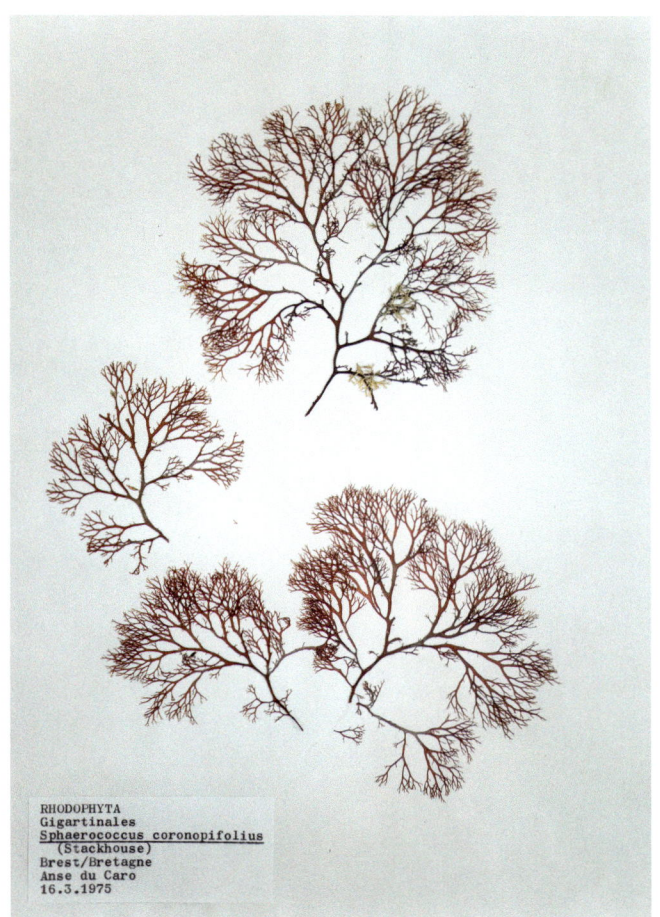

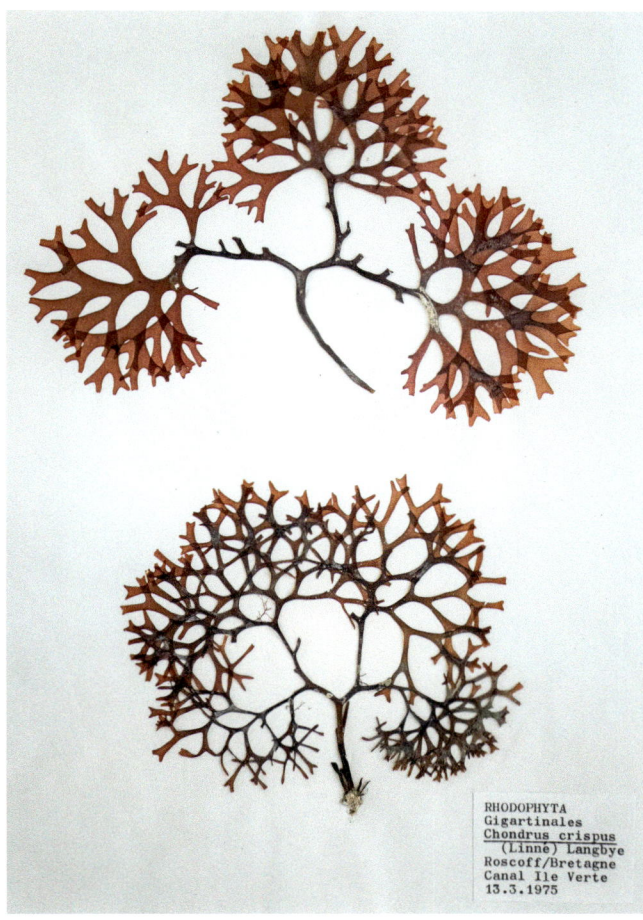

RHODOPHYTA
Gigartinales
Sphaerococcus coronopifolius
    (Stackhouse)
Brest/Bretagne
Anse du Caro
16.3.1975

RHODOPHYTA
Gigartinales
Chondrus crispus
    (Linné) Langbye
Roscoff/Bretagne
Canal Ile Verte
13.3.1975

↑ NATURAL HISTORY REFERENCES

Herbarium Specimen · Left: *Rhodophyta,
Gigartinales, Sphaerococcus coronopifolius
Stackh.* · Right: *Rhodophyta, Gigartinales,
Chondrus crispus Stackh.* · Each 29.7 × 21 cm
(11 11/16 × 8 1/4 in.) · Botanische
Staatssammlung München – SNSB

← NATURAL HISTORY REFERENCES

Plants preserved in alcohol in glass · *Opuntia
leucotricha DC., Cactaceae* · 30.8 × 10.5 × 4 cm
(12 1/8 × 4 1/8 × 1 9/16 in.) · *Musa sp., Musaceae* ·
30.5 × 20.2 × 10.5 cm (12 × 7 15/16 × 4 1/8 in.) ·
Euphorbia caput-medusae L., Euphorbiaceae ·
20.3 × 15 × 8 cm (8 × 5 15/16 × 3 1/8 in.) · Botanische
Staatssammlung München – SNSB

Particularly for his virtual gardens (see also pp. 109, 161) but also for his *Digital
Abysses* (started 2018; pp. 122, 124–31), Miguel Chevalier thoroughly studies
nature, researching botanical collections and getting inspired by objects from
▸ herbariums (p. 27). He is not only interested in visible structures such as special
flower shapes and ▸ fractals (p. 27) in plants like red algae or ferns, but also in the
internal structures that cannot be seen with the naked eye. (FS)

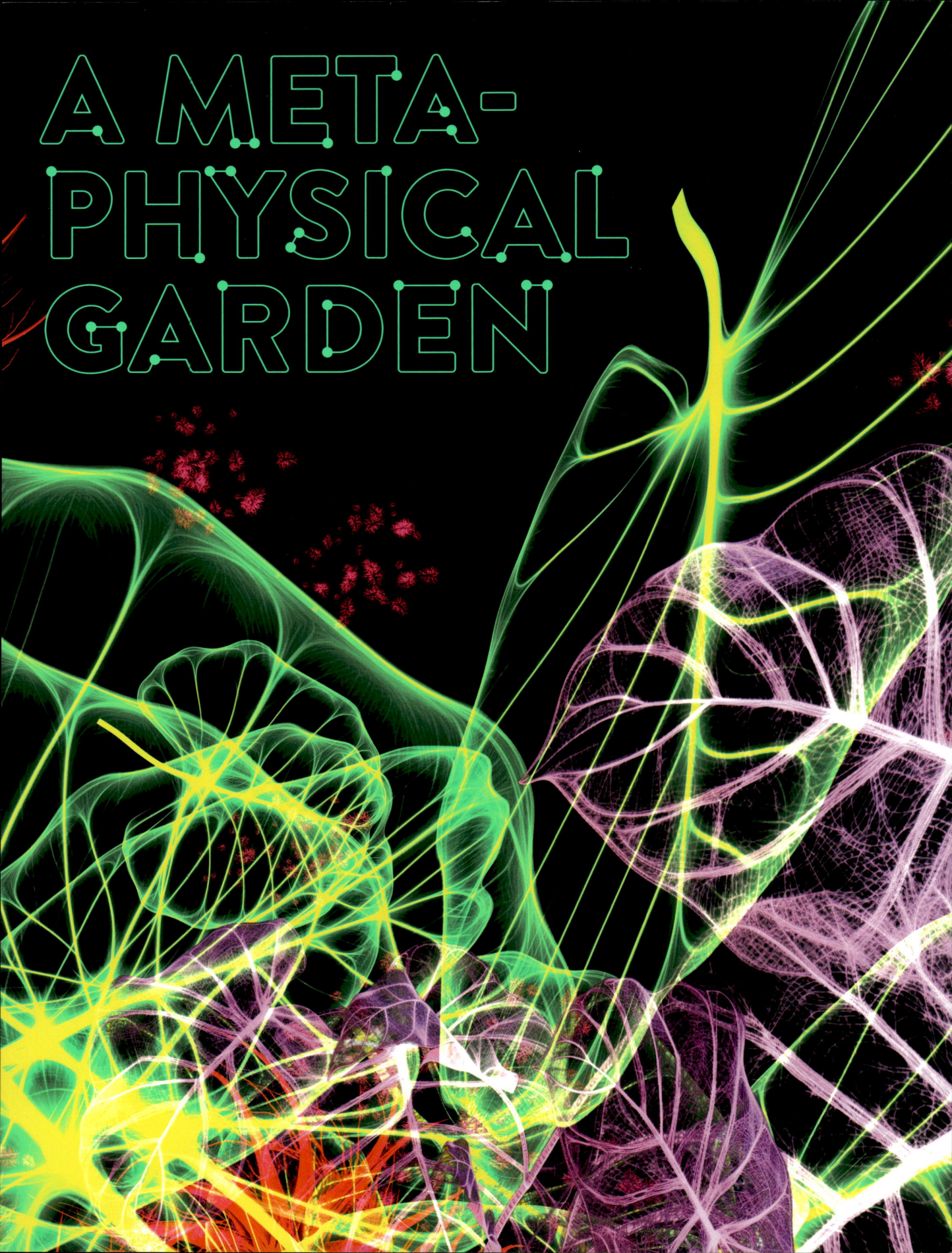

A META-PHYSICAL GARDEN

Meta-Nature AI, started 2023 · Generative and interactive installation · Dimensions variable · Software: Claude Micheli

● Since the 1990s, Miguel Chevalier has created several generations of virtual gardens, such as *Ultra-Nature*, *Trans-Nature*, and *Extra-Natural*, which are presented as installation projections. For each of these works, he produced a digital ▸ herbarium (p. 27), a defined collection of immaterial seeds that virtually follow a natural life cycle: they germinate and blossom, fade and die. Chevalier's plants grow in different places on the projection surface, in changing random rhythms, so that the gardens continue to develop endlessly and never look the same.

Meta-Nature AI (started 2023) is one of the most recent compositions within this body of work. This piece of ▸ generative art (p. 27) consists of two- and three-dimensional trees, leaves, and flowers. For the first time, Miguel Chevalier has included creations rendered by ▸ artificial intelligence (p. 26) in his database of specially created flowers and leaves. In this case, he used the AI-powered program Midjourney, which generates images from text. Chevalier clearly defined its field of activity. Using carefully phrased ▸ prompts (p. 29), he had the AI generate transparent flower or leaf shapes reminiscent of magnetic resonance imaging. These images were then recomposed using custom software developed in collaboration with Claude Micheli (b. 1957), resulting in a unique digital herbarium. With his transparent blossoms and leaves, Chevalier continues one of his fundamental themes, namely rendering visible that which cannot be seen with the naked eye (see also p. 16).

For centuries, botanical gardens and ornamental greenhouses have reflected the human desire to master, classify, and optimize nature. An interest in the beauty of plants and a scientific curiosity about them has traditionally been the main focus. In Chevalier's work, however, one can discern a critical voice as well: he reminds us that our rich and fragile ecosystem is now threatened by human intervention—whether through artificial hybridization or the exploitation of natural resources—and emphasizes what a vital foundation nature is. (FS)

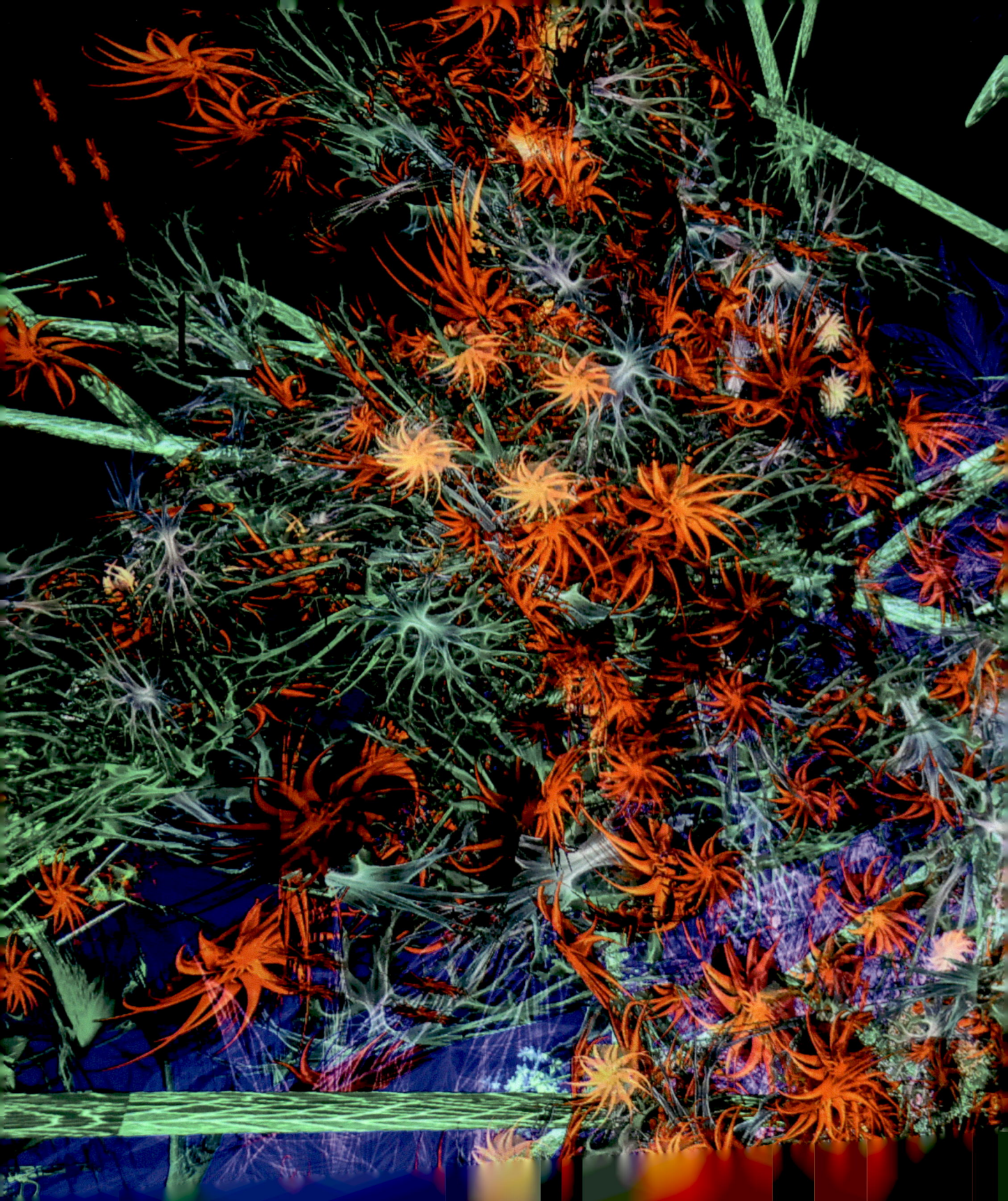

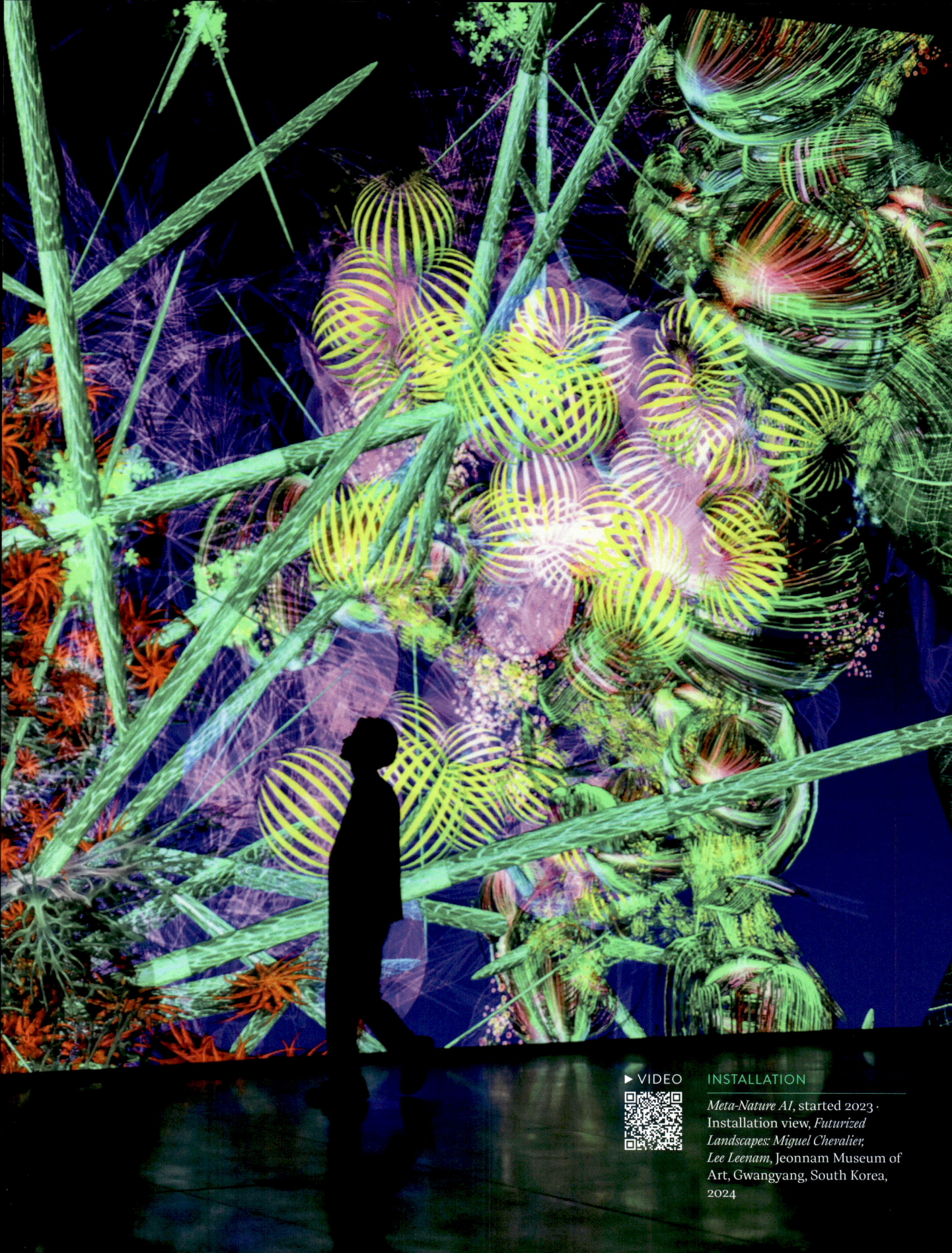

▶ VIDEO

INSTALLATION
_____

Meta-Nature AI, started 2023 ·
Installation view, *Futurized
Landscapes: Miguel Chevalier,
Lee Leenam*, Jeonnam Museum of
Art, Gwangyang, South Korea,
2024

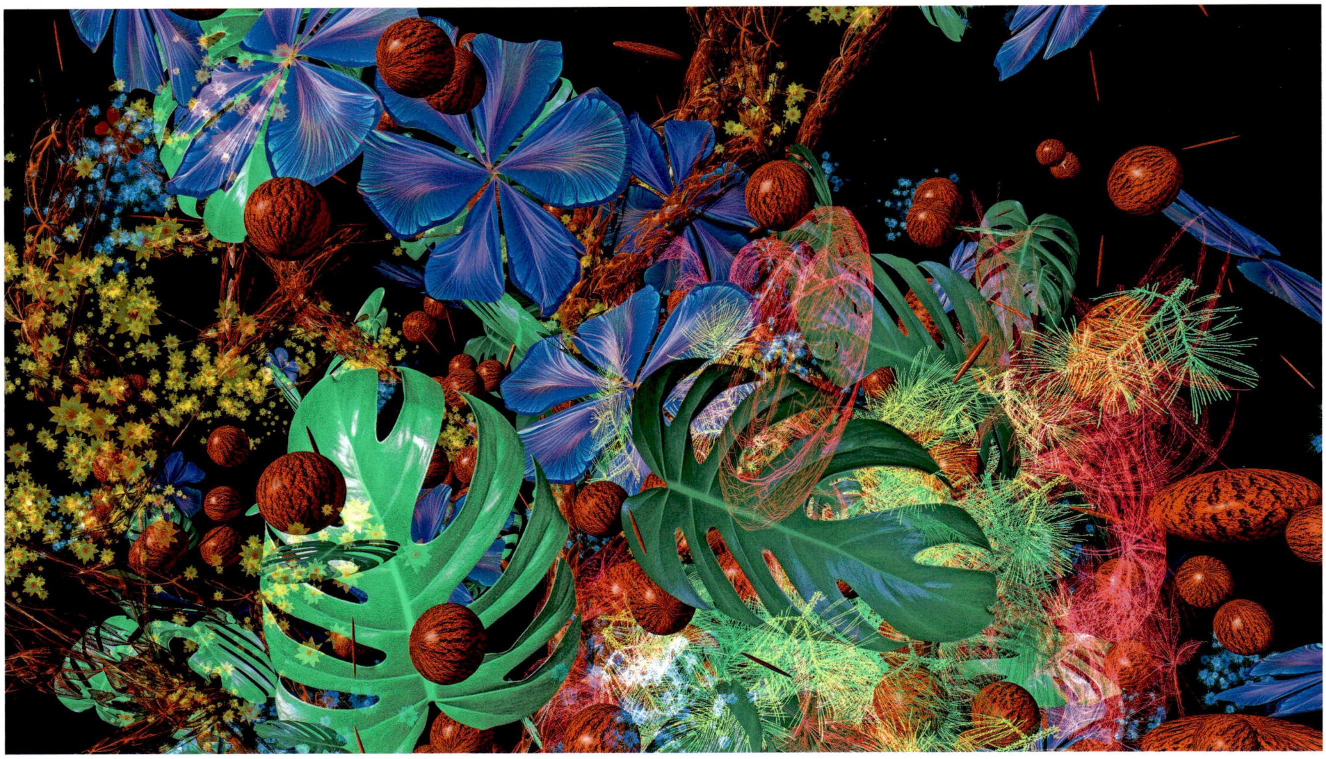

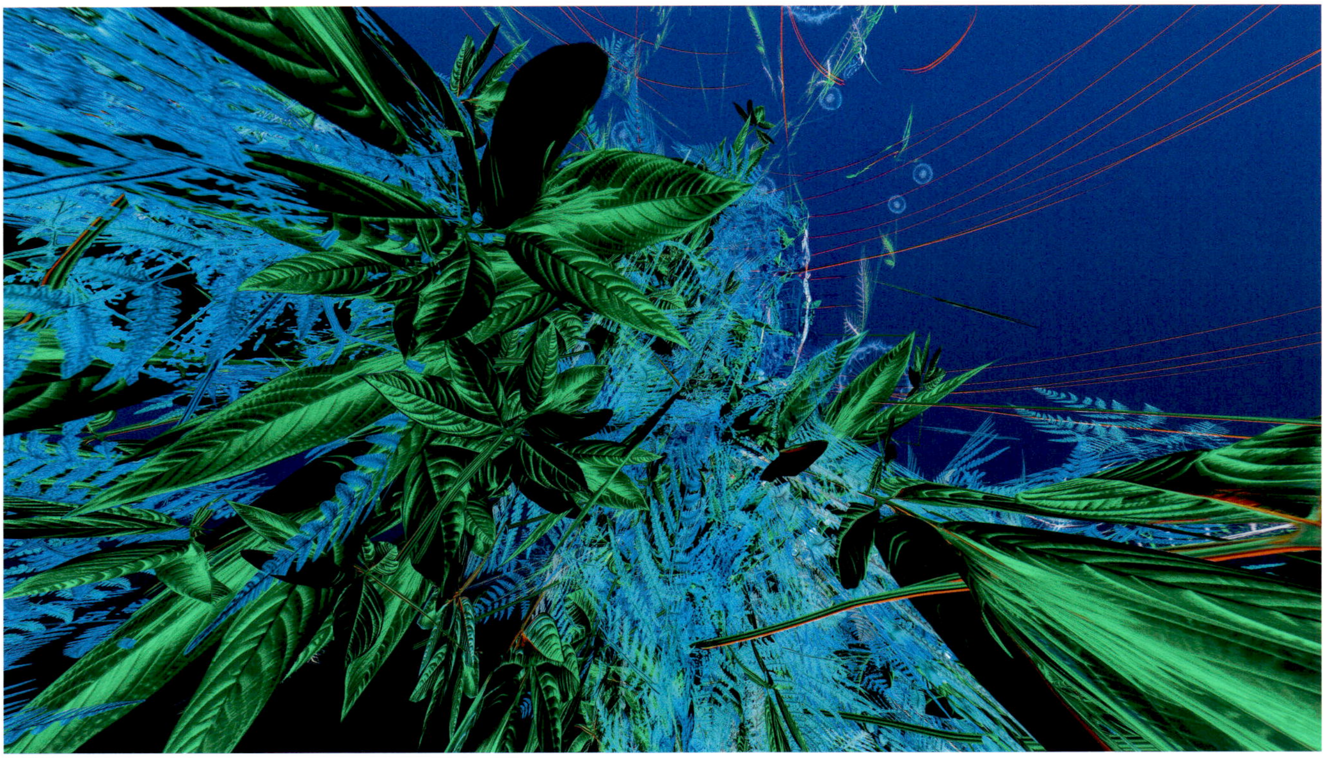

PATTERNS

Meta-Nature AI, started 2023

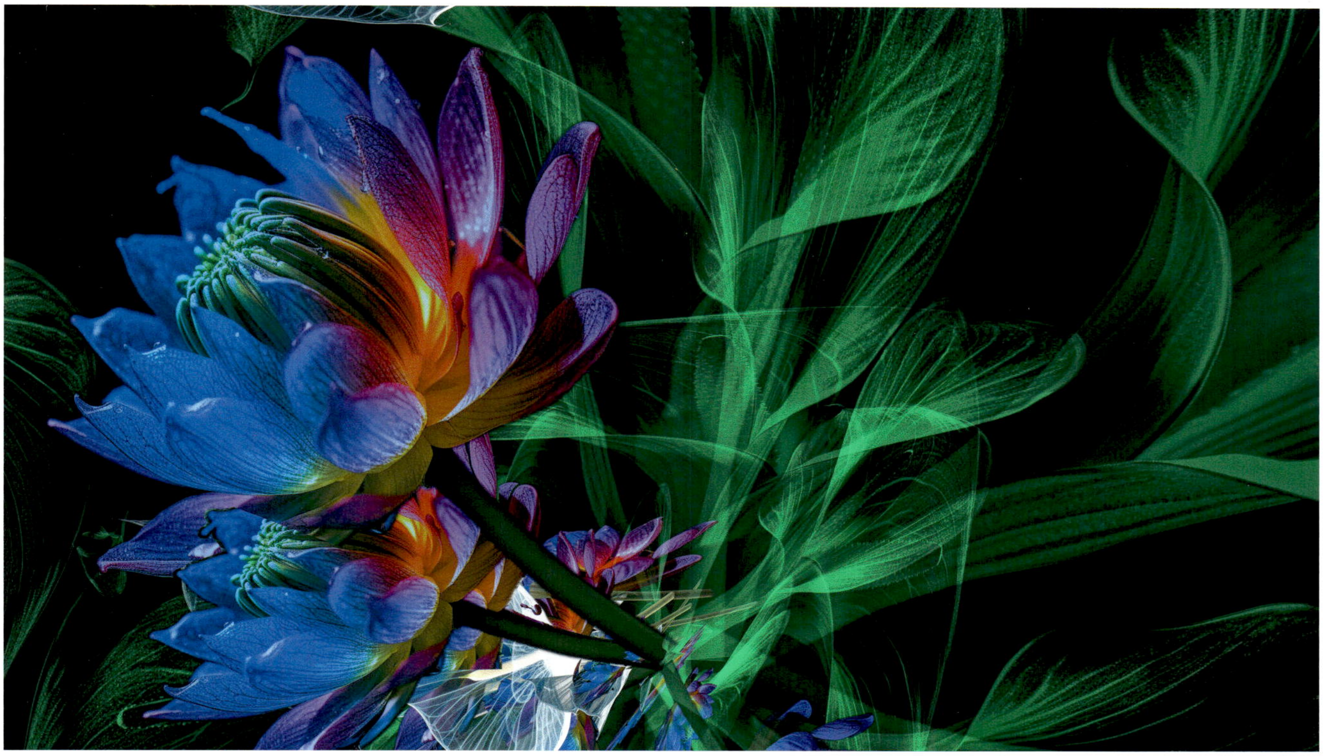

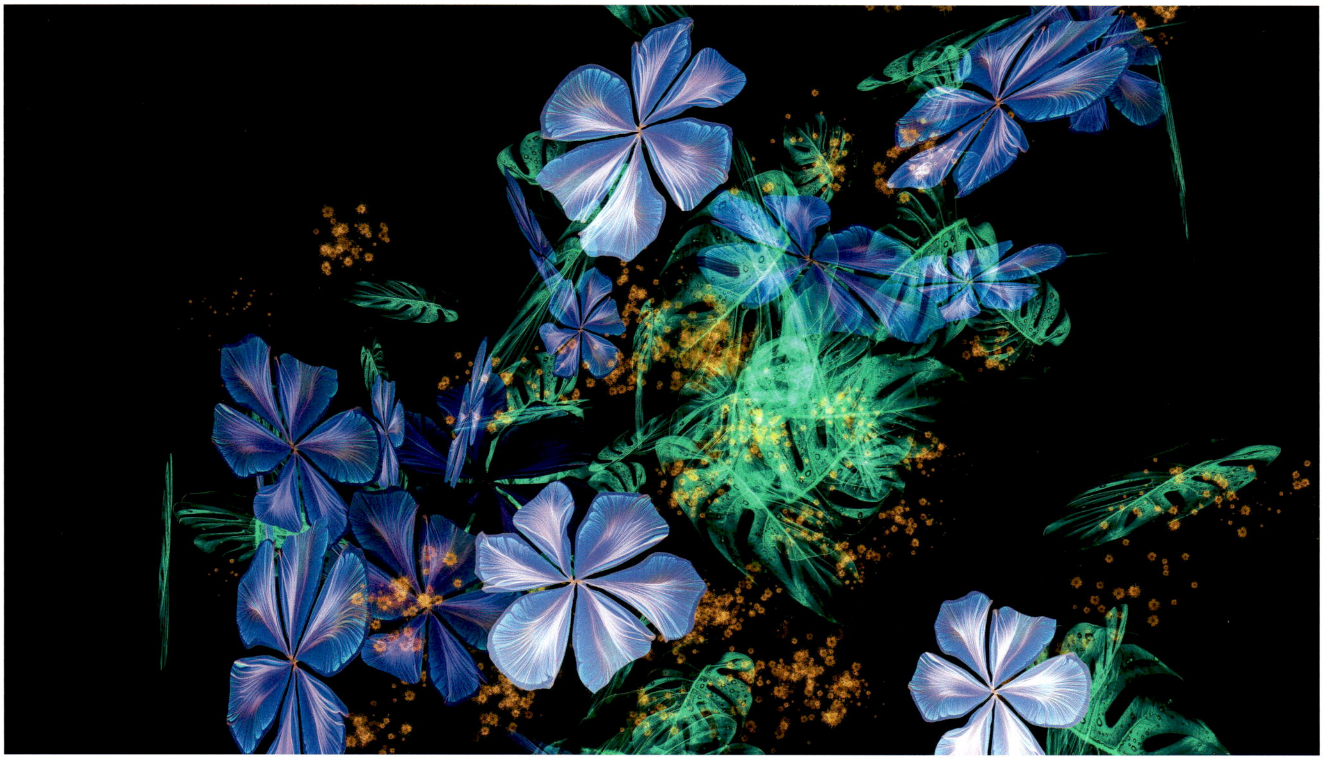

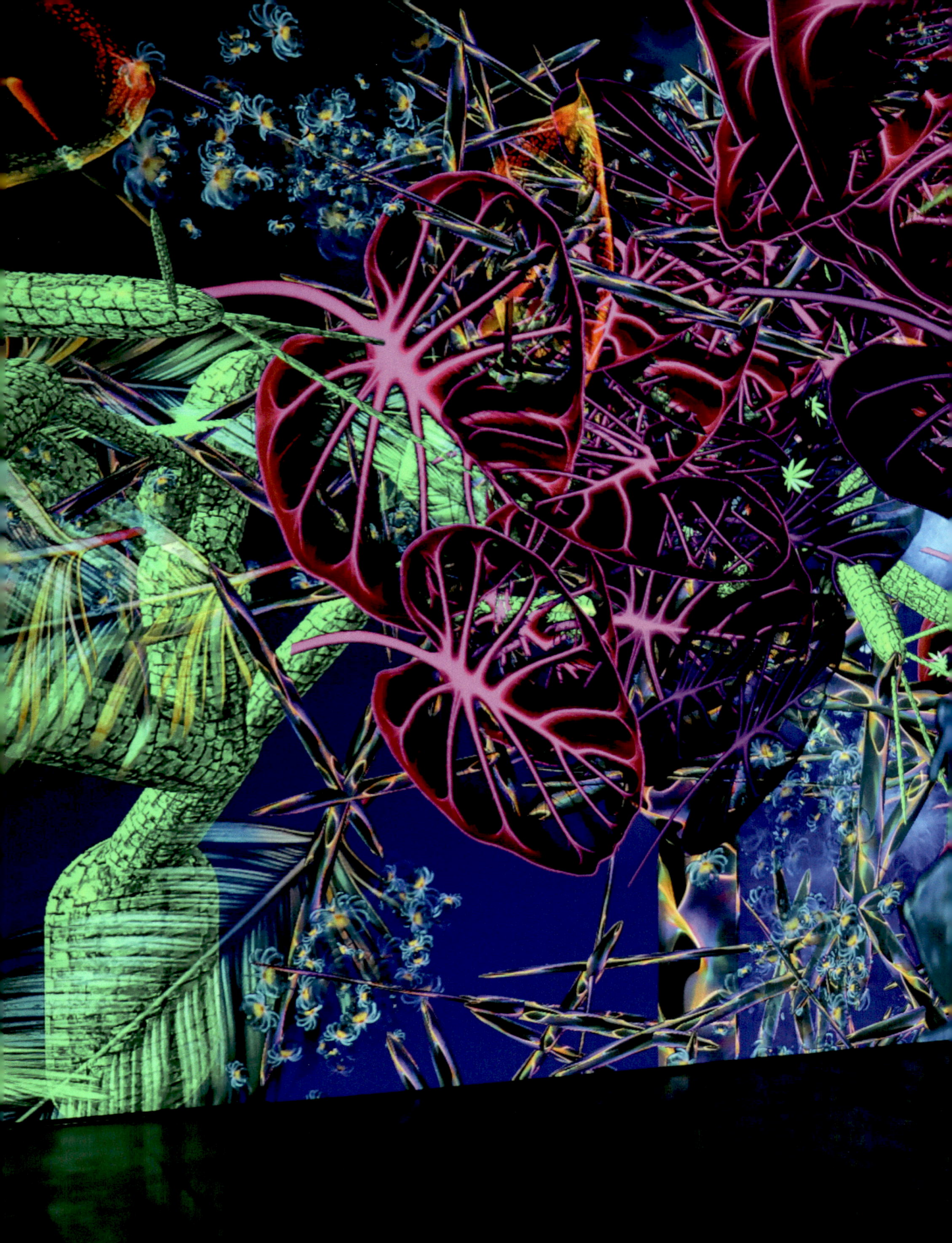

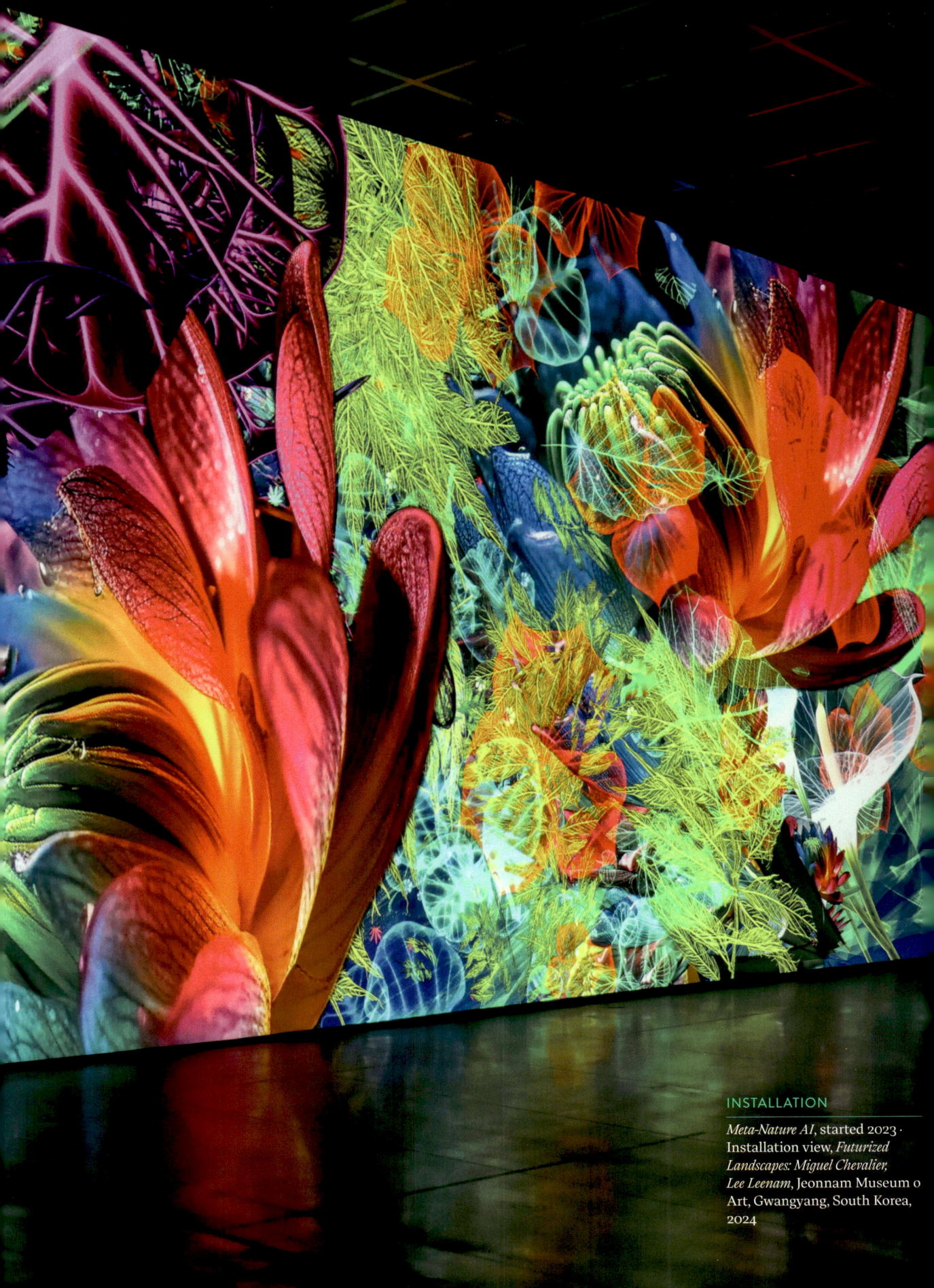

INSTALLATION

Meta-Nature AI, started 2023 ·
Installation view, *Futurized
Landscapes: Miguel Chevalier,
Lee Leenam*, Jeonnam Museum o
Art, Gwangyang, South Korea,
2024

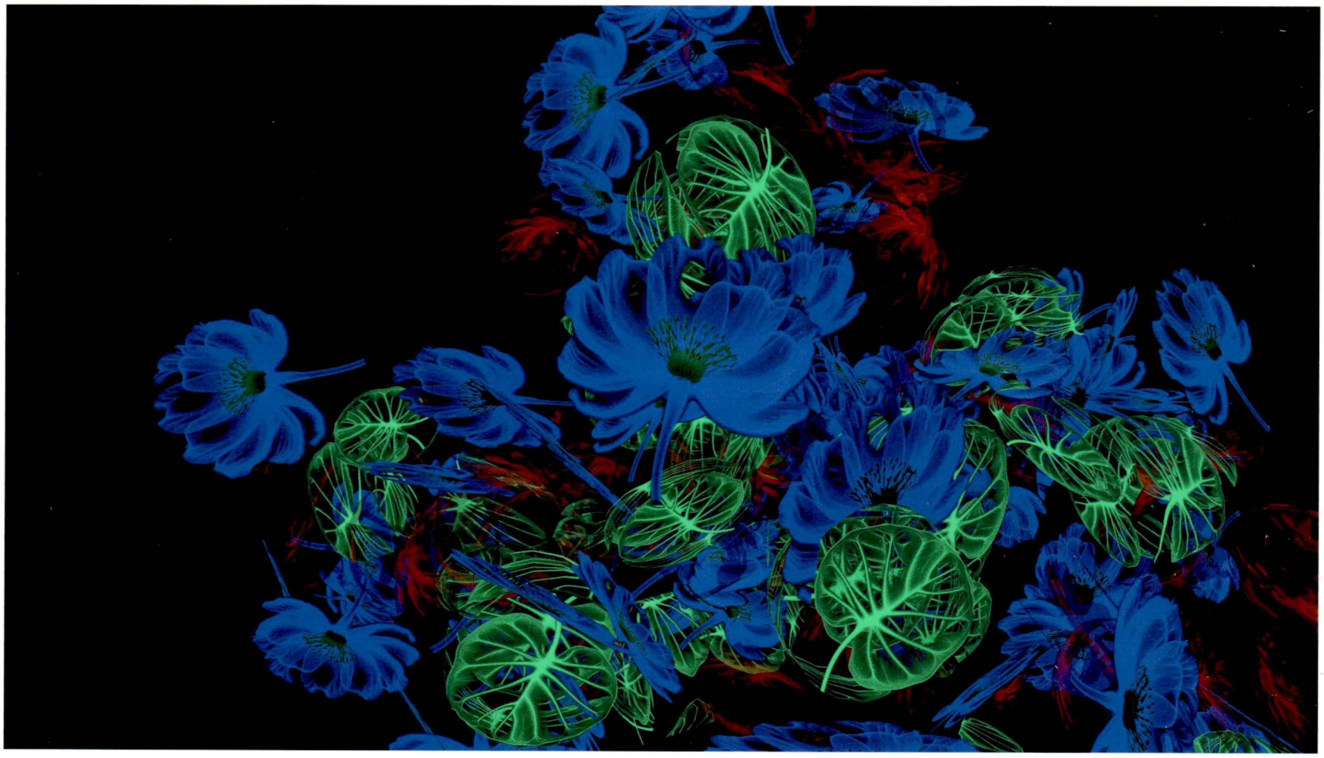

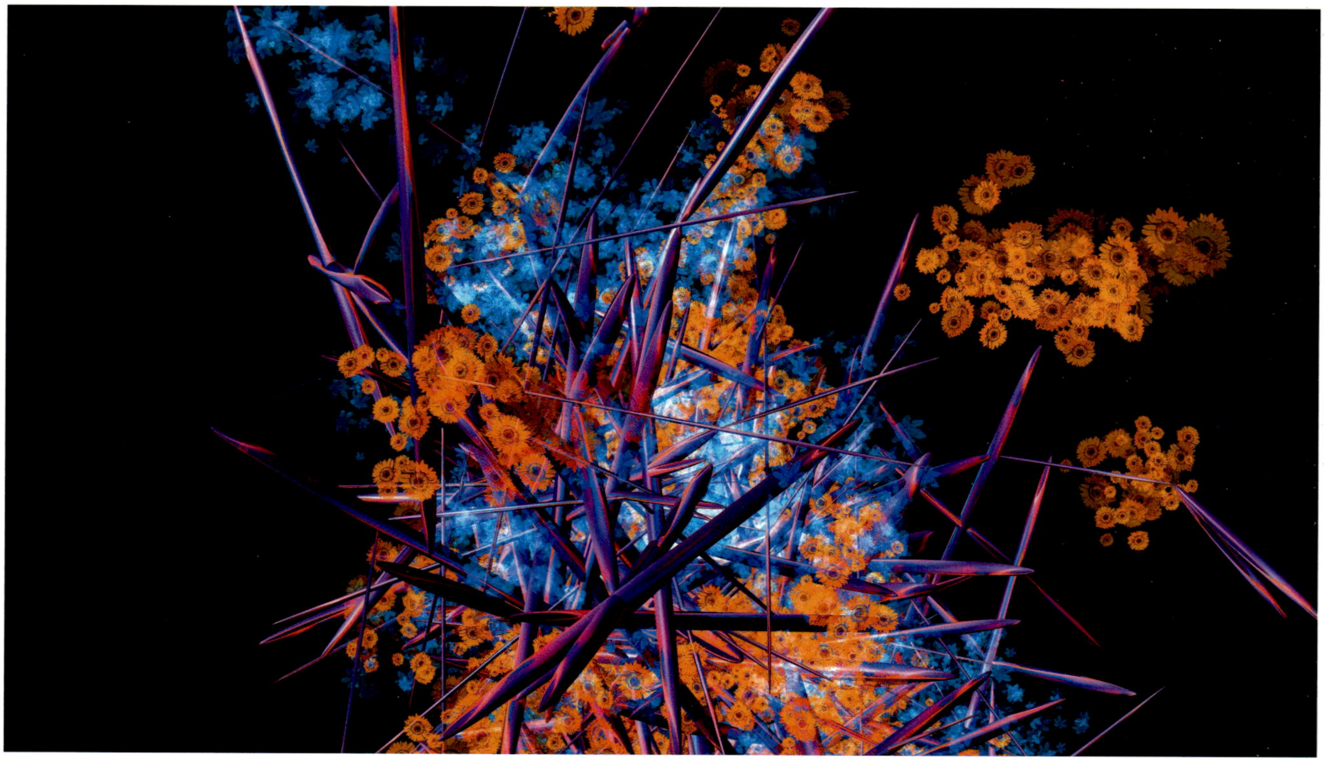

PATTERNS

Meta-Nature AI, started 2023

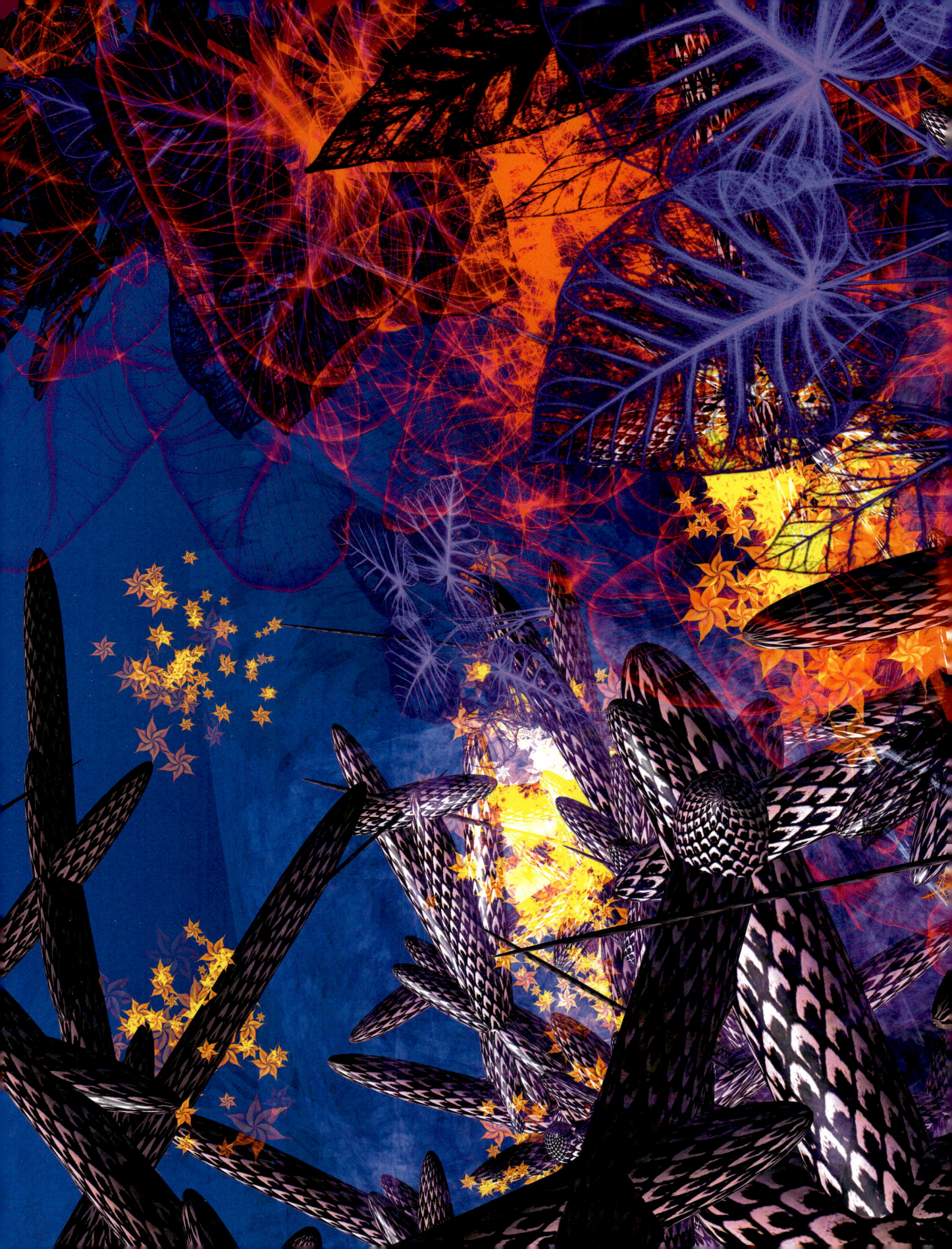

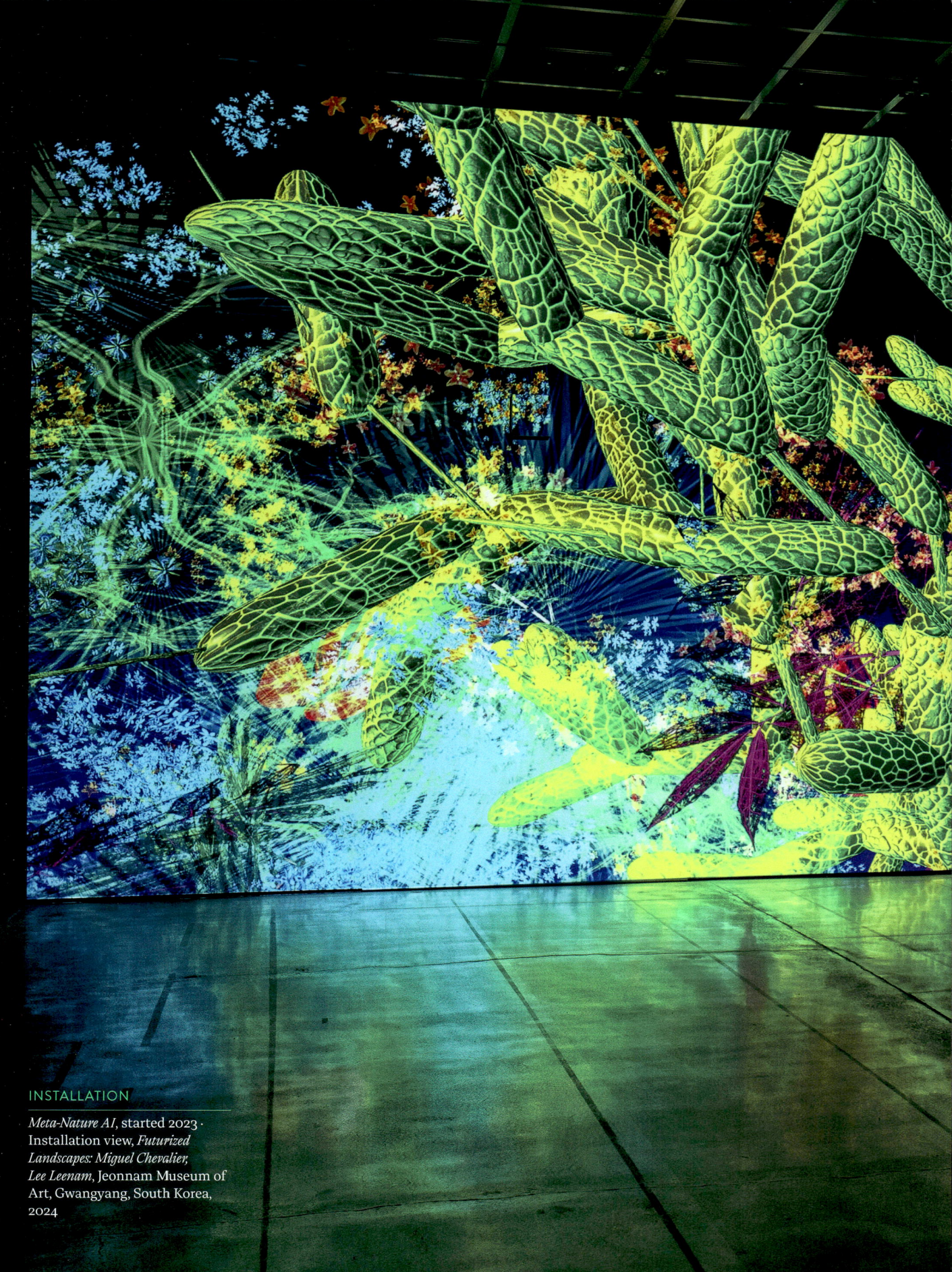

INSTALLATION

Meta-Nature AI, started 2023 ·
Installation view, *Futurized
Landscapes: Miguel Chevalier,
Lee Leenam*, Jeonnam Museum of
Art, Gwangyang, South Korea,
2024

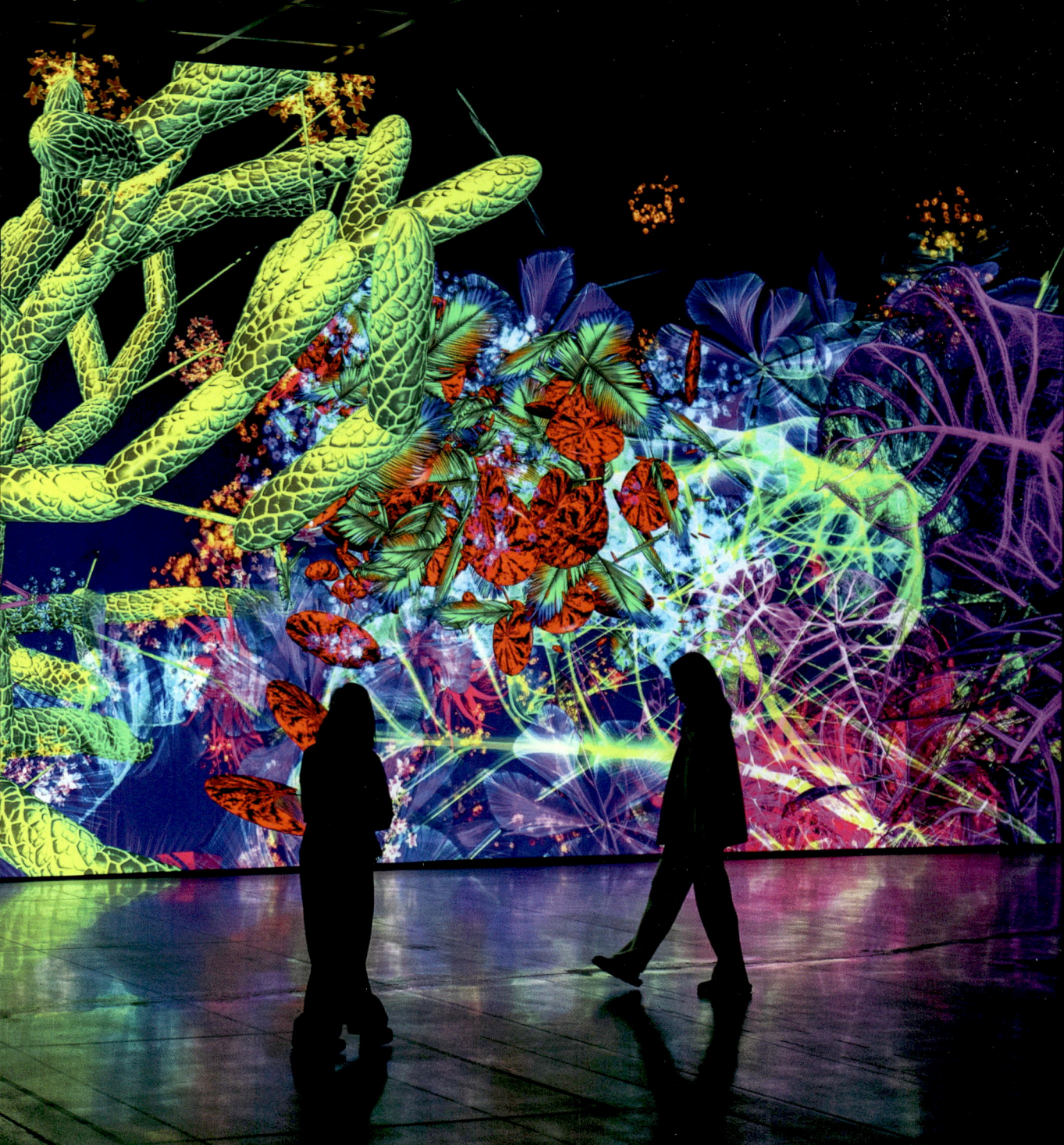

Biography

1959

Miguel Chevalier is born in Mexico City and lives there until the age of nine. His father, François Chevalier (1914–2012), a historian and director of the Institut Français of Latin America, regularly takes him to see the works of great muralists such as David Alfaro Siqueiros (1886–1974) and Diego Rivera (1886–1957).

1968–1976

Chevalier's family returns to Europe and settles in Madrid, where his father runs the Casa de Velázquez. Miguel Chevalier is impressed by Spanish art, particularly Gothic and Baroque altarpieces, as well as works by El Greco (1541–1614), Francisco Zurbarán (1598–1664) and Francisco de Goya's (1746–1828) *Black Paintings* (ca. 1820–23). These works heighten his sensitivity to the expressive power of light, the dramaturgy of composition, and the spiritual dimension that art can convey. He also learns about the Latin American kinetic art of Carlos Cruz-Diez (1923–2019), Jesús-Rafael Soto (1923–2005), and Julio Le Parc (b. 1928). He is enthralled by their work with light, optics, and the moiré effect.

1978–83

He studies visual arts and archaeology in Paris. Between 1981 and 1983, he graduates from the Université Panthéon-Sorbonne, the École Nationale Supérieure des Arts Décoratifs, and the École Nationale Supérieure des Beaux-Arts.

1982

Chevalier produces his first video installation, *Sweet Dream*, a blend of hand-painted film, video, and digital images.

1982–1983

With media and information technology (IT) increasingly present in society—but not yet taught in art schools—Chevalier is encouraged to explore the creative potential of innovative technologies. The engineer Serge Equilbey (b. 1950) gives him nighttime access to the powerful computers at the Centre National de la Recherche Scientifique (CNRS), which he uses to create his first digital works.

He learns the programming language Fortran and writes code to manipulate images.

Chevalier processes slides of greenhouses by removing parts of the gelatin layer. He then applies alcohol-based markers and stained-glass inks to create effects of transparency, filtering, and color. He digitizes the images and zooms deep into them to reveal the pixels. In this way, he creates his first links between painting, photography, and digital art.

1983–1984

A Lavoisier scholarship from the French Ministry of Foreign Affairs enables him to continue his research at the Pratt Institute and then at the School of Visual Arts in New York City. At both these schools he becomes familiar with computer graphics, thanks to the first computers, which were equipped with graphics palettes and drawing software. He also uses the Quantel Paintbox for the first time. With the latter, it is possible to combine two video images and, thanks to a kind of touch pad with a pen, digitally recreate a real painted line that resembles a brushstroke; it can also simulate various other media such as chalk. After his return to France, he is able to use the computers at the CNRS in a more targeted way to continue his artistic explorations.

Chevalier visits the exhibition *Electra: Electricity and Electronics in the Art of the XXth Century*, curated by Frank Popper (1918–2020) and Marie-Odile Briot (1939–1998) at the Musée d'Art Moderne de la Ville de Paris. He is impressed by the range of works as well as by the show's ambition and ability to make new approaches in electronic art accessible to a broad audience.

1985–1986

The exhibition *Les Immatériaux* by Jean-François Lyotard (1924–1998) and Thierry Chaput (1949–1990) at the Centre Pompidou in 1985 is a revelation for Chevalier and convinces him to pursue his research in the field of digital art. It is during this period that he acquires his first personal computer, an Amiga 1000 made by the company Commodore.

He produces the first video works illustrating the transition from analog to digital, recorded on magnetic tape and shown on television sets. One example is *Snow Pixels* (1986), which reveals the texture of screens switched on without a signal.

1987

He holds his first solo exhibition at Le Granit contemporary art center in Belfort. He exhibits *Greenhouse Effect*, which includes silkscreen works and a video installation consisting of a miniature greenhouse containing real plants and televisions showing *Baroque and Classical*. This six-minute digital video pays tribute to the South Korean artist Nam June Paik (1932–2006). Since then, Chevalier has presented his work in numerous solo and group exhibitions around the world.

1988

Chevalier becomes a member of the Institut des Hautes Études en Arts Plastiques in Paris. He is selected along with artists such as Philippe Parreno (b. 1964), Yan Pei-Ming (b. 1960), and Dominique Gonzalez-Foerster (b. 1965). The institute—created in the same year by Pontus Hultén (1924–2006), Serge Fauchereau (b. 1939), and Daniel Buren (b. 1938)—is inspired by the ideas of the Bauhaus and Black Mountain College. The institute in Paris aims to foster interdisciplinary exchange among young artists, focusing on research and discussion rather than on traditional teaching. Part of the curriculum is devoted to encounters with artists, architects, and thinkers such as Jean Tinguely (1925–1991), Renzo Piano (b. 1937), and Jean-François Lyotard.
The same year, Chevalier is selected for the exhibition *Ateliers 88 ARC* at the Musée d'Art Moderne de la Ville de Paris. On this occasion, he meets the art critic Pierre Restany (1939–2003), founder of the Nouveau Réalisme movement, who encourages him to pursue digital art.
He presents *Performance*, his first large installation in a public space, on the facade of the Panthéon in Paris.

1989–1990

Chevalier focuses on the changing modes of communication. Satellites, global trading on stock exchanges, telephones, and fax machines are the subjects of his creations, representing the close link between individuals and communication tools, as well as global connections. The binary system becomes an important motif in his oeuvre.

1993–1994

As a guest artist at the Villa Kujoyama in Kyoto, Chevalier explores the visual culture of Japan. With its meticulously orchestrated gardens, it is an important source of inspiration for the artist as he develops work focused on the connection between nature and the artificial.

1996

The Big Glass / Liquid Nature and *Digital Thinking* are the artist's first creations using images generated in real-time by two computers (software: Eric Wenger [b. 1961]). They also represent his first interactive works to incorporate projection, with viewers interacting with the image and modifying it using a trackball mouse.

1997

Art critic Henri-François Debailleux (b. 1955) and philosopher Christine Buci-Glucksmann (b. 1945) form the Fractalists group, along with Pascal Dombis (b. 1965), Carlos Ginzburg (b. 1946), Jean-Claude Meynard (1951–2019), Joseph Nechvatal (b. 1951), and Chevalier. The artists use fractal geometry while leaving plenty of room for the unexpected. The group disbands in 2002.
Chevalier begins a collaboration with Claude Micheli (b. 1957), who develops the software for the works *Massively Parallel* (1997) and later also *Pixel Dance* (1999), *Trans-Nature* (started 2012), *Fractal Cloud* (started 2013), *Meta-Cities* (started 2013), *Vortex* (started 2015), *Orbits* (2019), *The Eye of the Machine* (started 2019), *Digital Moiré* (started 2021), *Spatial Line* (started 2023), and *Meta-Nature AI* (started 2023).

2000

Chevalier sets up his studio La Fabrika in Ivry-sur-Seine, named after Andy Warhol's (1928–1987) Factory. The artist assembles a small team of computer specialists and technicians with whom he designs and tests the software for his creations.

2000–2003

Chevalier explores the notions of networks and flows, for example in the sense of data streams, that weave their way through our environment. Digital technology enables him to convey the intangible nature of the invisible world around us.

2004

The artist develops the generative and interactive work *Ultra-Nature* with the Music2eye collective. An herbarium made up of eighteen virtual seeds is used to generate interactive digital gardens that can be infinitely transformed. The installation, created for the Metropolitan Museum of Art in Daejeon, South Korea, is the artist's first major generative and interactive projection.

2005

Chevalier starts working with Nicolas Gaudelet (b. 1981), a specialist in IT solutions with a strong interest in art, who assists him in turning his ideas into reality and creating his monumental installations.

2007

Chevalier begins his collaboration with the programmer Cyrille Henry (b. 1977), who develops the software for the works *Fractal Flowers* (started 2008), *The Origin of the World* (started 2012), *Pixel Wave* (started 2011), *Complex Meshes* (started 2015), *Extra-Natural* (started 2016), *Oscillations* (started 2020), and *Fractal Arborescence* (started 2023).
Ever more powerful graphics cards and further improvements in the quality of video projectors encourage the creation of increasingly monumental and immersive works.

2008

The first sculptures produced using 3D printing (synthetic resin and powder or sand) enable the artist to bring his virtual creations into the analog world as physical objects. Today, he is exploring the potential of 3D printing in ceramics, recycled plastic, and fiber-reinforced concrete.

2013

Chevalier is invited to create a large-scale installation on the facade of the Palacio de Bellas Artes in Mexico City as part of the FILUX festival.

2016–2018

Chevalier works with curator Jérôme Neutres (b. 1970) to design and set up the group exhibition *Artistes & Robots*, which is shown from June 10 to September 10, 2017, in one of the pavilions of the international exhibition *Astana 2017* on the theme of "Future Energy" in Kazakhstan. The exhibition was also shown at the Grand Palais in Paris in 2018, curated by Jérôme Neutres and Laurence Bertrand Dorléac (b. 1957).

2022

He is named a Chevalier des Arts et des Lettres (Knight of the Order of Arts and Letters) by the French government.

2023

The artist introduces artificial intelligence to his creative process for the first time in *Meta-Nature AI*. It incorporates a database of images representing plant forms generated by AI. It is projected on the Dongdaemun Design Plaza in Seoul, designed by Zaha Hadid (1950–2016).

2025

Chevalier creates the new digital herbarium *Pixel Flowers*. For the first time in his work, people can create their own plants online or in the exhibition space and thus contribute to the artist's most comprehensive garden to date. It is presented in the exhibition *Digital by Nature: The Art of Miguel Chevalier*, his first major solo exhibition in Germany at the Kunsthalle München.

Miguel Chevalier lives in Paris.

www.miguel-chevalier.com
Instagram: miguel_chevalier

COLOPHON

This catalog has been published on the occasion of the exhibition
Digital by Nature: The Art of Miguel Chevalier

Kunsthalle der Hypo-Kulturstiftung (Kunsthalle München)
September 12, 2025 – March 1, 2026

EXHIBITION

Curator
Franziska Stöhr

Curatorial Assistant
Jasmin Gierling

Exhibition Design
Martin Kinzlmaier

Exhibition Production
Voxels Productions:
Nicolas Gaudelet, Emilie Lesne;
with assistance from
Thomas Granovsky,
Pascal Maillard, Elise Michel

Software Design
Cyrille Henry, Ollie Smith,
Claude Micheli, Samuel Twidale,
Antoine Villeret

Programming, Drawing Robot
Ludovic Mallégol

Musical Compositions
Jacopo Baboni Schilingi;
with assistance from
Gabriel Chouvet

The artist wishes to thank
· James Mayor and
  Christine Hourdé / The Mayor
  Gallery (London)
· Amanda and Alexandre
  Gaudelet
· Renata Sapey
· 3D Minerals
· Manufacture des Emaux
  de Longwy 1798
· Vangart

LENDERS

· Botanische Staatssammlung
  München – SNSB
· Miguel Chevalier
· Lélia Mordoch Gallery
· Mario Pauwels Mineral
  Collection, Belgium
· Najia Mehadji
· Mineralogische Staats-
  sammlung München – SNSB
· Vintage Computing Lab, Munich
· Domitille and Antoine Wargny

KUNSTHALLE MÜNCHEN

Director
Roger Diederen

Curators
Anja Huber, Stefan Kirchberger,
Franziska Stöhr

Curatorial Project Management
Juliane Au

Exhibition Management
Charlotte Ewers

Curatorial Assistant
Jasmin Gierling

Research Assistant
Francesco Alessandrini Lupia

**Exhibition Office and Visitor
Management**
Alina Kroos

Communications and Events
Theresa Scheuermann,
Anne Christine Thomé

Communications Assistant
Sabrina Benz

Technical Manager
Gerhard Karl

Management, Ticket Office
Gabriele Hauer

Management, Checkroom
Silke Mendel

Interns
Monique Burandt, Dilek Rüzgar

HYPO-KULTURSTIFTUNG

Board
Marion Höllinger (Chair),
Ljubisa Tesić (Vice-Chair),
Jörn Ebermann

Managing Director
Oliver Kasparek

Foundation Office
Juliane Wehrmeyer,
Charlotte Zeitler

Kunsthalle der
Hypo-Kulturstiftung
Theatinerstraße 8
80333 Munich
Germany

www.kunsthalle-muc.de
www.hypo-kulturstiftung.de

CATALOG

Editors
Roger Diederen, Franziska Stöhr

Editorial Team
Roger Diederen, Jasmin Gierling,
Franziska Stöhr

Authors
Jasmin Gierling (JG),
Franziska Stöhr (FS)

Image Editing
Emilie Lesne (Voxels
Productions); Jasmin Gierling,
Stefan Kirchberger
(Kunsthalle München)

Translation German–English
Lisa Contag

Translation English–German
Stefan Kirchberger,
Franziska Stöhr

Copyediting German
Holger Steinemann

Copyediting English
James Copeland

Design
Sofarobotnik, Augsburg &
Munich

**Project Management,
Hirmer Publishers**
Jutta Allekotte, Cordula Gielen

Production, Hirmer Publishers
Hannes Halder

Paper
MaxiSilk, 170 g/m²

Fonts
Thermal VF, Brandon Grotesque

Prepress
Reproline mediateam GmbH &
Co. KG, Unterföhring

Printing and Binding
Grafisches Centrum CUNO
GmbH & Co. KG, Calbe

Printed in Germany

**Bibliographic information
published by the Deutsche
Nationalbibliothek**
The Deutsche Nationalbibliothek
lists this publication in the
Deutsche Nationalbibliografie;
detailed bibliographic data are
available online at https://www.
dnb.de.

The publisher expressly points
out that external links contained
in the text could only be viewed
by the publisher up to the time of
publication of the book. The
publisher has no influence what-
soever on subsequent changes.
Any liability on the part of the
publisher is therefore excluded.

ISBN 978-3-7774-4587-8
(English edition)

ISBN 978-3-7774-4586-1
(German edition)

Hirmer Publishers
(Hirmer Verlag GmbH)
Managing Director:
Kerstin Ludolph
Bayerstraße 57–59
80335 Munich
Germany

www.hirmerpublishers.com
www.hirmerpublishers.co.uk

IMAGE CREDITS

This publication was made
possible by the support of

THE MAYOR GALLERY

KUNSTHALLE
MÜNCHEN

HYPO-KULTURSTIFTUNG

Supported by
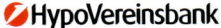

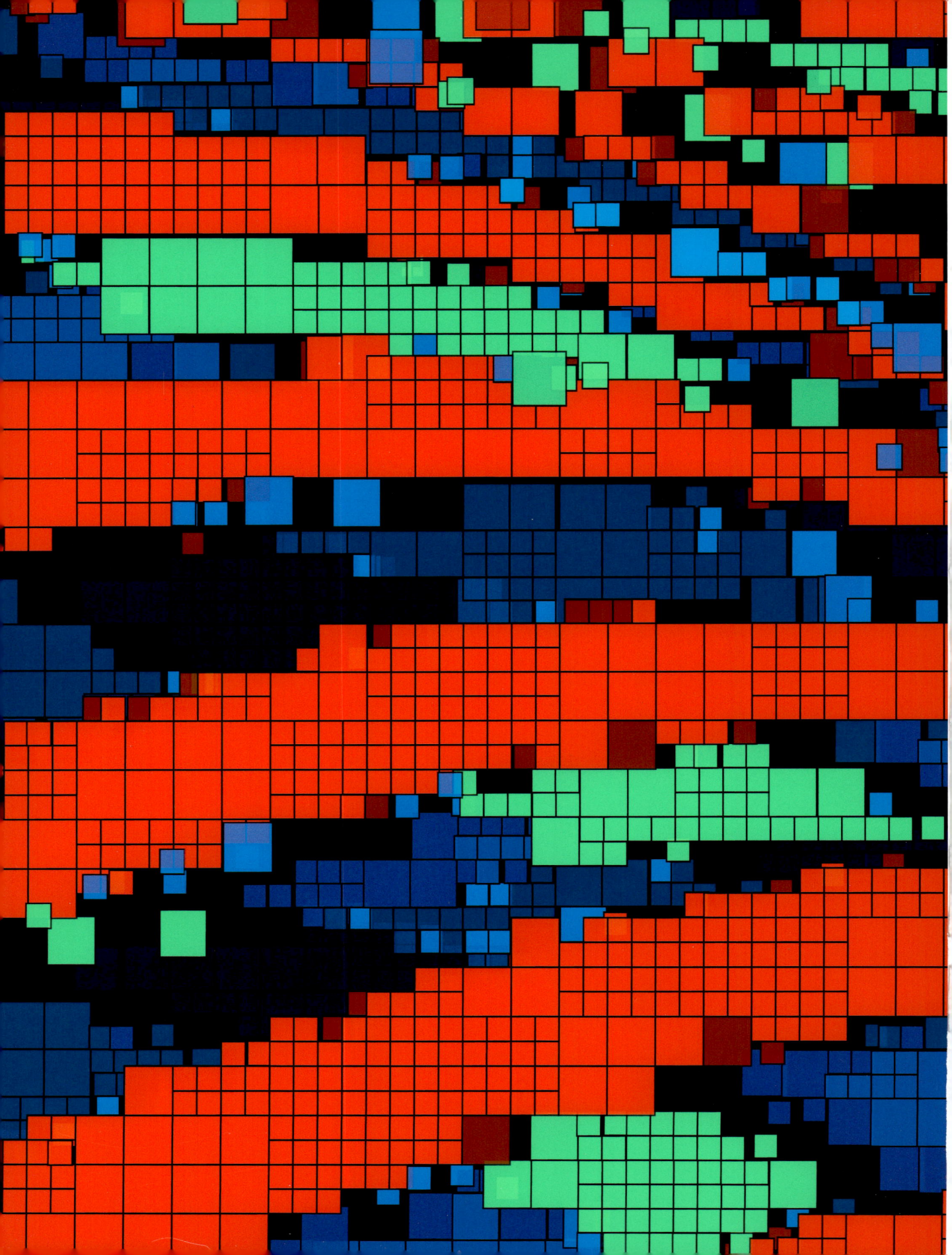